ST ANTONY'S SERIES
General Editor: Alex Pravda, Fellow of St Antony's College, Oxford

Recent titles include:

Mark D. Alleyne
INTERNATIONAL POWER AND INTERNATIONAL COMMUNICATION

Daniel A. Bell, David Brown, Kanishka Jayasuriya and David Martin Jones
TOWARDS ILLIBERAL DEMOCRACY IN PACIFIC ASIA

Judith M. Brown and Rosemary Foot (*editors*)
MIGRATION: The Asian Experience

Sir Alec Cairncross
MANAGING THE BRITISH ECONOMY IN THE 1960s: A Treasury
Perspective

Alex Danchev and Thomas Halverson (*editors*)
INTERNATIONAL PERSPECTIVES ON THE YUGOSLAV CONFLICT

Anne Deighton (*editor*)
BUILDING POSTWAR EUROPE: National Decision-Makers and European
Institutions, 1948–63

Reinhard Drifte
JAPAN'S FOREIGN POLICY IN THE 1990s: From Economic Superpower to
What Power?

Jane Ellis
THE RUSSIAN ORTHODOX CHURCH, 1985–94

Y Hakan Erdem
SLAVERY IN THE OTTOMAN EMPIRE AND ITS DEMISE, 1800–1909

João Carlos Espada
SOCIAL CITIZENSHIP RIGHTS: A Critique of F. A. Hayek and Raymond Plant

Christoph Gassenschmidt
JEWISH LIBERAL POLITICS IN TSARIST RUSSIA, 1900–14: The
Modernization of Russian Jewry

Amitzur Ilan
THE ORIGINS OF THE ARAB–ISRAELI ARMS RACE: Arms, Embargo,
Military Power and Decision in the 1948 Palestine War

Austen Ivereigh
CATHOLICISM AND POLITICS IN ARGENTINA, 1910–60

Leroy Jin
MONETARY POLICY AND THE DESIGN OF FINANCIAL INSTITUTIONS
IN CHINA, 1978–90

Matthew Jones
BRITAIN, THE UNITED STATES AND THE MEDITERRANEAN WAR,
1942–44

Anthony Kirk-Greene and Daniel Bach (*editors*)
STATE AND SOCIETY IN FRANCOPHONE AFRICA SINCE
INDEPENDENCE

Jaroslav Krejči and Pavel Machonin
CZECHOSLOVAKIA, 1919–92: A Laboratory for Social Change

Leslie McLoughlin
IBN SAUD: Founder of a Kingdom

David Nicholls
THE PLURALIST STATE, 2nd Edition: The Political Ideas of J. N. Figgis and
his Contemporaries

J. L. Porket
UNEMPLOYMENT IN CAPITALIST, COMMUNIST AND POST-
COMMUNIST ECONOMIES

Charles Powell
JUAN CARLOS OF SPAIN: Self-Made Monarch

Neil Renwick
JAPAN'S ALLIANCE POLITICS AND DEFENCE PRODUCTION

William J. Tompson
KHRUSHCHEV: A Political Life

Christopher Tremewan
THE POLITICAL ECONOMY OF SOCIAL CONTROL IN SINGAPORE

Jennifer M. Welsh
EDMUND BURKE AND INTERNATIONAL RELATIONS: The
Commonwealth of Europe and the Crusade against the French Revolution

State and Civil Society in Pakistan

Politics of Authority, Ideology and Ethnicity

Iftikhar H. Malik
Lecturer in History
Bath College of Higher Education

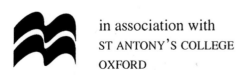

in association with
ST ANTONY'S COLLEGE
OXFORD

First published in Great Britain 1997 by
MACMILLAN PRESS LTD
Houndmills, Basingstoke, Hampshire RG21 6XS and London
Companies and representatives throughout the world

A catalogue record for this book is available from the British Library.

ISBN 0–333–64666–5

First published in the United States of America 1997 by
ST. MARTIN'S PRESS, INC.,
Scholarly and Reference Division,
175 Fifth Avenue, New York, N.Y. 10010

ISBN 0–312–16421–1

Library of Congress Cataloging-in-Publication Data
Malik, Iftikhar H., 1949–
State and civil society in Pakistan : politics of authority,
ideology, and ethnicity / Iftikhar H. Malik.
p.   cm. — (St. Antony's series)
Includes bibliographical references and index.
ISBN 0–312–16421–1 (cloth)
1. Pakistan—Politics and government.   2. Ethnic relations–
–Pakistan.   3. Ethnicity—Pakistan.   I. Title.   II. Series.
DS384.M2718   1996
320.95491—dc20   96–27847
                                                            CIP

This book is printed on paper suitable for recycling and made from fully managed and
sustained forest sources.

10   9   8   7   6   5   4   3   2   1
06   05   04   03   02   01   00   99   98   97

Printed and bound in Great Britain by
Antony Rowe Ltd, Chippenham, Wiltshire

To my parents

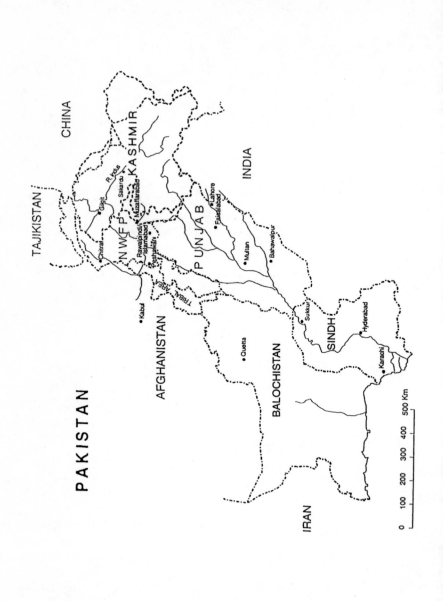

Contents

List of Tables

Acknowledgements

For quite some time, there has been a need for a comprehensive study to understand Pakistan's continuing dilemma in national integration with reference to the uneasy and unequal relationship between the state structure and civic institutions. The present study, based on theoretical and empirical evidence, attempts to analyse the country's problems in good governance. *Authority*, stipulating state structure both in the historical and political sense, is strictly anchored on the bureaucratic and military axis with the coopted elite from the landed aristocracy. *Ideology*, in the present study, signifies the enduring conflict between the traditionalists and modernists characterised by mutual negation and denigration rather than a dialogue. From official manipulation to a violent sectarianism, ideology remains a major factor in national politics.

The narrow nature of the state has constantly politicised *ethnicity*, finding momentum both from primordial and instrumental factors. Ethnic politics in Sindh is the latest spectre of Pakistani politics where the state machinery insists on administrative measures rather than compact politico-economic overhauling. External factors have not helped the tri-polar scenario as the continued difficulties with India help rationalise the continuity of the state structure besides growing expenditure on defence. However, due notice must be taken of ever-shifting ethnic identities, growing mobility within the society in the wake of all the necessary demographic changes and the positive contributions made in the economy, increasing awareness of women's rights, a vigorous press and intense debate on national and international issues. Such pointers can be helpful in building up a new contract between the state and society through political and civil processes allowing wider acceptance for ethno-regional diversity.

A predominantly Muslim society in the developing world, Pakistan provides a unique case study to understand the varying and mutual competitive forces of authority, ideology and ethnicity. It is hoped that this book will be of use both to specialists and to general readers interested in the issues of identity formation, state politics and civil society in the Muslim world. While being a critique of elitist manipulation of a state and society, the study pinpoints major areas which can help in establishing a more mediatory, dynamic and equitable equilibrium between the state structures and infantile institutions of the civil society. The book is the result of an effort spanning several years and various institutions and individuals across three continents. I am indebted to colleagues at St Antony's

xi

College, Oxford; Quaid-i-Azam University, Islamabad; University of Central Lancashire, Preston; and Bath College of Higher Education, all of whom provided me with intellectual stimulation and support to complete this research. My thanks in particular are due to the staff at the Bodleian Library, Oxford; India Office Records and Library, Public Record Office, London; and the Centre of South Asian Studies, Cambridge. Yunas Samad, Gurharpal Singh, Sameena Awan, Wiqar, Tim Farmiloe, Judy Mabro and Gráinne Twomey deserve my special gratitude for being so kind in their own ways. My special thanks to Nighat, Farooq and Sidra – my own family – for their help and understanding, and to countless Pakistanis who over the years have generously shared their time, thoughts and feelings with me. However, responsibility for the statements, hypotheses and any flaws in arguments or facts is solely mine.

Glossary

ajla'af	laity
alim	religious scholar
ashra'af	elite
awam	ordinary people/laity
babu	clerk: used by British for Western-educated South Asians
badla	vengeance
bait	allegiance
bap	father
baraat	marriage party
barani	rain-fed
bastis	temporary settlements
bazaari	urban petty bourgeoisie
burqa	veil
chaadar	veil
chardiwari	four walls (of seclusion)
crore	10 million
dabdaba	local authority
dargahs	shrines
dar-ul Islam	Islamic homeland
din	complete code of life
diwani	civil law suit
diyat	blood money
dunniya	world
dupatta	long piece of cloth worn by women, around the neck
faujdari	criminal law suit
gaddi nishin	successor to a *pir*
gheraojalao	siege and burn
goondas	ruffians
hadd	punishment under Islamic law
hakim	traditional healer
haq parast	truth worshipper
hari	landless peasant in Sindh
hathora	hammer
havelis	huge family houses
hijrat	migration
huddood	plural of *hadd*

ijma	consensus
ijtihad	intellectual innovation according to one's capabilities
ishtmaal-i-arazi	land consolidation scheme
izzat	honour, prestige
jagir	reward in land grant
jagirdar	feudal lord
jihad	struggle in the name of Islam
jirga	assembly of Pushtun elders
kameen	low-status rural professionals
katchi abadis	rural and tribal areas
khudi	self-knowledge
khalla	a woman's right to seek divorce
maddrassas	religious schools
mai	mother
malik	Pushtun tribal chieftain
mandi	market
mansabdar	a Mughal noble
mansabdari	administrative system of nobility introduced by Emperor Akbar
mashaikh	spiritual leaders
maulvi	Muslim theologian
millat	trans-territorial Islamic community
mofussil	hinterland
mohalla	urban locality
Muhajir	Muslim migrant
Muhajireen	Muslim migrants (usually refers to Urdu-speakers)
mujra	dance by a prostitute
murids	disciples
naukarshahi	the bureaucracy
nikah nama	marriage certificate
patharidars	influentials
pir	spiritual leader
purdah	seclusion
qabila	tribe
qaum	nation; also sub-caste
qazi	Muslim jurist
qisas	revenge
Raj	British rule in India
rawaj	traditions
safarish	recommendations
sajjada nishin	heir to a spiritual order

salami	reception
saleh	Muslim adult of good character
sardar	chieftain, usually in Balochistan and Southwestern Punjab
Sharia	Islamic law
shoora	advisory body
silsilahs	*sufi* orders
sonar Bangla	golden Bengal
subahjat	provinces
syed	descendant of the Prophet
tahsil/thana	administrative sub-division
taluqadar	land-owner in the UP
taqlid	blind conformity
tazir	punishment
ulama	Muslim religious scholar
ummah	community
umra	visit to the Hejaz other than Haj
ushr	tithe (tax at the ratio of one-tenth)
wadera	Sindhi landlord
walwar	bride price
zakat	charity at the ratio of 2 1/2 per cent
zameen	land
zamindar	land-owner
zan	woman
zar	wealth
zat	sub-caste
zina	adultery
zina-bil-jabr	rape
zulm	cruelty

List of Abbreviations

AIG	Afghan Interim Government
AIML	All-India Muslim League
ANP	Awami National Party (formerly the NAP)
APMSO	All-Pakistan Muhajir Students' Organisation
APP	Associated Press of Pakistan
APWA	All-Pakistan Women's Association
ATI	Anjuman-i Tulaba-i Islam
AZO	Al-Zulfikhar Organisation
BBC	British Broadcasting Corporation
BCCI	Bank of Credit and Commerce International
BNA	Baloch National Alliance
BNM	Balochistan National Movement
BSO	Baloch Students' Organisation
CDA	Capital Development Authority
CIA	Criminal Investigation Agency (Pakistan)
CIA	Central Intelligence Agency (US)
COP	Combined Opposition Parties
CPE	Council of Pakistan Editors
CPLC	Citizens–Police Liaison Committee
CSP	Civil Service of Pakistan
DIG	Deputy Inspector General of Police
EBDO	Elective Bodies (Disqualification) Order
FANA	Federally Administered Northern Areas
FATA	Federally Administered Tribal Areas
FIA	Federal Investigation Agency
FIR	First Information Report
FIT	Field Investigation Team
FML	Functional Muslim League
FSF	Federal Security Force
FSP	Foreign Service of Pakistan
IB	Intelligence Bureau
ICS	Indian Civil Service
IDA	Islamic Democratic Alliance
IJT	Islami Jamiat-i Tulaba
INC	Indian National Congress
ISI	Inter-Services Intelligence

JI	Jama'at i-Islami
JUH	Jamiat-i Ulama-i Hind
JUI	Jamiat-i Ulama-i Islam
JUP	Jamiat-i Ulama-i Pakistan
KKH	Karakoram Highway
KHAD	Khidmati-Itta'lat i-Daulati
LITE	Landhi Industrial Estate
MI	Military Intelligence
ML	Muslim League
MNA	Member of the National Assembly
MPA	Member of the Provincial Assembly
MQM	Muhajir Qaumi Movement
MRD	Movement for Restoration of Democracy
MSF	Muslim Students' Federation
NAP	National Awami Party
NGO	Non-Governmental Organisation
NPP	National People's Party
NPT	National Press Trust
NWFP	North-West Frontier Province
PATA	Provincially Administered Tribal Areas
PCO	Provisional Constitutional Order
PDA	Pakistan Democratic Alliance
PDP	Pakistan Democratic Party
PFUJ	Pakistan Federal Union of Journalists
PIA	Pakistan International Airlines
PIDC	Pakistan Industrial Development Corporation
PID	Press Information Department
PIF	Pakistan Islamic Front
PML	Pakistan Muslim League (formerly AIML)
PNA	Pakistan National Alliance
PNEC	Pakistan Newspaper Editors' Conference
PPA	Punjab Provincial Assembly
PPI	Punjabi-Pukhtun Ittehad
PPL	Progressive Papers Ltd
PPP	Pakistan People's Party
PRODA	Public Representative Offices (Disqualification) Act
PSF	People's Students' Federation
PSF	Pukhtoon Students' Federation
PSP	Police Service of Pakistan
RAW	Research Analysis Wing (Indian Intelligence Organisation)
SBNF	Sindh–Baloch National Front

SBPF	Sindi–Balochi–Pukhtoon Front
SHO	Station House Officer
SNA	Sindh National Alliance
TIP	Telephone and Typewriter Industries
UP	Uttar Pradesh
WAF	Women's Action Forum
WAR	Women Against Rape
WAPDA	Water and Power Development Authority

Introduction

Unlike many other countries in the developing world, Pakistan has been the focus of an impressive historiography with reference to regional and global developments. Similarly, domestic political developments such as the struggle for democracy, the intermittent imposition of martial law during almost two-thirds of the country's life span, ideological reshuffles in the name of Western liberal democracy, diluted socialism, and the orientation toward an Islamic form of socio-economic system, followed by privatisation and a guided economy, are the various subjects that have kept not only academics but the whole country engaged in speculation and discussions. However, the dilemma of nation-building and achieving good government has not been resolved. Pakistan's global policies, largely the result of her domestic and regional security imperatives – such as relations with India, the Afghanistan crisis and the situation in the Gulf – have brought her into relationships with most of the Muslim world and the superpowers, enhancing her stature.[1] The country's location as a junction between Central, Western and Southern Asia, and its proximity to China and the vital Gulf region, enable it to play a significant role in current world politics.[2] The emergence of Pakistan from the consolidated Raj in the teeth of opposition and its survival against many odds, despite expectations and fears to the contrary have also contributed to its importance. The constant struggle for democracy in the country, handicapped by various factors and overburdened with its praetorian nomenclature, has surprised many people. When General Zia ul-Haq died in a plane crash on 17 August 1988, along with several top military generals and the US ambassador, it was assumed that another military take-over was imminent. Nevertheless, it was democracy that once again emerged as the popular choice.[3] As a consequence, the military leadership and the acting president decided to hold party-based elections for the national and provincial assemblies. The electoral results interestingly presented a plural verdict resulting in a hung parliament with similar patterns for the provincial assemblies. This would have served Pakistan very well if it had not been for the mutual squabbling among the political leaders, who in the context of a larger national political malaise as well as their own stubbornness and naivety, mostly remained in bitter enmity. This state of affairs, based on a polarisation between pro-Bhutto and pro-Zia factions, persisted throughout the subsequent 20 months when Benazir Bhutto headed her first government at the centre. Immediately after her installation, apparently after

1

striking a 'deal' with the power elites (such as the military and bureaucracy) on vital national policies, rumours concerning a reimposition of
martial law began to appear from time to time in the world media.[4]

In keeping with the political instability that characterised the early life
of the country, between October 1988 and October 1993 Pakistan experienced three national and provincial elections with eight successive governments being formed. The dissolution of Benazir Bhutto's first government
by presidential decree on 6 August 1990 with allegations of inefficiency,
corruption and disorderliness (still largely unsubstantiated) was followed
by a brief interim period under Ghulam Mustafa Jatoi. Mian Nawaz
Sharif, the former chief minister of Punjab and Benazir Bhutto's main
political opponent from the forum of the Islamic Democratic Alliance
(IDA/IJT), claimed an overwhelming majority in the elections of October
1990 and succeeded Jatoi as prime minister. Following personal bickering
he was sacked by Ghulam Ishaque Khan in April 1993, exactly 40 years
after Pakistan's second prime minister, Nazim ud-Din had been dismissed
by an executive order from Ghulam Muhammad, the then governor-
general. Mir Balkh Sher Mazari, the interim prime minister, was unable to
complete his three-month term, because of an order from Pakistan's
Supreme Court which challenged the presidential dissolution order and
restored Nawaz Sharif and the National Assembly. The dissensions
between Ishaque Khan and Nawaz Sharif rather than being tempered were
intensified, until the army, led by General Abdul Waheed, intervened.
Through a brokered agreement both the president and prime minister
resigned allowing the establishment of the second interim government of
the year led by Moeen Qureshi, a former vice-president of the World
Bank. Finally, the elections in October returned Benazir Bhutto for the
second time as prime minister – three years after being dismissed by
Ishaque Khan. A month later, Farooq Leghari, a close confidante of
Benazir Bhutto, was elected president of the country, giving full authority
to the Pakistan People's Party (PPP) for the second time since the 1970s.
After quite a turbulent history the PPP rejoiced in the establishment of
their government, which was the fifth of 1993.

Although numerous successive elections and extended electoral campaigns with multiple alliances and counter-alliances may be taken to indicate a politicisation of the masses and the sifting of 'dead wood', they
could equally be seen as highlighting a long-term dilemma in the
country's history, namely the need to establish a mutually acceptable,
enduring and all-encompassing political order. Pakistan's governability
crisis is closely interlinked with the question of who runs the country. The
creation of Pakistan was achieved by a political and constitutional strug-

gle. From its pre-1947 historical burden to its political economy with an imbalanced relationship among the three pillars of power – army generals, bureaucrats and feudal politicians – it is the first two groups who have largely controlled the state while politicians have either played a secondary role or simply succumbed to internecine squabbles. Thus, Pakistan's failure to resolve the problems of governance, in a sense stems from a too powerful state and a fragile political culture, which is further vulnerable to individual or multiple machinations.

Once the identity of the *authority* in Pakistan has been established, it is easy to see that given its non-representative, elitist and ethnically discretionary composition, forces in authority have always tried to seek legitimacy by skirting around the prerequisites of a national, representative consensus. Indeed, legitimacy has been sought by non-representative regimes through a politics of cooption with intermediaries and dependence on an ideological rationale. In the 1960s, General Ayub Khan and his young team emphasised modernisation and development by denigrating the political processes and constitutional norms. In the 1980s, General Zia ul-Haq used Islamisation to legitimise his regime. Whereas in the 1950s the civilian bureaucracy, indirectly helped by the army, denigrated and manipulated the politicians and democratic principles, the successive military regimes of Generals Ayub Khan, Yahya Khan and Zia ul-Haq tried to bypass them. This was largely intended for self-perpetuation but it only weakened the process of national integration and allowed fragmentation of an already weak political culture. Even the elected regimes, largely motivated by personal whim, occasionally used authoritarian methods or simply became paralysed – to the detriment of the democratic process. Whereas generals and civil servants have played havoc with national institutions, politicians have fluctuated between greed and vendetta, which also dented national cohesion.

Significant themes such as constitutionalism,[5] political history,[6] the role of ideology,[7] the preponderance of elitism,[8] military take-overs by Ayub,[9] Yahya[10] and Zia,[11] the bureaucracy,[12] the army,[13] the separation of East Pakistan,[14] the populism of the 1970s,[15] the political economy,[16] geopolitics,[17] defence policy,[18] foreign policy[19] and Kashmir[20] have been amply discussed by various authors. Writers like Tariq Ali,[21] Selig Harrison,[22] Inayatullah Baloch[23] and Lawrence Ziring,[24] when discussing ethnic politics in Pakistan prophesied an eventual disintegration of the country. Hamza Alavi has found Pakistan's dilemma symptomatic of many post-colonial countries where the usual process of maturing into a nation before becoming a country has been reversed.[25] Anwar Syed[26] and Akbar Ahmed[27] believe that there are inherent ethnic tensions in society that pose conceptual problems for the policy-makers. Tahir Amin[28] and Mumtaz Ahmad[29] argue that ethno-regionalism, a major challenge to Pakistani nationhood, has to be seen in the context of foreign intervention, religion and the country's state structure.

Given the wide range of inter-related themes arising from the triangle of authority, ideology and ethnicity, there is a pronounced need for an integrated study that could provide a theoretical and historical framework for Pakistan's exciting but traumatic political career. The present study attempts to meet this challenge and has a simple thesis: that Pakistan's dilemma in being unable to establish good governance despite successive efforts, has largely revolved around a continuous disequilibrium between *state* and *civil society*. This postulates that the state[30] has successively refurbished itself at the expense of vital civil institutions, including the constitution, political parties, pluralism, an independent judiciary, a free press and other think-tanks and activist groups outside the public sector. As a consequence, the imperatives for the establishment of civil society have more usually been sidelined, creating a grave imbalance between the two. Such a dichotomy between state and civil society is closely linked with issues of legitimacy and authority. More significantly, this imbalance has only accentuated ideological manipulation, dissent and ethnic backlashes, since the forces of authority have been neglecting, bulldozing or simply exploiting ideological and pluralist forces. Pakistan is not unique in confronting such conflicts between the forces of authority, ideology and ethnicity. Nevertheless, its policy-makers' continued failure to establish a *possible* and workable synthesis of these three vital forces by means of a dynamic, integrated and judicious equilibrium between the edifices of the state and the vital institutions of civil society betrays their self-interest or lack of intellectual foresight.

STATE AND CIVIL SOCIETY: CONCEPTUALISATION

Whereas adequate material exists on Pakistan's state structure and historical origins,[31] its ideological and ethnic contours, and their complex relationship with multiple forces (including ideology and ethnicity) within society remain largely unexplored. Similarly, no study defining the concept, significance and imperatives of civil society and its interaction with the state has so far been undertaken.[32]

The concept of civil society might appear new, yet it denotes the interdisciplinary nature of a given community based on the supremacy of civilian-led institutions, anchored on distributive justice. In other words, institutions operating under the rubric of civil society aim to strengthen individual and collective rights and to restrain authoritarianism emanating from both the state and other societal forces. Generally speaking, a representative and responsive political system, popularly elected and enjoying a plural mandate, is the net result as well as the prerogative of a mature civil society. In the same context, while guaranteeing the sanctity of pluralism, a mature civil society rejects ideological totalitarianism, elitist monopolisation, majoritarian coercion and ethnic fascism. An ideal civil society in a case like Pakistan would imply decentralisation, democratisation and de-bureaucratisation, allowing greater populist participation in the composition and operation of the state structure. Pakistan's recurrent problems of governance, as in other countries, only add to segmentary politics and ethnic volatility, thus impeding the process of national integration. Civil society certainly means accommodating plurality, establishing egalitarianism, safeguarding human rights and stipulating basic need-oriented policies that give priority to development. In a larger sense, civil society is rooted in democracy, constitutionalism and issues pertaining to the national economy and security. It entails establishing public confidence in domestic and external policies through a corresponding system of accountability to discourage corruption and contain militarism. Such a society is an essential prerequisite for political culture, based on an independent press and judiciary, an efficient educational system and thoughtful planning in which the state encourages voluntary participation rather than operating as a coercive institution and embodies the broad principles of mutual acceptance and tolerance.

This positive image of civil society has evolved with global changes. As a 'second revolution of the developing world', Afro-Asian and Latin-American intellectuals have started exploring the dimensions of the concept. Faith in the state as the *only* vehicle for positive transformation has, in the light of titular, elitist leadership of generals, bureaucrats or coopted intermediaries through a politics of patronage, given way to demands for a new social contract between the state and civil society. In most of the developing world and the former Eastern bloc, the state has developed at the expense of vital civil institutions and this has only added to ideological divisions and ethnic turmoil. The emphasis given by the forces of authority to centralisation and monopolistic policies while lacking legitimacy and consensus has filibustered such unitary systems. A renewed discourse on the major issues of civil rights, academic freedom, a free press, an independent judiciary, deconstruction of elitist, discreet oligarchies, supremacy of the development sector in the national economy, tolerance for ideological and ethnic pluralism and the availability of multiple channels of accountability has already brought the unilateral role of the state under severe scrutiny.

There is no single definition of civil society. To some, it may simply mean a market economy and World Bank-led dictum of governance and governability, while to others it indicates a new definition of civil rights. There is a conscious effort, however, to differentiate it from a regionally specific cliché. To Afro-Asian and Latin-American thinkers, for example, civil society does not mean the rejection of egalitarian 'traditional' institutions as occurred with the proponents of modernisation in recent decades. On the contrary, civil society would imply a combination of both 'back-to-roots' and 'global-village' phenomena dealing with politics, sociology, economics and history. Thus, any discourse on the relationship between the state and civil society in a country like Pakistan would not separate itself from its political, ideological, sociological, economic, regional and global context.

The concept of civil society is not new and was in fact deeply rooted in the Enlightenment. In a definitional sense, it is about the 'fundamental experiential and relational connection between individuals going about their own lives and members of society doing what they are told'.[33] Philosophers like John Locke,[34] Adam Ferguson,[35] Jean Jacques Rousseau[36] and Immanuel Kant[37] wrestled with the idea of civil society in the seventeenth and eighteenth centuries. In a classical sense it was not considered separate from political society, as the wider notion of citizenship formed the basis for social order. Both 'civil' and 'society' were regarded as the opposites of barbarism and savagery. Civil society originally implied refinement of education, aesthetics and sophistication but it has subsequently come to symbolise differentiation between voluntary associations and institutional arrangements of the state. Under the influential views of John Locke and Adam Smith,[38] a clear segregation ensued with the state symbolising the sphere of political power and civil society denoting the free market and cultural and social interactions. However, civil society in Europe and America still largely symbolised a common struggle against despotic absolutism. To Karl Marx, civil society (*Burgerliche Gesellschaft*) was the bed-rock of the state and the economic infrastructure; it exposed the narrow basis of the state and brought into question the legitimacy of holding power over revolutionary classes.[39] However, civil society cannot be solely explained either by the autonomist school, which allows political and social forces a degree of autonomy from an economic foundation, or through the prism of the reductionist model, which sees the entire span of human history in terms of class conflict in which economic system is the sole determinant of thought in any given society. Against these two theoretical positions, Gramsci provided a middle ground between the primordial and the political, postulating a continuous contestation over norms and values. His model has become more relevant with the débâce of the former Soviet Union and Eastern Europe. By suggesting that 'between the economic structure and the State with its legislation and its coercion stands civil society' and that only the latter must be 'radically transformed' so as to avoid degeneration into 'economic moralism', Gramsci appears more relevant in the post-Soviet world.[40]

In contrast to a static concept, civil society is the culmination of deliberate processes of civilising individuals and social relationships. The establishment of civil society, especially in post-colonial societies, poses serious challenges. In the late twentieth century, civil society cannot be taken as a *given* reality, it has to be created and strengthened. The state, which ironically is also an institution based on a relationship, turns out to be the main rival. Civil society is to a large extent the milieu of private contractual relationships.

> It is a coming together of private individuals, an edifice of those who are otherwise strange to one another. ... As such, civil society is clearly distinct from the state. It involves all those relationships which go beyond the purely familial and yet are not of the state. Civil society is about our basic societal relationships and experiences; it is about what happens to us when we leave our family and go about our own lives.[41]

Like Benedict Anderson's idea of cultural nationalism, civil society is also *imagined*[42] as an historical and intellectual construct that is not directly known but from which knowledge can be acquired.

As stated earlier, the concept of civil society has changed over the centuries, as has the relationship between individuals, society and state. Civil society may mean all things to all people, but it is fundamentally a combination of democratic pluralism and protest against authoritarianism with sufficient allowance for state regulations and guidance. In earlier times, women did not take part in any debate on civil society but today they are its most crucial contributors. Similarly, the media, human-rights organisations and independent think-tanks or ethnic dissenters demanding wider participation in the polity are integral sectors of a present-day civil society. The medieval philosopher Ibn Khaldun's concept of civil society carried the sociological, generational model of transformation coming to towns from a rural–tribal milieu and completing itself within a life-span, whereas the Marxian encounter with civil society aimed at investigating the historical materialist forces that underlie or transform a given society. The

Gramscian model is partially useful in the case of South Asia as it is very time- and place-specific. Gramsci showed that the bourgeoisie mainly exercised power through the consent of civil society rather than through a coercive state, reflecting only the West European experience. In the West, the industrial revolution and the rise of the bourgeoisie preceded the extension of the franchise and the creation of modern, democratic political institutions. In post-colonial societies processes of state-formation have preceded nation-formation and, despite a wider use of 'nation-state', the state reflects a more complex phenomenon, more often suffering from legitimacy problems.[43] In a post-1989 perspective, it may be seen as a transition from bureaucratic socialism and economic statism to a constitutional, participatory democracy with wider economic opportunities. Thus, civil society is a reflection of the crisis of the modern state and is also a key word to explain the problems being confronted in the developing world following the imposition of the norms of development and modernity, largely exogenous to indigenous notions of community and tradition.

At present, proponents of this concept of civil society in Western democracies seek to eradicate sexism and exploitation of the third world and nature and to achieve a more harmonious relationship between individuals and society. On the other hand, the struggle to establish civil society is multiple, compound, challenging and protracted. Vestiges of colonialism, undefined issues of identity, powerful state structures defying social and individual prerogatives and ideological regimentation in the name of religion, modernisation or ethnicity have constantly weakened the forces of civil society. Trans-regional influences, mostly at the expense of national and civil priorities, have made the struggle towards establishing civil society more problematic. Even the formation of representative, plural and accountable polities remains the ultimate ideal for many in the developing world, consuming the meagre energies and resources at the disposal of weak civic voluntary groups. Thus, civil society in the perspective of the developing world is an interface between primordial social groups and political authority and is a continuum of changing processes and scenarios, with internal and global forces exerting an unbridled influence, in most cases contradicting the civic dictums of a given society.

Studies on the developing world in general and modern South Asia in particular are handicapped not only by the complexity and intensity of the polarisation between state and society, but also because the theoretical models used to understand these phenomena are more often derivatives of extrinsic historical experiences. Questions of identity, authority, legitimacy and universal welfare need to be seen in the geographical and historical context of the region.[44] To some social scientists, 'the problematique of change in South Asia involves the move (*not* linear) from hierarchy; insular, "little communities" and "social" order to egalitarianism, individual, law and "state" order.'[45] A host of studies from South Asia simply concentrate on themes such as communal, ethnic and border conflicts, ignoring the traditions endogamous to the region and consequently reinforcing the exogenous theoretical models. Pakistan is a useful case study where one finds two emergent schools of thought. The first view is that civil society is falling apart given the unresolved questions of identity, ideology and ethnicity further compounded by a monolithic state structure. According to this view the continued elitist monopoly in dysfunction with international forces has resiliently blocked the empowerment of the masses and the middle class. The second view, largely shared by this author, is more optimistic and sees civil society in Pakistan emerging from an abysmal state and redefining itself. Here, the emphasis is laid on civility, tolerance and decency as the moral grounds of civil society, which is being translated through an assertive press, diversified opinion groups and human rights activists. Politics of gender, exposure of corruption and similar distortions in all the areas of authority, ideology and ethnicity and a critical judiciary form major features of this *transforming* civil society. Erstwhile acrimonious debate on nationalism and trans-territoriality has been largely replaced by a new debate on national and ethnic identities. People have overwhelmingly supported the moderate forces in consecutive elections, and rapid urbanisation and consumerism mingled with more mobility and unlimited access to print and visual media have already unleashed new processes of communication. A comparatively youthful society, most of whose members have been brought up as *Pakistanis*, are not only demanding an efficient and congenial government but are also raising voices against a continued monopoly of feudal interests over politics. They are not comfortable with the existing oligarchic tripolar relationship between the bureaucracy, the military and politicians which smacks of age-old dynastic elitism and so the demands for accountability are becoming louder.

This discussion on the dilemma between state and civil society begins with an overview of the dilemmas of Pakistani political culture, where disregard for constitutionalism and emphasis on authoritarianism and praetorianism, mingled with the obdurate forces of geography, history and political economy, have distorted civil society and hampered the process of national integration. The vetoing state structure, following the colonial tradition in management rather than governance is (according to Punjab–Indus-Basin tradition) rooted in a trans-regional elitism which has been using ideological rhetoric merely to perpetuate itself. The present study, while improvising on the concept of elite/elitism as provided by Laswell,[46] accepts its different postulations. An elite group – social, economic or political – consists of those people 'who exercise power, influence and authority over others' operating as 'power-holders' in a given society.[47] As discussed in Chapter 2, the Pakistani polity is rooted in the colonial tradition of patronage, with the landed aristocracy frequently acting as willing partners and a coopted elite. On the other hand, ideological groups, largely suffering from internal splits resulting from an age-old yet largely undefined quest for identity, have been unable to provide any tangible alternative other than rhetoric. Regimes have often either benefited from such dissensions or, as in the case of the feudalists, have simply sought cooption from the religious elite. Whereas landed and ideological groups have both maintained a clientelist relationship with a vetoing state, a new intermediate class (apart from the business and professional elite) might signal a major change in the coming years.

As Chapter 2 investigates ideological polarisation and its exploitation by the state, Chapter 3 makes it evident that the Pakistani state, in a rigorous sense, is anchored on the uncontested primacy of bureaucracy and the military, which has become solidified over the years through a legacy of elitism and authoritarianism. Its opportunistic dallying with the feudal forces and religious–spiritual leaders has not allowed meaningful decentralisation and democratisation in a plural society like Pakistan and, in order to perpetuate itself, it has institutionalised a politics of corruption. An oligarchic alliance among the ruling elite continues to resist demands for land reforms and basic issues like legitimacy, empowerment of the people and long overdue reforms in the socio-administrative set-up. Chapter 4 is devoted to the study of feudalist politics in Pakistan. The landed elite, who have benefited from a politics of patronage and corresponding oligarchic polity, have consolidated their position and successfully transformed themselves into a trans-regional power group. The state, in alliance with the feudalists, has evaded the urgency of an honorific social contract with civil society, and damaged itself to the extent that an autonomous, invisible government run by intelligence agencies has unleashed its own forces of blackmail, harassment and torture. Chapter 5 is, thus, an attempt to seek the roots and operation of this parallel government, or the hidden hand, engaged in a war with civil society.

Chapter 6 is an in-depth study of the uneasy relationship between the state and civil society. Various sectors of civil society, including social welfare, education and health, have been the direct casualties of such a monopolist, narrowly based, *statist* elitism, with the administration ignoring demands for an independent judiciary, a free press and priority for the long-ignored development sector. Chapter 7 discusses the conflictive duality between state and civil society in the arena of gender politics. Through a theoretical and historical framework, the challenges and dynamics of an emerging area of civil society are explored. Based on a number of first-hand reports and statistics, this chapter highlights both the tribulations and responses of a new female political culture in Pakistan.

The dilemma of state and civil society not only hinges on the feudalisation of politics and bureaucratisation of the polity compounded by both domestic and external forces, it is also evident in the ethnic arena, which is still largely undefined despite its centrality in Pakistan's national experience. The last three chapters of this study show that if ethnicity is harnessed properly and judiciously, it can be a supportive factor in the evolution of a positive equation between state and civil society. However, actual experience has been the opposite. In Pakistan, ethnic pluralism is usually dismissed by the policy-makers and reduced to a mere law-and-order issue. The various forces operating in Sindh, especially in Karachi, may dismay any thinking Pakistani, especially after the separation of the former eastern wing in 1971. Though ethnic multiplicity in Sindh (despite the criminal acts by certain sections) is not secessionist, its comprehension and appropriate responses to it through tangible measures are a major challenge to the state and civil society. It signals the urgency of long-overdue reforms in the politico-administrative and economic systems, together with decentralisation and de-bureaucratisation. Thus, Sindh is a major test-case for Pakistan, which has strong reasons for entering the twenty-first century with renewed vigour and dynamic self-reliance.

The development of Pakistan from an idea to a reality in the colonial past is grounded in a political tradition inculcated through a constitutional struggle signalling the triumph of an infantile civil society over a state that was largely perceived as alien. Pakistan's survival against all the odds and its ultimate progress in a number of areas despite long spells of authoritarianism speak for the vibrancy of its people. The efforts of its political activists (supported by ordinary citizens) to establish a moderate, forward-looking, political system guaranteeing basic rights and curbing corruption and coercion, remain unstinted even though nepotism, vendettas and 'horse-trading' have disenchanted many Pakistanis. The role of an investigative press (in many instances where even parliamentarians have failed), the emergence of a cross-regional intermediate class of thinking and objecting citizens, a reawakened judiciary, active campuses and politicised masses led by an overwhelmingly youthful generation of leaders all provide hopes of more responsible and positive developments in the years to come.

1 Dilemma of Political Culture, National Integration and Constitutionalism

Pakistan's enduring intra-regional cultural attributes and fragile civic institutions have too often been jolted by major demographic developments, a politico-economic system lacking legitimacy, and authoritarian or quasi-democratic regimes bolstering themselves through centrist state structures. Despite shared historical and cultural traditions, economic interdependence and ecological integration, the problem of Pakistan's governability remains undiminished. In a symbiotic relationship, civil society which even in its embryonic form was weak and fragmented, has simply remained an appendage to the powerful state structure. Accountability, a decent educational system, egalitarian economic policies to help the have-nots and minorities, a non-partisan judiciary, a vigilant press, participation by women – all those necessary requirements of a vibrant civil society – have suffered from constant erosion. Such a dichotomous relationship has negatively affected the moral and cross-ethnic coherence in the country, otherwise embodied in the humane and folk traditions of the society. The process of national integration was ill-planned, officious and injudicious, with centripetal and centrifugal forces battling within the very *corpus* of the state which, true to its proto-colonial character, either chose to adopt the role of an indifferent observer or turned partisan.

The evolution of the country has been due to the triumph of political processes negotiated through constitutional means in a struggle against the well-entrenched forces of the colonial state and similar blocks. However, in the post-independence period, personalised politics and a total disregard for constitutionalism have often sunk the country into 'political paralysis', which emphasises the 'immaturity of Pakistan's democracy'.[1] The crisis of governance in Pakistan beginning with the dismissal of Nazim ud-Din as prime minister in 1953 and followed by elected governments until 1993, the use of strong executive orders, long phases of martial law, authoritarianism, further partition of the country and frequent conflict between the centre and the provinces or among ethnic groups, remain largely endemic. The failure to establish a viable, all-encompassing political culture despite positive idealism is at the root of Pakistan's inability to develop an integrated national cohesion or to guarantee its territorial integrity and economic development.

To many observers and commentators on Pakistan, the lack of a commonly defined and mutually shared political culture in the country since its birth has been the main stumbling block in the quest for nationhood. Major constraints on the achievement of this aim include crises of political geography, and political economy, and of representative, capable leadership; fragmented political parties and ever-changing loyalties; a disregard for constitutionalism; oligarchic elites and misplaced preferences; ideological rhetoric. In addition of course there have been regional and global influences.

In this chapter we consider the first three factors.

THE POLITICS OF GEOGRAPHY, ECONOMY AND IDENTITY

Difficult and conflictive forces of political economy, together with unfavourable geographic realities, may largely account for Pakistan's failure in establishing a common political culture, especially in the years before 1971. The sheer distance between the two former wings of the country, as well as their distinct demographic, cultural, economic and political differences have been held responsible for the divisiveness within the polity. Before the evolution of Bangladesh, both wings were typical of countries that were 'not yet nations in being but only nations in hope'.[2] Despite their differences, with geographic and political mutual dependence Pakistan might still have escaped the break-up in 1971. However, a very hostile Inida, reluctant to accept the independent Pakistan, exploited the geographic divide to its own advantage in order to humble a predominantly Muslim Pakistan.

Both before and after 1971, politics in Pakistan, as defined by Clifford Geertz, entails the dilemma of 'old societies and new states' and, as in many other developing societies, region-based 'primordial sentiments' are yet to be transformed into trans-regional 'civil sentiments'.[3] While East Pakistan presented a homogeneous 'political' society, West Pakistan appeared 'governmental', the bane of the civil and military bureaucracy. The common religious ethos was perhaps the only common denominator in the two regions other than a belated desire for self-determination, and this made the process of integration almost impossible, with official efforts being diverted mainly to government-building. Given the contemporary emphasis on the state as a vehicle of change, in Pakistan the state (with no

legitimacy and no mandate) took upon itself the role of 'deliverer' to bring
about modernisation and development, which were both considered essential for national integration. While in the developed world the state
evolved out of a developed nationhood, in most post-colonial countries
the state and nation had to be carved out simultaneously. State-building
and nation-building involve opposite and contrasting processes, though in
developing countries like Pakistan they were considered synonymous.
State-building implies refurbishing the administrative machinery and the
centralisation of authority, whereas nation-building stipulates dispersion
of powers, cooption of peripheral groups and decentralisation.[4]

Religion has certainly played a crucial role in the recent history of the
sub-continent and continues to do so, particularly in India, with a new-found
vigour. However, as mentioned earlier, after independence it was language
that was destined to create fissions – amply helped by geography and
uneven politico-economic development. As elsewhere in South Asia, linguistic and geographic factors in Pakistan have continued to play a
significant role in ethnic identification. Pakistan was and is a multi-lingual
and essentially plural society. By 1961, 55.48 per cent of Pakistanis spoke
Bengali as the mother tongue whereas Punjabi accounted for 29.02 per cent
in the total population; 5.51 per cent claimed Sindhi to be their mother
tongue whereas Pushto was spoken by 3.7 per cent of the country's population. Only 3.65 per cent and 0.02 per cent spoke Urdu and English respectively whereas Balochi accounted for 1.09 per cent of the aggregate figures.[5]
It would be a Herculean task to acquire a lingua franca for Pakistan given
this linguistic heterogeneity, although, at least in West Pakistan, Urdu was a
likely choice. Bengali was certainly subscribed to by an overwhelming
majority of Pakistanis (Bengalis) and, defined in the context of a territory, it
proved to be the threshold for Bengali (Bangladeshi) nationalism. Urdu, for
understandable reasons, had been considered synonymous with the Pakistan
Movement and the recent Islamic past in India. During the nationalist
period, even the 'Bengali' Muslim elites in the forefront of the struggle for
Pakistan spoke Urdu or Persian, giving it a rather elitist position, whereas
the regional, provincial and ethnic languages persisted with their own historic distinctness as cultural expressions. The Bengalis were the first to
resent the predominance of Urdu as the national language though it had
already become the lingua franca in northern India both as a literary language and as a common medium of conversation.[6] On the other hand, the
East Pakistanis felt that because of their numerical majority and the historic-
ity of their language, Bengali should have been designated the national language of the young Muslim state. When the expatriate Muslim elites in
Pakistan set up the triple forces of Urdu, Pakistan and Islam as the

cornerstones of the infantile Pakistani nationalism, the process of alienation began – largely in Muslim Bengal and, to a limited extent, in other 'smaller' provinces. Lingual commonalities in a given territory helped to politicise ethnicity. Demographic and historic claims and counterclaims were postulated on all sides to air the antagonistic feelings and, in a political vacuum with a thinly based state structure, relations between the 'core' and 'peripheries' turned increasingly sour.

Urdu had been used by great thinkers like Sir Syed Ahmed Khan and Allama Muhammad Iqbal to foster Muslim nationalism and Mohammad Ali Jinnah rightly felt that the nation needed a common national language and that Urdu, true to its assimilative traditions, might attain that status. However, it was not so much the language but the accompanying assertive and self-righteous sentiments that ultimately turned the Bengali-speaking East Pakistanis away from the language itself. Language and territory complemented each other in identity-formation while religion was neutral. To East Pakistanis, Urdu gradually came to symbolise the language of the ruling West Pakistani elite (Muhajir and Punjabi) and, as a reaction, Bengali nationalism in its Muslim formulation rooted itself in primordial traditions. Numerous analysts have provided the statistical details on the vast gulf between the two wings of Pakistan. Rounaq Jahan's meticulous study ably pinpointed such differences through numerous tables to prove that East Pakistan was on the receiving end. Nevertheless, such a comparative study can be made with reference to any country where inter-regional differences in terms of jobs, trade and economy underline parallel scenarios. In fact, for decades there has been an inherent divide between Western and Eastern Bengal despite the fact that both were the oldest part of the British empire in India.[7] Varied countries like India, the former Soviet Union, the United Kingdom, Canada or the USA embody variations in terms of economic development and underdevelopment, yet in Pakistan with its peculiar geographic location and a national consciousness still in the embryonic stage, economic unevenness accentuated language and region-based separatism. Thus, at one level it is simplistic to suggest that the inter-wing divide was symptomatic of an internal colonialism or a necessary result of exploitation of one province by another.[8]

Balochistan

Divergent but mutually intertwined forces of geography, culture and economy are still vital for understanding a persistent governability dilemma which prevents the evolution of a consensus-based political culture. Balochistan is the largest province in Pakistan, with the smallest share in national population.[9] There are more Balochis in Karachi than in the entire province, yet in the metropolitan population they are not a visible majority compared to Urdu-speakers. In Sindh, Balochi tribes over the past few centuries have formed the major land-owning *wadera* dynasties, but their politics revolve around personal interests or are simply *Sindh*-based and have nothing to do with any articulate *Baloch* ethnicity. Northwestern Balochistan is mainly populated by Pushtuns whose ethnic affinities lie with the Pushtuns in the neighbouring North-West Frontier Province (NWFP) and the tribals rather than with their Baloch neighbours.[10]

Within the Baloch tribes, there are further land-based loyalties fanning local clan rivalries. The Baloch diaspora in Pakistan, while confined to a limited section of elites and a small middle class, turns irredentist when it lays claim to Baloch territories in Afghanistan and Iran. Political developments in these countries have immensely influenced Pakistani Balochistan which is the historical and spiritual leader for all the Balochis.[11] However, despite closer affinity with the compatriots in Southwestern Punjab, the emphasis has been on an overarching *Saraiki* identity which, among others, includes Baloch tribes in Punjab, NWFP and upper Sindh but is not exclusively Baloch *per se*. Balochistan still remains outside the main economic activity zones such as the central Punjab and Karachi. An industrial zone at Hub remains on the industrial periphery of Karachi, and both Gwadar and Gaddani would need major efforts to become alternative ports with a wider communication network linking them to the rest of the country. Along a 400-mile-long coast of the Arabian Sea all the way from Hub to the mouth of the Gulf, Balochistan is still awaiting gigantic efforts in industrial development. Despite its geo-strategic significance and its mineral resources, Balochistan needs an efficient infrastructure in transport and communications. Balochistan provides natural gas, called Sui gas, to the whole of urban Pakistan but Quetta had to wait for years before it had a supply line installed. Even the establishment of an agricultural college becomes a coveted and contested proposition, which shows that the Baloch, like the rest of their countrymen, are anxious for their province to be developed. Although Pushtun–Baloch rivalries or inter-tribal disagreements can pose major problems, an administratively decentralised Balochistan could move towards self-sufficiency and peace. It could also relieve the added burden on Karachi's fledgling socio-economic infrastructure.

During the British Raj, it was mainly in Quetta and some parts of Pushtun Balochistan that initial institutions were established. For geo-political reasons, the British generally concentrated on wider issues and left the internal affairs of the area to the customary local tribal chiefs who owed a nominal allegiance to the Khan of Kalat.[12] Kalat[13] was the largest of all the tribal states and the British resident in Quetta negotiated with the chieftains of the Bugti, Marri, Mengal, Lashari, Khetran and Jamali tribes.[14] It was well after independence before Balochistan obtained the designation of a full-fledged province. Even today, the tribal agencies are still maintained within and around the province as part of the dualism that the Raj had introduced because of administrative and geo-political imperatives. During Zulfikar Ali Bhutto's rule in the mid-1970s, Balochistan passed through a very rough time when the Pakistani army engaged in a military operation against the Baloch guerrillas who were allegedly working for secession. Moved by his own whims and encouraged by an over-vigilant Shah of Iran, Bhutto engaged the armed forces in a futile exercise which only increased ill-feeling among the Balochis and other concerned Pakistanis. Many of the Baloch activists went into exile or engaged in guerrilla activities. It was under General Zia ul-Haq that the armed forces were recalled to barracks and the province returned to peace. However, with the presence of well-armed Afghan refugees and Iranian dissidents, inter-tribal and inter-sectarian tensions increased in Balochistan. In certain areas the Afghan refugees outnumbered the indigenous population. Gunrunning and drug trafficking, as well as the human traffic in political exiles across the three borders, created serious divisions within traditional Balochi socio-economic values. The Baloch Students' Organisation (BSO), a powerful student body representing lower middle-class Baloch intelligentsia and a training ground for many Baloch politicians, is an articulate and influential organisation holding liberal and leftist ideas. It aims at the abolition of the *jagirdari* and strives for the rights of the minority provinces. The BSO has provided cadres of workers and middle-level political leadership to parties like the Balochistan National Movement (BNM). Traditionally, the state has depended on the dynastic Baloch families and chieftains to represent the centre in the province, so making politics an exclusive affair on the whole. On the other hand, ethnic-based organisations such as BSO or BNM and the local press have been airing their dissatisfaction with the majoritarian system, perceived to be run by non-Balochi ethnic groups. Curiously, in Balochistan, the *ulama*, generally represented by the Jamiat i-Ulama i-Islam (JUI), have been coalition partners with the progressive and nationalist parties and have apparently shown a degree of pragmatism.

The Punjab

The Punjab itself, despite being one of the earliest provinces in British India to undergo an agro-based transformation by means of a highly

developed irrigation system and settlement, is hindered by its political tradition.[15] Its great size, and its administrative set-up, true to 'the Punjab
tradition', tend toward the apolitical.[16] In 1897 the British Punjab was the
last province to receive its own legislative council, where most of the seats
were allotted to the representatives of loyalist landlords – the intermediaries.[17] Such dynasties[18] maintained their hold on Punjabi politics through
strong political parties like the Punjab National Unionist Party which ruled
the province until 1947. The party came into existence in 1923 within the
Punjab Legislative Council due to the adroit efforts of Mian Fazl-i
Hussain. He had brought a group of predominantly rural landlords in a
supra-communal fashion to work closely with the provincial administration. India-wide organisations such as the All-India Muslim League
(AIML) and the Indian National Congress (INC) remained confined to a
few urban middle-class elites.[19] Provincial elites, coming from a feudal
background, dominated politics in the Punjab, UP, (Muslim) Bengal,[20] and
in the new province of Sindh[21] until independence; similar politics of
official preferences and patronage have been continued by successive
Pakistani regimes. The rural–urban divide frustrated national leaders like
Iqbal and Jinnah who considered it to be a major impediment to the development of an India-wide Muslim nationalism. 'Punjabi ruralism' defended
by the provincial/regional elites, like that of the NWFP and Sindh, served
the Raj faithfully but thwarted any effort from outside to break the local
isolationism.[22] The Punjab tradition embodying prioritisation of administration over governance and characterised by rural–urban splits along with
inter-religious dissent, did not allow a young political culture to develop
into a cohesive force – though in the late 1940s it appeared for a moment
that the Pakistan Movement had been able to dent the 'old' order.[23] For a
long time, the Punjabi political culture has remained static, true to its roots
in the Raj, with a hegemonic symbiosis between the landed aristocracy
and the services.

In the 1980s, however, a strong group of entrepreneurs, especially from
the small business community, had apparently emerged as a new political
reality. Zulfikar Ali Bhutto underrated the significance of this new intermediate class when he hastily nationalised the rice-husking mills in the
province. On the other hand, his successor, General Zia ul-Haq, himself a
Punjabi, courted this politically ambitious, economically industrious and
temperamentally conservative group, at the same time winning over the
loyalties of the traditional elites. During the early prime ministership of
Benazir Bhutto (1988–90) following a plural electoral verdict, Punjab confronted the central government for the first time and accused non-Punjabi
forces of 'Punjabi-bashing'.[24] Subsequently, Nawaz Sharif faced a revolt

from within the Punjab in early 1993 when Manzoor Watoo and other MPAs rebelled (interestingly many of them were from a rural background). In this largely inter-personal conflict, the Punjab was once again in revolt against the federal government. Nawaz Sharif was widely regarded as a representative of a cross-sectional intermediate group of entrepreneurs, though even as the leader of the Islamic Democratic Alliance (IDA/IJT) and as a prime minister he had to seek support from the traditional land-owning elites.[25]

The Punjab, being the oldest and the most prosperous of all the present federal units, has played a more visible role in the economy and in services. The former East Pakistan, however, despite its numerical preponderance and socio-cultural homogeneity found itself relegated to a diminished status. In a similar though less antagonistic way the elites from smaller provinces have had feelings of awe towards the Punjab and, over the years, 'Punjabi domination' has become a frequent reference in Pakistani political parlance.

Sindh

Sindh, the second largest province in the country with a significant share in the national population and socio-economic activities, was designated as a separate province in 1936. Previously, it had been a peripheral region of the huge Bombay presidency.[26] Predominantly rural in character, Sindh was largely like Southwestern Punjab under the clannish domination of various tribal dynasties, most of them Baloch by origin. However, economic and administrative powers lay with the Hindus. Educationally, economically and politically Sindh remained totally dependent on Bombay. Karachi was a much smaller town, so that even affluent Sindhis would send their children for higher studies and subsequently for jobs and business to metropolitan Bombay. Nevertheless, while Sindh remained attuned to Bombay its political ethos followed the Punjab tradition, and it also experienced a Punjab-like development of its irrigation system, being a part of the same Indus basin. The effect of this was to create divisions rather than unity over the distribution of water resources.

Predominantly a rural population under the traditional influence of the *sardars*, *syeds* and *pirs* lacked the urban component that the Punjab and united Bengal enjoyed with reference to Muslim politics in the subcontinent. The Sindhi *waderas* and *haris* both carried a strong grudge against the Hindu Baniya and, in the 1940s, idealised Pakistan as the ultimate source of deliverance.[27] It is noteworthy that it was G. M. Syed who, more than anybody else, presented a supportive resolution on Pakistan in the Sindh Assembly in 1943 by surpassing the other Muslim majority provinces. Sindhi politics, as we shall see in subsequent chapters, remained confined to a feudal elite until the predominantly urban Urdu-speaking refugees from India provided a turning point in its history.[28] With the exodus of the Hindu moneyed class to India in 1947, Sindhis believed that their adversities were over. But millions of well-educated, mobile and resourceful Muhajireen transformed the demographic, political and economic contours of Pakistani Sindh in their own favour. The socio-political cosmos was further compounded with the migration from up-country in the wake of Karachi's growing financial and industrial significance. Gradually, Sindhis found themselves in the difficult role of reluctant hosts to new pressure groups on their land; sentiments against the outsiders and 'settlers' increased. Alignment of the Pakistani state with the mobile Muhajireen at the expense of the natives left a lasting scar on Sindhi intellectuals, who found themselves being marginalised. Urdu and Pakistan symbolised a superior identity, while Sindh was left with plati-tudes like the title of *Dar ul-Islam* and being called a melting pot; there was also a renewed emphasis on Sindhi docility. The consolidation of a new power elite and the importance of the urban sector to the exclusion of the large number of indigenous Sindhis, whipped up strong feelings of *Sindhi* identity which had been sown in the campaign for a separate province. Since the Manzilgah incident in 1938, following Hindu–Muslim riots over a mosque and temple controversy in Sukkur, *Muslim* identity had overshadowed its *Sindhi* counterpart which stemmed from lingual, ter-ritorial and cultural commonalitics. In more recent years, the role of intel-lectuals like the late G. M. Syed, or the memory of Zulfikar Ali Bhutto who is considered to have been martyred by the Punjabi–Muhajir oli-garchy, have further substantiated slogans like 'sons of the soil'. The politicisation of ethnicity amongst the Sindhis and Muhajireen is deeply linked with migration, which has been steadily transforming the demo-graphic and resultant politico-economic realities in Sindh.

The North-West Frontier Province

The NWFP, like the other federating units in Pakistan, is a British cre-ation, which arose from purely administrative and geo-political considera-tions and which successive Pakistani administrations have continued. Since every province in Pakistan today is a frontier province, the title in a literal sense does not signify anything historical or cultural *per se*. In fact, even 'Pushtunistan' does not make much sense given the fact that there are so many Hindko-speakers in addition to a very vast expanse of Hazara region linking Pothowar in Punjab with the Northern Areas. In addition the tribal agencies, created a hundred years ago purely for geo-strategic reasons and crudely corresponding to the colonial definition and 'reorganisation' of the segmentary Pushtun tribal societies, represent another part of the NWFP, centrally administered and embodying a parallel political economy. In 1901 Lord Curzon, before partitioning Bengal, experimented on the formation of the NWFP – initially as a division under a chief commissioner and then as a province under a lieutenant-governor.

As in the Punjab, politics in the NWFP remained the preserve of a small middle class, originally activated by the Khilafat Movement and led by Khan Abdul Ghaffar Khan, generally known as the Frontier Gandhi. Politics on the Frontier like in Balochistan in the pre-1947 years – unlike the Punjab and Sindh – has been less communal and more ethnic.[29] Sahibzada Abdul Qayyum was one of the earliest benefactors of the province who pioneered modern educational institutions. Khan Abdul Ghaffar Khan organised his Red Shirts with his intellectual son, Ghani Khan, founding the Pukhtun Zalmai, a party of young Pushtuns. Khudai Khidmatgar or the Red Shirts was a regional party whereas the all-India parties such as the INC and AIML remained confined to a few urban Muslims.[30] While provincial politics centred around urban notables, tribal affairs were administered by political agents, representing the Indian Civil Service (ICS).[31] The local tribal *maliks* operated as intermediaries receiving remuneration, guns and individual benefits from the Raj and reciprocated by keeping their respective *ilaqajat* (territories) peaceful. Smuggling, gunrunning and tribal warfare did not matter to the Raj as long as they did not threaten imperial interests. The political agents masterminded day-to-day administration with the help of the *jirga* based on the *Pukhtunwali*, the Pathan code, whereas the Raj opted to leave the common tribals to their chieftains. Even after five decades of independence the tribal population remains largely disenfranchised with the *maliks* playing the role of intermediaries in the politics of patronage. The tribal chieftains not only exploit their own relations with Islamabad and Peshawar but also play power politics *vis-à-vis* Kabul by changing their loyalties.

Due to the almost complete absence of opportunities in their own mountainous regions because of internecine tribal warfare and the influx of millions of Afghan refugees, many tribals have chosen to settle in urban centres where they provide the bulk of the local blue-collar labour and staff inner-city transport. Mobility within tribal Pushtuns, unparalleled since the Gulf bonanza in the 1970s and the dissipation of romanticisation of 'Pushtunistan',[32] has led to interesting and far-reaching consequences both for the tribals and for the rest of Pakistan. All the way from Torkham and Karlachi to Karachi, the truck traffic, wayside restaurants and timber trade are largely run by the Pushtuns. Today, Karachi is the largest Pushtun city, way ahead of Peshawar or Mardan. Pushtuns have been mostly integrated into the Pakistani economy on a voluntary basis by 'push' factors such as population explosion, the situation on the borders and the Afghan crisis. In short, the divisions between the tribal and settled populations as well as the personality-centred politics in the NWFP have retarded the political processes in the province. The economic and professional integration of the province, so close to the Punjab and especially to Islamabad, has helped to enter mainstream national life. Pushtun students, bureaucrats, generals and merchants already outnumber their counterparts from Sindh and Balochistan and are competing with the Punjabis and Muhajireen. However, such a process needs conscious, well-planned efforts for national integration.

Northern Areas

Technically, the Northern Areas, comprising Gilgit, Diamir and Baltistan, like the tribal agencies in the NWFP and Balochistan, are administratively designated as the Federally Administrated Areas (FATA) with special quota allocation. Islamabad, the federal territory, did not have its own representation on the National Assembly or Senate for some time, whereas the tribal agencies did enjoy this privilege (though on the basis of a very limited and archaic franchise). Although the Northern Areas form regular districts they do not have any representation on the national electoral bodies and are administered through divisional and district bureaucracy. This might be explained by the contentious claims and counterclaims on the basis of their ambiguous relations with the former state of Jammu and Kashmir. However, such politico-administrative anomalies in this vital region leave ample scope for over-bureaucratisation resulting in a severe sense of alienation. While Kashmiris living in Pakistan since migrating from the Indian-occupied Kashmir after 1947 maintain their own system of separate electorates, Azad Jammu and Kashmir – despite being an independent territory with separate political parties, president and prime minister – is mainly administered by the Kashmir Council and the Ministry of Kashmir Affairs in Islamabad. The Karakoram Highway (KKH) opened in the early 1980s following collaboration between the Pakistani and Chinese engineers, has made the Northern Areas easily accessible to the rest of the country. Consequently, inter-regional migration, trade involving goods and tourism, have created enormous new prospects for the integration of these previously remote areas. The KKH serves as an example to the rest of the country to develop a technology-based infrastructure in communications to achieve national harmony. An important result of the KKH has been the increased demand for a realistic politico-administrative definition of these areas.

Existing anomalies characterising the continued crisis of governance in Pakistan thwart efforts for a cohesive *national* political culture embracing all the segmentary entities into a mainstream collective polity. The localisation and regionalisation of politics rooted in the colonial past continue to veto solitary efforts to express a trans-regional political consciousness. Similarly, geographic challenges in a vast country like Pakistan, accompanied by disputed claims over a narrow resource-base routinely exacerbate mutual antagonism. In the process, identity-formation falls to primordial, local and reactive factors rather than searching for shared traditions and horizontal linkages.

The ethno-political divisions and strategies involved in identity-formation have been discussed in a subsequent chapter, but it will be of interest now to consider how the Urdu-speaking migrants from India have added to political plurality in the young country. Mainly urban, better educated and politically more active in the mainstream political parties like the AIML or INC or JUH, these refugees very ably created a niche in the new power structure in Pakistan. Whereas Biharis resisted assimilation into mainstream Muslim Bengali culture, their compatriots from the UP or Hyderabad state, gradually alienated the native Sindhis by emphasising their own socio-cultural exclusivity. Although this cultural separatism is easily understood in the context of the Pakistan Movement, it has nevertheless resulted in a vast gulf in present-day Sindh where Urdu and mobility have been equated with Muhajir dominance in the new state.[33]

On the other hand, migrants from eastern Punjab and adjoining areas seem to have easily assimilated into mainstream Punjabi society. Language did not turn out to be a divisive factor since most of them spoke Punjabi or were familiar with it. Moreover, urban Punjabi plural traditions did not cause any pulls or pushes either for the migrants or the natives. A successful process of acculturation in the Punjab over the preceding five decades saved it from becoming another Sindh in the late 1980s.

The interplay of territory, language and cultural homogeneity, cemented together through a sense of political alienation in a state structure rooted in specific prerogatives, formulated various communitarian responses in Pakistan. The politicisation of ethnic interests mainly hinges on forces governing and emanating from the political economy in the country. While economic development has assisted the emergence of an intermediate class in the country, the elitist state structure is largely anchored on support from land-based intermediaries. With increasing urbanisation and diversification of the economy, the intermediate class might eventually operate as a reformative force, but for now it remains marginalised because of the traditional power structure. This new class of entrepreneurs may seek occasional refuge in ethnic identification until it becomes a trans-regional group, though it would be premature to assume that ethnicity as a factor in Pakistani politics will disappear altogether in the future.

Since 1949, while trying to adjust to post-1947 trauma, Pakistan followed a twin-track economic policy, allowing private-sector and market forces to guide the economy and the state-led sector to help fill the gaps.[34] During Ayub Khan's period, when the state was visibly more involved in the economy, market forces were left to alleviate poverty.[35] Mahbubul Haq, one of the authors of the Second Five-Year Plan in the early 1960s, like other contemporary planners believed that prosperity would filter down to the underprivileged sections in society. The contemporary rationale was that a stable, modernising government of strong men (even/without any democratic pretensions, but working for total development) was preferable to the 'soft governments' of the anti-colonial elites.[36] Haq and many of his generation were soon disillusioned as the national wealth was confined to a few industrialist families.[37] In this atmosphere, Zulfikar Ali Bhutto criticised private capital and pursued a policy of nationalisation. This created its own difficulties, however, as rather than increasing output and equity it only bureaucratised the vital economic sector. General Zia ul-Haq, helped by foreign remittances and aid, tried to denationalise some areas, while since 1990–91 Pakistan has set herself on the course of full-fledged privatisation and liberalisation of the economy, granting complete autonomy to market forces.[38] It is too early to know the results of this policy, although poverty seems to be less acute and there is more economic activity in the country. Contrary to Zia's period of consumption, Pakistan in the 1990s aims at reaching the threshold of newly industrialised countries. It has certainly entered the middle-income group, yet major policy changes in national economic strategies, ever-increasing defence expenditures, multiplying foreign loans, a budgetary deficit, increased migration and urbanisation compounded by the high proportion of young people in a constantly growing population have all unleashed parallel processes of percolation and dislocation.[39] Recently, Pakistan has been looking for models of economic development; the examples of South Korea and Malaysia, as well as Japan, demonstrate the need for well-planned and stable policies guaranteed by political stability and a continued era of peace. Despite its receding regulatory role, the state would remain a major guarantor and arbiter in the process of economic development and that is where a new equation is needed to epitomise processes of national integration.

NATIONAL LEADERSHIP CRISIS

An agonising legacy for the Pakistani polity, over successive decades, obstructing the evolution of consensus-based political culture and national integration, has been the absence of national leadership. It is common to hear Pakistanis from many walks of life bemoaning the absence of an honest and capable national leadership with the necessary diligence, tolerance and foresight to cement the disparate politico-geographic regions and traditions into a mainstream national consciousness. Textbooks deplore the leadership crisis as the main misfortune for a young country born in adversity. Jinnah's untimely death left Pakistan with his successors claiming authority but seriously lacking legitimacy and the ability to lead the country out of its many problems. The leadership crisis was evident at the second-tier level even during the 1930s and 1940s when Jinnah was coopting Muslim elites. Within the AIML, most of the leaders came from traditional feudal or bourgeois urban classes and had no contact with the grass-roots. Many of these Leaguers, who were later to become rulers of Pakistan, were mere figureheads or regional elites welded together thanks to the acumen of the Quaid and by the overarching ideal of Pakistan.

Religious parties run by Muslim *ulama* in addition to their inherent technical weaknesses, lacked a consensus-based programme for Indian Muslims. On the one hand, many of them like Abul Kalam Azad seriously doubted the credentials of Muslim nationalism as spearheaded by the AIML, and they ended up supporting national parties like INC. Other Muslim parties like the Ahrars, Jama 'at-i Islami (JI), Khaksars, or Jamiat-i Ulama-i Hind (JUH) showed strong reservations if not sheer antagonism towards the AIML, regarding it as a party of westernised Muslims paying lip service to Islam. In an ideal democratic set-up, such parties would have benefited from the debate on Muslim identity but they chose to negate the very *raison d'être* of Pakistan. Nevertheless, once Pakistan came into being these groups joined a hectic race to convert it into a theocratic state.

The fragmentation of the Muslim elites and absence of a healthy and productive dialogue created an ongoing split within Muslim politics, allowing it frequently to fall back upon regionalist, segmented identities. In India, Muslims were left leaderless while in Pakistan they were confronted with theocratic claims on the nascent polity. Liaquat Ali

Khan, a long-time associate of the Quaid, could not hope to imitate the nation-building process that was taking place in neighbouring India under Nehru and Patel. Pakistan lost its small generation of founding fathers within a few years of its inception, whereas India escaped such a tragedy. Many Leaguers and former critics of the Pakistan Movement, in particular those lacking vision and constituencies, began to milk the young country by engaging in a race to acquire wealth and property. The majority of parliamentarians were seduced by money, ministerial positions and material gains. Soon after independence, a number of influential Pakistanis submitted false land claims left in India and obtained vast tracts from the evacuees' property. Regimes encouraged such foul play in order to buy loyalty. Jinnah's death opened up a bonanza for the *nouveaux riches* and the foundations of the civil society were thus laid on shifting sands.

Liaquat's mysterious assassination[40] on 16 October 1951, left a huge void which, in the wake of fragile political traditions and insecure politicians, was filled by an ambitious bureaucracy. In 1953, Prime Minister Khawaja Nazim ud-Din, an honest but weak Bengali Leaguer,[41] was dismissed by the self-opinionated governor-general, Ghulam Muhammad, who had never held electoral office and came from the railway administration. He surrounded himself with a group of ambitious bureaucrats who deeply abhorred politicians and political processes. They preyed on his ill-health and forced him to take certain crucial decisions that left Pakistani politics to an overpowering bureaucracy – commonly known in Pakistan as *naukarshahi*. The chief executive of Pakistan unashamedly and without any real reason dismissed the prime minister, who still enjoyed a majority in the constituent assembly.[42] Pakistani ambassador to the USA, Mohammad Ali Bogra, who was a Bengali by birth, and was currently on vacation in Pakistan, was picked up from Karachi airport by the first commander-in-chief of the Pakistan Army, General Ayub Khan and the defence secretary, Iskander Mirza, and taken to the bedside of the governor-general, known for his unintelligible muttering and swearing.[43] To his utter shock he was informed that he had been designated the next prime minister of Pakistan.[44] The cabinet, which had been dissolved only a few hours earlier on allegations of corruption, was reinstated with the addition of two new members.[45] The same chief executive, egged on by a coterie of advisers, dismissed the first elected assembly of Pakistan in 1954 on flimsy grounds, although it had recently passed the national budget.

Earlier in 1953, martial law had been imposed in Lahore to suppress the anti-Qadiani movement which, as later researchers show, was a command performance by the ambitious Punjabi chief minister, Mumtaz

Daultana – an aristocrat, who in collusion with the Muhajir–Punjabi bureaucracy, tried to create problems for the Khawaja.[46] The Sindh High Court, in an historic verdict, annulled the gubernatorial dissolution but the Supreme Court, led by Justice Muhammad Munir, then upheld the official decision, pioneering a long phase of submission to the executive by the country's judiciary.[47] For some time to come, the mutilated press and the judiciary, otherwise the strong-arms of any civil society, generally validated such extreme measures in Pakistan. However, the remains of a democratic tradition did survive in Pakistan before the bureaucracy and army again united to strike a decisive blow to the political process. On 7 October, Iskander Mirza, a bureaucrat-turned-president, promulgated martial law in collaboration with General Ayub Khan. He was an old hand from the Indian political service who had been jockeying for power since 1948 and from a secretarial position had manoeuvred himself into the highest office of the country without contesting a single election, even for a local council. It is not surprising that Pakistan had six prime ministers and one commander-in-chief in eight years (1950–58), whereas in the same period India had one prime minister and six commanders-in-chief. In 1956, Pakistan had opted for a presidential system and Mirza, following his mentor, Ghulam Muhammad, and with the connivance of the military and bureaucracy, landed himself with the position.[48]

Backstage conspiracies eased Mirza out within three weeks and Ayub Khan and other generals assumed the restructuring of the polity under the direct supervision of the state itself. Politicians, constitution, elections, political debates and parties, independent judiciary, think-tanks and freedom of the press all became taboo subjects and Pakistan formally came under authoritarian rule. Ayub's junta tried to depoliticise Pakistanis by claiming that, unlike people in the West, they were not ready to run electoral politics and that politicians were all corrupt.[49] Everything was to be monitored and guided in the name of efficiency and development,[50] and Pakistan was totally controlled by generals and bureaucrats.[51] The country remained under martial law for the next four years, though Ayub remained in power until a popular uprising ousted him in 1969. Contrary to his own constitution of 1962, he bequeathed power not to the speaker of the national assembly but to his successor in the army, General Yahya Khan. The state had struck again. Yahya drifted from democracy to ideological rhetoric and dithered on the transfer of power to the majority party – the Awami League of Sheikh Mujibur Rahman – which, after a futile military venture, led to the break-up of the country in 1971.

The policies of Zulfikar Ali Bhutto promising radical reforms turned out to be very timid. His army action in Balochistan, the use of troops to suppress the protest movement against ballot rigging in 1977 and dependency on the *naukarshahi* and coopted elite isolated him in the country and the army finally moved in to stage Pakistan's longest period of martial law. However, Bhutto's tenure, described as 'authoritarian populism' had reinvigorated Pakistan through the Constitution of 1973 and other confidence-building measures.[52] Most importantly, he politicised the laity in Pakistan and exhibited a defiance that eventually cost him his life. Through his personal insecurity and in order to preclude any further military coups he had selected Zia as the next army chief-of-staff over the heads of six senior colleagues, believing his nominee to be an apolitical professional soldier. Bhutto's own fear of a powerful state striking against him turned out to be true.[53]

Zia used Islam, the *ulama*, entrepreneurs, bureaucrats and Pakistan's intermediate class to his maximum benefit, while Afghanistan provided a timely balm for mending relations with the United States and other former Western allies. Factionalism within the political opposition over the years helped him to consolidate his power in the country. An economic boom, due to remittances from Pakistani expatriates in the Gulf and bumper crops at home, was also favourable to him. Zia suspended the Constitution of 1973, but frequently reiterated that national elections would be held. Under various pretexts they were delayed and democracy was scorned as an alien machination, foreign to Islam. Zia nominated a Majlis i-Shoora to meet the reservations of his Western detractors and to appease the Islamicists within the country. These nominated individuals, who had no electoral base and lacked both authority and legitimacy, were simply an advisory group of people taken from the traditional ruling elite and the intermediate class. They were neither parliamentarians nor legislators and were a constant burden on the national exchequer. Pakistan's authoritarian polity had been institutionalised, though neither ordinary citizens nor political activists ever took these members of the Shoora seriously. However, the officially controlled media gave full coverage to the empty rhetoric and irrelevant speeches in the chambers.

Zia's mockery of the nation materialised in the notorious referendum of 1984. Apart from its very low turn-out, it made Zia and Islam integral to each other in Pakistan's state structure and he took it as a vote for his presidency until 1991. In reality the army was his constituency, and Zia maintained the duality of being the country's president and the army chief until his death in 1988. Given that he was not an elected representative and had come into power through his preeminent position in the government's hierarchical structure, he continually gained ludicrous extensions in his office as chief of staff. The major political parties in the country were intentionally kept at bay during his tenure and were either harassed or adapted to his own personal needs. With Zia's personal blessing, M. K. Junejo's government came into existence in 1985 from within a partyless House. Junejo was acceptable as long as he was not a personal challenge to Zia, but he was abruptly dismissed the moment he began to criticise the military and bureaucrats after the Ojhri arms-dump explosion of April 1988 that followed the signing of the Geneva Accord to end the war in Afghanistan. All the assemblies in the country were dissolved at the personal whim of an individual. Already various martial-law ordinances had been given constitutional indemnity under Zia and Junejo, through the Eighth Amendment in the Constitution which clipped most of the prime-ministerial powers contained in the Constitution of 1973. This Amendment gave the president more unilateral powers with the prerogative of appointing chiefs of the armed forces and the discretion to dissolve parliament. His successor, Ghulam Ishaque Khan, a seasoned bureaucrat, dissolved three national assemblies in August 1990, April 1993 and July 1993; however, in an historic verdict in May 1993, the Supreme Court restored the national assembly and the government of Nawaz Sharif.[54] Ishaque Khan reluctantly restored Sharif's government, and then used provincial assemblies to defy the federal government, so creating a deadlock that was eventually broken through the mediation of the army. Benazir Bhutto, who had met a similar fate earlier, was now supporting Ishaque Khan in her political strategy to outwit both her opponents. The army-brokered agreement eased out Nawaz Sharif and Ishaque Khan and installed a government of retired bureaucrats and generals as an interim arrangement to conduct impartial elections in the country.

Looking back at these long decades of uncertainties in Pakistan, it is clear that the politics and administration of the country have revolved around personalities, so-called strong men who by virtue of being non-representative and simply authoritarian, refurbished governmental control over the country. The mutilation of political opponents, muzzling of the press, thwarting of the judiciary and educational institutions, and the manipulation of power have all combined to hinder the evolution of an acceptable Pakistani political culture. They have also produced persistent street agitation and violence to defy these regimes, given that no other politico-constitutional mechanism was available. In the 1950s, 1980s and 1990s, the centre has used provincial governments to browbeat its political opponents and, in the process, Pakistan has lost its eastern wing and is still struggling against fissiparous and centrifugal forces.

PARALYSIS OF POLITICAL PARTIES

One leading Pakistani historian believes that the main reason that Pakistan has not been able to steer its way to a stable, consensus-based political culture leading to national harmony is the absence of national parties.[55] Khalid B. Sayeed felt that a parliamentary form of government only works well among homogeneous societies and that Pakistan, which is heterogeneous both physically and culturally, could not sustain the unity that had developed from the Indian Muslims' resistance to being absorbed into the wider Hindu culture.[56] However, there was more to it than this. When the possibility of Pakistan being created seemed to be moving closer, people who had formerly been critics of the AIML movement joined the bandwagon out of self-interest. Obtaining a separate state of Pakistan turned out to be an objective that submerged all personal or factional interests. Similarly, ethnic diversity was temporarily subsumed in the wholeness of a Pakistani Muslim identity. After 1947, when the time came to transform it into a full-fledged party the AIML, now the Pakistan Muslim League (PML), lost its core leadership and failed to provide a *national* agenda. Submerged differences resurfaced and the League itself became the first casualty of a politics where personal loyalties overrode party interests. Problems of membership and of formulating a viable manifesto together with the absence of a realistic policy based on a synthesis of the polarising forces of religion and reformism catapulted the PML into chaos. The disintegration of the party led to a coercive attitude towards other dissenters.

> The Muslim League, which took credit for establishing Pakistan, was essentially a party which lived not by program, but by its leaders. After Muhammad Ali Jinnah's death, it languished as a coalition of Punjabi–Bengali groups, with the Frontier and Sindi groups sulking on the sidelines. There was no one to challenge Liaqat Ali Khan and, with his enormous prestige, he could at least prevent the Punjabis and Bengalis from flying at each other's throats.[57]

The foundation of the Awami League (in 1949) and other ideological and regional coalitions only incurred the League's suspicion and wrath. The case of Huseyn Shaheed Suhrawardy can be considered here. A veteran Leaguer from Bengal and, until independence, the chief minister of British Bengal, he found, on repatriation to his newly adopted country (Pakistan), that his seat in the constituent assembly had been revoked and that the membership of thousands of League workers had been suspended. Although he was a well-known attorney, he was not allowed to practice in any major city in Pakistan and eventually went to Sahiwal, a small town in the Punjab, to continue his law practice.[58] Chaudhary Rahmat Ali, who had coined the name 'Pakistan' during his days in Cambridge in the 1930s, left Pakistan heartbroken as the state set intelligence agencies after him. Similarly, the former Red Shirts got a raw deal even though they had been rejected by the NWFP in the referendum for Pakistan in 1947.

Instead of developing itself into a full-fledged party, the PML turned out to be a coalition interested only in gaining power. Its higher echelons engrossed themselves in intrigues and ignored the imperatives of nation-building. The League aligned itself with the non-representative ruling elites who have used its name and cadres ever since for their own interests. Ghulam Muhammad, Iskander Mirza, Ayub Khan, Yahya Khan, Zia ul-Haq and Ghulam Ishaque Khan all used the League to acquire legitimacy. Similarly, Suhrawardy and others were acceptable to Mirza[59] when he manufactured his own Republican Party which harnessed the energies of predominantly power-seeking Leaguers. During Ayub's time there were three Leagues in existence simultaneously, a phenomenon that has occurred again in more recent years. The electoral defeat of Fatima Jinnah by Ayub Khan in the presidential contest of 1965 was unashamedly manoeuvred by some of her former colleagues in the PML who switched their loyalties to the general. In a later decade, at a single stroke, Zia converted the partyless House in 1985 into a League-dominated administration. Junejo, who owed political and spiritual allegiance to the Pir of Pagara, became the head of the League-run government and resuscitated a dormant faction of the PML. Malik Qasim, a former close associate of Ayub Khan, led his own faction of the Lahore-based Qasim Moslim League, which had supported the Movement for Restoration of Democracy (MRD) in its struggle against Zia. In addition, throughout the periods when Junejo, Benazir Bhutto, Nawaz Sharif and Moeen Qureshi were prime ministers in 1988–93, the Pir was promoting his Functional Muslim League as an alternative to all other 'official' Leagues.

Other political parties in Pakistan have been similarly personality-centred or region-based. The Pakistan People's Party (PPP) is still confined to the dynastic preeminence of the Bhutto family. Despite a clear manifesto and personal appeal, Zulfikar Ali Bhutto's party never held party elections for various offices, even when it was in power. During the elections of 1970 in the formerly united Pakistan, the PPP and Awami League had massive electoral triumphs but proved to be *regional* parties at the most. The PPP leadership allowed a drift in national politics when street agitation in 1977 enabled its opponents to confirm to the armed forces that it had failed to manage national affairs.[60] Since the early 1980s, however, both the Awami League and the PPP in Bangladesh and Pakistan respectively, have valiantly resisted onslaughts from the ruling elites and ethnic militancy and proved themselves to be formidable *national* forces. Nevertheless, in order to mature into strong parties there must be a move away from personalities.

The religio-political parties present the most pathetic aspect of Pakistan's party politics. Of these, the JI has been the most organised party in Pakistan. Since its inception in 1941, it has gone through a number of phases but is not yet mass-based and so its political ambitions cannot be realised through electoral politics.[61] It has usually supported authoritarian, non-democratic regimes like those of Generals Yahya Khan and Zia ul-Haq.[62] Moreover, its attitude towards plural forces and its aggressive role on the university campuses through its student body, the Islami Jamiat-i Tulaba (IJT), have lately alienated it from grassroots[63] and ethnic groups.[64] It has efficient and far-reaching media and devoted cadres (both civil and military) to spearhead its cause, yet its elitism has remained its main hurdle. The JI has established its research institutes over the past decade, both in Pakistan and abroad, yet its exclusivity in terms of its theological explanations of Islam, its membership and the specific intermixing of religion with politics have posed problems in terms of popular appeal. Equally, as with other religio-political parties, the JI has not been able to come to grips with the sensitive and mutually conflictive forces of nationalism, ethnicity, folk culture, democracy and Islam. Its problems with Bengali nationalists during the war in 1971 and its confrontation with ethno-regional forces in contemporary Sindh illustrate this difficulty. It has played a decisive role both in Afghanistan and Kashmir by supporting religion-based resistance movements, while on Pakistani campuses its student organisation has run an anarchic and violent form of politicking through gunrunning, kidnap and intimidation of nationalist or liberal student groups to the extent of regular battles. It has systematically tried to eliminate opposition from educational institutions and attempted to gain a monopoly over the official and private media by applying pressure. These policies have not only brought it into disrepute but also provided models for other ethnic organisations like the Muhajir Qaumi Movement (MQM).[65] Under the leadership of Qazi Hussain Ahmad, a native Pushtun, the JI appears to have accepted a combination of Islam and nationalism in Pakistani experience, which is a unique ideological shift, though not an openly acknowledged one. However, in the elections of 1993 the JI, despite assuming a populist stance, overwhelmingly lost to the national parties (PPP and Muslim League), confirming that Pakistani voters are not convinced by religio-political parties.

Other religio-political parties such as Jamiat-i Ulama-i Islam (JUI) and its various factions reflect personal differences among the *ulama* rather than any specific ideological schools. They are the offshoots of the JUH which supported the INC against the AIML during the nationalist era, although a few prominent *ulama* such as Shabbir Ahmed Usmani and Zafar Ahmed Ansari did support the demand for Pakistan. The Jamiat-i Ulama-i Pakistan (JUP) represents the Brelvi school of thought and enjoys a major following among the masses in Pakistan which it has not yet been able to convert into an enduring political constituency.[66] This might be because Pakistanis would rather hand over the electoral mandate to secular parties than to warring *ulama* whose vagueness on Islamic order and their mutual intolerance are a disappointment to their supporters. It might be easy to bring people out in the name of Islam in order to topple a government but it is virtually impossible to establish a government on the basis of Islam enjoying a consensus from *ulama*. Furthermore, Shia–Sunni differences often turning violent, ethno-regional divisions within the *ulama* and, worst of all, Saudi–Iranian competition in Pakistan to carve out favourable constituencies, have all discouraged Pakistanis from making a total commitment to the religio-political parties. As we shall see later, Islam has for centuries survived and prospered in the areas of present-day Pakistan as a tolerant and receptive force, and any coercion in the name of religion either by the state or by the religio-political parties only exacerbates existing divisions.[67]

Regional parties like the Awami National Party (ANP) or Balochistan Milli Party remain bound by charismatic figures like Khan Abdul Wali Khan and Nawab Akbar Bugti. Similarly, the MQM, which is the third largest electoral party in the country, is basically a regional organisation espousing *Muhajir* identity by revolving around the figure of its founder, Altaf Hussain. The ANP in its former incarnation (NAP), led by Ghaus Bux Bizenjo and Khan Abdul Wali Khan, tried to establish trans-regional alliances but was branded as pro-Moscow and pro-Delhi. Despite a short-lived reign in the NWFP and Balochistan in the early 1970s in alliance with the JUI, the NAP was finally outlawed by Zulfikar Ali Bhutto. Earlier, in East Pakistan, Maulana Abdul Hamid Khan Bhashani, the charismatic Bengali leader, had severed his part of the NAP, which eventually lost to a more powerful rival – the Awami League under the fiery leadership of Sheikh Mujibur Rahman. Following his own interests and under pressure from the Shah of Iran, Bhutto readily suppressed the NAP by setting up a treachery trial against its leadership, known as the Hyderabad Conspiracy Case. The trial followed a military action in Balochistan, both eventually being called off by General Zia ul-Haq. Wali Khan and Bizenjo resisted supporting the martial law regime despite various temptations and intimidation and subsequently joined the MRD led by the Bhuttos and Nawabzada Nasrullah Khan, the leader of the small centrist Pakistan Democratic Party (PDP). Once Benazir Bhutto had become the premier, she ignored the sensitivities of her former colleagues and in fact pushed them towards her opponent, Nawaz Sharif, who had masterminded an umbrella alliance called the Islamic Democratic Alliance (IDA/IJT).

Pakistani political parties have been characterised by a lack of scruples in the formation of alliances and counter-alliances. At any time, there may be more than a hundred parties. The self-interests of about fifty dynasties, consolidated by inter-marriage and common business ventures, have always dictated a politics of opportunism. The elitist nature of the state itself, as we shall see in the next chapter, has hindered the development of ideology-based, competitive and nation-wide parties. It is little wonder that most of the parties are silent on the issues of land reform, agricultural tax, redistribution of wealth, decentralisation and devolution of power in line with the demographic and historic realities of Pakistan, human rights and welfare. They virtually never debate the role of the military, ethnicity, or *ulama* in politics; at the most they would attack the bureaucracy – *naukarshahi* – in an abstract, non-obtrusive manner just to appease a few educated voters. Thus, the basic restructuring needed for the establishment of a civil society has been missing from their manifestos and personal ambitions. Given the mind-frame of most traditional politicians so well-entrenched in the system, the evolution of a dynamic grassroots political culture still remains a distant reality. Politicians prefer fighting among themselves to pursuing higher goals of national interests. The worst experience of this was provided in the years 1988 to 1993 when Benazir Bhutto, Nawaz Sharif and their allies and opponents routinely changed alignments, eventually leading Pakistan to a complete standstill in 1993.

DISREGARD FOR CONSTITUTIONALISM

An additional yet equally significant factor that destroys efforts for a vibrant political culture and national unity and blocks the evolution of a civil society has been the dismal record of adhering to constitutional norms in the country. As mentioned above, Pakistan's constitutional problems[68] stem from the dearth of a political consensus, weak political parties and a state structure that hindered the evolution of a constitution at a formative stage in the country's life. Various constitutional reports, schemes (including the One-Unit to bring about parity between the two wings of the country), basic democracies through limited franchise, frequent martial laws and unilateral amendments have persistently dented and delayed politico-constitutional processes and eroded official respect for constitutionalism. It is not surprising then that after almost five decades the country still awaits basic constitutional guidelines and has yet to decide between a presidential and a parliamentary form of government.[69] Prolonged and futile discussions intended to serve executive interests on non-issues such as *shoora*-based Khilafat, trans-territorial Pan-Islamic remedies and democracy versus Islam, all blurred the real issue of an efficient and accountable government elected by universal adult franchise and with an independent judiciary and free press. Such a clear demand by South Asian Muslims since the 1940s has been misinterpreted or twisted to such an extent over the decades that the nation seems to have lost patience and confidence in both the state and politicians. India acquired its constitution soon after independence, apparently with a common consensus despite many deterrents and grave impediments; the Pakistani state, notwithstanding numerous favourable factors, wasted its youth in polemics. But the damage has been done and the waywardness and fragmentation in society demonstrate the absence of common objectives and a tangible identity that such a constitution could have provided.

It is interesting to see how efforts for a constitutional framework accredited to the central legislature have fallen victim to the state-led structure. At the time of writing this book, Pakistan's tenth elected parliament is near the completion of its tenure and the debate on the form of government continues; in many quarters, however, it is felt that the parliamentarians have successively failed the nation by the horse-trading and corruption that are exposed by a vigilant press from time to time.

The seventh national assembly of Pakistan (1985–8), based on partyless elections and reminiscent of the 1950s and 1960s, was elected under the umbrella of martial law. By approving the Eighth Amendment, the House gave indemnity to all the martial-law regulations and ordinances besides transferring vital powers from the office of prime minister to the presidency. It was dissolved, along with the dismissal of the Junejo government, by General Zia on charges of corruption and inability to Islamize the country. The eighth national assembly of Pakistan (1988–90) followed the death of General Zia in 1988 and was elected on a party basis in an atmosphere of euphoria and polarisation between the Bhuttoists and Ziaists.[70] The elections, as illustrated in Table 1.1, resulted in a plural verdict, though the PPP of Benazir Bhutto held a majority in a 237-member house:[71]

The Senate, since the days of General Zia, had held a predominant majority of non-PPP members. On 6 August 1990, Bhutto's government

Table 1.1   Regional Distribution of Seats for the National Assembly, 1988

Province/area	Seats won
Punjab	115
Sindh	46
NWFP	26
Balochistan	11
Islamabad	1
FATA	8
Total	**207**

Source: 'Elections: The Verdict of History', *The Herald*, Karachi, November 1988, pp. 3–24. *Notes* (1) The total electoral turn-out was reported to be around 42.03 per cent. (2) The total of 207 seats represents the total of contested seats. The rest were allocated for women and minorities.

Table 1.2   Party Position in the National Elections of 1988

Party	% of votes obtained	Seats won
PPP	38.70	93
IJT	30.60	55
Ind.	13.40	40 (including 13 MQM+8 FATA)
MQM	5.25	13
JUI	2.00	8
ANP+PNP+BNA	2.80	4
PPA	4.50	5
Total		**218**

Source: As for Table 1.1.

was finally dismissed along with the national assembly by President Ghulam Ishaque Khan on charges of widespread corruption and disorder in the country. The ninth National Assembly of Pakistan came into being after party-based elections on 24 October 1990, which returned the IDA/IJI led by Nawaz Sharif with a clear majority. The break-down of seats won in the national assembly by various alliances and parties and the ratio of votes obtained by them are shown in Table 1.3.

Soon after the elections, the People's Democratic Alliance (PDA) claimed that large-scale rigging had occurred at the behest of the interim

Table 1.3   Party Position in the National Elections of 1990

Party	% of votes obtained	Seats won
PDA (PPP-led alliance)	36.65	45
IDA/IJT	37.27	105
MQM	5.6	15
ANP	1.68	6
JUI	2.93	6
Ind.	10.61	13
Others	2.67	8
Total		**198**

Source: Adapted from 'The Fall of the People's Empire', *The Herald*, November 1990, pp. 8–15.

government to manoeuvre a victory for the IJI, though international observers did not find any 'serious report of fraud'.[72] Mian Nawaz Sharif, the former chief minister of the Punjab and main architect of the League-led IDA, took over as the new prime minister. The continuing polarisation between the government and opposition and the president and prime minister eventually led to a major political and constitutional crisis in early 1993. There was an atmosphere of apathy at the grassroots level caused by the irresponsible behaviour of politicians and the common disregard for national prerogatives.[73] Sharif challenged presidential powers under the Eighth Amendment to appoint military chiefs and to dissolve elected assemblies, and this led to a long battle of nerves. Many parliamentarians activated the politics of factionalism for purely selfish reasons and the country came to a standstill.

On 18 April 1993, President Ghulam Ishaque Khan dissolved the National Assembly, on the same charges against Nawaz Sharif that he had earlier applied against Benazir Bhutto. However, in a landmark decision, the Supreme Court restored the Assembly only 39 days after its dissolution. In the interlude a pro-president provincial government had been established in the Punjab challenging Nawaz Sharif on his home ground. With the deadlock between the president, the prime minister and the opposition exacerbated by tensions between the federal government and 'rebel' provincial governments, life in Pakistan came to a halt. With an army-brokered agreement, both the prime minister and the president, by now arch enemies, resigned and caretaker governments of retired technocrats and military commanders were established in the centre and the provinces.

Before tendering his resignation, Nawaz Sharif advised the outgoing president to dissolve the ninth national assembly of Pakistan, which, as mentioned earlier, had already been dissolved once through a presidential decree. The Eighth Amendment had enabled the country's chief executive to dissolve national assemblies four times within five years (1988–93). In between, five prime ministers were sworn in while the country prepared for the tenth assembly in October 1993.

Pakistan's tenth national assembly came into being after nation-wide elections in October, supervised by the army and considered to be the fairest in the country's history. While the religio-political parties contesting from forums such as the Pakistan Islamic Front (PIF) were virtually rejected by the voters, the PPP, led by Benazir Bhutto, and the ML, under the leadership of Nawaz Sharif, emerged as the two nation-wide parties. Tables 1.4 and 1.5 show that the PPP won an overall majority in the centre and in the provinces of Punjab and Sindh. While maintaining its core support of 38.1 per cent, the PPP lost in crucial urban constituencies like Lahore and Rawalpindi where the ML made visible gains as well as noticeable inroads in Sindh. A faction of the Muslim League (the Junejo group), which had earlier supported Ishaque Khan against Nawaz Sharif, aligned itself with Benazir Bhutto. Regional/ethnic parties like the ANP and MQM maintained their support – although the MQM had boycotted the national elections but participated in the provincial elections, obtaining all the 27 seats. Benazir Bhutto, with the support of various groups and independents, formed the government in the centre and Sindh and in the crucial province of Punjab.

Table 1.4   Party Position in the National Elections of 1993

Party	% of votes obtained	Seats won
PPP	38.1	86
ML(N)	39.7	73
MQM	1.1	2
ANP	1.7	3
PIF	3.1	3
Ind.	7.4	15
Others	8.8	20
Total		**202**

Source: Adapted from 'People's Verdict', *Newsline*, October 1993.

Table 1.5   Party Position in the National Elections by Province, 1993

Party	Punjab	Sindh	NWFP	Balochistan	Islamabad	Fata	Total
PPP	47	33	5	1			86
ML (Nawaz)	52	10	10	–	1		73
ML (Junejo)	6	–			–	–	6
PIF		1	2		–	–	3
MQM	1		1		–	–	2
ANP	–	–	3		–	–	3
Ind.	5	1	1	1	–	7	15
Others	1	1	3	9		–	14
Total	**202**						

Source: As for Table 1.4.

In November 1993, Farooq Leghari, a landlord from Dera Ghazi Khan and a senior office-holder in the PPP, was elected as president of Pakistan by defeating Wasim Sajjad, the acting president and chairman of the Senate. For a moment it appeared that Pakistan was finally emerging from the throes of political instability despite a plural verdict, resumption of confrontational party politics and unresolved vital political and constitutional issues. Pakistanis had once again rejected the religio-political parties and affirmed their support for a plural, accountable, vigorous political culture, which lay bruised by inter-personal conflicts and a legacy of administrative unilateralism over *national* prerogatives. Nineteen ninety-four dawned amidst hopes that, learning from the mistakes of the past, the Pakistani elite would help civil society play a dynamic role in bringing about a more equitable relationship with the institutions of state, allowing Pakistan to obtain national cohesion and develop as a nation. But such expectations were short-lived due to internecine polarisation between the PPP regime and the opposition led by Nawaz Sharif, followed by heightened sectarian and ethnic conflicts in Karachi making the city ungovernable.

2 Elite Formation, Politics of Ideology and Cooption

Given the constant mutilation of political processes, violation of the electoral mandate, contempt for a representative system and disregard for the national Constitution by the forces constituting the *state* in the country, the growth of civil society in Pakistan has constantly been blocked. The absence of a cooptive, consensus-based *national* political culture (augmented by a free press and independent judiciary), together with an imbalanced economic development, have occasionally strengthened ethno-regional forces. Confused rhetoric, a dislike of political parties and the depoliticisation of the masses by successive centrist, non-representative regimes have seriously damaged the evolution of an accountable political culture. Overpowering elitist oligarchies have formed and monopolised the Pakistani polity for some time and their narrow base, limited capability and efforts, non-representative nature, legitimacy crisis and ethnic specificity help to explain the recurrent governability crisis in the country. These elites have dominated decision-making processes, monopolised debate, preferred self-preservation over national prerogatives, and opted for executive/administrative measures rather than political/constitutional solutions. Their short-term, personality-centred, manipulative and anational characteristics in terms of a multi-ethnic society like Pakistan have done irreparable damage to the country and the institutions essential for national cohesion. Certainly the Pakistani *state*, at so many crucial junctures in the country's history, has appeared blind to societal pluralism and the dictates of civil society like political culture, civic institutions and human resource development. The non-representative elites, with no mandate or legitimacy in a wider national political context, have adopted a neo-colonial role to usher Pakistan into the modern era, assuming the absolutist role of pre-democratic European oligarchies.

In the present chapter and the following one, after first identifying the Pakistani elite groups such as the *ulama*, the landed aristocracy, the bureaucracy, and the military, we shall attempt to investigate their respective role in the polity and their antecedents in colonial tradition. Ideologically, Pakistani elites generally belong to two major groups, traditional and modernist, while in terms of their professional classification, they fall into the following main categories: religious/theocratic elites; landed aristocracy/feudals; civil bureaucracy; khaki bureaucracy/military; industrial and professional elites. Excepting the last category, the rest of the groups do

40

maintain an ideological divide in addition to their respective rural–urban backgrounds and specific provincial–ethno-regional identifications.

MUSLIM ELITE FORMATION IN THE SUB-CONTINENT

The conversion of the indigenous South Asians to Islam, through its emphasis on equality and dynamism, was largely due to the efforts of Muslim publicists, both theological (*ulama*) and spiritual (sufis), who came from Muslim Western and Central Asia. The foundation of the Muslim empire in Delhi under the sultans and the Mughals indirectly helped the propagation of Islam, though the majority of rulers were more interested in worldly affairs. Without underrating the significance of religion as a legitimising force, the sultans owed nominal allegiance to the Caliphate in Baghdad and subsequently in Constantinople, funded certain Muslim *maddrassas* (Muslim schools) and patronised a few leading Muslim scholars; yet they avoided a mass conversion of the Hindu population even though they might privately have wanted it. However, Islam was a solidifying force for the Muslim elites with their cross-regional diversity (Arabs, Persians, Afghans and Turks with a sprinkling of a few indigenous Muslims). Until the nineteenth century the elites asserted their non-Indian origins.[1] Affinity outside the region, especially with the Muslims in Central and Western Asia, has significantly permeated the Muslim ethos with recurrent exposure through migration, invasions and movements like the Khilafat,[2] the pan-Islamism of Jamal ud-Din Afghani and Muhammad Iqbal and the teachings of successive religious scholars.

Akbar (1556–1605), the grandson of Babur,[3] true to his imperial dream of a united India, introduced his Din i-Ilahi in 1582. It was a conscious effort by the state to impose a superior unity and identity on the disparate Indian communities. When his Afghan predecessor, Sher Shah Suri, had faced a similar dilemma, he fell back upon the tribal fraternity of the Pushtun/Afghan elites as well as establishing an organised administrative unity based on efficient land settlement, a vigilant judiciary, police reforms, appropriate defences and development of means of transportation. Such state-led efforts in sixteenth-century India indicate the recognition of an uncomfortable element of plurality and its resultant socio-administrative impediments. Despite his personal ambitions Akbar wanted to broaden and diversify his elitist base so as to indigenise the Mughal empire. However, he annoyed the predominantly Muslim religious elites who could accept the secular role of the Mughal state but would not allow it to interfere in the Islamic belief system so as to perpetuate the imperial goal. Akbar's successors, Jahangir (1605–27), and Shah Jahan (1627–58) both used Islam to legitimise the empire without involving themselves deeply in intricate theocratic matters. Their secular outlook and matrimonial alliances with the Hindus (mostly Rajput princes) continued uncensured by the Muslim clergy as long as the state did not challenge their theological suzerainty.

The unwritten pact underwent a transformation with Aurengzeb (1659–1707) who considered himself to be a soldier of Islam with a revealed mission to purify the *Dar al-Harb* (House of War). Aurengzeb's emphasis on the Islamic and Sunni orientation of the state, coupled with the regionalist and fissiparous tendencies among the *mansabdars* (Mughal nobility), especially in peripheral areas, fuelled the dissenting forces in the empire.[4] Aurengzeb spent his life fighting heterogeneous elements in India who defied the state either for religious (as in the case of Mahrattas and Sikhs) and sectarian reasons (as in the case of Deccan's Shia principalities), or because of sheer tribal/ethnic separatism (as was the case with the Uzbeks and Pushtuns, especially the latter under the fiery leadership of Khushal Khan Khattak). Aurengzeb's dependence and emphasis on Islam, as opposed to Akbar's statism and his own father's secular postures, shrunk the Mughal roots.

During the next 150 years, the state, like its counterpart in medieval Europe, suffered from a schismatic and extremely anarchic feudalism, with regional elites becoming autonomous from Delhi and an internecine jockeying for power. Ethnic and ideological idioms were used to justify and negate claims to power. The emphasis on Islam to hold the fledgling and already narrow base of the Mughal state increased non-Muslim defiance in both the core and peripheral areas. The arrival of the Europeans further added to a complex situation where regional and personal loyalties in the absence of a wide, all-encompassing and dynamic ideological superstructure enabled the sub-continent to be easily conquered. The Mughals had created an empire but they had utterly failed to create a genuine nation, and the emphasis remained on temporary expediency or restoring the excessive state structures.

REORGANISATION OF THE MUSLIM ELITES IN BRITISH INDIA

Loss of political power to Europeans and autonomous non-Mughal principalities across the sub-continent coincided with the economic and intellectual decline of the Muslim community. Whereas the elite fell into mutual squabbling and chaos, the Muslim laity suffered from a severe sense of loss. The absence of industrial changes or commercial expansion – as characterised by the long-held traditions of a predominantly agrarian, feudal economy – took its toll. Both the *ashra'af* (elite) and *ajla'af/awam* (laity), in the absence of a binding middle class, looked for scapegoats. Religious revivalists like Shah Wali Allah and others hoped that Ahmad Shah Durrani's Afghanistan would provide the external push factors to revive the community but the malaise was not confined to Muslim India.[5] The Indian Muslims realised to their chagrin that they would have to deal with a non-Muslim majority eager for change within a non-Muslim yet politically dynamic and technologically far superior colonial structure. There were a variety of Muslim responses to the new radical challenges, including complete defiance based on armed resistance as was the case with Tipu Sultan, Siraj ud-Daula, and the leaders of the Tehrik-i Mujahideen led by the descendants and followers of Shah Wali Allah and the sepoy militants of 1857.[6] Another response to the new overwhelming challenges was articulated in the form of cooperation based on complete subordination to the Raj as exhibited by the Muslim princely states and the feudal families. The third kind of response, mainly found in urban centres, involved seeking pragmatic measures to find a synthesis between Islam and Western knowledge by acquiring them both. Such a group included reformers like Sir Syed Ahmed Khan (1817–98) and Allama Iqbal (1875–1938), who have generally been known as Muslim modernists.

The failure of successive armed revolts encouraged the Muslim intelligentsia, especially revivalists, to establish schools of Muslim learning and religious education, for example those at Deoband and Rai Bareli in the United Provinces. These Muslim ideological elites, known as traditionalists, distrusted Western civilisation and advocated separatism based on convictions like 'back to pristine Islam'. They believed that Muslims had lost their political power everywhere due to their negligence of *din*, a complete code of life. While the Tablighi Jama'at aimed at Islamic revival among Indian Muslims through a sense of commonality, Jamiat-i Ulama-i Hind and Jama'at-i Islami emerged as religio-political parties rejecting the modernists' viewpoint of working 'within' the system. The feudal classes, the *pirs* and the *sajjada nishin silsilahs* (also very feudal in composition and character) sided with the British state though ostensibly they appeared to be apolitical. Their role as intermediaries was a boost to their own individual and class interest besides providing stability to the Raj. While both the urban-based modernists and many traditionalists, making a core of reformists, debated political and ideological issues, the land-based Muslim elite, predominantly in rural and tribal areas, prided themselves on collaborating with the regime. By the early twentieth century, the chasm between ideological and non-ideological groups (urban versus rural) and factionalism between the modernists and traditionalists became more marked, with the state exhibiting discretion towards the non-ideological, non-reformative groups. In addition, given the low rate of literacy, the absence of a press and worst of all the rural–urban divide, the emergence of a common Muslim opinion in India remained an unrealised ideal. The absence of a trans-regional Muslim middle – intermediate – class in a largely rural, divisive society in Muslim South Asia, operated as a major stumbling block to the evolution of a consensus on community issues. Whereas the traditionalists had their local mosques and *maddrassas* to spearhead their cause, the modernists' appeal was confined to like-minded urban Muslims. The populations of vast outlying *mofussil* areas (rural hinterland) were unconcerned and apolitical thanks to the collaboration between the state and regional–local intermediaries.

As well as the landed aristocracy, the British colonial state in the subcontinent, through its institutions and politico-economic policies, depended on two other major indigenous support groups. The British Indian Army provided a strong tier of defence throughout the empire in addition to its frequent role as the guardian of law and order during emergencies. Mainly led by British officers until well into the twentieth century, the army indirectly politicised many ethnic and caste groups by pursuing highly selective and ethnically preferential procedures in recruitment. True to its loyalist traditions, the Indian Army never revolted against its own superiors or against the Raj. Another strong, well-knit and cohesive institution created for imperial administrative purposes was the Indian Civil Service (ICS), which operated as 'the steel frame' of the state. Most of the early civil servants were recruited in Britain and trained in Oxford or Cambridge until recruitment started within South Asia. It was not until much later that Indians were entrusted with important positions in the civil service, though even then all the sensitive positions were reserved for the British. Totalling less than 70 000 at its peak, such as during the Second World War, the ICS and British military personnel constituted the *de facto* British colonial state in India.[7] Thus, along with the landed aristocracy, the native junior officers in the Indian Army and ICS proved to be pillars of strength for the Raj, and were inducted as a class of influential locals. British educational policies were already directed towards creating this 'class of persons, Indian in blood and colour, but English in taste, in opinion, in morals and in intellect'.[8]

British influence in South Asia proved to be all-pervasive and polarising; it unleashed an unending debate on the formation of Muslim identity and raised pertinent questions, such as: Did the Muslims form one community or were they as divided as others? Must trans-territorial loyalties supersede and submerge local, ethnic, national and regional identities? Is Islam a religion or a code of life? Should Muslims return to their religious roots by rejecting contemporary challenges, institutions, ideologies and systems? How would the Muslim renaissance come about? Who is to be blamed for discord and backwardness among Muslims? How can Islam, nationalism, ethno-nationalism, democracy, liberal arts and Western education co-exist? These and many related issues have kept Muslim religious leaders, intellectuals and statesmen engaged in an intense debate, not merely within the sub-continent but wherever Muslims reside.

It is not easy to generalise about Muslims in British India without referring to their ethno-regional or sectarian variations, despite the idealism that yearned for an overarching *Muslim* identity.[9] Given the non-existence of a Muslim middle class in British India, the elite formation largely depended on interactions with the state. The following configuration of Muslim elite groups resulted in British India with an enduring and reinvigorated influence in post-1948 Pakistan:

1. **'Muslim' positions in India**
   i. Islamic traditionalists: the Deobandis
   ii. Islamic traditionalists: the Brelvis and Pirs
   iii. Islamic fundamentalists: Maudoodi and his JI
   iv. Islamic modernists: Sir Syed Ahmed Khan and Allama Iqbal
   v. Secular and nationalist Muslims: M.A. Jinnah and others
2. **Non-communal Muslim positions**
   vi. Secular/trans-communal rightist provincial politics: Punjab Unionists, various political groups in Sindh
   vii. Secular non-communal provincial politics: Krishak Proja Party in Bengal
   viii. Secular non-communal nationalists: Ruling Congress in NWFP.[10]

Though the Deoband school of Muslim theology did not come into being until 1867, the religious scholars of this ideological orientation had already been involved in religio-military activism – both by reinterpreting Islam in its pristine form and by defying non-Muslim political threats like those of the Mahrattas and the Sikhs. From the early twentieth century, the Deobandi *ulama* became extremely anti-colonial and joined country-wide organisations. They participated in the Khilafat movement, established Jamiat-i Ulama-i Hind and followed pro-INC policies, as was articulated by Hussain Ahmed Madani, Ubaidullah Sindhi and Maulana Azad despite the fact that they preached a pan-Islamic outlook and derided westernised nationalist elites in the AIML.[11] Many other *ulama*, with a similar ideological outlook, established their own parties like the Tehrik i-Khaksar and Majlis i-Ahrar in the 1920s and 1930s with strong anti-colonial, anti-League creeds. On the other hand, the Brelvi *ulama* and the *pirs* – the latter espousing spiritual powers – were local or regional influentials, lacking country-wide programmes. Many *murids* (disciples) of these *pirs*, like their mentors themselves, came from strong feudatory dynasties traditionally pursuing very pro-establishment policies. The predominantly rural-based *sajjada nishin* and their land-holding *murids* made the most conservative elite group, and the AIML had to make special efforts to solicit their support given the social, political and economic influence they held in their territories.

Islamic modernists like Sir Syed and Sir Iqbal, who were aware of the deep cleavages among the Muslim elite and the narrow intellectual base of the *ulama*, were equally concerned about the growing backwardness of the Muslims and espoused a Muslim renaissance through multiple activities. Sir Syed pinned his hopes on a Muslim revival through modern education and a rational approach to religion, while Iqbal, like Sir Syed rejected *taqlid* (blind conformity) and emphasised *ijtihad* (intellectual innovation according to one's capabilities). He believed that Muslim nationalism was vital for Muslim survival and exhorted *khudi* (self-knowledge) at both the individual and collective levels so that Muslims would shun inactivity and morass. To Iqbal, *ijtihad* would lead to *ijma* (consensus) and their communitarian approach would spearhead the new Muslim era that he visualised. Iqbal was strongly opposed to the obscurantism and narrow-mindedness of the *ulama* and was equally uncomfortable with feudalism and colonialism. It was through the pervasive efforts of modernists like Syed and Iqbal that 'Pakistan' eventually emerged as the common creed, for the *ulama* and other influential Muslims were opposed to the idea of a separate Muslim state to the extent of confusing nationalism and pan-Islamism.

Islamic fundamentalists (Islamists) like the JI considered nationalism to be a conspiracy to divide the Muslim *ummah* (community). According to Maulana Maudoodi, the founder of the JI, Islam is cognitive of cultural variations among Muslims but is entirely opposed to modern territorial nationalism since it negates the existence of an all-encompassing transterritorial community. Maudoodi, unlike the INC, rejected the idea of a composite Indian nationalism as he believed in a multi-national India. Unlike Madani and Ubaidullah Sindhi, he felt that by accepting a unitary Indian nationalism, Muslims would lose their cultural, educational and historical distinction. But the AIML's stance for Pakistan was equally unacceptable to him as demonstrating that its leaders were not Islamic and were working for their own elitist interests.[12]

The Maulana opposed the campaign for Pakistan because he believed that it would not become an Islamic state. He maintained that 99.9 percent of the Indian Muslims were thoroughly unregenerate. They had little or no knowledge of Islam, their moral and intellectual orientations were un-Islamic and in many cases, they could not tell right from wrong. It was therefore foolish to expect that a majoritarian democracy in Pakistan would steer the government of that country, if it came into being, toward Islam.[13]

Later on, in 1942, Maudoodi observed that if the Indian Muslims persisted in nationalism he would not concern himself with them and they could 'go to hell'.[14] Maudoodi, despite his erudite scholarship and sincerity to the Islamic cause, could not keep up with the tempo of Muslim political aspirations, which saw in Pakistan altogether a new hope. As Syed noted: 'His expectation that he would be able to convert any considerable number of non-Muslims in a Hindu-dominated Indian polity may have been naive. But then perhaps the preacher's arithmetic is different from that of others.' The elitist character of the JI, its very limited membership due to strict preconditions, and the rejection of the beliefs and practices of 99.9 per cent of the Muslims as non-Islamic prevented any popularisation of Maudoodi's religio-political creed.[15] On the other hand, the Muslim nationalism advocated by Iqbal and Jinnah superseded the ideal of a composite and arithmetical Indian nationalism (including the Jamiat, Ahrars, Khaksars) and the schemes of thinkers like Maudoodi or the Shia theocrats.

Iqbal regarded Islam as a means of social action to mobilise and unite the people, but by 1930 he had realised this would not come about without a political and territorial definition in a multiple society like India. To Jinnah, Islam was a solidifying and activating force, which gave an identity to the community whose only alternative was to accept the position of a permanent minority. Iqbal, in his letters to Jinnah, expressed his fears that in a united India Muslim cultural identity would be at stake, so Pakistan was a necessity, at least in Muslim majority areas, not merely for economic reasons but for cultural preservation. He was weary of 'Punjabi ruralism' as espoused by the Punjab National Unionist Party since it compromised Muslim identity to the combined interests of rural feudal elites and imperial forces. Likewise, Jinnah saw India's problem as not merely a *communal* but rather an *international* problem underscoring the need for Muslim nationalism. Jinnah, after the creation of Pakistan, referred to Islam as a solidifying force for Pakistan, though in his well-known speech of 11 August 1947 he had candidly observed: 'You are free, you are free to go to your temples, you are free to go to your mosques or to any other places of worship in this state of Pakistan. You may belong to any religion or caste or creed – that has nothing to do with the business of the State.'[16] Being a pragmatic statesman, Jinnah recognised that after the creation of Pakistan it was vital that an integrated Pakistani nationhood be strengthened in opposition to the communal, sectarian and provincial prejudices that threatened the new state. In response to the welcome address from the Quetta municipality, Jinnah advised Pakistanis to love their country more than their own town or area, saying: 'Local attachments have their value but what is the value and strength of a part except within the "whole"?'[17]

'Secular' Muslim elites like the Unionists in the Punjab and elsewhere concentrated more on regional issues, thanks to British policies, especially after the promulgation of the reforms of 1919 which shifted the political centres to the provinces, at least in the case of Indian Muslim politics. Punjab will be studied in a separate section; although the Krishak Proja Party in Bengal led by Fazl ul-Haq, was quite different from the Punjabi Unionists, both maintained an essentially regional characteristic. As regards the secular Muslim nationalists, there were cases like Humayun Kabir or Mian Iftikhar ud-Din who, unlike the regional–provincial secular elites, moved in the mainstream nationalist–ideological movements.

Another way to look at the Muslim elites in British India is to see them in terms of their regional–provincial affiliations. Historically, there was no unitary *Indian* identity as such and religion, region, language and *biradari* (kinship–based) provided such an identification. Bengalis were Bengalis, since they came from Bengal and spoke Bengali. Whether Muslim or Hindu, it was profession and economic standing that determined status in addition to tribal and caste affiliation. Ethno-regional identities emerged with the administrative and political divisions of the British empire when these provinces and regions provided a larger identity along with religious differentiation. The caste or profession-based classification came along with the tribal origins of the *provincialised* subject of the empire. Thus region, sometimes denoting merely history, or geography or language, in a primordial sense, solidified ethnic (provincial) identities. By the early twentieth century, provincial and regional identities like Punjabi, Balochi, Sindhi, Bengali, Tamil, Kashmiri an so on had already become quasi-historical. In addition, there was the dilemma of younger national identities like Pakistani, Indian, Sri Lankan or Bangladeshi coming face to face with these consolidated identities. Pluralisation had multiplied in the imperial set-up with complex overlapping. For instance, one could be a Punjabi at one level, but that was not sufficient. One might be Sikh, Muslim or Hindu – denoting a second level of identity. Then, rural or urban origins along with profession and caste would determine further levels of identity to be capped by citizenship of the British empire. In the case of Muslims, regional identities espoused through forums like the Unionist Party, the Krishak Proja Party, the Khudai Khidmatgar or the Kalat State National Party represented strong ethno-regional elites who, in the late 1940s, witnessed the emergence of Pakistan as a super-ordinate identity, basing its case on the largely historic Muslim identity promising socio-economic welfare and political egalitarianism. If Pakistan had followed these ideals, such a spectrum of mutually competitive identities would have added to its dynamism and cultural richness. However, as discussed in a separate section, the imbalance and state-led ethnic unilateralism naturally caused varying degrees of both reaction and rejection.

PAKISTAN: LEGACY OF ELITE POLARISATION

As the above resumé shows, polarisation and fragmentation within the Muslim elites in the British sub-continent dented the development of a cohesive and well-integrated political creed. While the religious elites seriously differed among themselves on doctrinal issues that were not of the greatest significance, they devoted rather more of their energies to refuting the modernists and nationalists. This was injurious to the case for Pakistan. After independence, all these groups randomly turned on the young nation-state demanding that it 'Islamise', although, being a Muslim majority country, it was clear that Islam would not be on the agenda for debate. The founders of Pakistan very rightly considered Islam and Pakistan to be mutually inter-dependent and supportive rather than antagonistic so there was no need for slogans like 'Islam is in danger' once the country had come into existence. Rather than working for a participatory system responsive to the needs of all the regional, provincial and ethnic components of Pakistan, the rhetoric turned to self-assertion. With the Quaid's death in 1948, there was increased pressure from ideological groups on a state which faced a crisis in legitimacy. In a constitutional vacuum, the elites turned to a game of hide-and-seek among themselves while jockeying for power. Both religious elites and the state followed a policy of convenient offence and tactical retreat towards each other. The institutions essential for civil society were totally ignored as the emphasis was on self-preservation. Moreover, since efforts to establish such institutions would have ended the jockeying for power and hollow rhetoric, it suited everyone to carry on the legacy.

This ideological confrontation at the very core of Pakistani nationhood in its early years was accompanied by regional elites espousing ethnic separatism (provincialism as it is called in Pakistani political parlance). Bengalis, Pushtuns and Balochis felt that Punjabis and Muhajireen were collaborating to deny them their due rights. Suddenly, Pakistan and Islam became controversial issues, for ethnic elites found them being used by dominant elites to perpetuate their dominance. It is interesting to see that provincial elites like those from the Punjab or expatriates (Muhajireen) dominated the state and denied similar privileges to their counterparts from the other provinces although expediency and common sense suggested a different course.

Pakistan's polarised divisions among the elites accruing from their ideological, ethnic and professional dissensions together with a pervasive rural–urban divide has hindered national integration in many ways. First it has dented the process of mass-based political culture and, secondly, it has blocked the evolution of a nation-wide middle class; though in recent years there has been an emergence of an intermediate class, admittedly very localised. Thirdly, and equally significantly, it has allowed the *state* to fill the vacuum with more emphasis on administration than on governance. In addition the government, usually led by a bureaucratic, military and feudal axis, has exhibited an ethnic discreetness and oligarchic manner which has only added to the disenchantment of centrifugal forces. It is not that the elites have lacked patriotism, rather it is the absence of basic *national* credentials that has damaged the promotion of civil institutions. Efforts were turned to self-preservation, centralisation, bureaucratisation and depoliticisation, thus creating a serious credibility crisis. Civil society was scorned as it would have meant strengthening political institutions, decentralising power, safeguarding human rights, prioritising basic needs and development sectors and egalitarian power sharing – all certainly anathema to the Pakistani ruling elites.

THE SAGA OF RELIGIOUS ELITES

While power elites manipulated the state, established clergy created serious fissures in the national outlook by confronting the very concept of Pakistani nationalism, taking it to be a negation of *millat* (trans-territorial Islamic community). Many of them questioned such institutions as elections, political parties, parliaments, a consensus-based constitution, an adult franchise and women's rights. They scoffed at modern education, science, research in humanities and the co-educational system. Such a dismissive attitude on the part of established *ulama*, who otherwise could not agree on the definition of a *Muslim*, provided an ideological justification to successive non-representative elitist oligarchies in Pakistan. All the rulers except Jinnah have used Islam to legitimise their authority and to avoid electoral politics and accountability. Like the Mughal state, the Pakistani state found many voluntary and willing supporters amongst the *ulama*. Many religio-political parties, which could not otherwise win more than a handful of seats in the assemblies, however favourable the circumstances, found it more convenient to work in league with the non-representative regimes. It is no wonder that in all the elections, partyless or party-based, religio-political parties have fared very badly (which may perhaps keep them close to the authoritarian regimes). On the other hand, the country's electoral history since 1946 demonstrates the maturity of the voters, whose verdict has been for 'mundane' and nationalist programmes. Jinnah had openly declared that, in Pakistan, religion, creed and caste would have 'nothing to do with the business of the state'.[18] According to the vision of the founder of the country, Pakistan would never be a 'theocracy or any thing like it'.[19] Time and again, some of the influential religious elites would take anti-populist stances, rejecting the democratic basis for Pakistan.[20] The young state, while coopting the religious elite to build a consensus from above, adopted the Objectives Resolution in 1949 which was incorporated with minor modifications in the successive constitutions of 1956, 1962 and 1973 (in the latter case by General Zia ul-Haq). However, the ruling elites and the religious elites were not always mutually supportive; the anti-Ahmadiyya Movement in the Punjab in 1953 and then the objections to the Family Laws Ordinance of 1961, which placed restrictions on polygamy and traditional divorce patterns, epitomised opposition to the state. The *ulama* sometimes contradicted themselves as well. For instance, in 1965 several religio-political parties and personalities supported the candidacy of Fatima Jinnah for presidency against General Ayub Khan, declaring that a woman as 'Head of State is not against the Shariah'.[21] Then, two decades later, many of the *ulama* and their followers questioned the candidacy of Benazir Bhutto as chief executive in 1988–90 solely on the grounds of her being a woman. Pakistani ruling elites have generally tried to pacify the religious elites through cooption rather than coercion. Ayub Khan enjoyed a rapport with certain religious leaders and declared the Pir of Daiwal, an influential *pir* from Pothowar, to be his personal spiritual guide. Yahya Khan, in his hour of trial, invoked Islam to crush Muslim Bengalis, and the voluntary cooperation from many religious and ethnic groups even from former East Pakistan was available. Bhutto, in the Constitution of 1973, declared Pakistan to be the Islamic Republic of Pakistan and then held an international Islamic summit in Lahore the following year. He appointed

Maulana Kausar Niazi as a federal minister, tried to win over religious sections by declaring Pakistan a dry country and changed as the weekly holiday to Friday instead of Sunday.

More recently, the religious elites did on the whole cooperate with the military regime of General Zia ul-Haq and even dismissed electoral politics as un-Islamic. The army had intervened when the movement led by the Pakistan National Alliance (PNA) against Z. A. Bhutto demanded his resignation after the rigged elections of 1977. Zia raised the slogan of *Nizam-i Mustafa* (Islamisation) while promising elections and a return to democracy within 90 days, which became 11 years. The manipulation of the political, judicial and educational systems and a complete reorientation of the socio-economic order in the name of Islamisation fragmented the nascent civil institutions to which ordinary citizens applied for redress. In legal issues, for instance three parallel traditions co-existed: the Anglo-Saxon legal traditions, the martial-law regulations and the Huddood ordinances to give the legal system a back-to-Sharia outlook. This parallelism lacked a mandate and electoral legitimacy and frequently led to confusion and official high-handedness in addition to official manipulation at the expense of civil liberties. Many criminals were surreptitiously given the option to select one of the three traditions depending upon their influence and affluence. This was occurring at the same time as many *ulama* were preaching that democracy was irreligious, that political parties were unnecessary and that women should be confined to *chardiwari* (four walls). Journalists, lawyers, academics, several labour leaders and many independent intellectuals in Pakistan have always stood against authoritarianism. But their job became more difficult as the regime coopted many *ulama*, *pirs*, landed aristocracy and other faithful whose influence in their respective constituencies aimed at isolating the masses from mainstream political processes. Naturally, people fell back upon local, *biradari*-based or sectarian identities, thus causing further cleavages in the nationhood.

Even since Zia, the tensions between established institutions and ideological pulls for an Islamic system have caused serious rifts within both society and state. In an attempt not to offend people Benazir Bhutto wore the *chaadar*, performed *umra* to the Hejaz and was even shown in the national media rolling her beads.[22] Two recent examples from among many are tensions over the banking system and Pakistan's Afghan policy. The Federal Sharia Court, created during Zia's time to Islamise the system, has taken strong positions on various legal and financial issues and so exposed the conflict between the establishment and ideological pronouncements. For example, in a ruling in late 1991 the Sharia Court decreed that all financial dealings should be placed on a non-interest basis. It declared that interest should be considered usuary, forbidden by the Holy Quran, and found 32 laws dealing with financial matters to be 'un-Islamic'. This ruling alarmed Pakistani bankers, foreign creditors and the IDA government, which feared that such an action would affect its privatisation policies. A petition against the ruling in the Supreme Court of Pakistan was submitted by two private banks – not by the government itself – to reconsider the verdict. The petition is pending before the special Sharia bench of the Supreme Court rather than an ordinary court following the usual Anglo-Saxon law. The banks do 'not intend to challenge the substance of the ruling, only [desire] to delay it while viable alternatives are found'. The then federal minister for law was quoted as saying: 'The government does not challenge the contention that interest is against the Koran, but the system is so deeply entrenched that it cannot be eliminated overnight. There is no alternative system in place anywhere in the world.' Qazi Hussain Ahmad, the Amir of the JI, advised against petitioning the Supreme Court on the grounds that 'If there are any differences over imple-mentation, they can consult the religious experts and *ulema* [clergy].'[23] Mian Nawaz Sharif, while distancing himself from fundamentalism, had 'been working hard to burnish Pakistan's image as a stable and progressive place for foreign investors. The state of economy gives him little choice.'[24] In view of the acute energy shortage leading to long hours of load-shedding and black-outs, the government underlook a very ambitious project for power generation near Karachi, the biggest in Asia involving a total expen-diture of $1.3 billion. The Hub Project was to be financed through an inter-national consortium of foreign donors and the work was to begin in March or April 1992, but because of the injunction of the Sharia Court the entire project fell in the doldrums. Without an interest mechanism, the foreign creditors did not find the project feasible.[25]

On the issue of Afghanistan, both Benazir Bhutto and Nawaz Sharif fol-lowed General Zia's policies for a Mujahideen-led solution to the crisis. However, internecine warfare among the Mujahideen and their inability to make a major political or military breakthrough, the retirement of tradi-tional Pakistani army officers like Generals Aslam Beg and Hamid Gul who espoused a more forward policy *vis-à-vis* the Kabul regime, pressure from the United States for a political solution and Pakistan's eagerness to develop closer relations with the young Muslim Central Asian republics, all underlined the need for a major rethinking of official policy. The regime in Kabul had withstood many setbacks while former king Zahir Shah still carried a symbolic appeal, among many Afghans, so the shift came about. In early 1992, Sharif's government openly supported UN pro-posals and urged the Mujahideen to enter into negotiations for a broad-based interim government in Kabul. It demonstrated its displeasure with the hardliners and stopped military assistance to them. Such a policy brought problems for Nawaz Sharif from his coalition partners like the JI in the IDA.[26] Sharif's overture on Afghanistan received wider acclaim within the country and abroad, showing a civilian–military consensus on the issue, though it equally manifested strong ideological 'pulls' on the regime itself.[27] Eventually, the JI quit the IDA for not supporting its favourite warlords in Afghanistan and remained critical of the Sharif government throughout the subsequent months.[28] These two examples show the ongoing polarisation within the society and state structures that has occasionally produced severe instability and waywardness in foreign policies. For the Pakistani polity, the best course would be to synthesise the forces of idealism and realism in a balanced and pragmatic manner.[29] The country cannot ignore its Islamic roots any more than it can progress with a siege mentality.

Another disquieting aspect of the religious elites is their doctrinal and sectarian disunity which in many cases is reduced to the *personal* rather than the *ideological* or the intellectual. Traditionally, Islam does not allow any established clergy, and religious piety is a matter between the Creator and the individual. Over the centuries, however, the *mashaikh, ulama* and *pirs* have developed their own hierarchical orders and this has led to an intellectual stalemate arising from orthodoxy, narrow-mindedness and intolerance. The emphasis has been on self-preservation rather than on the study of sacred and secular subjects. Such a phenomenon has fuelled sectarian violence among Muslims in addition to an intolerant attitude to both natural and social sciences. Islam has been reduced to a religion of rituals and rote by semi-literate *mullahs* and pretentious *pirs*. From mosque to mosque and mohalla to mohalla, personality-based rifts presented as *ideological* and doctrinal, have permeated Muslim societies the world over. In Pakistan, along with Shia–Sunni differences[30] leading to violent outbursts, inter-mosque, inter-*ulama* differences have constantly generated strife that has engulfed vital financial and human resources. At times, it appears that each mosque has become a pseudo-discipline to itself promoting a nefarious kind of sub-localism.[31]

[The] ulema today have no knowledge of contemporary sciences, natural or social, they are no match even as religious personages to the better educated clergymen or the Jewish rabbis whose understanding of the world and the society is wider and deeper. Quite often the intellectual capabilities of the ulema are spent in hair-splitting and they tend to give much greater importance to insignificant details and, in their exaggerated zeal for them, create dissensions among themselves and their followers. This loses for them a good deal of respect of the well meaning, better balanced and more sophisticated classes.[32]

These *ulama* are simply rejectionists when it comes to the imperatives of civil society. Academically, their feedback follows a very simplified routine course, developed centuries earlier, which they acquire without any major academic effort and which is indicative of a wider malady that has been confronted by Muslims for a long time.[33] The trans-territorial affiliations and support bases for certain religio-political parties in the Near East, however genuine they might sound, add to the mutual antagonism and have serious side-effects on general Pakistani morale.[34] The lack of genuine debate and inquiry among Pakistani clerical groups is partially explained by their non-academic base, dependency on authoritarian regimes and trans-national financial sources.

PUNJAB TRADITION OR INDUS-BASIN TRADITION?

When discussing the collaborative role of the ruling elites in Pakistan, questions arise about Punjabi domination of state apparatuses and national resources. Since the Punjab accounts for almost 70 per cent of the Pakistani population with almost the same ratio in resources and job allocations, it is easy to accuse Punjab of manipulation and exploitation. As seen in the previous chapter, the political, geographical, economic and demographic imbalance within Pakistan's polity that has existed since the Raj, has been carried on through a countinued oligarchic tradition sustained by elitist pressure groups. The landed aristocracy, mostly from the Punjab, true to its loyalist and cooptive traditions, supported the colonial state structure anchored on a powerful bureaucracy. The civilian bureaucracy, representing an ethnic mix of Punjabi and Muhajir elites, coopted the military elite who were also overwhelmingly from the Punjab. The Bengali salariat was the largest, the most homogeneous and the most articulate in all Pakistan, but it could not withstand this new hegemonic collaboration that thrived on centralisation and depoliticisation. A similar fate awaited its counterparts from Sindh (rural), Balochistan and the NWFP. Therefore, the Punjab provided an obvious and more visible focus, as the Urdu-speaking Muhajireen constitute less than 7 per cent of Pakistan's population and Urdu had already been adopted as the national language. While not absolving Punjabis from their domination of national affairs, it is the case that diversity and unevenness within the Punjab has been overlooked by critics.

Another important issue is the apolitical history of the entire territory of present-day Pakistan since the time of the British when the emphasis was logically on administration and regionalisation rather than governance and politicisation. The Punjab was the first province to experience a strong administrative tradition; the conditions that created this were rural–urban differences and a preference for stable and apolitical administration through a powerful bureaucracy with the cooption of intermediaries.[35] Thus, in order to understand Pakistan's dilemma in establishing powerful civic institutions based on a dynamic political culture symbolising an integrated nationhood, one has to understand this background. Moreover, as mentioned above, similar patterns were emerging in other near by Muslim-majority regions. The Punjab retains all the tribal, rural and urban diversities that characterise socio-political realities in other provinces in Pakistan. Given the fact that it is the hub of political activity, the heartland of Pakistani nationalism, the granary for the country and is both praised as a trend-setter and attacked as a scourge of the system, its role is bound to create controversy and awe among non-Punjabis.

Thus while urban movements might bring down Pakistani regimes, it is the feudal families with strong diffused roots, inter-matrimonial alliances and trans-ethnic partnerships who dominate the representative institutions in Pakistan. More mobility, a higher rate of literacy, a strong middle class with a reservoir of vast goodwill from the masses on the basis of a reformist and trans-regional ideology – all the essential characteristics of a civil society – could radically transform the Punjab/Indus Basin tradition for the general welfare of the masses.

3 The Supremacy of the Bureaucracy and the Military in Pakistan

The oligarchical relationship among the narrowly based ruling elites in the young country predated independence. It was mainly in the areas constituting West Pakistan that the traditional land-based feudatory system guaranteed through official patronage existed. In the Southwestern Punjab, Sindh and the tribal areas of the NWFP and Balochistan, there was a persistence of the tribal and aristocratic traditions owing allegiance to 'localism' and reinforcing 'ruralism'. After independence, with a clear 'bias' for an administration-oriented rather than politics-based system, the civil bureaucracy and the feudal pressure group coopted the armed forces. As suggested earlier, this development disturbed non-Punjabi and non-Urdu speaking communities. East Pakistanis, excluding a few landed elites, were the main losers in the new state formation. In West Pakistan, suave, westernised and highly mobile bureaucrats forged closer bonds with the rural aristocracy in a relationship which had its antecedents in the Raj. The economic interests of the *zamindar*, *wadera*, *pir* and *maulvi* found more in common with the forces and functionaries of the state than with their respective tenets, followers or the fragile politicised urban middle class. The evolution of this new oligarchy shifted the political balance in favour of West Pakistan.

BUREAUCRACY: BED-ROCK OF THE CENTRALISED STATE

While the Pakistani polity over successive decades has been vulnerable to the pressure of feudalists and the military, its civil service has largely been the bed-rock of the state. In terms of rhetoric, both the military and political rulers have continually hurled attacks on the *naukarshahi*, the unbridled and monopolistic civil bureaucracy. Once in government, however, they have relied upon the institution itself. Some politicians like Z.A. Bhutto enjoying populist support or generals like Ayub Khan tried to control the bureaucrats through 'purges' or structural changes, yet the bureaucratic hold on the state has essentially remained undiminished. Indeed, Pakistan has become a highly centralised and over-bureaucratised polity with politicians and everyone else largely dependent on the state structure and official largesse. The civil service has suffered a serious legitimacy crisis due to its anational composition and ubiquitous hold on power. Its preference for bypassing political and constitutional processes and representative institutions has entailed a cost for bureaucracy itself. It lacks credibility among intellectuals and the masses, to whom it is seen as neither sincere nor capable of developing the civic institutions that may eventually circumvent its unilateral power, forestalling its discretionary, authoritarian and elitist prerogatives. They consider the military and the civil service to be part and parcel of the same bureaucratic set-up, lacking a national character but sharing a common antipathy towards full-fledged, accountable, representative and mandated institutions.

Typically, a bureaucratic attitude that symbolises a sense of superiority at both generalist and specialist levels and dismisses democracy and decentralisation, betrays a strong colonial tradition. The monopolisation of power from the grassroots to the top echelons by bureaucracy, its huge economic cost,[1] together with inherent corruption,[2] and worst of all its lack of a balanced ethnic composition, have seriously eroded its standing in society. By July 1993, nine Pakistani prime ministers had been dismissed by six heads of state, three of whom were generals and three senior bureaucrats.[3] Equally, the manipulation of political institutions in the country by coopting the army was first done by bureaucrats. In terms of decision-making the civil service may have enlightened cadres, but at the level of implementation it is extremely coercive. To understand the Pakistani state structure and its immense powers, one needs to assess the colonial origins of the civil service, its set-up and training facilities in the post-1947 era and the various half-hearted measures for improvement.

THE STEEL FRAME OF THE RAJ

The British ruled India through a centralised bureaucracy, the Indian Civil Service (ICS), which was the kingpin of the Raj. The selection and training of ICS officals (ICSs) in Britain stemmed from the theory that as the representatives of the Raj they must (a) maintain law and order, (b) collect revenue and other taxes, and (c) plan and implement development plans. In line with Lord Macaulay's exhortations, Indians were inducted at the lower sub-divisional levels and even in the 1940s their representation in the highest cadres remained minimal. For a long time the ICS remained a monopoly of generalists with academic backgrounds in liberal arts from the prestigious British universities. First through an apprenticeship and then at the job, they acquired professional specialisations.

The ICS officials were supposed to be strictly professional in their relationship with the politicians who in any case were not generally very assertive or intrusive. The training and natural inclination of these officials did not lead them to work with politicians on an equal basis. Their isolation from the natives was intended to guarantee their impartiality in a very paternalistic environment. They were the *mai bap* for the Indian subjects as they each led entirely separate lives. The total number of ICSs in British India, even during the peak years, never exceeded a few hundred. The Raj maintained a highly centralised system, in order (among other reasons) to keep expenses at a minimum. Consequently, huge districts and divisions were preferred over smaller and more homogeneous administrative units. Typically, one well-placed British ICS official would run a district with the help of a dozen low-paid local clerks.[4] In 1947, Pakistan inherited a strong, centralised and powerful civil service from 'their imperial predecessors'.[5]

The colonial administrative structure was completely biased in favour of a strong executive. The administrative head at the district level looked after routine law-and-order matters as well as the duties of the district magistrate. Such dualism was repeated at the *tahsil* or *thana* (subdivisions) level where the local magistrate was a civil administrator with his judicial duties trailing behind his routine administrative prerogatives. Further down the ladder, the *tahsildar*, basically the sub-divisional revenue official, also held the court session in the *tahsil* (mostly for civil matters) besides as assisting the magistrate in administrative affairs. In some cases, civil judges were appointed to look after the civil (*diwani*) suits yet the magistrates held regular courts on criminal (*faujdari*) offences. This dualism allocated immense powers to the executive at the expense of a separate and independent judiciary. Moreover, the same hierarchical system was maintained at divisional, provincial and central levels. As the viceroy held unilateral powers at the centre as the representative of the Crown over everybody else, the governors in the provinces wielded *de facto* powers. The India Act of 1935 solidified gubernatorial authority over the assemblies who, by virtue of clauses like section 93, could simply dissolve the elected assemblies and promulgate governor's rule on the province.[6] Long after independence, the same Act, aided by the Independence Act of 1947, operated as the *de facto* Constitution for Pakistan.

THE CIVIL SERVICE IN PAKISTAN

In 1947 there were 1157 officials in the Indian Civil Service (including the Indian Political Service), of whom 608 were British and 448 were Hindus and others. The total number of Muslim officials was 101, out of whom 95 opted for living in Pakistan (83 from the civil service and 12 from the political service).[7] Most of these Muslim officials were Urdu-speakers from Muslim minority provinces; one-third came from the Punjab, while only one or two belonged to Muslim Bengal.[8] Since there was no single bureaucrat with a designation equivalent to that of secretary, vacancies were filled by quickly promoting the renamed CSP (Civil Service of Pakistan) officials and retaining several senior British civil servants. Within the CSP, the PSP (Police Service of Pakistan) and FSP (Foreign Service of Pakistan) were considered to be more prestigious than services like accounts, income tax and customs and excise, though the selections were made by the Public Service Commission on a merit basis.[9] In the early years, at the Civil Service Academy in Lahore, vigilant British administrators instilled the probationers with the 'sense of belonging to a privileged group which had a major responsibility for the future governing of Pakistan'.[10] The Academy, 'the manufacturing laboratory' created 'Anglicised officials' true to Macaulay's dream, who held political leaders in contempt.[11] According to Braibanti, the trainees were being 'steeped in the ethos of British colonial administration'.[12] While Jinnah acknowledged the urgency of an efficient civil service in the young country, he advised the bureaucrats to adopt a more nationalistic and realistic attitude by functioning as the 'servants of Pakistan'.[13]

The civilian bureaucracy of Pakistan has tried to meet three challenges. In a collective sense, it has operated as a secular and modern institution and has generally resisted efforts to convert Pakistan into a theocracy. In the national context of a multi-ethnic society, it has stressed integration, which has generally produced a severe backlash. Finally, it has confronted the issues of uneven political and economic development.[14] In fact, bureaucracy has been playing concurrently executive, judicial, legislative, political and technical roles (such as economic planning and implementation) in the state structure while at the same time regimenting the status quo.[15]

BUREAUCRACY OVERRULES POLITICS

As a 'viceregal system',[16] the bureaucracy has constantly overstepped, bypassed, dismissed and denigrated the mass verdict by simply opting for authoritarianism. It has underrated its own citizens and their acumen. Without understanding the dilemma of politicians and political parties in a young country like Pakistan, the public servants have acted as masters and king-makers, missing no opportunity to malign them among the people. While politicians have been presented as mischievous, corrupt and inefficient, their favours have nevertheless been sought to legitimise authoritarian regimes from Malik Ghulam Muhammad through to Ghulam Ishaque Khan. A constant erosion in civil authority has been matched by an all-transcending state power. As LaPorte says on the Zia period, 'The political leaders are episodically replaced, but the power of the administrative system and the authority of the bulk of its officers is impervious to change.'[17] During the premiership of Liaquat Ali Khan, the provincial governors (many of whom were civil servants) routinely sent him secret reports on the chief ministers and cabinet members.[18] Eventually, the West Punjab Legislative Assembly was dissolved in January 1949 with the governor citing Section 93 (a) of the India Act of 1935. The PRODA (Public Representative Offices (Disqualification) Act) was used against the politicians in Sindh as well, though Khan Abdul Qayyum Khan's provincial ministry in the NWFP survived such pressures. In East Pakistan, PRODA was used against Hameedul Haq Chowdhury, a provincial finance minister, and the provincial chief secretary 'revealed in September 1950 that under instructions from Central Government he had effectively stopped the export of steel drums to India which had been ordered by Mr. Chowdhury'.[19] The provincial secretaries even began to dismiss ministers on the basis of alleged corruption or for disorderly misdemeanour.

The earliest blatant instance of the attitude of civil servants to politicians was Nazim ud-Din's dismissal by Ghulam Muhammad in 1953. The Bengali prime minister, a colleague of the Quaid-i Azam and a seasoned political leader, enjoyed support among the legislators. After Jinnah's death, he had assumed the office of chief executive of the country and allowed Liaquat Ali Khan to function as a very assertive prime minister. At the time of Liaquat's assassination in October 1951, Mushtaq Gurmani, Ghulam Muhammad and other senior military and civil officials were present in Rawalpindi and they asked Nazim ud-Din to form the next government.[20] He preferred to become prime minister and Ghulam Muhammad, a bureaucrat, was selected as the governor-general. The latter busied himself in palace conspiracies fearing that the prime minister would sweep the polls by means of the Bengali ethnic majority. He was duly assisted by Iskander Mirza, a cunning civil servant with 28 years experience, and General Ayub Khan, the ambitious commander-in-chief who was eager to establish closer relations with Western powers in order to build Pakistan's defence establishment. Iskander Mirza was appointed minister for the interior in Ali Bogra's cabinet in October 1954 while Ayub Khan, the army chief, also acquired the additional charge of the ministry of defence. Chaudhary Muhammad Ali, a senior Punjabi bureaucrat, liaised closely with this ambitious trio and, with no apparent justification, assumed the position of secretary-general to the central government which he made the hub of the administration. He was then appointed the minister of finance.

While politicians fought for offices and ignored the task of framing the Constitution, the bureaucracy and the military leadership grouped together and struck at the first opportunity. Nazim ud-Din was the first but not the last casualty and few tears were shed over the unceremonious dismissal of an elected prime minister and close associate of Jinnah. At one stroke, the Bengalis in particular and politicians in general had been thwarted and a message was sent to other 'to behave'. Ghulam Muhammad used the India Act of 1935 to justify his action on the basis of the law-and-order situation both in East Pakistan and Punjab. In Bengal, there had been riots over the language issue in 1952; in Punjab there had been anti-Ahmedi riots in 1953. The Punjab ministry led by the wily Mumtaz Daultana wanted to capture power in the centre by ousting the Bengali prime minister. In the event, the riots were controlled by a partial martial law, Nazim ud-Din was dismissed and Daultana gained nothing at all. The state had succeeded in creating a further polarisation of the factionalist politicians.

Another example of the bureaucratic manipulation of the state structure is the establishment of the One-Unit scheme which was ingenuously conceived to counterbalance the Bengali majority in any elected assembly. It delighted many Punjabi politicians as it facilitated their domination of the four provinces in the Western wing and gave them parity with East Pakistanis. The fear of Bengali domination held by these politicians and their benefactors in the state was justified when the United Front won a clear majority over the Muslim League in the provincial elections of 1954 in East Pakistan. While the Front, led by stalwarts like Fazl ul-Haq, H. S. Suhrawardy and Maulana Bhashani won around 300 seats, the League had only 10. The Front aimed to rule the whole of Pakistan given the chance, and their 21-point manifesto promised land reforms, the formulation of a constitution and social-welfare-oriented measures that disturbed the Indus-Basin landed aristocracy and Pakistani bureaucracy. Consequently, Ghulam Muhammad imposed governor's rule on East Pakistan, sending Iskander Mirza to replace the veteran politician, Khaliquzzaman, as the new provincial governor. Fazl ul-Haq was detained on charges of treason and the provincial assembly was dissolved on 30 May 1954. Iskander

Mirza threatened the Bengali politicians with the imposition of martial law and mobilisation of troops in East Pakistan. The state structure had shown once again how far it would go to preserve its own petty interests.

Chaudhary Muhammad Ali, the bureaucrat turned-prime-minister, gave the country its first constitution in 1956, modelled on the India Act of 1935, which safeguarded a strong centre, preserved parity between the two wings and guaranteed One-Unit in West Pakistan. During the absence of the opposition members from the assembly, hastily formulated clauses were inserted in the Constitution to protect the bureaucrats from being dismissed without the authorisation of the president. Thus, the civil service obtained a higher position than the elected assemblies and the national constitution without giving up its attempt to wield more powers. The colonial legacy of divide and rule was operating to the full at the expense of political institutions. The ordinary people in Pakistan were treated with contempt by state functionaries who behaved virtually like 'brown Englishmen'.[21] Naturally, this accentuated the ethnic divide in the country as the Bengalis especially resented the Muhajir–Punjabi domination of the country. Ataur Rahman Khan, then chief minister of East Pakistan, summed up the feelings of most Bengali politicians when he observed in a parliamentary debate:

> As a matter of fact I may tell you, it may be a great weakness with me that I feel a peculiar sensation when I come from Dacca to Karachi. I feel physically, apart from mental feeling, that I am living here in a foreign country, I did not feel as much when I went to Zurich, to Geneva or Switzerland, or London as much as I feel here in my own country that I am in a foreign land.[22]

On the whole, East Pakistani politicians and some West Pakistani dissenters were effectively marginalised by the bureaucratic 'combine' which had been coopting opportunist politicians and bringing Islam into the political idiom to legitimise their hold on power. H. S. Suhrawardy mourned the state of affairs in the country: 'In Pakistan, however, the administrators have taken upon themselves the task of making and unmaking Ministries. The result is that at present the country is being ruled by a coterie of foolish politicians and the "king-maker" administrators.'[23] When Suhrawardy became prime minister it was generally assumed that he would restore the supremacy of the political processes. To his chagrin, he realised that virtually all the powers lay with the president, Iskander Mirza, who could break the Awami League–Republican Party coalition headed by Suhrawardy. When the prime minister requested the convention of the national assembly, the president 'wrote back a letter refusing to call a meeting of the National Parliament stating that he knew about the position of the parties and called on me to resign by 11 o'clock in the morning otherwise he would take action'.[24] Suhrawardy should have realised that earlier recommendations by foreign experts concerning the control of the bureaucracy had been foiled by the ruling elites.[25] On the other hand the civil service, while stressing its role as the agent of modernisation, had undertaken the leadership of semi-autonomous corporations like the Water and Power Development Authority (WAPDA) and the Pakistan Industrial Development Corporation (PIDC).

Ayub Khan's martial law signalled the ascension of bureaucratic rule since the military itself was part of the bureaucracy and the state structure itself depended on civil servants from the grassroots to the governorship of the provinces. A senior Punjabi bureaucrat, Aziz Ahmad, with no experience of military service was even appointed martial-law administrator of East Pakistan for a while. Subsequently another civil servant, Akhtar Husain, was appointed as the governor of West Pakistan. Ayub Khan depended heavily on bureaucrats like Altaf Gauhar and, despite some feeble anti-bureaucratic rhetoric, nothing substantial was done to rein them in. On the contrary, the politicians bore the brunt. The Constitution of 1962 was another brain-child of Ayub's advisers from the bureaucracy, which made political institutions and parties hostage to bureaucrats all the way from the sub-divisional level to the national assembly.[26] A limited electoral college allowed blatant tampering with the elections and this came out quite openly during the presidential campaign against Fatima Jinnah when the Pakistani civil service made it impossible for the opposition to campaign for votes. Yahya Khan's retrenchment of 313 civil servants on allegations of corruption was more of a political ploy and, in the absence of a durable political order, smacked of opportunism. When the dissolution of the One-Unit came about, it had already irreparably damaged the polity. Like any other military government, martial law was a mere facade and decisions were made by a small coterie. The administration at divisional and district levels went on as usual, but the state would not allow politicians to run the country and refused to honour the results of the 1970 election. In fact, the bureaucracy had assumed that the electoral verdict would be more split, for it did not appreciate the extent of damage done to nationhood by the high-handed and partisan policies of the state apparatus in the preceding years.

Bhutto recognised that the period of *naukarshahi* was over and set out to reorganise the administrative set-up.[27] His reforms, largely implemented in 1973, integrated the civil service into a single unit with divisions dealing with specific areas like district management, foreign service, income tax, commerce, information, secretariat, postal service and railways. Mobility within these cadres was made possible and specialised academies to train the cadres were established. However, this was not a radical reorganisation since the bureaucrats operated as *de facto* administrators with nominal allegiance to the ruling political party. Nevertheless, the induction of lateral entrants and quota systems to bring personnel from less developed regions were innovations that caused chagrin to the established civil service.

> The emergence of the party as a powerful instrument in the state made the bureaucracy withdraw into the background where they merely followed government's directives. In a country with a scarcity of skills and expertise, such an attitude sabotaged Bhutto's programmes. The BE [Bureaucratic Elite] were not a spent force for they remained busy with their personal rather than national interests. They were known to tout for illicit gain and in some cases became CIA agents to sell information from countries like China.[28]

Bhutto's nationalisation of financial and industrial institutions provided ample new opportunities for the civil service to increase its influence. This not only hampered the growth of the banks, insurance companies and a number of industrial concerns by denying them incentives but also made them the personal fiefs of the civil service. Within a few years, all these concerns had become a major burden on the national economy as they were in deficit – though the official statistics gave a contrary picture. Once the jobs were secure, output either became stagnant or totally dropped, while financial institutions began issuing immense loans to favourites, bypassing moral and technical strictures. These nationalised banks replicated bureaucratic institutions, with an added financial attraction for the state to win favour from politicians – as was seen during Pakistan's longest martial law under General Zia ul-Haq.[29]

The Absence of a Trans-Regional Character

Even after decades of independence, the bed-rock of the Pakistani state lacks national character and a more indigenous outlook. It is true that because of the colonial inheritance of Pakistan, the Punjab provided the bulk of the military and civil bureaucracy. In 1948, only 2 East Pakistanis held top positions in the civil service compared to 16 West Pakistani senior officials (both Punjabis and Muhajireen).[30] By the mid-1950s, Bengalis were outnumbered by West Pakistanis in the ratio of five to one.[31] The regionalisation of the civil service promoted provincial and regional loyalties at the expense of a national outlook.[32]

THE QUOTA SYSTEM AND BUREAUCRACY

The redistribution of positions in the civil service on the basis of regional quotas was due to a growing consciousness of regional and ethnic pluralism in society, together with variations in terms of economic and political development. Overlapping populations in several provinces because of post-1947 migration both from outside and within the country as well as accelerated urbanisation motivated this policy of positive discrimination to make the civil bureaucracy a truly national institution. Language is the bed-rock of ethnic identity, and Table 3.1 shows the distribution within Pakistani society as seen in the last census (1981).

Added to such ethnic diversity, there are further variations in terms of rural, urban, tribal, developed and 'backward' regions. Even within a province like Punjab there is differentiation according to economic criteria. Similarly, the federal territory of Islamabad – highly developed and urban – federally administered areas (FATA) inclusive of tribal agencies, the Northern Areas and Azad Kashmir have their own separate allocations on the basis of population. Introduced in 1949, the quota system was intended to redress the imbalance between the two wings of Pakistan, while after 1971 the intention was to ameliorate inequalities 'between "more developed" and "less developed"' regions. The argument was that the quota was a necessary expedient designed to close the gap between the levels of development while promoting national integration. The second principle, that of proportional representation, has been invoked both as a goal and a strategy for effecting the compensatory principle.'[34] The domicile of each candidate determines his/her candidacy for the quota to be administered by the Federal Public Service Commission through its examination system.

Table 3.1   Language Groups as Percentage of Total Population

Punjabi	48.2
Pushtu	13.1
Sindhi	11.1
Saraiki	9.1
Hindko	2.4
Balochi	3.0
Brohi	1.2
Urdu	7.6

Source: Government of Pakistan, *Main Findings of the 1981 Population Census*, Islamabad, MPCPP, 1983, p. 13.[33]

The quota was introduced in Pakistan initially for five years and despite various recommendations it still continues and is still controversial especially in urban areas like Karachi. The ongoing arguments in favour and against have made it impossible even to incorporate minor amendments in its technicalities. Criticism that the quota system is vulnerable to corruption, manipulation and reverse discrimination, especially in the case of urban Punjabis and Muhajireen, has been countered by low development and lack of sufficient institutional support in the less-developed areas. It appears that the decision-makers will retain the quota system for some time to come.

During the 1980s, the combined civil service, inclusive of all attached departments and autonomous organisations, superseded the total figures of united Pakistan both in numbers and expenses. There were 13 784 public servants working in the parent organisations in the federal secretariat, while in attached departments the figures had already reached 137 191 in 1983. In the autonomous and semi-autonomous organisations, the total number of public servants had reached a staggering figure of 400 000. Officials employed by the central secretariat at the senior-cadre level in National Pay Scale 17 or above constituted 19 per cent of the total while in the attached departments they represented only 7 per cent.[35] After defence and debt-servicing this is the third major area of expenditure for the Pakistani exchequer. On the eve of the budget in 1992, it was leaked to the press that Prime Minister Nawaz Sharif had been appalled at the number of civil servants and the enormous expenses involved. There was speculation that a few ministries and divisions

Table 3.2 Regional Distribution (per cent) of Pakistan's Bureaucracy
(Grades 16–22) 1973–83.

Region	Quota	Actual strength
Punjab	50.0	55.8
NWFP	11.5	11.6
Urban Sindh	7.6	20.2
Rural Sindh	11.4	5.1
Balochistan	3.5	3.1
FATA & N.Areas	4.0	3.4
Azad Kashmir	2.0	0.9

Source: Government of Pakistan, *Federal Government Civil Servants Census Report*, January 1983, Islamabad, MPCPP, 1984.

would be wound up in 1992–93, both at the federal and provincial levels, but nothing came of it.

Over the years a number of Pushtuns have emerged as partners in the state structure through a growing participation in the bureaucracy, yet the Urdu speakers and officials from the Punjabi domicility outnumber other linguistic or regional sections. For instance, in 1983, the Muhajireen held 20.2 per cent of the total gazetted posts and 18.3 per cent in 1986. The Sindhis held only 2.7 per cent of gazetted positions in 1973 compared to 5.1 per cent in 1983 and 6.7 per cent in 1986. 'At the officer level, Muhajirs held 30.2 per cent of posts (grade 16–22) in 1974 and 14.8 per cent in 1989; Sindhis 4.3 per cent in 1974, and 6.1 per cent in 1989. Of the senior posts, 46.8 per cent were held by Muhajirs in 1974 and 31.5 per cent in 1985; Sindhis held 3.6 per cent of the comparable posts in 1974 and 6.8 per cent in 1983.'[36] In the military, the Muhajireen were also disproportionately over-represented. In 1968, they held 11 of the top 48 senior positions above the rank of brigadier, making their representation 23 per cent of the total. In the private sector, Sindhis were totally outnumbered by the others.[37]

CENTRALISED OR UNITARY STATE?

Several examples of the state taking powers to itself have been shown already. In addition, there have been military actions from the most disastrous and unnecessary of all in the former East Pakistan to similar ones that followed in Balochistan and Sindh. In Sindh, the state apparatus operated in two ways: first, it tried to restrain the nation-wide political threat to its authority and legitimacy by playing a partisan and opportunistic role in parallel ethnic loyalties, and secondly, it tried to curb political dissent by identifying the activists as bandits. Under General Zia, the ISI (Inter-Services Intelligence) and other intelligence-gathering agencies, vied for influence and propped up ethnic leaderships, otherwise poles apart, to counter the threat from the MRD and the PPP. The MQM was used as a pawn to wrest urban political power from the PPP, while in rural areas the Sindhi nationalists were implicitly allowed to carry on their tirades against the PPP and other country-wide political forces. The ethnic riots taking place in the 1980s and 1990s helped government functionaries to extract benefits for a centralist state. After all, Junejo, Bhutto, Jatoi and then Nawaz Sharif faced their greatest challenges in Sindh, to the extent of being ousted from the seat of government or simply acquiescing to the executive demands. Such meddling not only hurt the rubric of Pakistani society, it damaged its feeble political and economic institutions and demoralised the entire nation.

Sindh, as will be seen later, is a story not only of administrative mismanagement, but also of executive high-handedness that could have been avoided. The role of agencies like the police, the Criminal Investigation Agency (CIA), Federal Investigation Agency (FIA), Intelligence Bureau (IB), ISI and others such as Military Intelligence (MI) and the army's Field Investigation Team (FIT) simultaneously operating in Sindh have raised many questions about their long-term usefulness. The implementation of administrative measures at the expense of political dialogue, egalitarian policies and the overhauling of an archaic, unbalanced system, has taxed Sindh and Pakistan irrevocably. Consequently, inter-ethnic dialogue has given way to violence, banditry and torture-houses followed by frequent cleansing by paramilitary forces and the ethnic outfits. Sindh represents the failure of the Pakistani state system towards its own people. In the 1980s, the Al-Zulfikar Organisation (AZO) provided an easy scapegoat by which to settle accounts with the political critics of Islamabad. Incidents like the killing of several young men by Pakistan Navy patrol boats (the official explanation was that the youths were on their way to India for military training), the death of four Sindhi activists in military custody and the killing of nine non-political *haris* near Jamshoro in early June 1992 exposed the dire limitations of governmental intentions and actions. Similarly, the exposure that the MQM was operating torture-houses in 1992 and that it was carrying out a continuous campaign of terror in Karachi in 1994–95, both with the knowledge of the state, explains the very partisan, time-serving and shifty nature of the state structure. How the state could overlook the existence of such heinous practices and justify the credentials of the perpetrators in the province for so long when kidnapping and extortion were the order of the day, cannot be explained.

Many cases are not reported to the police or the press for fear of retaliation. Some of the worst incidents in Pakistan's history like the parades of nude women at the behest of local police or feudalists, have gone unpunished. Most cases of rape are not registered for fear of loss of reputation and further unnecessary interrogation. Occasional voices, usually from urban areas, reach the press, where they are eventually hushed up through an official 'press advice' or by sheer intimidation. The gang rape in November 1991 of Veena Hayat, a Karachi socialite, the mysterious murders of numerous citizens by a *hathora* group (hammer group), frequent *choolah* deaths (deaths allegedly due to exploding kerosine cookers), gunrunning by student and labour 'leaders' belonging to various parties, the sexual manipulation of innocent women by influential men, the muzzling of the press by local gangsters, or the lid placed on the stories of bonded labour and child trade to the Gulf for camel races, are all initially underplayed and then gradually eased out of the media. Administrative high-handedness may at times inspire awe among the people for the official machinery but public anger erupts as well. Quite often villagers and townsmen block the traffic on main roads and torch the local police station to register their protest against the authorities. Politicians, ironically, come to the rescue of the state and calm the protesters and a number of movements die in a vacuum because of official obstinacy and the absence of organised groups to defend civic rights, especially in the rural and tribal areas.

BUREAUCRACY AND UNEVEN DEVELOPMENT

Apart from the immense defence burden, the huge borrowing from foreign and domestic sources has caused a severe dependency syndrome in the national economy. Even in defence procurement, official discretion, personal choices, individual whims and ambitions have overruled the development of an indigenous infrastructure. The acquisition of huge loans was easy in the geo-political environment of the 1980s, but their role in national construction has been limited and they have increased national obligations. In fact, in more recent years, Pakistani debt-servicing has already outdone the allocations for the defence sector. Priorities have been drawn up to serve specific interests such as the evasion of crucial issues like land reforms, agricultural tax and expansion of the tax base.[38] Since the civil servants staffing the vital institutions in the central government formulate national five-year plans, prepare annual budgets and negotiate deals with foreign governments and agencies,[39] their personal limitations in terms of professional training and exposure to objective realities are often revealed.

Civil servants, with the exception of a few technocrats, generally lack the necessary wherewithal and professional acumen to handle sensitive issues.[40] The saga of Pakistan Steel Mills, Karachi, is an example of this. Established with generous Soviet assistance as one of the largest of its type in Asia, it has suffered from underproduction and mismanagement. Reflecting Karachi's uneasy ethnic situation, unrealistic and unnecessary recruitment to appease the MQM was made, with the mills becoming a new drain on the national exchequer. Decision-making positions are held by people without the necessary specialisation and experience while various hostile labour groups exhaust their energies and institutional resources in mutual struggle. The Pakistan International Airlines (PIA) is another ongoing story of inefficiency and official corruption. With an excessive number of employees on its pay-roll, its services and revenues have been the subject of debate for many years. Usually headed by a retired air marshal, this 'pampered' organisation has monopoly over national routes and lucrative business in the Gulf. Yet it has a history of squabbles, inefficiency and corruption; many of its employees have been found dealing in drugs and so the airline has become suspect at European and North American airports. In addition, the Pakistan railways, various insurance corporations, numerous state-run industrial and commercial concerns as well as the country's missions abroad present a sorry state of inertia, alienation and lack of commitment reminiscent of the decadence of the later Mughals, while ordinary citizens toil laboriously, unrecognised and unappreciated.

The official monopolisation of financial and semi-autonomous institutions by public servants has also resulted in increasing corruption. The executive positions enable financial deals, including huge commissions on contracts with foreign companies. The two major crises in Pakistan's recent history have involved the official plunder of public institutions. Grants of soft loans involving millions of rupees on fictitious grounds were eventually written off without reimbursement in the late 1980s, and though widely debated in the media and by the public, remain unaccounted for. Even the names of the beneficiaries were not released to the public[41] until the interim government led by Moeen Qureshi in mid-1993 officially published the long lists of defaulters on loans and taxes.[42]

Another financial scandal of immense proportions that affected almost every middle-class family in the Punjab was the bankruptcy of a number of cooperative societies in 1991. They had promised huge dividends on individual investments but squandered all the money. Many civil servants and politicians, including a few ministers, have been involved in this scam, which again has not been accounted for. Such intermittent frauds[43] have created a moral dilemma and, moreover, have directed attention to making easy money through shoddy real estate, loan defaulting, tax evasion, drug-trafficking and other underhand practices.[44]

THE MILITARY ELITES

Pakistan's polity has been under the influence of the military through most of its history, and even when not in power it has been 'behind the steering wheel'. The preponderant role of military elites both in national politics and in the formulation of regional and foreign policies as well as the ever-escalating defence expenditure in terms of resource allocation in the national exchequer, has occasionally raised (admittedly muted) queries and questions. Academically, the military in politics and decision-making processes has generated a body of theory about 'the man on horseback' and praetorianism. Equally, the vital questions of modernisation and national integration are substantive themes in contemporary literature on the military and politics. Pakistan's continuum of martial laws or military-led regimes (1958–71 and 1977–88), the military's indirect role as the power elite or arbiter in the early years and during the post-martial-law interludes in the country, its unchallenged position in the formulation of economic, foreign and defence policies have attracted an increasing number of studies in recent years. In addition, the ethnic composition of the military (especially the army) and attendant issues like the role and adoption of ideology, legitimacy and the cooption of other elitist groups, together constitute a body of significant yet complex academic themes.

In a country such as Pakistan, the army's hold on power has been justified frequently as a means of eradicating corruption (usually attributed to inept politicians), guaranteeing national security and improving law and order. In the 1950s and 1960s, it assumed the role of moderniser; in the 1970s it battled with the alienated political forces in former East Pakistan and Balochistan; and in the 1980s it adopted an additional role as the defender of ideology. In the 1990s it withdrew to a less visible yet crucial role of being the most powerful member of a 'troika' with the president and prime minister as the other members. It played a crucial role in brokering deals among the feuding politicians.

During 1947–48, the military elites had taken a back seat in policy-making processes and helped in the rehabilitation of refugees. In 1953, while they served as custodians of the law for a brief period during the anti-Ahmedi riots in the Punjab, the GHQ based in Rawalpindi began to assume a more decisive role. Powerful bureaucrats like Ghulam Muhammad, Iskander Mirza, Ikramullah and Chaudhary Muhammad Ali helped draw the defence establishment into domestic politics, duly reciprocated by an ambitious army chief. With the erosion of political authority both at the central and provincial levels, the bureaucrats and generals assumed the role of the state with willing feudalists ready to play a subordinate role. Eventually, the army emerged as the power-broker and moved to take complete control, which was eventually consummated through a formal take-over in 1958. As in the case of other military regimes, the top Pakistani officers could not handle the politicised ethnicity in the former eastern wing, which demanded its share of power after the electoral victory in 1970. The military leadership became partisan and triggered a civil war, while active foreign intervention converted ethnic dissent into a national liberation movement. Having failed to manage the state, the military rulers temporarily assumed a low-key profile by allowing Z.A. Bhutto to run the country. Politicians were always difficult to handle, many were ruthless and self-motivated and their loyalties never went further than material gains. In 1977, Pakistani politicians both in government and opposition, gave the army another chance to stage a come-back as the country embraced the longest martial law in its history. Without the fateful plane crash in August 1988, Pakistan would still be under military-led ad-hocism presided over by the late army chief of staff.

In both Pakistan and Bangladesh the military used ideology and threats to national security in order to gain legitimacy as well as blaming politicians for all society's ills. In Pakistan, after Zia, the rigidity and bi-polarisation apparently disappeared as the new army leadership claimed to believe in democratic processes; but the divisions and cleavages among politicians have enabled the military to play the role of a moderator and effective arbiter. Under Generals Ayub Khan, Yahya Khan and Zia ul-Haq the military has been shifting its role from veto regime to clientelism.[45] In Bangladesh, and to some extent in Pakistan, the divided political opposition and a stubborn India did not help the development of mature democratic order.

Ayub Khan and Mirza were the earliest and most obvious representatives of the two major branches of a headstrong bureaucracy. They aborted the elections of 1958 through a coup only to fall out three weeks later. Iskander Mirza left and Ayub's new cabinet included nine civilians holding portfolios such as interior, information, finance, commerce and communications. Despite seemingly drastic purges only 13 civil officials were dismissed, while all sorts of harsh measures (including PRODA and EBDO) were applied to the politicians and political activists. Thousands of them were barred from holding any public office with retrospective effect from 14 August 1947.[46] The state had become blatantly coercive and the alliance between its two strong arms had matured into a firm bond. Ayub Khan, speaking for his colleagues, considered that the Pakistani masses were too unsophisticated and illiterate to exercise their democratic rights in a parliamentary democracy.[47] His idea of basic democracy was to win legitimacy without going through a mass-based political process, which would also conveniently thwart the Bengali majority. This manipulation of the political system and the Constitution to suit his own interests hastened the split between the two wings of the country. By the time

Yahya Khan tried to hold back power it was too late: 'The break-up of Pakistan was largely the result of the failure to build institutions based on popular consensus and the determination of the civil–military bureaucracy to monopolise decision making to the exclusion of political elites with a broad base'.[48] The separation of East Pakistan could have been possibly averted or at least achieved by a mutually acceptable, peaceful and honourable arrangement. However, the West-Pakistan-based ruling elites underestimated the situation as a simple law-and-order problem.

Military defeat in the former East Pakistan sent the armed forces back to barracks for a few years, though not a single person was taken to court even after such a national catastrophe. Bhutto tried to rein in the generals through constitutional guarantees, which were not sufficient deterrent for any power seeker however. The PNA movement was hijacked and eventually Bhutto was executed since he 'was the only national leader who could keep the armed forces under political control and his extermination was therefore essential'.[49] Pakistan had come full circle. Democracy was taboo and ad-hocism became the order of the day. Afghanistan provided a prop to acquire foreign assistance yet the political institutions and the Constitution remained in a shambles. Ideology and physical coercion were used to sidetrack the real issues. Suppression of the MRD in 1983 further proved that the army, at least at the command level, wanted to stay at the helm and that politicians and bureaucrats would only be allowed a surrogate role. Legal, political, educational, judicial and economic institutions were reoriented to eradicate any dissent and ideology was used to superimpose conformity and docility. Civil society was degraded by extensive government intervention in matters from dress styles to broadcasts, amendments to the Constitution and press advice, lashes and summary military courts, special ordinances to curb nominal university autonomy and subordination of the judges to martial law. Pakistan was in its worst time, nationalism lay bruised, people turned to earlier identities and the state was triumphant in its ascendancy over its own people and institutions. A severe sense of dejection and alienation prevailed among intellectuals, who felt that 'The military, the bureaucracy and the unrepresentative leaders have one thing in common: the fear of the masses.'[50]

Nevertheless, it is true that Pakistan's defence policy has hinged on the crucial pillar of national security since the country's inception. It has been compounded by hostility from its larger neighbour, often articulated by the leaders of the Indian National Congress desiring annulment of the partition, or through successive feuds over princely states, assets, water distribution and relationships with outside powers.[51] Not only India, but

Afghanistan has also exhibited aggressive hostility and irredentism with serious ramifications for Pakistan's national security.[52] A post-independence war over Kashmir in the wake of mass migration and little in the way of defence infrastructures except for a few scattered cantonments (but no ammunition factories), made Pakistan follow a rigorous policy to overcome its handicaps. The dominant elite with an obvious pro-Western orientation and a bi-polarised world provided incentives to enter into an alliance-based relationship. However, it is not clear to what extent such elitist preferences have been effective in overcoming Pakistan's deficiency in conventional weapons.

At the leadership level, the military in 1947 presented a very dismal picture as compared to the present, with only 4 lieutenant colonels, 42 majors and 114 captains and there was no single unit that could be called truly Muslim. Partisan decisions governing the boundary award,[53] the overruling of Liaquat's formula of April 1947 for further specification of the Indian Army before independence along with Marshal Auchinleck's suggestion for a shared defence, laid the ground for Indo-Pakistani misperceptions. This mistrust increased with Kashmir's annexation in India's favour.[54] Pakistan's preoccupation with the security threat and the attendant priority for defence, partially led to the supremacy of the defence ministry and the GHQ in the wake of weakened parliamentary processes in the post-Jinnah years. While reminding the army commanders of their oath of 'allegiance to the Constitution and the Government of the Dominion of Pakistan', Jinnah had always emphasised 'the supremacy of the civilian government'. To him, the armed forces 'were the servants of the people', since he believed in strong parliamentary institutions. Under Liaquat, while he himself held the position of defence minister, the GHQ being in Rawalpindi, the defence ministry and the army command tended to be more autonomous at the behest of powerful bureaucrats like Iskander Mirza. There was an erosion of civilian/political control of the armed forces and formulation of the defence policy shifted from the political sector to its supposedly subordinate bureaucratic–military counterpart. Ayub Khan, Mirza, Ikramullah, Ghulam Muhammad and their cohorts made and pursued Pakistan's defence policy entirely according to their own biases and ambitions, mostly over and above the political authorities.

Although Liaquat had a pro-US orientation, he nevertheless followed a non-aligned policy; yet Pakistan's defence-needs as advocated by the defence establishment, helped by the cold war and Nehru's dismissal of the USA, pushed Pakistan into closer relations with America. As P. I. Cheema explains:

Four factors seem to have compelled Pakistan to abandon the option of non-alignment: the fear of India, the domestic political and economic problems, the ruling elite and the dictates of the international climate. But far the most important factor was the perception that even after the partition India was not reconciled to the establishment of Pakistan and would do everything to destroy the new state at the first opportunity.[55]

The repercussions were significant:

Not only did the agreement change the entire training patterns of armed forces that were, hitherto, akin to British modes of training and introduced the American pattern of training but gradually it made Pakistan heavily dependent upon American weaponry. Pakistan's options but [sic] other sources of arms procurement were also not properly explored. Consequently when the Americans decided to impose an arms embargo during the 1965 Indo-Pakistani War, it was Pakistan that was seriously hurt.[56]

In the 1980s, the Pakistan Army was better poised to derive benefits from its American allies without losing its nuclear option, though certainly many American liberals criticised their government for supporting a martial law regime.[57]

THE HISTORY AND DEVELOPMENT OF THE PAKISTAN ARMY

The British Indian Army, originally divided into various regional set-ups, was finally integrated into a cohesive, unitary and country-wide organisation after the Mutiny of 1857. Lord Roberts of Kandhar, espousing a predominant view in the Indian government during the 1880s and 1890s, preferred recruitment from the so-called martial races, mostly from the Punjab and the NWFP. Kitchener's reforms were introduced to meet a possible Russian threat from the north and again the northern areas were prominent in strategic thinking. Pursuing the demands for Indianisation, the Skeen Committee was established in 1925 to make recommendations in that direction. Jinnah headed a sub-committee which toured various European countries to familiarise itself with the training facilities at these places. By 1947, 80 per cent of officers in the Indian Army were Hindus, though the soldiers were motivated by a complex blend of symbols, loyalty, rewards and honour. The British Indian Army basically played the role of defending the empire both within and outside the sub-continent. In addition, on occasions, it was called in to assist in the maintenance of law and order. 'During the British period, formal drills and exercises were developed by the military to enable it to deal with violent crowds or trouble-some areas; the location of the Indian Army units in cantonments adjacent to major cities was certainly no coincidence.'[58]

After independence, the Pakistani armed forces emphasised Islam as the unifying force, though the basic structures remained largely based on the British model. In 1950, General Akbar Khan suggested the establishment of a nation-wide people's army but Sandhurst remained the model at the decision-making levels. Stephen Cohen, the author of an influential work on the army, who had unique access to classified archives and institutions, finds three distinct generational phases in the history of the Pakistan army: the British generation (1947–53); the American generation (1953–71), and the Pakistani generation (1972 onwards). Especially under Zia, organised efforts were undertaken to induct an Islamic dimension at the officer level. The lower middle-class middle-rank officers accepted the army's enhanced role not only as defenders of the country but also as soldiers of Islam.[59] Islam replaced the symbols of the British Indian Army. To some, the army's dominant role in the body-politic is neither interventionist nor praetorian,[60] but is more complex than that. For example,

The military–state relation conceptualizes a dialectical relationship between Islam, Pakistan and the military. Without Islam, Pakistan would not have come into existence; without Pakistan the military would not be able to exist; and without the military, Islam and Pakistan would be threatened. In perpetuating such a state, the military was per-petuating Islam.[61]

Such an interpretation is not correct, however, since it is only recently that the military has assumed the role of introducing Islam in the country; also, although this was genuine at various levels, for many it was simply a ploy to acquire legitimacy. As far as Pakistan's security is concerned, it entered into war – even for defensive purposes – only when it was under a military ruler. One cannot deny the inter-relationship between Islam, Pakistan and the army, but to regard the latter as the guarantor for the others is an over-simplification, as Muslim society even under non-Muslim colonial rule produced dynamic leaders like Syed Ahmed Khan, Jinnah and Iqbal.

Moreover, the composition of a supposedly national institution is a sen-sitive issue in a multi-ethnic society like Pakistan. There has been no dearth of public outcry at the military's capture of power, for Pakistanis feel strongly that even a corrupt and weak democratic government is preferable to any form of dictatorship.[62] The fall of the Soviet Union is clear proof that only a shared political and economic system within a plural society can guarantee the longevity of a state or country. Enormous defence expenditures are already crippling South Asian economies which have the world's highest concentrations of poor people. The problem of underdevelopment can be addressed if the South Asian elite begin to think in terms of substantial demilitarisation on a regional basis. Militarism is not an isolated phenomenon as it gradually replaces tolerance and humanity within a society and unleashes the forces of bigotry and intolerance which are further accentuated by the problems of inequality and social stratification.

Compared to its counterpart in the pre-independence era, the Pakistan army is a very different set-up. Its officers have gradually obtained more social status and political power. In the early years, it lacked the continuity in formation, leadership and institutions which its counterpart enjoyed and given Pakistan's emphasis on Islamic identity the army had to adapt to this. The Indian army, on the other hand, accommodated itself easily in a secular state. In addition, 'The Pakistan Army developed quite early and close ties with foreign military establishments (especially that of the United States) out of necessity, whereas the Indian Army has been deliberately kept away from such contacts.'[63] The Pakistan army has been more dependent on foreign sources for weapons and equipment and the efforts for self-reliance began much later. There are a number of other denominators and variables which distinguish the Pakistan army and its role from that of its counterpart across the eastern borders.[64]

'PUNJABI DOMINATION' OF THE ARMY

As mentioned earlier, the Pakistan army traditionally has been dependent upon recruitment from the Punjab and NWFP, an issue which has become increasingly polemical and controversial. Given the plural and multi-ethnic nature of Pakistani society, with the military the most organised country-wide institution and an effective part of the state in the socio-political and economic sense, this dependence is significant. Apart from being a symbol of status, service in the military (undoubtedly the major public employment sector[65]) brings comparatively higher and more stable economic prospects.[66] So, in an over-populous society with an increasing number of unemployed youth and educated unemployed, where forces of friction are stronger than those of tolerance and integration, a sense of group deprivation can be a very explosive issue.

Initially the Bengalis and then the Sindhis and, to a lesser extent, Balochis resented the 'Punjabi domination' of the state. Geo-politically,

India has always maligned the Pakistan army as an aggressive, regionalist and power-hungry institution. Intermittent martial laws, the military's role in alliance-building with foreign powers,[67] the East Pakistan crisis and the military's pronounced role during the Afghanistan crisis (in the context of ISI's involvement with the Mujahideen) are all used by Indian and some Pakistani critics to portray the army as a Punjabi institution of an otherwise ruthless state out to conquer its own people.[68] Factually, it is from the less developed districts like Attock, Chakwal, Mianwali and Rawalpindi that the bulk of the soldiery comes and that could be explained in economic and historical terms; similarly Kohat and Bannu contribute more than the settled, fertile Peshawar valley. Central Punjab, the most developed in the province, or even Southwestern Punjab, much more advanced than *barani* (rain-fed) Pothowar, have a very meagre share in army enlistment. However, it is a fact that the Punjabi share, if one extends the term indefinitely, is proportionately higher and even that of the NWFP is many times higher than that of Sindh, the second largest and most populous province in the country. The existence of the Northern Command in Rawalpindi since the British era has left a continuing legacy in favour of the Punjab and the neighbouring Frontier. Cohen, however, believes that the theory of the Punjabi domination 'is the product of the actual numerical imbalance between the Punjab and the other provinces and the bluff, rough Punjabi style (which has an undercurrent of treachery, according to Mengal and others), complicated by a Punjabi-centred strategic orientation'. Moreover, it is concerned with 'the strategic core area' that the province had obtained.[69] To army generals and other thoughtful Pakistanis, the continuing ethnic imbalance for whatever reason is perplexing and demoralising.

In a representative political culture, the establishment of military cantonments or military assistance in the maintenance of law and order under a civil authority would not have caused an uproar against the institution itself. But martial laws, the execution of Z.A. Bhutto, generous land grants to former military and civil personnel, the suppression of MRD-led protests in Sindh, apprehension concerning the after-effects of the Kalabagh Dam and the presumed patronage of the MQM through ISI, all exacerbated Sindhi reservations against Islamabad. Thus, the army was viewed as the instrument of specific regional interests and its assumption of the country's leadership for so long has exacerbated this image. Since Zia's death this has led to a 'new thinking' and within the army many echelons realise the extent of erosion the institution has suffered due to its interventionist and vetoing role in domestic politics. With each military take-over, deeper fissures have appeared in the polity which affect the professional capabilities of the institution itself. For many army officials this has presented a difficult choice especially when there is no tradition of 'Young Turks' taking on the senior generals. Cohen summed this up succinctly: 'There are armies that guard the nation's borders, there are those that are concerned with protecting their own position in society, and there are those who defend a cause or an idea. The Pakistan Army does all three.'[70] Further dynamic efforts may be needed to help 'disengage' the army from its complex and equally baffling multiple roles. A weak, mutually divisive, economically underdeveloped and politically fragile Pakistan would never be able to afford a huge defence establishment. Similarly, the non-interventionist generals can help politicians in evolving a common viable political culture based on plural, democratic and accountable traditions.

4 Feudalists in Politics: Trans-Regional Elitist Alliance

Historically speaking, the feudal lords lost their politico-economic ascendancy in Europe and North America to an ambitious, highly literate, and urban-based middle class, forerunner of modern Western civilisation. In predominantly agrarian societies elsewhere, especially in colonies like the South Asian sub-continent, the emergence of a bourgeoisie was a slow and largely state-dependent process.[1] The colonial state harboured suspicions towards the professional elites and therefore coopted the landed elites[2] and attempted to ensure their preservation as regional potentates. South Asia essentially remained segmentary due to a marriage of convenience among the tripolar forces of the land-holding tribal, feudal and imperial hierarchies. The consolidation of ruralisation under the Raj reflected the very imbalance in the demographic realities of the sub-continent where three-quarters of its population lived in villages depending on agriculture. Industrialisation and the resultant urbanisation had been relatively recent developments in British India. Cross-border migration in 1947, ambitious plans for rapid industrialisation, mechanised agriculture leading to the green revolution of the 1960s, migration to the UK and, in the 1970s, to the oil-rich Gulf states, were all decisive factors in the development of South Asian mobility. Job opportunities and better civic facilities attracted peasant and tribal communities to the cities and, especially in the 1980s, new socio-political forces and tensions were unleashed.[3] Although this could be seen as a fortuitous development, despite the unprecedented scale, apparently breaking the age-old hierarchical order in the countryside; a deeper scrutiny of the underlying forces testifies to the contrary. Migration to urban areas might provide emancipation from an oppressive and stale socio-economic order, yet ghettoisation has rendered the unskilled masses vulnerable to city-related traumas including volatile ethnic divisions.

In Pakistan, feudalism itself has undergone a dramatic transformation. With their role and influence redefined and regimented under the Raj, the feudal dynasties, like the European medieval lords, have turned out to be change-resistant but, unlike the latter, have continuously redefined their roles so as to guarantee their self-preservation. Adjustment to new socio-economic and political realities, as long as they do not threaten their own interests, has safeguarded their survival and entrenchment. During the British period this ensured that they remained the main beneficiaries of favours from the Raj. For instance, they sent their children to schools like Aitchison (also called Chiefs' College); were eager to get them enlisted in the British Indian Army; assumed administrative cum judicial responsibilities in their respective areas of influence; purchased expensive urban properties initially for residential purpose and then for commercial as well; and most of all, they contested elections for the local and provincial legislative bodies mainly to strengthen their local/regional status. Their hobnobbing with colonial officials guaranteed them increased influence and affluence. Certainly, the landed aristocrats of the early twentieth century in the Punjab and Sindh were a different breed altogether.

Since 1947, they have provided the bulk of Pakistan's parliamentarians; have dominated party politics in the country and, through matrimonial and economic alliances, have assumed the role of a trans-regional elite. Forward-looking aristocrats have been investing in urban property and industrial concerns in cities; a new generation of aristocrats with degrees from privileged Western universities and with urbane and cosmopolitan life-styles have seen to it that their near-monopoly of national politics and the economy remains unchallenged. In lieu of political support to a regime, whether military or quasi-democratic, feudalists exact favours through ministerial positions, loans and property allocations. They have regularly defaulted in repayments, evaded taxes and, in many cases, even evaded payment of the electricity bills for their farms and estates. They have also been able to obtain the most expensive urban properties in Pakistan through political bribes. Regimes, anxious to gain support, have always avoided overdue measures such as land reforms, the imposition of an agricultural tax and reorganisation of the electoral constituencies which could alienate the landed interests. In more recent years, both the military and post-military regimes have been writing off loans worth billions of rupees owed to the national exchequer by the landed aristocracy. Such practices done in the name of 'horse-trading' have consolidated the tradition of state patronage and institutionalised corruption. Thus, the consolidation and overwhelming importance of feudal influence in the polity has not only retarded Pakistan's transformation into a viable, egalitarian society but has also made its millions of people hostages to an elitist oligarchy thriving on unbounded corruption and cooption.[4]

CHARACTERISTICS OF THE FEUDAL CLASS

The feudal class is traditionally land-based.[5] Given the patriarchal nature of a rural/agrarian society, it is property and land that largely determine the social status and politico-economic role of an individual/family.[6] Feudalism is simply dynastic and the clearest manifestation of its influence is at the local level. Especially in rural Sindh, Balochistan, Southern NWFP and Southwestern Punjab certain families, in a very tribal manner, prefer a *regional* role over any other. In several cases, trans-regional matrimonial alliances have refurbished the dynastic feudal interests.[7] In other cases, the feudal classes extend matrimonial relations with non-feudal yet powerful families of industrialists, senior army officials and civil servants.[8] The desire for such a relationship is mutual.[9] In such cases, the feudalist's status in his respective area and clan is perceived in terms of his land possessions and socio-political clout. The syed landlords would prefer syeds or *sajjada nishin* of similar genealogical background as would the Pagaras of Sindh, syeds of Jhang and Khanewal and the Makhdooms of Multan and Hala.[10]

In recent times cross-regional and cross-ethnic marriages among the feudal families have emerged, though the Baloch clans in southern Punjab, rural Sindh and neighbouring Balochistan have always maintained cross-regional alliances. But such alliances are again *ethnic*. The marriages among the Pushtun feudal families were strictly *tribal* (limited to one's own clan, tribe and region) but among certain educated families new patterns of seeking bonds outside the *qabila* are emerging. On the other hand, the Punjabi feudal families are the most mobile and diversified of all in terms of matrimonial bonds, although socio-economic stature remains the main criterion. Feudal marriages are generally discreet when it comes to inter-denominational marriages, with Sunnis marrying into Sunni families and Shias seeking Shia suitors. Any transgression could mean losing prestige (*izzat*) and local authority (*dabdaba*).[11]

Since the early decades of the present century there has been a growing tendency to acquire higher education as a symbol of honour and influence. Many feudal members of Pakistan's assemblies are former graduates of English-medium public schools, although this does not apply to women. In many traditional families women stay inside the home behind *chaadar* and *chardiwari* (veil and four walls).[12] A few of the educated amongst them, otherwise quite liberal in an urban environment, resume their traditional role once back in their native areas.[13]

In terms of political views, the feudal class is extremely conservative, oppressively status-quo-oriented, and in nearly all cases it is totally resistant to change.[14] At least on the local level, the worst and most co-ercive form of feudalism reflects itself in the treatment of tenants, *kammis* (low-caste professionals and artisans), women and other dependents.[15] In this the feudalists remind one of the pre-French Revolution aristocracy in Europe.[16]

The landed aristocracy is non-ideological and their politics, irrespective of their ethno-regional background, is simply self-preservation. The best example of this is their total opposition to land reforms and agricultural tax. Similarly, they are averse to decentralisation, redefinition of smaller constituencies, politicisation of the masses or any such radical transfor-mation in the social sector. Even the economic diversification of resources, job opportunities on a wider scale or simply the development of an urban-based economy are anathema to Pakistan's land-based aristocrats. Their emphasis has been on acquiring grants, soft loans and foreign assistance through official channels to build up dairy or fruit farms. Such open biases for an agro-based economy are obvious to any observer of Pakistani socio-political structures.

The feudalists contest elections in order to retain their influence and, in a complete ideological void, such campaigns are simply extravaganzas to impress others.[17] Huge expenditures are exacted by seeking patronage from the provincial and national regimes. To all such families, electioneer-ing is merely a business to invest money and then to reap the highest benefits from the provincial and metropolitan bidders. There was an attempt to restore *controlled* democracy in the country from 1985 onwards but, in an ideological vacuum filled with corruption, regime after regime showered its supporters with loans (eventually written off), rural and urban property and tax evasions. Some assembly members engaged in drug trafficking were allowed to carry on their practices so that the regimes did not lose their 'supporters'. As was seen in Chapter 3, it was not until mid-1993 that the government of Moeen Qureshi published lists of loan defaulters, drug barons and tax-evaders.[18]

Given the huge expenses involved in electoral campaigns and the vast outstretched constituencies, it would not be wrong to suggest that the current electoral system helps to perpetuate the feudal monopoly over politics in the country. Ideology-based parties would not venture into *mofussil* areas since they would not have resources and cadres to run the campaigns. In the event that they did attempt such a move, their camp followers would be chased out by local influentials or the ballot boxes would be hijacked. Thus, there is no opportunity for a new, representative and reforming leadership to emerge at regional and national levels. Consequently, the masses and the middle class in the country have become increasingly apathetic about the entire process.[19] The tribal chieftains, largely from tribal agencies in the NWFP and Balochistan, follow similar patterns to their rural counterparts, though in a more conventional form, touching on crudity in some cases. Their attitudes towards women, the menial classes or rival tribesmen are very archaic. In terms of politics, they are extremely conservative, lacking any ideological commitment except for self-interest. They are always on the 'right' of the state if not in the centre and would not allow any transformation of the outdated electoral franchise. Special favours, land grants, import licences and weapons are the main enticements used by the state to attract their loyalty.[20] On occasions, chieftains on both sides of the Durand Line would shift their loyalties between Kabul and Islamabad to suit their own interests.

Basic tribalism permeates Pakistani feudal traditions in terms of vengeance (*badla*) and resolution of conflicts through intrigues and sheer force.[21] According to folk wisdom most of the feuds and law suits in rural Pakistan are over *zan, zar* and *zameen* (woman, wealth and land). If the other party is strong, then efforts are made to gain official connivance or support from paid ruffians. If the other party is weak, then ruthlessness will know no bounds – involving parades of woman in the nude, gang-rapes, kidnaps, arson, robberies and assassinations. The spirit of vengeance at its worst brings out the most abominable in a typical Pakistani feudalist.[22]

Our analysis of Pakistan's predominant feudal traditions would not be complete if we simply considered them from a regional perspective. In order to be part of any government, ambitious feudalists readily adopt surrogate roles. The assumption of extra-territorial loyalties is motivated by the need to remain in power as *mai* (mother) and *bap* (father) for their local clans and areas; staying as part of the regime is voluntarily institutionalised in Pakistani polity. Admission to select academic institutions, seats on the district council or membership of any assembly or public office is guaranteed to those from the noted landed dynasties. If they do not receive what they consider to be a birthright a dramatic shift occurs in personal party loyalties.

An example of this behaviour is found in a former governor/chief minister of the Punjab, who, coming from a *zamindar* family, was one of the founders of the Pakistan People's Party with Zulfikar Ali Bhutto in 1967. His early career was as a quiet back-bencher like many of his parliamentary colleagues who only knew how to serve the party or personality in power at the time. Bhutto's flamboyant style of politicking transformed the young Ghulam Mustafa Khar from a rustic playboy to an urban mixer.

His forays into Lahore politics and various scandals eventually cost him his mentor's favour. After a brief alliance with the opposition, he rejoined the PPP which soon lost power to Zia's martial law in 1977. Khar, apparently working as a go-between for the deposed Bhutto and the generals, was guaranteed a safe exit from Pakistan by the military rulers. While in exile in London, the former chief executive of the Punjab entered into secret negotiations with Indian diplomats; he collaborated with the RAW (leading Indian intelligence organisation called Research Analysis Wing), visited India a few times and, with military and economic support from New Delhi, conspired towards an armed revolt in Pakistan. The former 'lion of the Punjab' plotted for an Indian military attack on Pakistan in the style of the liberation of Bangladesh so that he could regain power.[23] A few years later, after the dismissal of Benazir Bhutto in August 1990, he was installed as a minister in Islamabad in the interim government of Ghulam Mustafa Jatoi, a former PPP stalwart but now heading his own Pakistan National People's Party. The state against which he had conspired only a few years earlier recently welcomed him as the head of a ministry. In 1993, he re-emerged as a PPP stalwart in the Punjab offering his services to Benazir Bhutto against the urban industrialist, Mian Nawaz Sharif, whose major supporters in the province came from the landed aristocracy.[24]

It is intriguing that a feudal-based power politics, personal loyalties often supersede family ties. For instance, while Ghulam Mustafa Khar lived in exile, his own brothers worked in close cooperation with Zia's regime at home. One of his brothers subsequently contested an election against him. In Pakistan, it is usual to see personal loyalties overtaking pseudo-ideological loyalties. Former Unionists in the British Punjab joined the Muslim League on the eve of independence as did their counterparts in Sindh and other places. Mian Iftikhar ud-Din, a Lahore-based feudalist and the former president of the Punjab National Congress, patronised the communists in Pakistan, though he never volunteered to live the life of a commoner. This was also true of Z. A. Bhutto who emerged as the leading spokesman for the downtrodden in Pakistan but surrounded himself with feudalists and the bureaucratic elite. The former Muslim Unionists were among the 'pioneers' who shifted their loyalties to Pakistan in the late-1940s once it had become a consensus among Muslim masses across the sub-continent. In many areas like Bengal, the freedom movement coincided with the lessening of feudal influence in politics, but in the areas of British India that subsequently constituted West Pakistan, the feudalists were consolidated under continued official patronage. However, the colonial state kept discretionary prerogatives to itself without leaving the grounds totally open for the landed elites whom it considered to be its beneficiaries. In the young country, the lack of counterbalancing forces at the state level yielded a vacuum which enabled these elites to establish themselves as the pillar of the state structure. Indeed, the Pakistani state structure has become a permanent hostage to the landed dynasties, on occasions the state even appears to have assumed the former clientele role of the landed elites.

POLITICS OF THE LANDED ARISTOCRACY

Without a cohesive political culture adhered to by a *national* middle class, the feudal families have been able to monopolise politics at both the grassroots and national levels. The feudalists in Pakistan, especially in the early years, competed against each other ruthlessly without any recourse to ethics. Between 1947 and 1955, the Noons and Daultanas caused numerous ministerial changes both in the Punjab and at the national level. The Mamdot ministry gave way to the Daultana faction which, through intrigues, eventually was taken over by the Noon faction. In Sindh, Ayub Khuro's cabinet (1947–48) was followed by six ministries formed respectively by Pir Ilahi Bakhsh (1948–49), Yusuf Haroon (1949–50), Qazi Fazlullah (1950–51), Ayub Khuro (1951), Abdus Sattar Pirzada (1953–54) and, once again, Khuro (1954–55).[25] 'Deposed leaders formed opposition parties and in their struggle for power challenged members of their previous parties. Some even made reforms that would adversely affect their landed interests, such as those introduced by the Daultana ministry in 1952 and annulled by the Noon ministry in 1953.'[26]

The landlords aligned themselves with the successive military rulers, though in 1958 Iskander Mirza and then Ayub Khan temporarily sought military and business elites for support. Despite its early shock from the land reforms of 1959 under Ayub Khan's martial law, the landed aristocracy staged a come-back by joining his Convention Muslim League. Through his Basic Democracy system, Ayub recreated a dependency relationship with the landlords. His greatest instrument of power in West Pakistan was Amir Mohammad Khan, the Nawab of Kalabagh and an archetypal feudalist who, as a governor, ran the province ruthlessly. The Nawab was Ayub's strongest link with the landed aristocrats while the Pir of Daiwal provided another strong bond with the *sajjada nishin* families. Z. A. Bhutto, formerly a cabinet minister and subsequently critic of Ayub Khan, had earlier defended the system: 'It was unjustifiable on the part of the politicians to shift their guilt to the bureaucrats, the feudal landlords and the bourgeoisie.'[27] Bhutto's own PPP was completely dominated at the decision-making level by the feudalists although he did introduce the myth of *awam* (ordinary people) into the political vocabulary. Liberal colleagues and urban ideologues in the PPP were not satisfied with the land reforms of 1974 and many of them either deserted the ranks or were simply chased out of the PPP. In the 1977 elections, the PPP high command overwhelmingly selected land-holding candidates, a tradition largely upheld in later elections as well. Even General Zia's hand-picked Majlis i-Shoora exhibited the same discretionary patterns although he tried to include a sizeable number of professionals and urban-based pro-government individuals along with 'the traditional families of note'. The partyless elections for the National Assembly in 1985, despite a surprisingly high ratio of 'young blood' belonging to the forties age-group, and with a higher rate of education, retained a sizeable majority from the land-holding class. Out of an elected total of 200, 117 belonged to the landed aristocracy[28] and a similar ratio was observed in the subsequent party-based elections of 1988, 1990 and 1993.

Elections in Pakistan are contested for prestige as well as for reaping the attendant benefits that feudalist politicians have come to assume as their birthright. Such blackmail has more often resulted in Pakistan affording the largest cabinets during the prime ministership of Benazir Bhutto and Nawaz Sharif. In a very non-ideological, interest-oriented and personality-centred political system, the regimes spend most of their time, energies and resources on 'buying' or warranting such shifting loyalties. Endemic corruption haunts the corridors of power, where loyalties are routinely traded in. Sidelining of the masses even in an otherwise representative system has generated widespread dismay and an all-encompassing nationalism has been eroded. Personal and parochial loyalties seem to have overtaken *national* prerogatives by eroding the supremacy of law and permeating the governability crisis. In Pakistan, like other countries in the region, folk wisdom attributes implementation of the law according to the status and nuisance value of the parties involved. Many thinking citizens have seen a brazen hijacking of their rights by the powerful forces above. Thus, feudalist manipulation of the vital electoral institutions and domination of local and national affairs to suit their own interests have damaged the civic institutions. Such a loss of trust in the civil institutions has not augured well for Pakistan's nascent political institutions. Authoritarian forces have been able to claim that democracy is not suitable for Pakistan and the masses would be better off under a benevolent authoritarian regime.

COERCIVE LOCALISM

In the early days of Islam, the state's efforts 'to strike a balance between the rights of the more powerful citizens and the rights of the weaker individuals was presumably designed to strengthen the sense of communitarian spirit among the believers'.[29] Jinnah certainly talked of democracy patterned on Westminster's parliamentary traditions and inspired by the above-mentioned Islamic principles of welfare and social justice. Iqbal, while reinterpreting Islam, observed that democracy and social welfare meant the same: 'For Islam the acceptance of social democracy in some suitable form and content with the legal principles of Islam is not a revolution but a return to the original purity of Islam.'[30] While the landed elites might have had their own reasons for supporting the movement for Pakistan, the masses usually saw their redemption in a more egalitarian future. But Pakistan's post-independence rulers were not prepared to change the politico-economic structures and the exploitation of the toiling masses in rural and tribal areas continued exactly as Sir Malcolm Darling had described in the Muslim Punjab two decades earlier:

> The peasantry, almost to a man, confesses themselves the servants of one true God and of Muhammad his Prophet, but in actual fact they are the servants of landlord, moneylender and pir. All the way down the Indus from Hazara in the north to Sind in the south, these dominate men's fortunes; and though they are around in greater or lesser degree all over the province, nowhere are they so powerful.[31]

Mukhtar Masud, a Muslim ICS, while writing his note of dissent on the *Report of the Government Hari Enquiry Committee* on the plight of the Sindhis in 1947, had succinctly observed:

> Fear reigns supreme in the life of the hari – fear of imprisonment, fear of losing his land, wife or life. The Zamindar might, at any time, get annoyed with him and oust him – he might have to leave his crops half ripe, his cattle might also be snatched and he might be beaten out of the village.[32]

The monopoly of the landlords over local services has put the peasants in permanent bondage. This bondage is solidified through superstition if the *zamindar* simultaneously happens to be a syed, *pir* or *sajjada nishin*. Fatalism fosters such a dependency-based relationship especially among the rural and tribal Pakistanis who, like the Hurs of Sindh, would go to any length to win the pleasure of their *pirs*. The *zamindari* system in Pakistan revolves around the central role of the landlord and whenever a peasant/*hari* or a share-cropper is in trouble, he assists him. When the peasant has problems concerning, for example,

> his lack of finance, his social relations with his fellowmen, his implication in police cases, the ill-health of members of his family, the abduction of his women, the loss of his bullock, the procurement of his home necessities in consumer goods, the recruitment of casual labour to aid him in harvesting and weeding his crops or for other reasons, it is to his zamindar that he first appeals for help.[33]

The entire socio-economic system revolves around the possession of land and agriculture; it is not merely a means of livelihood in Pakistan but an enduring way of life:

> It is natural, therefore, that there should be a universal urge for the possession of agricultural land ... The status of a man on land and his right to the use of land also defines his social status in society. ... Those who do not own land are relegated to a socially inferior position with all the disabilities of that position.[34]

While rural Pakistanis largely remain dependent upon the landowners, they have the right to vote; their tribal counterparts, however, have remained disenfranchised since British rule, and the electoral college remains strictly limited.

LAND REFORMS

Land reforms intended to change the balance of land ownership in Pakistan to create a more equitable and efficient system guaranteeing amelioration of the peasants' sordid state of affairs, providing finances to the government through agricultural tax, is still an unrealised dream. Such reforms would not only redress politico-economic injustices at both local and national levels, they would also provide tangible incentives for intensive productive farming. This may go a long way towards eradicating poverty and strengthening civic institutions in the country. The entire political structure would become more participatory, viable and responsive to the needs of the masses rather than pampering a few thousand people at the top.

In 1959 and 1972 there were two half-hearted efforts to bring about some change. Ayub Khan, in an effort to project his image of a Pakistani Nasser and a great reformer, introduced land reforms which put a maximum ceiling of 500 acres of irrigated and 1000 acres of non-irrigated land for holding. The owners were allowed to maintain an extra 150 acres for orchards or livestock and were allowed to 'gift' their land to relatives. At that time, 6000 land-owners representing 0.10 per cent of the total agricultural population in the country possessed 7.5 million acres of land estates over 500 acres, making altogether 15 per cent of the private land in the country. On the other hand, more than 2.2 million persons owned less than five acres and another 2.5 million landless farmers were either *haris*, share-croppers or simply tenants. The farmers with small land-holdings also equally suffered from land fragmentation for which the *ishtmaal-i-arazi* (land consolidation scheme) was adopted in the reforms of 1959.

As can be seen in Table 4.1, 6000 *zamindars* and *waderas* owned 1236 acres on average, compared to the national average of 9.5 acres. Acquisition of the 'extra' land was almost impossible due to bureaucratic bottlenecks, transfer of land to other members of the family and, in particular, the timid nature of the reforms. Only 5 per cent of land was surrendered to the government.[35] Many observers felt that Punjabi domination of the military and the landed interests of the officers prevented the martial-law regime from adopting any radical measures.[36] The Ayub regime could not afford to alienate the landed gentry and the reforms were simply a cosmetic treatment of an age-old malady. Mir Ghulam Ali Talpur, a leading landlord of Sindh felt that the reforms were very generous to the landed aristocrats 'because of the big heart of the President'. Arbab Noor Mohammad Khan, a leading land-owner from the NWFP, exaggerated the reforms and claimed: 'Had these reforms been delayed longer a violent revolution might have taken place destroying the present goodwill between tenants and landlords.'[37] The landlords benefited from the mecha-

Table 4.1 Land Ownership in West Pakistan, 1959

Average landholding (in acres)	Percentage of landlords	Percentage of land owned
5 or less	64.5	15.0
5 to 25	28.5	31.7
25 to 100	5.7	22.4
100 to 500	1.0	15.9
500 and more	0.1	15.9

Source: Government of Pakistan, *Report of the Land Reforms Commission*, (1959), Appendix 1.

nisation of agriculture under the green revolution as the peasants felt uprooted and looked for employment in urban centres. 'This left considerable resentment among the peasantry and the rural middle sectors, who later gave their support to Bhutto.'[38]

The PPP, in its election manifesto in 1970, declared land reforms to be 'a national necessity' and raised the well-known slogan of *roti, kapra aur makkan* (bread, clothes and shelter). According to Bhutto's land reforms of 1972, the maximum ceiling for a land-holding in the case of irrigated land was brought down to 150 acres and 300 acres in the case of non-irrigated land. State lands were to be distributed among the landless peasants. Civil servants would not be allowed to possess more than 100 acres and land acquisition by military officials near the defence belt of the border areas was cancelled. All previous records and land transfers were to be scrutinised so as to plug the loopholes in the early reforms. A system of cooperative farming through self-sufficient agrarian villages was planned for the long term. As usual the bureaucracy gave out exaggerated figures on land transfers to the peasants and raised their expectations. In 1976, a Peasants' Week was organised which promised that the government would distribute 25 million acres among 2 500 000 families. It is not known how far the land reforms were implemented, given the usual corruption and the ascendancy of the feudals in the system. According to one estimate only 1 per cent of cultivable land was distributed among 130 000 tenants.[39] However, many landlords had preempted the reforms by transferring land to their immediate relatives without risk of loss.

During General Zia ul-Haq's time the land-tenure system continued unchallenged and unchanged. The stagnation of the agricultural sector led to migration to urban areas and the Gulf. Despite conducive weather and good harvests and the influx of foreign remittances, Pakistan's economy remained stable but the problem of poverty continued. In its search for legitimacy, the military regime spared the landed aristocracy from reforms or agricultural tax. The landed elites derived all sorts of ministerial, fiscal and managerial benefits for supporting the system. Their heavy representation on the Majlis i-Shoora, local bodies, provincial assemblies, the national assembly and the senate have guaranteed their perpetuation in the state structure. Even the Sharia Court, in a verdict on an appeal against the land reforms, decreed the irrevocability of the Islamic guarantee of private property and questioned the legality of the land reforms. What more could the landed aristocrats desire? To sum up, both the state and the propertied elites have already established a dependency relationship which is both exclusive and partisan. It operates as the vehicle for the continued disenfranchisement of the masses and intermediate class, who, in desperation, turn parochial or sectarian. The multiple nature of this elitist oligarchy hampers the growth of a responsible, egalitarian and dynamic civil society which may eventually result in the devolution of powers.

5 Unilateralism of the State: 'Invisible Government' at Work

The symbiotic relationship between state and civil society in Pakistan is obvious in vital areas such as the civil liberties of women, religious minorities, political activists, dissenters, the judiciary, independent intellectuals and journalists. Whereas the narrowly based regimes of so-called strong men coopted intermediaries from the regional feudal families or willing religious elements from the *ulama* and *pirs*, vast sections of civil society remained marginalised. Under General Zia ul-Haq, in particular, Pakistan suffered the most suffocating years of its existence and, in the wake of depoliticisation, regimented ideas like *chaadar* and *chardiwari* denoted women's place in the home, democracy was portrayed as anathema to Islam and the media was made use of to silence the opposition. A demagogic emphasis on religion promoted obscurantism and unleashed sectarian violence which jeopardised the polity. Mainstream politics held at bay serious dilemmas like ethnic violence, sectarian feuds, drug addiction and polarisation on university campuses; social banditry became the order of the day.

Important security agencies that were intended to protect the country from sabotage were engaged in subverting national institutions. These agencies were largely geared towards protecting the limited interests of the military regime, or simply pursuing their ideas. While Zia ridiculed the nation's Constitution as simply a piece of paper and declared that elections and democracy were un-Islamic, members of his junta headed federal ministries, assumed unchallengeable gubernatorial positions and, in numerous cases, obtained executive jobs in autonomous corporations. Both the civilian and khaki bureaucracy enjoyed undisputed powers and kick-backs such as commissions in deals with foreign companies or benefits like expensive urban property, and ambassadorial positions exposed the unrepresentative and vulnerable nature of the Pakistani regime. During this period many military officials, who were not otherwise professionally qualified, routinely headed summary military courts dishing out fast, partisan and repressive judgements. Politics became taboo; women activists were charged with libertine ideas; several teachers were charged with 'poisoning' the youth with sedition; mediamen were lashed in public; the judiciary was dictated to and coerced; and Pakistan was said to be on 'the right track'.

Following the military coup of 1977, the national Constitution was 'held in abeyance' since its outright abrogation was treachery to the nation and under 'the law of necessity' martial law was justified by the tame judges of the superior courts.[1] The martial law regulations which followed each other superseded civil procedures to complete the process of dehumanisation and decimation of civil liberties. While the regime did have its own apologists who considered Zia a latter-day reformer (in league with his claims as the representative of one thousand million Muslims of the world), the dissenting voices continued – though apparently overshadowed by the forces of conformity and sycophancy.[2] A separate study is needed of the martial-law regime in Pakistan which, as the 'secret hand' or 'invisible government', and in contravention of the national Constitution and individual rights, tampered with civil liberties to a damaging extent. Harassment and blatant torture were undertaken routinely by the police and public servants through agencies like the provincial Criminal Investigation Agency (CIA), the Criminal Investigation Department (CID) and the Intelligence Bureau (IB). Ironically, defence-related security agencies such as the Inter-Services Intelligence (ISI) and Military Intelligence (MI) went beyond their professional domains to conduct surveillance on civilians and political opponents of the military regime as well as masterminding alliances of coopted politicians.[3] In some cases, they helped to create ethnically based movements by hammering out deals. It is only by recognising the extra-professional activities of such agencies that the extent of the irreparable damage done to civil society in the country will be known.[4]

SECURITY AGENCIES AGAINST CITIZENS

True to the tradition of previous rulers of Pakistan, General Zia used the intelligence agencies to curb political dissent and create fear among his critics. The MI, the ISI and the largely civilian security outfits like the IB were used to spy on people and to mastermind alliances and counter-alliances. Earlier, Zulfikar Ali Bhutto, concerned that security was essentially a military domain and wanting to keep a safe distance in civil matters, founded the Federal Security Force (FSF), a force parallel to the regular police which operated as Bhutto's private army to coerce his opponents and former allies into submission. The FSF was reputedly involved in gross human-rights violations including the murder of the father of one of Bhutto's opponents. It was disbanded by Zia who used some of the files and former officials of FSF as prosecution witnesses to establish cases of serious crimes against Bhutto and his colleagues.

With a freer and more responsible press, such conflicting interests and their effects on the nation at large are revealed. In Islamabad, the IB, as 'Pakistan's premier civilian intelligence is believed to be modestly staffed, its role has long exceeded its prescribed function of counter-espionage and monitoring the activities of the hostile foreign powers and their diplomatic missions in Pakistan.' It 'has been involved not just in keeping tabs on opposition politicians and tapping telephones, but recruiting informers from among journalists, and above all, manipulating politics. Its activities have included blackmail, harassment, disinformation campaigns against opponents as well as keeping watch over other intelligence agencies.' During 1991–92, it was headed by Brigadier (retd) Imtiaz Ahmed, formerly a 'director of the ISI's internal security wing' who 'earned the nickname "green-eyed jackal" when as a protégé of the late ISI chief, General Akhtar Abdul Rahman, he played a key role in suppressing political resistance to martial law'.[5] Brigadier Imtiaz was rehabilitated with the installation of Nawaz Sharif as premier in 1990 and resigned after the dissolution of the regime by Ishaque Khan in April 1993.

The ISI, known for its collaboration with the US CIA and other Western intelligence agencies during the Afghan war,[6] has its headquarters in the national capital. Its cooperation with the CIA during the Soviet venture into Afghanistan provided the Americans with a chance to bleed them in their 'Vietnam'. Zia was personally responsible for allowing the CIA to operate in Pakistan to train and arm the Afghan resistance:

> Most crucial was President Zia's willingness to allow the CIA to funnel growing amounts of paramilitary support to the Afghanistan rebels through Pakistan. [William] Casey, the CIA and Reagan Administration all wanted Zia to stay in power and needed to know what was going on in his government. The CIA station in Islamabad was one of the biggest in the world.[7]

The premier Pakistani intelligence agency is reputed to have collaborated in the 1980s with Israeli secret agents in redirecting to Tehran crucial weapons originally earmarked for the Afghan Mujahideen.[8] The ISI, though mainly a military organisation and originally established to deal with national security from foreign threats, has been used,

> both by elected leaders but more so by military dictators. This had made them so politically effective that they have been used by powerful

figures in the Establishment to even destabilise an elected government. This has been highlighted by recent disclosures about army officers associated with the ISI trying to subvert the loyalties of PPP MNAs during the no-confidence motion moved in 1989 against the then Prime Minister Benazir Bhutto. The Midnight Jackals affair in fact strengthens the growing impression that an intelligence agency can itself become a key player in the political power game.[9]

Z. A. Bhutto had added an internal wing to the ISI when it was headed by General Ghulam Jilani Khan, who tipped off Zia about his possible retirement by Bhutto, hastening the army chief of staff to make a preemptive strike. General Jilani enjoyed wide contacts among the opposition leaders, and this subsequently helped him in his gubernatorial position in Lahore. By the time of his departure to the Punjab, he had initiated the ISI on the campaign to stabilise the unpopular martial-law regime which was intent on crushing the PPP. General Jilani, when governor of the Punjab, was also instrumental in launching the political career of Mian Nawaz Sharif and a number of other young politicians as a counterweight to the PPP. The ISI overshadowed a largely civilian IB. The Afghanistan crisis consolidated its position as a powerful state organ dealing with both domestic and external policies. Under General Akhtar Abdul Rahman, a close confidante and relative of Zia, the much-feared ISI conducted the Afghan war, which turned out to be the most covert operation in its history.[10] The ISI, as recorded by Mohammad Yusuf – the liaison between the CIA and the ISI on Afghanistan and chronicler of the joint venture – kept a 'careful watch on the generals to ensure their reliability to the regime'. Not only civilians but even generals were frightened of the influence of the ISI.[11] A few years later, however, the honeymoon ended when the United States planned to brand Pakistan a terrorist state.[12]

Much to his annoyance, Zia's hand-picked prime minister from a party-less house, M. K. Junejo, wanted to contain the ISI's unchallenged influence so as to negotiate a political settlement of the Afghanistan crisis through ongoing UN-led indirect talks at Geneva.[13] Zia would never allow a politician of his own choice to assume an autonomous position on national and regional matters, while Junejo himself desired empowerment so as to exhibit the independence of his government. During the Zia–Junejo diarchy (1985–88), Zia used the ISI to spy on Junejo while the latter used the IB to report on Zia. Junejo insisted on replacing Rahman with his own appointee, but Zia was able to manoeuvre General Hamid Gul's appointment as the new head of the ISI and Rahman was elevated to the chairmanship of the joint committee of chiefs of staff. General Gul harboured his own ideals and illusions which he tried to accomplish with a religious zeal. Apart from General Zia, he was one of the select few who dealt with vital issues of national security ranging from domestic opposition to the Afghan war. Despite the death of Zia and a number of senior army officials in the air crash in August 1988, the army maintained its veto power and the ISI as its constituent wing continued to enjoy wider powers in the national political spectrum. Undoubtedly, 'Hamid Gul crucially influenced the role that the army defined for itself in the post-1988 period. This itself showed the power that the head of the agency wielded in this crucial transitional period which shaped the future power structure in the country.'

Since the army leadership could not block the elections of 1988, it tried its best to deny the PPP a landslide victory as Gul accepted the responsibility of creating 'a countervailing force to the PPP otherwise democracy could not have been restored'[14]. The then army chief, General Aslam Beg, gave the ISI the task of creating a parallel political force in the body of the Islamic Democratic Alliance, commonly known as IJT, so as to deny the PPP a landslide electoral victory. General Gul, the head of the ISI, is himself on record as acknowledging that 'the ISI created the IDA to promote democracy after the August 1988 death of President Zia ul-Haq in an air crash ... Without the IDA, Gul claimed that Pakistan could not have returned to electoral politics.'[15] It was the first time in the history of Pakistan that an intelligence agency had been asked to craft and sponsor a political alliance.[16] Presumably no civilian was involved in the formation of the IJI as it was solely accomplished by the ISI. Simultaneously, General Beg through Wasim Sajjad, chairman of the Senate, advised the Supreme Court against the restoration of the unlawfully dissolved Junejo government and assemblies.[17] Furthermore, to undermine Benazir Bhutto's appeal in the Punjab, Brigadier Imtiaz Ahmed, the then additional director-general of national security in the ISI, introduced slogans fomenting *Punjabiat*.[18] Benazir Bhutto was portrayed as a Sindhi leader enjoying dubious links with the Al-Zulfikar Organisation (AZO) working against *Punjabi* interests.[19] Even a controversy on the nuclear issue was fed to the press claiming that the PPP leaders were playing to foreign audiences and would compromise on Pakistan's vital security interests.[20]

When the PPP was allowed to form the government in November 1988, the scepticism of the army leadership towards the new administration was obvious. Thanks to the Eighth Amendment in the Constitution engineered by Zia, the office of the president had already been vested with discretionary powers *vis-à-vis* the tenure of the prime minister and the existence of the elected assemblies. Benazir Bhutto, despite a popular electoral mandate, was the weakest element of the 'troika' precariously lodged between discretionary presidential powers and a powerful army establishment unwilling to revert to a strictly professional role. Her efforts to assert her office eventually led to her dismissal by the two other stronger and vetoing counterparts in the tripolar set-up.[21]

Even after the formation of her first short-lived government, Bhutto was not allowed to function normally, for the high cadres in the civil and military establishment did not trust her. Given their close collaboration under martial law, these officials and their 'intermediaries' feared that their crimes and scandals would be exposed. Zia had created an exaggerated scare among the leading generals and bureaucrats of a PPP-led backlash to avenge Z. A. Bhutto's execution. A well-orchestrated media campaign concentrating on character assassinations of the Bhuttos and other PPP activists as well as a number of white papers on the previous administration, led officials in the Zia regime to look towards the military dictator for protection. Zia knew that these officials would have to remain loyal to him and his policies out of sheer personal insecurity, and he relished this. In addition, he created a wider constituency among the Punjabi–Pushtun lower middle classes and small business groups as well as coopting the religious elite. All these elements (including some of the politicians involved in the anti-Bhutto campaign of 1977) felt safe under a centralist anti-PPP facade. In addition, as subsequent chapters will show, the patronage of ethno-regionalist demagogues in Sindh was aimed at containing the PPP.[22] Thus, Benazir Bhutto had a formidable task in dealing with such a wide range of hostile forces. Her youthfulness, her demeanour as a resolute, assertive woman and her very inexperience as an idealist politician, unnerved her opponents who took advantage of the conservative values in society to begin a smear campaign against her. By evoking doubtful religious orthodoxy, ample propaganda was applied to discredit her as a *woman* politician lacking the essential religious credentials and legality to lead a Muslim society. As far as the masses in Pakistan were concerned such a contention was unlikely to be effective.

Soon after her installation as prime minister, Benazir Bhutto had to confront a powerful opposition from the IJT-led government in the Punjab and the over-enthusiastic PPP activists who had naively believed that the PPP was 'in power'. In fact the PPP regime, suffering from constitutional blocks, did not have any control over the country's vital policies dealing with the nuclear programme and Afghanistan. The ISI's sole monopoly over the Afghan operation since the time of Zia had remained largely unchallenged though Junejo, to some extent, had tried to influence it indirectly. Some of the ISI officials planned to topple the PPP regime by winning over the members of the MQM and some PPP MNAs in the national assembly. As early as spring 1989, Bhutto discovered that General Gul and other senior officials of the ISI had secretly met the 13 Sindhi PPP MNAs in an effort to persuade them to vote against their prime minister during the budget session. She determined to replace General Gul and the opportunity came with the ISI's fiasco over Jalalabad. In the wake of the Soviet withdrawal from Afghanistan in February 1989, the ISI, after establishing a hand-picked Afghan Interim Government (AIG) in Islamabad, had mounted a military operation to capture Jalalabad from the Kabul regime. The abortive offensive turned out to be the most expensive venture in the 11 years of Afghan resistance, and thousands of Mujahideen and many innocent civilians were killed, with the city staying faithful to President Najibullah. The ISI was subjected to a barrage of domestic and international criticism.[23] Benazir Bhutto, encountering such a God-sent opportunity, tried to wrest its leadership from General Gul by replacing him with her nominee, General (retd) Shamsur Rahman Kallue, who proved to be a total disaster.[24] He was largely ineffective as the ISI officials refused to cooperate with him. The appointment of a retired general dismayed his serving counterparts who felt that the Bhutto regime did not trust them at all. This feeling was erroneously interpreted by strong elements in the army command as Bhutto's disenchantment with it as an institution. Simultaneously, she established a high-profile commission to investigate the unspecified and often contradictory operations of the intelligence organisations which occasionally ran contrary to their own original charters. The commission was headed by Air Marshal (retd) Zulfikar Ali Khan and sought to systemise the operations of security agencies. Before its report could see daylight, however, Bhutto's government had been dissolved, and the appointment of the Zulfikar commission only added to the list of her enemies.[25]

With the ISI becoming the subject of national and global media attention, a number of its political assignments were transferred to the MI by the GHQ. Like the ISI, the MI overstepped its charter by involving itself in domestic political activities. Its enhanced role under its head, General Assad Durrani, 'a trusted associate of Beg' included political surveillance, contacts with politicians and developing a 'strategy to deal with a government with which the Army became increasingly estranged'. Aware of such hostile moves, Bhutto activated the IB led by a 'figurehead', Noor Leghari, assisted by Masud Sharif, a retired major and the *de facto* schemer. 'It was a sting operation masterminded by Masud Sharif code-named Midnight Jackals that culminated in GHO's dismissal of Brig. Imtiaz and Major Aamer from the Army in October 1989.' On 1

November 1989, Benazir Bhutto survived a no-confidence move in the national assembly in which the MQM had voted against the prime minister.[26] It was the second time, as confirmed in 1992 by Nisar Ali, an IJT minister, that the army had 'delivered' the MQM to the IJT's fold.[27] Despite the failure of the no-confidence move against Bhutto, Generals Beg and Gul persisted with their efforts to oust her. Bhutto had also antagonised the powerful president by insisting on her powers as prime minister to retire and appoint the chief of joint staff committee and the chief justice of Pakistan. Her own ambitious and, in some cases, unscrupulous associates made her position more vulnerable.

Her lack of attempts at bringing in legislation and her ambiguity on a number of policy matters, partly due to the obstacles arising from the tripolar nature of the Pakistani government, provided fuel for disinformation campaigns. Stories of corruption received exaggerated coverage and Bhutto, despite a whirlwind diplomatic initiative on Kashmir, seemed to be bogged down in unending intricacies further compounded by polarisation in Sindh. The Punjab was already under a defiant chief minister while Sindh experienced social banditry and ethnic criminalisation. Such a hostile atmosphere gave ample opportunity to the intelligence agencies and opposition to build up stronger anti-PPP coalitions. The Pakistan Army's own insistence on wider powers to curb disorder in Sindh accentuated Bhutto's estrangement with her powerful counterparts. Finally, in early August 1990, under pressure from General Beg, the president dismissed the prime minister and all the assemblies and 'the MI was assigned the responsibility of on-ground implementation of that order'. Without any apparent need[28] for preemptive measures, 'the MI supervised the whole operation in which troops took control of TV, Radio and other key installations and sealed the offices of the IB as well as the Prime Minister'.[29]

As was confirmed later, the army chief, General Beg, desired a presidential order to dismiss the PPP government though, at the time of his retirement he claimed to have defended the democratic set-up in the country.[30] Benazir Bhutto, apparently to assuage hostility from the generals, had even called Beg the defender of democracy, though it was apparent to everyone that the army's influence in national politics remained undiminished. Exposures by some former generals, substantiated by a number of influential politicians, tarnished General Beg's image as the champion of democracy.[31] General (retd) Alam Jan Mahsud, a general of unimpeachable professional integrity, in a number of interviews to the press, 'accused Beg of constantly interfering with the governments of Bhutto and Sharif. Mahsud claims to have irrefutable proof of Beg's attempts to destabilise the Bhutto government. He implied in the interview that Beg was prevented by other senior commanders from declaring military rule before Bhutto was dismissed by President Ghulam Ishaq Khan'.[32] Within a week of Benazir Bhutto's dismissal General Beg appointed General Assad Durrani as the head of the ISI.

The unilateral powers and uncontrolled activities of the security agencies continued even under Nawaz Sharif who, despite constant unease, had been a beneficiary of their operations – especially against the PPP. His relationship with Beg was not at its best when he removed General Assad Durrani from the ISI. Sharif, like Bhutto, began to depend on the IB and appointed Brigadier Imtiaz Ahmed as its director. During the Gulf crises, Sharif and Beg exhibited divergent views, 'triggering open conflict between the ISI and IB'.[33] After Beg's retirement, Sharif, at the behest of the IB director, appointed General Javed Naser as the head of the ISI. The new director, apart from being a non-assertive religious person, was reputed to be a close relative of the IB director. They both sought retirement after the dismissal of the Sharif government.

True to the tradition of mutual antagonism among the ruling parties and opposition, Pakistan's recent history is witness to an element of vendetta webbed around palace intrigues. The coalition opposed to Nawaz Sharif, the Pakistan Democratic Alliance (PDA) including the former interim prime minister, Ghulam Mustafa Jatoi, had alleged wide spread rigging in the elections of 1990. In addition, the PPP (the main component of the PDA), constantly complained of harassment and imprisonment of its workers, especially in Sindh, accusing the IJI government of high-handedness. Asif Zardari, the husband of Benazir Bhutto, remained incarcerated for more than two years on unsubstantiated charges of corruption. Even the former prime minister had to run between various cities to appear in courts to respond to a wide variety of charges, which, if upheld, might have debarred her from holding any public office for a considerable time. Such tactics increased the bi-polarisation, though the PPP claimed to have extended an offer of cooperation in the early months of the Sharif government. The government, on the other hand, felt that the PDA was intent upon bringing it down long before its stipulated tenure.

Massive disenchantment in the Punjab in 1992, due to embezzlement of the finances of cooperatives, added to the PDA's pressure on the IJT and this again hardened the bi-polarity. Under the leadership of Benazir Bhutto, the PDA decided to organise protest marches beginning on 17 November. The government, despite an initial accommodating attitude, reacted harshly by banning the marches and arresting thousand of activists in preemptive measures.[34] Benazir Bhutto's march was considered to be a gamble since, in the worst scenario, the army would have moved in. Some observers felt critical of Bhutto's strategy to acquire power through street agitation: 'By setting out, with yesterday's march, to use mass protest to compel the formation of a "national consensus government" pending fresh election, she has shown in turn that she ranks the pursuit of power higher than the ballot box.'[35] Benazir Bhutto was able to reach the rally but the reaction by the security forces to the protesters, including women, was considered unnecessary and harsh by neutral observers. It was believed that some ministers in the cabinet advised political negotiation but eventually the hardliners in the Sharif regime vetoed moderation. Such a coercive strategy added to Bhutto's moral stature.[36] Retaliatory measures were both crude and inflammatory:

> An estimated 15 000 people were arrested across the country on the pretext that they might be travelling to Islamabad for the march; trains were halted and searched 1000 miles from the capital; and journalists were beaten up in the streets. Even in Pakistan's turbulent history, it was a draconian crackdown: the first time a leader of the opposition had been prohibited from the capital.[37]

The generals were reported at one stage to have planned to take over. However, it was only five months later that the rivalry between President Ghulam Ishaque Khan and Prime Minister Nawaz Sharif enabled Benazir Bhutto to stage a come-back in late 1993. Now the intelligence agencies started shadowing the opposition led by the former prime minister. With an increase in ethnic and sectarian conflict in Karachi in 1994–95 the inability of the intelligence agencies to provide advance information on the terrorist activities and their failure in tracing the perpetrators raised a number of serious questions about their motives and usefulness. Various opinion groups even accused them of fostering crime.

The important question to be asked is why the 'invisible government' was allowed to operate in Pakistan with impunity even when there were assemblies and a comparatively freer press. In order to provide an answer many dimensions must be considered.

The Pakistan Army has enjoyed great status and power in the internal affairs of the country with an ever-increasing involvement in regional and extra-regional affairs. From the early years of Pakistan, the army began to play a cooptive role along with civilian bureaucrats until it finally took control of the country directly in its own hands in 1958. General Ayub Khan and powerful bureaucrats like Ghulam Muhammad and Iskander Mirza derided the politicians and virtually ran the country after the death of Jinnah. The army chief even carried out defence agreements with foreign countries without the prior knowledge of the contemporary prime minister.[38] Iskander Mirza, initially as the defence secretary and then as the president, used armed forces to advance his personal ambition, until the forces themselves took over the steering. The intelligence agencies, like other official mouthpieces, were used more earnestly to defend the military regimes of Generals Ayub Khan and Yahya Khan which lacked electoral bona fides. Operations against dissenting politicians, objective intellectuals and other activists were carried out through systematic harassment, disinformation campaigns, fictitious trials, kidnaps, torture and assassinations. The bureaucracy, the military and the landed aristocracy engaged in depoliticisation of the nation which eventually harmed the democratic processes and resulted in further martial law. The agencies only hastened the divide between the two wings of the country and failed to advise and forewarn the policy makers on the deteriorating political situation in East Pakistan. The separation of East Pakistan was the turning point in the national psyche and people looked to Z. A. Bhutto for a reprieve. Bhutto, true to his temperament and feudal background, utilised state agencies for his personal purposes while Zia's regime, suffering a complete legitimacy crisis, relied on intelligence agencies to operate at both national and regional levels. For most of its history Pakistan has remained directly and indirectly under military rule with the state structure providing support to the military regimes. Given such long-held practice, the agencies have taken it upon themselves 'to guide' the political destiny of the nation.

Weak political traditions and fragile democratic institutions, largely dented by an elitist state structure, have lacked the vitality to prevent the intelligence agencies from playing an extra-constitutional role. In addition, weakened civic institutions like the press, the judiciary, academia and human rights groups have, for a considerable time, lacked the wherewithal to expose and restrain the extra-constitutional role played by such agencies. It was in Pakistan that, as late as 1988, the chief of army staff could dissuade the country's Supreme Court from restoring an elected government unconstitutionally dissolved by a military ruler.

Ambiguity about the roles and prerogatives of such agencies has allowed personal whims and priorities to supersede institutional and national interests. The rising tide of corruption has allowed powerful employees to operate as 'king-makers' and to amass both influence and affluence.

The exclusivist nature of policy-making processes – especially on regional issues like Afghanistan – have precluded these agencies from any public scrutiny and reprimand. Disastrous ventures like the Jalalabad fiasco, the Ojhri arms-dump explosion or many other ill-planned operations in Karachi and elsewhere at the cost of numerous lives and properties have never been called to account and have added to the self-importance of these agencies.[39]

The supply of unlimited and unaudited funds[40] in an atmosphere of total secrecy has allowed these agencies and their decision-makers to continue in ventures which are often an infringement of individual rights and might even clash with national interests. Since the issue of security remains out of bounds for parliament, the press and other public-opinion groups, its constituent bodies have assumed enormous proportions with generous funds at their disposal. Never in the history of Pakistan has any austerity scheme in the realm of defence and security-related expenditure been broached. Similarly, the unlimited funds at the disposal of the ministry of the interior and its organs have left agencies like the FIA, the CIA and the IB amply provided for.[41] Indeed, budgetary allocations for the police department alone, excluding the IB, are almost equal to national allocations for education and health together.[42]

Undoubtedly, the extent and nature of the external threat to Pakistan, given its difficult relationship with a bigger and hegemonic neighbour and its uneasy western borders, combined with the internal political crisis, has necessitated extra vigilance. It is also beyond any doubt that many influential Pakistanis have proved to be vulnerable to foreign temptations and ignored national prerogatives.[43] Patriotic members of the security intelligence agencies would certainly expect such individuals to be investigated and treated according to the law rather than elevated to important positions in the government.

It is important to bear in mind 'the India factor' when studying the general and official mind-set in Pakistan. India has always been reluctant to appreciate and acknowledge the security imperatives of the young Muslim country. Disputes over princely states like Kashmir, Hyderabad and Junagarh and the distribution of assets and water resources have patterned a relationship based on bi-polarity where both the contenders have adopted various offensive and defensive measures. While India has routinely accused Pakistan of interfering in Kashmir and the Punjab, Pakistanis see Indian involvement in Sindh. Pakistanis are cognizant of the fact that it was with India's encouragement and active intervention that their former eastern wing separated from them. In this aura of mutual antagonism characterised by 'hot' and 'cold' wars, both countries employ numerous means to cultivate lobbies. India's official support for Sindhi nationalists and some MQM leaders has been aimed at involving Pakistan in a low-intensity conflict. India holds the Pakistan Army (and especially the ISI) responsible for all the sores in Indo-Pakistan bilateral relations. In

a condescending manner, it is claimed that India is the friend of civil liberties and democracy in Pakistan, but the army puts obstacles in the way of
democratisation and the normalisation of relationships. More recently, the
ISI has become the major focus of Indian propaganda, being held responsible for bomb blasts and armed support across the country.[44] Needless to
say, this widens the gulf between the two countries and provides
justification for vigorous intelligence agencies. By exaggerating the role of
the ISI and the MI, India only helps to create an inflated sense of self-
importance among some of the officials in these organisations. In addition, it serves the needs of the Indian government to use both the Pakistan
Army and the ISI as convenient scapegoats. Pakistanis respond to Indian
allegations in the same manner, with the RAW accused of masterminding
subversion in Pakistan. The net result is that the organisations on both
sides justify their respective roles and thus help the status quo.

The presence of the intelligence agencies at places of higher learning,
research institutes, universities and other semi-autonomous organisations
is generally irritating and obvious to the institutions, who feel that they are
under observation by agencies for no reason and with no justification.
While agencies have their own sleuths among the students, employees and
labour leaders, teachers consider it an infringement upon their rights by a
very obtrusive establishment which doubts everybody else's patriotism. A
tradition since the colonial days has assumed very crude, and in many
cases ridiculous proportions in terms of their visibility and activities on
campuses.[45]

Like any other sovereign country, Pakistan of course has every right to
establish intelligence organisations. It is the abuse of power by some of
their members that attracts criticism. An open debate on the workings and
operations of such agencies is certainly not to underrate their usefulness in
the larger interests of the society. Once their rationale has been established
it is essential to streamline their purposes and processes through a rigorous
system of training. It has been seen that many personnel in sensitive positions in the police, the CIA and Special Branch are neither properly
equipped and trained nor adequately paid to perform their jobs. Stories of
corruption, high-handedness and intimidation are attributed to such forces
by society at large whereas a cognisant reciprocity is needed on all sides.

With the opening of society in the post-Zia years, the average Pakistani
has access to more information and investigative media. People now
expect more human and equitable treatment from the police and other
security agencies, but they also bemoan the role of prominent opinion-
makers who dish out alarmist, scare-mongering stories based on yellow
journalism. Many journalists and academics have suffered retaliation

because of their courageous exposure of corruption and coercion, whereas some of their colleagues have been willing partners and conduits for smear campaigns against their fellow citizens 'planted' from outside.[46] It is only in recent years that the press, assisted by 'whistle blowers', has begun to unearth some of the scandalous ventures of the intelligence and law-enforcement organisations, although even now information about such agencies and their operations remains scanty. By invoking the national interest and security, or by applying brutal force and intimidation, a few mavericks have retained control of the agencies as their exclusive domains. The establishment of a number of bodies to review their operations has turned out to be a useless exercise. More recently, the Zulfikar commission appointed by Benazir Bhutto submitted the most exhaustive report of its kind, suggesting proper laws to govern and regulate the functioning of these agencies. The report was never made public and its recommendations were put in cold storage. It is believed that it recommended a complete reorganisation of the intelligence agencies, making them more efficient and accountable. In addition, a watch-dog committee has been suggested to coordinate and supervise operations and to function as a filter point for the 'raw' intelligence so as to avoid unnecessary wastage of resources and energies.

THE POLITICS OF MALICE AND TORTURE

In addition to tampering with the country's constitutional norms and making and breaking governments at their will, for a long time the intelligence agencies in Pakistan have been used to carry on smear campaigns against critics of officialdom. Where harassment, surveillance and phone-tapping have not been successful, torture has been resorted to. In 1991, the Pakistani and foreign press reported two major sex scandals in which such agencies were said to be involved indirectly. These cases serve to demonstrate the rising graph in official activities to malign Pakistani citizens. In Karachi, a number of unidentified men broke into the house of Veena Hayat, the daughter of Shaukat Hayat, an old associate of the Quaid-i Azam. As confirmed by her and her father, she was molested and gang-raped by the men who, she claimed, were sent by Irfanullah Marwat, the son-in-law of Ghulam Ishaque Khan and adviser on administration to the chief minister of Sindh. In his capacity as adviser, his status was that of a provincial minister for he made vital decisions on a day-to-day basis regarding the provincial police and related agencies like the CIA and the FIA. Although he denied it, the Hayats and their kinsmen insisted on the complicity of Marwat since the victim was a close friend of Benazir Bhutto, the then opposition leader. The entire issue, as will be seen in a subsequent section, raised a number of vital moral and legal issues, but until 1993 it remained mysteriously hushed up – though the elderly father had been 'promised' retribution by a tribal *jirga*.

The other incident involved a religious *alim* and a senator from the NWFP who was alleged to frequent a brothel in Islamabad. Maulana Sami ul-Haq, a close associate of General Zia and a great propounder of theocracy in Pakistan, claimed to have been a victim of a smear campaign in order to soften his criticism of official policies regarding the promised promulgation of Islamic order in the country. The police had apparently raided the brothel in a smart locality on 24 October 1991, and booked the madam. 'Annoyed that none of her powerful clients was prepared to bail her out, Madame Tahira soon spilled the beans, or more literally her telephone index and visiting-card catalogue. Her "confession", full of prurient detail, was secretly recorded and then leaked – presumably with the government's connivance.'[47] Maulana Sami ul-Haq was named as one of many frequent clients, including a few other influential people. He claimed that 'the campaign had been begun by malicious elements and was baseless and concocted'. Even the opposition felt that such campaigns were 'not a healthy sign'.[48] The speculations caused Maulana to tone down his criticism of the Sharia bill being contemplated by the IJT government, although the matter subsequently seems to have been hushed up.[49]

Over the years, torture by police and other investigation agencies following unlawful incarceration has become a norm. These bodies have routinely maligned, imprisoned, verbally and physically abused numerous political detainees, and interrogation centres like the Lahore Fort and Attock Fort became proverbial for the brutality of their extremely inhospitable treatment of 'the prisoner of conscience'. The criminalisation of the administrative infrastructure in Sindh especially during the 1980s is the culmination of the policies based on brutalisation. The military regimes under Mirza, Ayub Khan and Yahya Khan, despite apparent liberal persuasions, institutionalised the practice of torture in police structure. Ayub Khan's feudal governor of West Pakistan, the Nawab of Kalabagh, was known to patronise criminals across the country for personal purposes. A number of political activists, journalists, labour leaders and students were 'eliminated' by the *goondas* on orders from the governor. A similar reign of terror was unleashed in the former East Pakistan by its governor, Abdul Munem Khan, a protégé of Ayub Khan.

Institutionalised tampering with electoral processes took place during the Ayub era when the regime used its officials to manage a presidential victory over Fatima Jinnah. The basic democrats were tempted, purchased or simply coerced by the civil service and state agencies to vote for the incumbent president. Where the functionaries failed, *goondas* were deputed to keep the voters intimidated.[50] Yahya Khan's military regime carried the brutal policy to its extreme when it withdrew its promises to hand over power to the elected representatives. Facing a mass-based rebellion in East Pakistan, the state turned to punitive action and the intelligence agencies, both military and civil, administered the province by brutal force. Since most of the military and civil personnel running these agencies came from the western wing, Bengali hatred for West Pakistanis – generally referred to as Punjabis – knew no bounds. It was Bhutto who, through his manoeuvres at Simla in 1972, earned an umbrella reprieve for these military and security officials whose trials by special tribunals made sense to Bangladeshis and many others.

Bhutto's interlude was supposed to differ from the preceding regimes but it suffered from its own special type of paranoia.[51] Rationalising the continuation of the state of emergency and underlining the need for the FSF, his interior minister, Abdul Qayyum Khan, told the national assembly: 'Efforts have been made to topple this government by disturbances, by language riots, by spreading regional feelings, [and] by growing sectarian hatred.'[52] Bhutto applied coercion against his former allies and used the military in Balochistan on flimsy grounds. His successor, Zia, issued a general amnesty for Baloch and Pushtun detainees but unleashed his own reign of terror against political dissidents. Using Islam as a straitjacket to legitimise his rule, Zia introduced a number of special martial-law regulations and presidential ordinances which handed out summary verdicts varying from flogging to imprisonment. The contemporary reports on Pakistan by Amnesty International are detailed accounts of the widespread and excessive use of torture. In order to escape legal retribution, Zia managed an indemnity for all the harsh measures undertaken during the martial-law years by incorporating the Eighth Amendment in the constitution. By then the deinstitutionalisation of the judiciary, the press, education and women's rights was complete. Junejo, despite resistance from Zia, took giant strides towards the restoration of human rights in Pakistan by ending the emergency and restoring press freedom. His policies were followed by those of Benazir Bhutto, who has maintained a mixed record in the preservation of human rights in the country. While she showed tolerance towards a critical print media, she instituted 160 court cases against Nawaz Sharif in June 1995 including a more serious charge of sedition.

During the 1980s, when the military regime persuaded the intelligence agencies to engineer ethnic and political alliances, a new chapter in the history of torture began.[53] The agencies brazenly violated human rights, while simultaneously the ethnic groups began mafia-style campaigns to eliminate their rivals. Thus, Pakistan entered a new phase of administrative bankruptcy and social banditry. In Sindh, both the Sindhi nationalists and the MQM engaged in extortion, kidnap for ransom and assassinations. Ordinary Sindhis have been subjected to the most debilitating kind of feudalism.[54] With the police and related agencies also patronising criminals, torture and violations of human rights have been institutionalised in a multi-tiered fashion with the feudal fabric of society being joined by the strong arm of the state.[55] When the police and investigation organisations are unable to find alleged criminals, they round up their relatives so as to compel their surrender. The practice, widely known to all in the country, was rebuked by a senior judge in the Sindh High Court: 'You have started arresting the brothers, sons and fathers of wanted persons and next you will arrest their sisters, daughters and wives.'[56] The mismanagement in Sindh has been so pervasive that an army official, motivated by his own whims and those of a corrupt landlord, killed 12 unarmed *haris* in a so-called 'encounter' near Hyderabad. Major Arshad Pervaiz simply went berserk in June 1992, when he shot down these poor peasants at Shah Bilawal. It was initially announced that the dead were dacoits killed in an armed provocation, but subsequent to a public outcry an army tribunal found Pervaiz guilty of killing innocent, unarmed citizens. During that same week, four Sindhis died in official detention, although all sorts of alibi were used to avoid responsibility for their deaths.[57] The exasperation of the police and intelligence agencies with human-rights activists knows no bounds. Such a policy has already resulted in total public alienation from the police and other law-enforcing agencies. In the summer of 1995, while various factions of the MQM were fighting among themselves, they were equally engaging the security forces in regular gun-battles by using rocket launchers and car bombs. The police were helplessly marginalised with Karachi being dominated by the terrorists who were killing 12 persons per day.

The mutilation of the country's judicial system has caused a serious erosion of civil liberties, giving police and other agencies a freer hand to violate basic rights with impunity. The tampering with national judicial institutions by manipulation of rules, appointments, retirement and forcible transfers of judges has resulted in further taming of the judiciary.[58] The dissolution of the first Pakistani parliament was upheld by the Supreme Court as 'constitutional' while Zia's martial law was belatedly justified under the 'law of necessity'. Similarly, Zia's Provisional Constitutional Order (PCO) produced a grave powerlessness in the judiciary. Zia's drastic measures in the name of Islamisation – the establishment of Qazi courts, the promulgation of the Huddood Ordinances and similar punishments and a rhetorical emphasis on the Sharia – eroded the country's judicial system. There is no doubt that several judges resigned over these unilateral changes with a direct bearing on individual liberties, but it appears that the courts resigned themselves to the docile role imposed by a strong executive. Even at present, despite electoral promises to separate the judiciary from administration, the latter continues to monopolise judicial prerogatives. Under such circumstances, it is no wonder that the abuse of power by state functionaries remains unchecked. After Zia's death, the Pakistani courts gave historic verdicts, for example declaring his dissolution of assemblies in 1988 to be 'unconstitutional', but the subordination of the judiciary to an ambitious executive has become reality.[59]

Thus, the malady causing the evolution of parallel government by intelligence agencies is, to a large extent, a necessary result of the subjugation of the judiciary to the whims and fancies of an overpowering executive. According to Pakistani legal tradition, any accused was allowed automatic bail after being in jail for two years. In September 1992, Ishaque Khan changed that law through a special presidential ordinance not allowing the benefit of bail to Asif Zardari. Moreover, on 14 December 1992, another special presidential ordinance prohibited the high courts from allowing bail to parties whose cases were under consideration before special courts. Asif Zardari's bail had been under consideration before the Sindh High Court since October 1992 and the new presidential ordinance barred the court from even conducting a hearing on the petition. 'Lawyers and human-rights activists said the move was directed against Asif Ali Zardari, the imprisoned husband of the opposition leader Benazir Bhutto who has been in prison for more than two years on a variety of charges ... "To keep one man in jail they are willing to jeopardise the liberty of hundreds of people", said Asma Jehangir, a prominent lawyer and secretary general of the Human Rights Commission of Pakistan.'[60] Protest and indignation were expressed throughout the country over these two ordinances which were interpreted as a major infringement of individual rights.[61]

Stories abound of police brutality, unlawful incarcerations and continued detention of innocent, poor individuals,[62] who in many cases are children and women.[63] According to a documented study in 1991, there were 12 198 children/minors waiting to be tried in the jails in Punjab alone. Of these, 2095 were finally tried and sentenced, 129 of them aged below 14. Earlier, in 1989, 13 125 minors were reportedly awaiting trial and of these 752 were below 14. In 1990, the total number reached 14 353 with only 883 finally sentenced by the courts, the rest being simply held in police custody. Most of the girls and women in jails are routinely subjected to multiple rapes. For instance, in December 1988, Saima Aasim, a 16-year-old girl, was raped by five or six police officials in Sindh and subjected to physical torture. She was released in September 1990 after appeals were lodged with the prime minister and the president but until the mid-1990s, not one tormentor had been punished.[64]

THE CIA AND SINDH

Like its sister agencies, the Pakistani CIA has acquired ill repute not only through violations of human rights but also by becoming an active party in organised crime in the turbulent province of Sindh. During its heyday under Jam Sadiq Ali and Irfanullah Marwat, the CIA practised victimisation, personal vendetta, forgery, car theft, kidnapping, torture of innocent citizens including cases of gang rapes against women and operated as a parallel organisation pursuing its own kind of interrogation. The CIA was originally intended to help the police in criminal investigation, but political patronage and the exclusive nature of its leadership helped the agency to run a reign of terror in Sindh until the death of Jam Sadiq Ali in early 1992.

After the dismissal of Benazir Bhutto's first government in 1990, Sindh had been given into the titular custody of Jam so as to marginalise the PPP irrespective of means. Jam, a former founder of the PPP, had forged alliances with the MQM, the powerful Pirs of Sindh, and taken Irfanullah Marwat as his adviser on internal security. Jam and Marwat had paralysed the PPP by using elaborate tactics. Aftab Nabi, the former DIG of the CIA in Karachi and a brother of Islam Nabi, the MQM minister, was eased out and replaced by Samiullah Marwat in June 1991. 'Even prior to his out of turn elevation to the position of the DIG, Samiullah Marwat had a reputation for acting independently, though he was supposed to be tiers below the chief of the Sindh police. The reason was that he was very close to the home advisor, to whom he was directly reporting.' As an organisation, the CIA allowed itself to cover a wider terrain, including surveillance of the opponents of the government.

The CIA had always been an organisation that had a reputation for terror, something out of a gory horror film. Since its job was to investigate heinous crimes, the interrogation of accused persons formed part of its duties. Like the rest of the police in this country, the CIA has always employed medieval tactics, the old third degree methods, to extract confessions. The list of those who have been killed in CIA custody, or maimed for life, is as long as it is horrifying.[65]

Insiders who discovered details of murders committed at the behest of the CIA, were also 'flushed out'. An example is the 'disappearance' of Malik Ehsan, an inspector in Karachi, who had gathered facts on the death of Saeed Mighty, a notorious criminal who died mysteriously in Jinnah Hospital. A post-mortem was not allowed on the body. Mighty had been privy to important information on car thefts and serious violations of human rights by the CIA. Many observers believed that he had been administered poison in his food as the doctors had submitted a fitness report on him only a day earlier. Malik's own death remained a mystery and 'his widow was forcibly prevented from addressing a press conference, where she was believed to be ready to make sensational disclosures about her husband's death'.

Another story of the type of torture routinely perpetrated by the CIA on political activists is of Raheela Tiwana, a woman activist from the People's Students' Federation (PSF), who after a 'harrowing ordeal of torture' at a CIA centre of investigation, was admitted to the psychiatric ward of the Jinnah Hospital on 3 January 1991, 'for physical dysfunction and a condition known as radial nerve neuropexia'. Along with Shehla Raza, another PSF activist, she was subjected to torture in custody for two weeks before the police officially declared their arrest. She was hung upside down and beaten up routinely by male interrogators and tormentors in order to squeeze a confession of her complicity in terrorist activities on behalf of the AZO. In an interview in hospital when she described her ordeal in custody, she observed: 'I don't know how I survived it.'[66]

Such investigative findings published in responsible magazines like the *Herald* and *Newsline*, alerted the nation to the sordid side of the law-enforcment and intelligence agencies and caused widespread fury. The October 1991 issue of the *Herald* became a best-seller in the country and was reprinted many times until the editor announced their inability to keep up with public demand. However, the initial response from the CIA was that it would forcibly remove the magazine from the shops. Carrying a picture of Irfanullah Marwat on its cover under the title 'Inside the CIA', the magazine heralded a new defiant, courageous and maturer phase in Pakistani journalism. Despite widespread public demand for his reprimand, Irfanullah was not removed but Samiullah was transferred to a less 'visible' position. He remained *persona non grata* in Pakistani public opinion and his alleged involvement in sex scandals made the headlines.

At the same time, quite a few journalists were roughed up in Karachi and the editor of the *Herald* (a woman) had to seek special military protection.

Various intelligence agencies represent a brutal and confused form of the state and operate without well-defined objectives. In most cases, they humiliate and coerce the civil society. Individuals from the opposition, minorities, academia, the press and human rights groups are the usual victims of their repression. It is an area of conflict between the state and civil society which has not attracted major attention yet has been continuously eroding the moral stature of the state. It is only through strengthening rather than annihilating the voices of civil society that the state in Pakistan will be able to resolve this dilemma.

6 State and Civil Society in Conflict

The awakening of civic institutions like an empowered parliament, an independent judiciary, a free press and public opinion forums, private think-tanks, human-rights groups, dynamic educational institutions, energetic research organisations and other non-governmental organisations providing institutional restraints on a growing elitist state have added to the forces of despondency in various cross-sections of the society. While the state authorities were involved in corruption and coercive activities or suffered from inertia, the public waited for a messiah to deliver them from oppression. With a diminished belief in the administrative set-up, polarisation between rich and poor increased and the demographically youthful society turned to guns and drugs on a horrendous scale. The interventionist role of the army and monopolisation of power by the bureaucracy made the civil institutions mere appendages of a state which suffered from a dual crisis in mandate and legitimacy. The way in which civil society was gradually beleaguered can be understood in terms of the administrative and economic priorities of the state as reflected in the annual budgetary allocations which have led to a weakening of institutional civic foundations.

The study of various sectors which have become non-priority areas as a result of official policies may illustrate the failure of civil society in Pakistan to arrest the monopolistic, centralist and elitist preferences that harm its own citizens. The persistence of poverty, the marginalisation of the social sector including vital areas like education and health, the exclusion of women from many aspects of national life, the muzzling of the press for so long as well as an extremely narrow tax base and the evasion of overdue measures like agricultural tax and land reforms – these all point to the failure to establish an enduring and plural civil society. Such a scenario, which is essential for national well-being, would certainly be a nightmare for non-representative regimes which thrive on non-accountability.

If we look at the society with hindsight, it must be admitted that Pakistan has managed to overcome several of the internal and regional constraints that it faced at its inception. A dismal natural average life expectancy of 32, almost zero industrial base and a mainly agrarian, rural economy as well as an acute security dilemma were reminders of the events of 1947 and the huge influx of refugees into the new country. Pakistan's growing middle class, its impressive technical achievements (including the acquisition of nuclear and sophisticated computer technology) and indeed its own survival despite various odds are not insignificant achievements. In recent years, Pakistani expatriates have made important contributions to the national economy while working in sometimes unfriendly circumstances in the Gulf region. Overall, the nation economy registered healthy growth despite institutional restraints (Tables 6.1 to 6.7). Pakistan has the ability to cross the threshold of middle-income countries if it develops a civil society that will guide the nationa and state. Pakistan's GDP compared with other countries is shown in Table 6.1; regional comparisons are shown in Table 6.2.

In 1992–93, the rate of national growth was halved due to floods and other adjustment problems in the wake of dwindling foreign assistance

Table 6.1   GDP Growth in Pakistan and Selected Countries, 1980–92 (per cent)

1.	Botswana	10.1
2.	Korea	9.4
3.	China	9.1
4.	Bhutan	6.9
5.	Hong Kong	6.7
6.	Thailand	8.2
7.	Pakistan	6.1

Source: The World Bank, *World Development Report* (1994)

Table 6.2   Comparative Regional Indicators in the World Economy (per cent)

Region	Real growth of GDP		Growth of export volume	
	1980–89	1990	1980–89	1989
Industrial	3.0	3.6	4.8	7.6
Sub-Saharan	1.0	1.8	0.0	10.1
East Asia	8.4	7.7	14.7	8.1
South Asia	5.5	5.2	6.1	9.6
E. Europe	1.4	0.0	3.8	2.0
Middle East & Europe	2.9	2.2	6.4	1.4
L. America	1.6	1.8	4.9	4.4

Source: The World Bank, *World Development Report* (1990 and 1994).

and decreasing exports. In addition, economic growth has been less egalitarian given almost matching increases in population and defence expenditures in a conflict-ridden region like South Asia. Defence, the servicing of foreign loans and upkeep of the bureaucracy and administration take almost three-quarters of the national budget, with little left over for the social sector (see Table 6.4). Ever-increasing government expenditure and additional loans have been consuming the limited foreign-exchange

Table 6.3   Comparative Defence Expenditures, 1980–88 (percentage of GNP)

Year	Pakistan	India	S. Asia	LDCs	World
1980	5.4	3.2	3.3	6.1	5.4
1981	5.5	3.3	3.4	6.3	5.4
1982	5.8	3.5	3.6	6.7	5.7
1983	6.8	3.5	3.8	6.5	5.7
1984	6.5	3.6	3.8	6.4	5.6
1985	6.8	3.5	3.8	6.1	5.6
1986	7.0	3.6	3.9	5.5	5.5
1987	6.9	3.8	4.0	5.2	5.4
1988	6.9	3.5	3.8	4.3	5.0

Source: *World Military Expenditures and Arms Transfer 1989*, Washington, DC, 1990.

Table 6.4   Military Expenditure and Social Sectors (Education and Health) 1991

	1	2	3	4	5
Mexico	0.3	5	45	0.2	2
Malaysia	3.1	48	26	0.7	19
Turkey	4.0	87	1 233	1.9	13
Sri Lanka	4.8	107	33	0.4	25
India	3.1	65	2 447	0.3	4
Pakistan	6.5	125	697	1.5	9
South	3.5	60	–	0.6	19
North	3.4	37	–	0.7	16

Notes: 1. Per cent of GDP; 2. Per centage *vis-á-vis* social sector; 3. Annual arms imports since 1988 (in $ millions); 4. Ratio of armed forces per teacher; 5. Ratio of armed forces per doctor.
Source: UNDP, *Human Development Report* (1992 and 1994).

reserves along with a vertical increase in the national debt and annual deficit.

Pakistan's defence expenditure might be rationalised in terms of specific geo-political vulnerabilities and the ongoing security threat from India. Nevertheless, however justifiable it might be, this increase has been taking place at the expense of the vital social sector. It is also worth noting that 90 per cent of the defence equipment is imported from foreign sources and indigenous technology can meet only the remaining 10 per cent. In addition to the political and psychological-costs, such a heavy dependence on foreign supplies has exacerbated the flight of scarce reserves from the country. The combination of all the factors mentioned above has pushed South Asian countries like Pakistan down the ladder on the global human index (see Table 6.5).

Table 6.5   South Asia on Human Development Index (Ranking in the World)

Country	Rank number	Value
Sri Lanka	90	0.665
Pakistan	132	0.393
India	135	0.382
Bangladesh	146	0.309
Afghanistan	171	0.208

Source: UNDP, *Human Development Report* (1994).

THE POLITICS OF POVERTY

A constant problem in Pakistan has been the long-standing duel with poverty given its uneven development, rural–urban differences, feudatory land-holding patterns, narrow tax base and huge non-development expenditure. The dwindling of the social sector in some decades despite projections to the contrary in the five-year plans, has been exacerbated by a huge increase in population and created an enduring problem. The rhetorical emphasis on reli-gion during the 1980s hampered serious efforts for family planning while the country continued receiving refugees from Afghanistan, Iran, India, Bangladesh and elsewhere. The uneven development during the 'decade of development' in the 1960s added to unemployment while rapid nationalisa-tion in the 1970s only resulted in economic stagnation. Recent liberalisation and privatisation of vast sectors of the public economy may yield similar discrepancies if not properly and judiciously envisioned. Similarly, an inability to address basic needs and an absence of land reforms have increased the numbers of urban and rural poor. Today, Pakistanis may be more mobile, better fed and proportionately better clothed, yet the basic inequalities within society are as visible as ever. Poverty remains the biggest challenge for the country although there are apparently no dramatic cases of starvation. Table 6.6 indicates the general patterns in Pakistan at the beginning of the 1990s.

Table 6.6   Regional Distribution of Poverty, 1985–2000 (in millions)

Region	1985	2000
South Asia	500	350
Sub-Sahara	175	250
East Asia	225	50
Europe, Middle East	50	50
Americas	75	50

Source: UNDP, *Human Development Report 1990.*

The population increase in South Asia, especially in Pakistan in the 1980s, equally took its toll, as Table 6.7 shows.

Table 6.7   Human Development Indicators in Pakistan

Life expectancy	1992	58.3
Access to health (per cent)	1991	56
Access to safe water	1991	50
Access to sanitation	1990	24
Percentage of daily calories required	1990	101
Adult literacy	1992	36
Primary and secondary enrolment ratio (per cent)	1990	24
GNP per capita (US$)	1991	400
Real GDP per capita (PPP$)	1992	1 970
Fertility rate	1990	6.2
Urban population	1992	33
Infant mortality rate	1992	0.09
Population per doctor	1990	2 940
Population per nurse	1990	1 720
Scientists per thousand	1988	4
Radios per thousand	1988	86
Television sets per thousand	1990	18

Source: Taken from *Human Development Report (1990–4).*

According to the UN, there are altogether 1200 million individuals in the developing countries who live below the income level commensurate with essential food requirements; of these India, Bangladesh and Pakistan make almost half the total.[1] In 1990, Pakistan had altogether 37 million poor people while during the period 1977–84 the figures stood at 34 million. Both per capita expenses and household income are used as barometers to measure standard of living but it includes other important sectors of welfare like life expectancy, health, literacy and access to public services. According to the World Bank, poverty is 'the inability to attain a minimal standard of living', which certainly hinges on a specific income value.[2] In Pakistan, poverty has two separate rural and urban manifestations.[3] In 1990, 55.2 million Pakistanis did not have access to health services; 54.6 million lacked access to safe water and 100.3 million were without sanitation facilities, which certainly makes poverty more than a routine calorie/income-centred issue. A major consequence of poverty in the country has been the prevalence of child labour. In 1961, the rate stood at 38.3 per cent increasing to 39.5 per cent in 1971 and a decade later it decreased to 34.7 per cent of the total labour force.[4] In terms of actual figures, given the rise in population, there has been a steady increase in figures to 10 million, constituting two-thirds of young adults. The accompanying incidence of female child labour is equally astounding but remains unmeasured and generally unpaid. In fact, child labour largely falls in the unregulated, informal sector of the economy as a major portion of the bonded labour that has persisted in Pakistan for years, involving generations of under-paid families working as odd-jobbers on kilns, construction sites, quarries and other privately owned industries. Any kind of dissent voiced in urban quarters has been hushed up until the inception of the Anti-Bonded Movement in Pakistan, which carried on an impressive campaign at regional, national and global levels, resulting in a growing consciousness of the inhuman institution of slavery.

During the 1960s, the government stressed the need for rapid industrialisation and economic growth without bringing about any structural changes. The proponents of 'modernisation' enthused that industrial change, urbanisation and economic growth would lead to national cohesion and development and a loosening of traditionalism. However, the net result has been the concentration of wealth in a few families of urban entrepreneurs while the landlords benefited from mechanisation of agriculture without any change or challenge to basic land-holding patterns. With rising unemployment and economic discontent throughout the country, there was a reemergence of fissiparous tendencies and eventually political suffocation superimposed by the military regime. East Pakistan went its own way. The PPP, recognising the economic disparities, had sounded the clarion call for social justice, reaching the disgruntled echelons of Pakistani society. However, its nationalisation policies only consolidated the unchallengeable transcendency of the state over vital financial institutions and led to added stagnation. The land reforms were largely 'cosmetic' and failed to change the traditional land-holding patterns given the feudal vetoing power in the PPP regime. Indeed, 'barely 1 percent of the landless tenants and small owners benefited from the 1972 land reforms'.[5] Ever since, successive regimes have been held to ransom by vested interests in order to ward off any basic economic structural changes. The imposition of the agricultural tax[6] has been resisted by feudal groups on the plea that, given the low agricultural income, realisation of such a tax would be difficult. Notwithstanding this argument 'it is used as a tax shelter by the rich. This has seriously eroded the tax base and contributed to the regressive nature of the tax system in Pakistan.'[7]

The population of Pakistan, estimated at around 122.6 million in 1990, is still unconfirmed due to suspension of the census in 1991 and 1992. The annual growth rate is around 3.0 per cent, higher than that of Bangladesh with 2.8 per cent, Egypt and India with 2.4 per cent each and Indonesia 2.2 per cent.[8] Basic education on such matters, bold initiatives on the remodelling of the economy, land reforms, conducive environmental policies, broadening of tax reforms, and effective employment strategies such as the search for overseas markets for skilled Pakistani labour would certainly help to alleviate the country's chronic problem of poverty.

EDUCATION, HEALTH AND THE PRESS

Education

On questions of education and health, which are the basis of any civil society, Pakistan's record has been less than impressive. Rationalised by a constant security threat, defence spending and the resultant increasing expenditure in non-development sectors have been increasing and eating away scarce resources that would otherwise be available for development. In spite of a persistent increase in population, there has been a reduction in funds and other inputs for education and health. Adult literacy rates have declined or have stayed low while the number of drop-outs from schools has been multiplying. In addition, teachers remain underpaid though education is the largest employing sector in the national economy after defence. Given the lack of incentive both at primary and higher levels, neither students nor teachers sustain a steady interest in progress. Abandonment of the profession as well as the criminalisation of the entire system by manipulation of examinations and final results, demonstrate the extent of the problem, which certainly cannot be understood in terms of mere figures.

As Table 6.8 amply illustrates, education has never been a national priority even though the increase in population and greater need for skilled and semi-skilled personnel within and outside the country demands generous investment in this sector. On the contrary, compared to Sri Lanka which is torn by ethnic warfare, Pakistan's contribution to education has decreased. The mushrooming of private educational institutions at the primary level in the 1980s catered for the middle class, leaving rural, tribal and poor areas solely dependent on public schools. Such schools usually have a wretched infrastructure, a scarcity of trained and committed teachers and a huge drop-out rate. Most of the schools in the country lack proper buildings, suffer from an absence of proper library and laboratory facilities and even in many cases basic sanitation facilities. They present a pathetic picture compared to some of their counterparts in the private or semi-autonomous sector providing for the needs of the elite. This uninspiring educational system, together with physical punishment and an emphasis on cramming rather than learning, is the breeding ground for infantile civic institutions. The religious schooling in *maddrassas* is equally outdated with an emphasis on rote-learning Arabic rather than learning and comprehension of the message itself and is handled by incapable, intolerant and repressive individuals holding the exalted litle of *ulama*. Properly designed courses in a medium understood by the pupils and teachers in the

Table 6.8   A comparison of Expenditure in Pakistan and Sri Lanka (per cent)

	Year	Pakistan	Sri Lanka
Defence expenditure as per cent of GDP	1960	5.5	1.0
Defence expenditure as per cent of GDP	1991	6.5	4.8
Public expenditure on education as per cent of GNP	1960	1.1	3.8
Public expenditure on education as per cent of GNP	1990	3.4	2.7
Adult literacy rate	1970	21.0	77.0
Adult literacy rate	1994	36.4	89.1

Source: *Human Development Report* (1994).

context of their daily lives, with an adequate physical infrastructure would ensure that the pupils were not only attracted to the schools and *maddrassas* but would also find the atmosphere less humiliating.

Funds for education become entangled in the long ladders of bureaucracy all the way from the federal level to the sub-divisions and very little filters down to the grassroots. Donor agencies such as USAID have pursued other areas in Pakistan that reflect the geo-political priorities of their respective countries. Similarly, the NGOs have suffered from personality clashes and corruption or become controversial because of negative social pressures. While the Aga Khan Foundation has concentrated on Ismaili-populated areas in Hunza, Gilgit and nearby Chitral for social uplift programmes, neighbouring Baltistan, Chilas and Nagar, for quite some time, remained outside its purview. The veteran social worker and leading administrator, Akhtar Hamid Khan ran his highly respected Orangi Pilot Project on a self-help basis throughout the turbulent 1980s and 1990s in Karachi's slums but its achievements have been more often maligned by local thugs and mullahs whose preference, given their own petty interests, is the status quo. One of Khan's poems written mainly for children was made controversial in 1992 so as to chase him out of the area and the local mosques were used to incite the public against him.[9]

At the graduate and post-graduate levels, the 22 Pakistani universities and hundreds of colleges run in the public sector reflect a similar saga of alienation, lack of infrastructure, absence of motivation among the teachers and the taught and resultant frustration. Such an atmosphere has been conducive to growing problems like factionalism, gun-running and drug addiction. Political parties, otherwise banned from mainstream national and provincial politics under Zia's martial law, found willing recruits amongst students to their opportunistic causes. Campuses became hotbeds of violent politicking and capturing the unions became both a motive and a strategy to add to the activism. Funds, arms and legal protection were provided to so-called student leaders who engaged in battles with their 'opponents' and committed crimes like kidnapping, lynching and murder. Regular gun-battles during the 1980s symbolised the rise of a 'Kalashnikov culture' that saw student bodies like Islami Jamiat i-Tulaba (IJT), Anjuman i-Tulaba i-Islam (ATI), All-Pakistan Muhajir Students' Organisation (APMSO), Baloch Students' Organisation (BSO), People's Students' Federation (PSF), Muslim Students' Federation (MSF) and Pukhtoon Students' Federation (PSF) organising themselves as regular junior cadres of militants fighting over petty matters.

This social criminalisation, which stemmed from a tacit understanding and patronage from the martial law regime and various political groups, subsequently degenerated into organised banditry in both rural and urban Sindh. The regional groups profited from regionalist identities which were fertile ground in a constantly fragmenting national political culture and eroding civil society. The JI, taking advantage of its experience in training young cadres from the schools and from its own field experience in the former East Pakistan and in Afghanistan, concentrated heavily on spearheading its student wing, IJT. A sympathetic martial-law regime looking for tacit support and eager to curb rival political factions, on occasions became totally dependent on the IJT to 'control' the universities. The IJT, which eventually provides members to the JI, benefited from the Afghanistan crisis by sending its youth on training and querrilla missions – with the result that the hostels on Pakistani university campuses became storehouses for arms. The Punjab University was virtually captured by the IJT; all appointments from vice-chancellor to peon, the selection of teachers, research staff and their promotion were all conducted with the Nazim of the IJT dictating to the university and provincial administration. The IJT chased all opponents from the campus and only students who had clear IJT sympathies or were able to prove their neutrality were given admission and hostel accommodation. Even after allocating lodgings, IJT activists would regularly monitor the premises for any sort of 'intrusion'. In the Quaid-i Azam University, Islamabad, the IJT and pro-PPP faction (PSF), usually ended up with a hung union and used pressure tactics and hostage-taking to broaden their membership and solidify their respective influence. Fascist tendencies resulted in the division of hostels with the IJT and PSF allocating rooms to their sympathisers as 'favours'. In times of confrontation, three hostels became battle-grounds. Similarly, in the University of Sindh at Jamshoro, the Jeeye Sindh students had a unilateral policy against non-Sindhis, with a timid administration bowing to their dictates. In 1992, the University hostels were the dens of dacoits, kidnappers and extortionists.[10] The University of Karachi was for a long time an IJT monopoly which received major support from the Urdu-speaking community in the city. The IJT's high-handedness and changing ethnic contours were challenged by a new generation of Muhajir students in the 1970s who felt that under PPP rule the Muhajir had been given a rough deal. The All-Pakistan Muhajir Students' Organisation (APMSO), building on localist loyalties, gradually emerged as the main challenger to the IJT and other groups and ultimately overran both the university and the city. The university remains a total MQM fiefdom, with security posts manned by rangers and police maintaining a semblance of tranquillity.[11] Balochistan University reflects an ethnic mix with the BSO rivalling the rightist IJT which includes emigrants and Pushtuns. In the NWFP, earlier, student politics revolved around 'locals' and 'non-locals' or Pushtuns versus non-Pushtuns. Punjabis, Hazarawals and Urdu-speakers would support the IJT or MSF but Pushtun students, reflecting the politics of the former Red Shirts, emphasised inter-Pushtun solidarity. Pushtun student politics, as in present-day Sindh, remained centred on regional loyalties while in other campuses it reflected the pseudo-ideological polarisation that has permeated the dissensions. The BSO, Jeeye Sindh, and Sindhi Shagird Tehreek have been simultaneously ethnic and ideological groups with leftist and secular/liberal leanings, while the APMSO has been secular but not leftist in its orientation and the MSF advocates views of national and centrist shades. All these student groups embody the regional, lingual and ideological variations in the main regionalist or religio-political parties.

This volatile politicisation of the campuses began under Ayub Khan's martial law which had stifled the general political atmosphere in the country. The movement to topple Ayub Khan began in Rawalpindi following the death of a student in 1968 and subsequently engulfed all the major campuses in both wings of the country. Dissenters like Zulfikar Ali Bhutto and Mohammad Asghar Khan were massively supported against Ayub Khan while Sheikh Mujibur Rahman, himself a former student leader and supporter of the demand for Pakistan, gave a clarion call to his student followers to strive for *sonar Bangla*. Bhutto's regime had both supporters and critics amongst the student groups in universities and colleges. While the PSO (currently PSF) defended Bhutto, the IJT tried to build wider support against liberal elements and eventually spearheaded the PNA movement in 1977. The Zia years were the worst period of student polarisation as political avenues and processes nation-wide had been closed by the regime. The state-run intelligence agencies infiltrated student bodies and, in many cases, ethnic and regionalist loyalties were promoted to create fissures within political circles. The IJT, like the JI itself, consolidated its hold over campuses and judiciously avoided destabilising Zia's regime. But its growing influence left many in the government uneasy, and they used the ethnic card to challenge its unilateral hold on campuses in Sindh. The APMSO and certain Sindhi groups did receive official patronage in order to contain an overpowering JI and its student constituent, IJT. This see-saw game led to frequent closures of the campuses because of violence and kidnapping. The Afghanistan crisis had already opened up unlimited reserves of weapons and drugs to the universities, which became centres of gunrunning and related crimes. Elections to the student unions were farcical, and sporadic incidents of lynching, murder and communitarian banditry became a norm until the unions were banned in 1984. By which time the malady had become all-pervasive. The

Benazir Bhutto government lifted the ban on student unions but with more openness in society and general tolerance toward political activities, the campuses gradually awoke to the new realities. The years of political suffocation and neglect of education in the country have left their indelible effects and the banning and unbanning of the unions was not sufficient to solve the problem.

After a short lull, organised crime, both on- and off-campus, began to increase until in 1992 the Sindh High Court and the Supreme Court of Pakistan took judicial initiatives to contain violence on campuses. Student bodies were declared illegal and the students were asked to submit affidavits, duly signed by parents and magistrates, committing themselves to serious studies. Wider and well-planned measures are, however, needed to eradicate inefficiency and corruption from the educational system. The sanctity of the examination and emphasis on merit rather than on pressure and recommendation (*safarish*) have to be restored. Simultaneously, the educational institutions need major and urgent uplifts both in institutional and professional areas by providing sufficient incentives to qualified teachers and discouraging the bureaucratisation of the campuses. Pakistan has a serious dilemma in attracting competent teachers given that they face serious economic handicaps and are routinely victimised by the local and provincial educational bureaucracy. In the whole country, there are only a few hundred people holding Ph. D.s and, despite their professional competence, in most cases they are not able to make both ends meet. Basic needs such as housing, reasonable food, appropriate health facilities and a good education for their children remain the ultimate ideals for this minority of highly educated and well-trained academics. Efforts to train Ph.D. candidates indigenously face similar economic, institutional and professional handicaps. Some of the country's capable graduates scorn teaching and research as professions and prefer lucrative and powerful positions in the civil service. In addition, Pakistan has been a victim of the brain drain, losing its trained and skilled professional to foreign institutions. Basic economic insecurity and professional hazards have, over the years, induced between 80 per cent to 90 per cent of Pakistani graduates to seek employment and residence in the West. A few individuals trickle back into the country, soon to suffer from increasingly insurmountable, frustrating and unnecessary barriers.

The research institutes to promote science and technology and devise programmes for both rural and urban areas in the education, health and agriculture sectors suffer from lack of funds, incentives and proper infrastructures. Since the funding and planning for these institutes is done by the relevant ministries and administrative divisions, their autonomy and initiative for research become secondary to the dictates of the funding agencies. The experts heading such organisations spend most of their time struggling for budgetary allocations and appeasing officialdom with research becoming secondary. Decisions are made on personal whims and the emphasis is on survival rather than planning and professional achievements. Professional inefficiency, corruption and a preference for short-cuts have become national problems. Various centres of excellence and area study centres across the country otherwise headed and staffed by some of the most capable specialists, suffer from bureaucratic inertia in the wake of centralisation and official indifference. Table 6.9 shows some of the effects by comparison with other countries.

Cheating in examinations, the leaking of papers in advance, sale of 'easy' examination centres and even of forged degrees are frequently reported in the Pakistani media.[12] On the whole, students justify such incidents and administrators look the other way. Another malady has been the parallel working of a number of educational systems in the country. Whereas rural and tribal schools are understaffed, lacking even basic physical facilities, urban schools in the public sector are overcrowded and have poor facilities. Insecurity turns some science teachers to private tutoring to make ends meet, which is affordable by only a certain section of the urban population. Many tuition centres, originally started to compensate for inefficiencies in the public sector, turned out to be good schools. For economic reasons and because of tough competition in the

Table 6.9 Human Capital Formation, 1992

Country	Literacy Rate per cent			Scientists R & D	
	Total	*Male*	*Female*	*(per 1 000)*	*scientists*
Mexico	89	91	86	64.4	6.1
Malaysia	80	89	72	–	4.0
Turkey	82	91	72	26.3	3.7
Sri Lanka	89	94	85	–	2.2
Iran	56	67	45	7.6	1.1
India	50	64	35	3.5	2.5
Pakistan	36	49	22	4.0	1.5
Dev. South	69	79	58	8.8	3.2

Source: *Human Development Report* (1994).

open market, such centres followed rigorous plans but paid meagre salaries to their teachers. With their nationalisation in the 1970s, the teachers felt a sense of security as their jobs were now officially guaranteed. However, the quality of education slumped. With the reemergence of the private sector in schools, the middle and upper classes are the main beneficiaries while the foreign-administered schools in Islamabad, Lahore and Karachi as well as a number of pre-1947 elitist schools such as Aitchison in Lahore, Lawrence College, Murree, Karachi Grammar School, or missionary-run schools maintain higher standards and charge exorbitant fees way beyond the means of an average Pakistani family. Even the military-run schools geared to train young cadets and the civilian-run model schools in cities exude an atmosphere of class-based exclusivity, leaving almost the whole of Pakistan to *moffusil-* and *mohalla*-based schools in the midst of financial, psychological and professional crises and controversy over the medium of instruction.

While private and foreign-sponsored schools teach entirely in English, the state-run schools and colleges use Urdu as the medium of instruction. English is taught as a compulsory language from sixth class until undergraduate level, but trained facilities are few and modern methods and aides are not available to the pupils. English-medium schools teach Urdu as a compulsory subject in addition to basic information on Islam and Pakistan. Language has been a highly politicised issue for a long time, and in many cases is the bed-rock of political or ethnic identity; provincial governments therefore make special arrangements for provincial languages to be taught at primary and secondary levels. In both the Punjab and Azad Kashmir the situation is slightly different since here Urdu was adopted as the medium of instruction quite some time back. A number of ways have been suggested over the years to help increase literacy in the country including the introduction of the mother tongue as the medium of instruction, a change in the script or the simple imposition of Urdu. Such strategies need wider debate for the evolution of a consensus, given the volatile history of ethnic pluralism in the country and the importance of language in the formation of identity. However, without an end to the cold war in South Asia, it is idealistic to expect that there will be a unilateral demilitarisation and reorientation of national priorities. Education in South Asia is not merely a *local* issue, as it has its regional and intra-state antecedents.

Health

The other major casualty in the largely-ignored social sector in the region is health, which has a low priority in budgetary allocations. For a long time, South Asian doctors have worked abroad while the indigenous populations still lack basic infrastructures and both funds and medicines are scarce. State-run hospitals and dispensaries are over-worked, under-staffed, over-crowded and poorly equipped. Proper tests, diagnosis and relevant treatments are simply erratic. It is quite common for vital test results to be misplaced, while seeing a consultant within state hospitals means proper contacts at the right places. Underpaid staff lack both interest and incentives with many of them referring patients to private clinics, which are staffed by hospital doctors. The health system, like education, embodies various parallel systems operating largely on the principle of 'each according to his status and wealth' (see Table 6.10). The rural dispensaries, primary health centres and hospitals in towns and cities operated in the public sector suffer from all the above-mentioned problems, whereas the private clinics thrive. It is only in these clinics that one may see a consultant, though otherwise 95 per cent of them are full-time government employees. In addition to private practice, many of the specialists are on the faculty of the medical colleges, leaving them with little time or incentive to carry on further research. Where proper, judicious planning is needed at all three levels, the severe brain-drain has to be stemmed as well. Pakistani tax-payers spend millions of rupees on training doctors who often leave for better prospects in the West and Middle East or simply become money-minting machines.

Table 6.10   World Health and Nutrition Indicators

Country	Life Expectancy		Mortality under 5		Daily calories
	1960	*1992*	*1960*	*1992*	*1988–90*
Mexico	57.1	69.9	92	36	3 060
Malaysia	53.9	69.9	73	14	2 670
Turkey	50.1	66.7	190	57	3 200
Sri Lanka	62.1	71.2	71	24	2 250
Iran	49.6	66.6	169	41	3 020
India	44.0	59.7	165	89	2 230
Pakistan	43.1	58.3	163	99	2 280
Dev. South	46.2	63.0	149	69	2 480
North	69.0	74.5	35	13	

Source: *Human Development Report* (1994).

The statistics in Table 6.10 reveal that health is still not a national priority in Pakistan, since it receives the lowest budgetary allocation in terms of its share of GNP in comparison with other South Asian countries. Its national fiscal contributions to the health sector during the 1980s remained almost half the average of the developing world. Consequently, only 55 per cent of its population compared to 64 per cent in the developing world have had access to health services while the same proportion had access to safe drinking water compared with an average of 68 per cent in the developing South. Although fewer people were smoking tobacco, one doctor served 3000 people and one nurse tended 5000 inhabitants on average, which is lower than many other regions. Such trends were noted in the mid-1980s and still continue without any radical change.

The profession of nursing has suffered immensely in Pakistan due to social taboos and the lack of any serious efforts to change attitude. Muslims take pride in reminding one another that the wives of the Prophet nursed the wounded in the wars, yet they shy away from seeing their own female relatives opting to enter the nursing profession. Given the clericalisation of Muslim culture over the centuries, societal attitudes towards nursing reflect rigidity toward females. Like women's education, any outdoor female activity, however healthy and significant it might be in the familial and social sense, has been decried by Muslim conservatives. Nursing is still largely looked down upon as a profession for non-Muslim minority women. It was during the British period in India that the official and missionary hospitals, facing opposition from both Muslim and Hindu families, began recruiting local Christian women as midwives and nurses. Eventually, nursing emerged as a predominantly Christian domain largely staffed by European and local Christian women. Whereas the Muslim urban elite and rural feudal classes were contemptuous of nursing, Muslim women from the laity negotiated their own routine localised life largely served by a traditional untrained *dai* (midwife). Since antiquity, traditional Muslim families and upper-class Hindus have equally depended in childbirth upon illiterate midwives whose primitive methods and absence of hygiene contributed to a high rate of infant mortality.

During the 1960s, several low-income families, who were attracted by the new economic prospects arising from the opening of primary health-care centres and family planning units, allowed their daughters to obtain training in nursing, midwifery and basic health care. But such individual decisions did not reflect any major shift in public attitudes towards nursing which, even today, remains an unspoken social taboo. Additionally, the long working hours and very low salaries in a predominantly male environment with fears of sexism, have proved to be decisive disincentives. Pakistan is still a long way from having an adequate number of trained nurses even in good urban hospitals. The military hospitals have better job prospects for nursing though recruitment can be a cumbersome procedure given the availability of a vast majority of male nurses. Female nurses are mainly based in urban military hospitals situated in cantonment areas whereas male nurses can be moved around more conveniently. Some of the trained nurses quit the profession after marriage, and without a steady stream of new entrants there have been serious setbacks. In the 1970s, a number of trained nurses sought employment in the Gulf and North Africa, which helped them financially and professionally but had an adverse effect on the profession at home.[13]

Parents from diverse socio-economic backgrounds prefer to send their daughters to regular medical colleges to obtain a professional training in medicine. This is considered to give social status and to be an economically secure profession. Despite a large number of women practitioners in Pakistan, they are still under-represented in vital areas like paediatrics, gynaecology, physiotherapy, rehabilitation and psychiatry. Like the nurses, many women doctors quit their jobs after marriage and turn to child rearing. In most cases, it is the well-placed husbands who are unable to stand the social pressure, and therefore compel their female partners to revert to domestic roles. Ironically, female medicine turns out to be a mere economic gambit circumscribed by social superficialities. This dilemma is compounded by the lack of proper, standardised medicines which, if purchased on the market, are very expensive.

Since government hospitals are over-crowded, under-staffed and under-funded, patients often do not receive the right treatment at the right time.[14] For instance, in a country where there are daily road-side accidents, there are only 150 orthopaedic surgeons and they are only in a few cities.[15] Affluent patients end up at the private hospitals which mint money by conducting all sorts of unnecessary tests, charging huge consultation fees and bed charges. Like the private schools, running private hospitals is a growing, immensely profitable business. Many specialists either form cartels to run such hospitals or simply work in them on a part-time basis. Their employers expect them to bring in revenues and the usual course is frequent referral for hospitalisation and operations even for apparently minor medical ailments. City-based specialised doctors have established their own clinics where they run laboratories to conduct basic tests including x-rays. Patients are advised to visit such clinics periodically, where after the routine but costly tests, a prescription is given. Usually no records of the patients are kept except for the prescriptions written on letter-head paper which the patients carry around to seek further consultations from suggested specialists or merely to buy medicines.[16]

In small towns, private practitioners operate dispensaries attached to their clinics. They may not charge exorbitantly as their dispensaries mainly play a compensatory role. Given the expensive nature of allopathic medicines, and partly out of sheer desperation, many patients turn to *hakims* who claim to have a traditional herbal treatment for every disease. Others turn to homeopathy which keeps thousands of practitioners employed. Some of the big names among traditional and homeopathic practitioners spend very little time on a patient as the 'consultation' time is spent in scribbling down a *parchi* – a small chit for the dispenser, who is generally the key figure in the establishment. Simple folk are exploited mercilessly without any redress or accountability. Given the huge population and the resultant health problems, despite apparent multiple choices patients are simply on the receiving end. Never in the history of Pakistan has any medical practitioner been taken to court for prescribing wrong medicines, running unnecessary tests, causing radiation, or conducting unnecessary and often fatal operations. It is ironic that many unscrupulous doctors are not even taken to task by an otherwise alert media.[17] Vedic and homeopathic treatment thrives because it is within reach of an average Pakistani. However, it may be harmful to youths since many *hakim* alert them to almost non-existent, sexual diseases. In a society where even talking of sex is a taboo and youths have no understanding of physiological changes, so-called experts advertise strange-sounding sexual diseases varying from impotency to lack of stamina which the adolescents start internalising. From newspaper commercials to billboards, various sexual 'weaknesses' are advertised to the wavering, semi-literate young population. So-called potency potions are sold to such adolescents who are coaxed into believing that they actually do suffer from serious sexual deficiencies.

Another usual recourse, in the case of terminal illnesses, is to consult *pirs* and *sanaysi* charmers who operate as natural healers. While bureaucrats, military personnel and politicians spend millions of dollars from the national exchequer on foreign consultations and treatment abroad for themselves and their dependents, employees of the semi-autonomous corporations and ordinary citizens lack basic health care.[18] Many academics, journalists, lawyers and writers believe that since the current system suits its own architects, there is no hope of change in the near future.

While vital fields in medicine are still neglected or under-represented in Pakistan disciplines like counselling, psychotherapy and applied psychiatry are totally barren areas. In a transitional society with so many overpowering and coercive problems of a socio-economic and politico-psychological nature, there is certainly a need for expertise and advice on rehabilitation. The growing youthfulness of society, high drop-out rates, ethnic and sectarian violence and drug-related crimes make the need undeniably urgent.

Education and information on basic health-related subjects like sanitation, smoking, periodic medical check-ups or even an urgency like family size are minimal. The low rate of literacy, pervasive poverty and the predominantly rural composition of a society simmering under a stagnant feudal system largely neutralise official efforts for public health. While the Indus Valley civilisation prided itself on minute details of public sanitation, the present-day rural and industrial Pakistan appears to have forgotten all that. The lack of proper drainage, the pools of stinking water around factories, the stench of saline water, heaps of rubbish in the streets and the absence of public facilities have been major causes of disease in Pakistan. An absence of statistical data on pollution and lack of interest in environmental concerns both at the public and private levels have added to the health hazards in a country which could otherwise be proud of the clean, fresh air across its length and breadth. Nevertheless, compared to 1947, an average Pakistani has doubled his/her natural age and is more health-conscious and better clothed than many of his/her counterparts in the rest of South Asia.

The Press

Given the significance of the press as the Fourth Estate and, in some ways, its elevated status as the most effective watch-dog of individual rights, a separate full-length study would be in order. It is safe to assume that the press in Pakistan has suffered enormously because of authoritarian policies and draconian laws. The press has played a very important role in the political awakening of the South Asian masses, though the establishment of a modern, independent press has been a comparatively recent innovation in the sub-continent. With the launch of *Hickey's Bengal Gazette* in 1780, followed by Raja Ram Mohan Rai's *Mirat-ul-Akhbar* (1822) in Persian, the press in British India emerged as the most powerful vehicle of political ideas in the early twentieth century. From government to missionaries to political parties newspapers and magazines became both the medium and instrument of change.[19] During the 1940s, the Congress and the Muslim League, like their political parties, maintained their own influential mouthpieces carrying views and news on their respective political creeds, whereas the government wrestled hard to publish its viewpoint. Official censorship and frequent reviews of various papers and magazines were routinely applied, especially during emergencies including wars and non-cooperation movements.

After a brief interlude, the early years of quasi-democratic regimes in Pakistan were marred by organised efforts to muzzle the press. Regular press 'advices' – a colonial tradition – were sent daily by the ministry of information and its provincial constituents to the editors in order to tone down or twist the news and editorials in favour of the government. In addition to this system, regular black-listing, withdrawal of official advertisements, restrictions on newsprint quotas, law suits and individual harassment of journalists through intelligence agencies were used to pressure editors and newspaper proprietors. Press-gagging was one of the main instruments employed to achieve the depoliticisation of the masses, especially under non-representative regimes. Where coercion failed, temptations were offered instead. Also, inter-personal rivalries or ideological conflicts among powerful editors like Altaf Husain of *Dawn* and Majid Nizami of *Nawa-i-Waqt* were exploited to the maximum so as to keep the national press divided and ineffective. These two editors headed parallel organisations: The Pakistan Newspaper Editors' Conference (PNEC) and the Council of Pakistan Editors (CPE). These bodies competed for official favours while the press in general remained directionless.[20] Anti-communist propaganda and undefined 'national interests' provided successive regimes with pretexts to witch-hunt journalists. In particular, the *Pakistan Times* and *Imroze*, two prestigious dailies launched by Progressive Papers Limited (PPL) under the respective editorship of leftist intellectuals Faiz Ahmed Faiz and Ahmed Nadim Qasimi joined by the *Weekly Lail-o-Nihar*, edited by Syed Sibte Hasan, proved irritants to the establishment because of their bold and objective journalism. However, while the pre-1985 regimes were uncomfortable with the journalists, they resisted the temptation to impose radical curbs on the press. Instead, a Press Commission was established to recommend the systemisation of the print media and the standardisation of wages. It submitted its report in 1954 but there was no official attempt to implement its recommendations.

Pakistan's worst period in the history of the press began with the promulgation of martial law under Ayub Khan in 1958. Apprehensive of the powerful press and its growing contribution in generating a political consciousness in the masses, the military-bureaucracy establishment undertook a series of drastic steps to curtail it. Within a few days of the coup, the military regime arrested Hasan, Qasimi,[21] Faiz,[22] Mazhar Ali Khan[23] (editor of the *Pakistan Times* after Faiz) and other journalists. On 18 April 1959, the regime forcibly took over the PPL and the administration of its four papers under the Pakistan Security Act and appointed its own administrators and editors. The ministry of information headed by secretary Qudratullah Shahab, took over the administration of these papers, which began mud-slinging against their former owners and editors. Shahab, a seasoned bureaucrat and a close aide to various 'strong men' in the brief history of Pakistan, aimed at neutralising intellectual and popular resistance to Ayub Khan's dictatorship. He bought and bullied dissenting journalists and writers across the country. By striking a close collaboration with leading financiers like the Admajees, Saigols and others, he established a number of awards and organisations with which to shower obliging Pakistani journalists, poets and authors. He instituted the Pakistan Writers' Guild with the money from such sources to reward pro-regime intellectuals.[24] Its secretary, Jamil ud-Din Aali, was a known columnist and poet. Even Altaf Husain, 'the king-maker' and an early critic of the military take-over, was made to join Ayub's regime as a minister for industries and natural resources.[25]

Where the Ayub regime failed to coopt journalists and writers it used coercion and institutionalised corruption to 'tame' dissenters. A number of authoritarian laws were promulgated through special ordinances to curtail press freedom. Five years after taking over PPL, the National Press Trust (NPT) was established in the public sector in April 1964 to take control of the papers and to implement the national press policies being introduced by the ministry of information to suit the temperament and prerogatives of the Ayub regime. NPT is considered to be the brain-child of Khawaja Shahab ud-Din, Ayub's minister for information, and Altaf Gauhar, the federal secretary for information, who carried on Shahab's policies slightly more vehemently. Gauhar, a professional bureaucrat with literary qualities, rose to the highest pinnacle of power by winning the confidence of Ayub Khan who made him his information secretary. Gauhar engaged in 'building up' the field-marshal as a latter-day messiah for Pakistan. From Ayub's book, *Friends Not Masters*, to his speeches, award schemes to encourage pro-establishment intellectuals and the introduction of major ordinances curbing the residual freedom of the press, Gauhar has earned himself a controversial reputation in the history of Pakistan. Like Shahab, he refused to assume responsibility for curbing press freedom and the right of free expression in the country.[26] However, there is no denying the fact that the powerful establishment was responsible; in the words of a veteran journalist, 'Those were the days when Altaf Gauhar, in the office of the Central Information secretary, was the virtual "Editor-in-Chief" of 1, 597 dailies, weeklies, fortnightlies, monthlies and other periodicals, and the regional PID officials were the "Resident Editors" of the papers in their jurisdiction.'[27] Gauhar's Press Information Department (PID) not only dished out 'advices' but also tried to buy the loyalties of a number of media men and intellectuals:

> During the trial of Ayub's Information Secretary Altaf Gauhar in 1972, a disclosure was made that quite a few members of the Press succumbed to the corruptive influences of the dictatorial regimes of Ayub and Yahya. It was revealed that some members of the Fourth Estate were in the pay of various official agencies, doing assignments of purely political character, more often outside the ambit of the institutions they belonged to. Their role was part of the corrupt and unjust dispensation that had to be suffered all these years.[28]

However, along with Shahab and Gauhar, Brigadier F. D. Khan and Manzur Qadir were advising the general to restrict freedom of speech and political expression in the country. There were already 12 restrictive laws in force in addition to martial-law regulations coercive enough to inhibit resistance to the government. Ayub ignored the basic recommendations of the Press Commission of Pakistan (1954) which had found Pakistani journalists to be patriotic and introduced the Press and Publications Ordinance of 1960, an exhaustive document of 30 pages dealing with printing presses, newspapers, periodicals, books and other publications. Accordingly, the government asked for security deposits from the printing presses to be scrutinised by the sessions judges under whose jurisdiction the press lay. These judges took action on the publication of any 'objectionable material' and the appeals could be made only with a special bench of the High Court. The government was empowered to forfeit the deposit and prohibit the publication of any paper, magazine or book. In addition, all publishers were made to show that they had sufficient financial resources to carry on the publication of a newspaper or magazine. Editors were required to have sufficient professional education and a written nomination from the publisher(s). Any writing against the armed forces, police or any attempt to create hatred against the government, evasion of taxes or libel against any official would render the publication liable to a punitive action. Even the head of the princely states were given such rights of indemnity.

After lifting his martial law, Ayub introduced various ordinances in 1963 in both the wings of the country raising the amount of security deposit and adding more restrictions on editors and journalists. The 'blackest of the black law was promulgated to make the Press *conform* to recognised principles of journalism and patriotism, to encourage feelings of responsibility and not to place any reasonable fetters on the Press and finally to allow the Press to grow and help to maintain healthy journalism'.[29] Further amendments along with the existing laws made the entire ordinance cumbersome and restrictive. Various press organisations including the Pakistan Federal Union of Journalists (PFUJ) agitated against it but to no avail.

The ordinance continued to be used in subsequent years and the NPT carried on publishing its papers, which had become full-fledged organs of the state. Under the military regime of General Zia, additional martial-law regulations were issued 'protecting the ideology' of Pakistan – a powerful weapon which had been added by General Sher Ali Khan, Yahya Khan's information minister. From 1977 to 1985, Pakistan witnessed the most repressive measures against the press. NPT papers, state-owned news agencies like the Associated Press of Pakistan (APP), radio and television were used by the regime to defend and advocate its policies. The ministry of information, headed by General Mujibur Rahman, a close associate of Zia, almost surpassed the era of Shahab and Gauhar in building up the military regime. The intention was mainly meant to establish credentials for a non-representative regime lacking both mandate and legitimacy. A number of apologists were hired to air pro-regime views and, where temptations and rewards failed, imprisonment and flogging were ordered by the summary military courts. Intelligence agencies shadowed the journalists while the favourites were rewarded with property, positions and foreign visits. The situation was desperate:

> The hypocrisy of the shackled Press produced or promoted political parasites, sanctimonious humbug and self-advertising charlatans who dominated the scene for over three decades; its servility helped the powers-that-be to destroy democratic institutions and fortify authoritarian regimes. The bureaucratic grip is tightening with every passing day, without any accountability whatsoever. In these circumstances one sees no silver lining on a darkening horizon, and many senior respected newsmen honestly feel that unable to bring out their potential, they really led a wasted life.[30]

Politics of temptation and coercion had almost debilitated a vital institution of the civil society.[31]

With the establishment of the Junejo government in 1985, the disappearance of martial law was followed by winding down of the state of emergency. During the last ten years, the print media has mushroomed and, despite a long period of suffocation and oppression, has apparently rediscovered its potential as the journalists are engaged in investigative journalism. Benazir Bhutto's regime restored the freedom of the press to a great extent though her successor had his moments of confrontation on issues like the bankruptcy of the cooperative societies in Punjab in 1991–92, and the CIA-led crime wave in Sindh. Nawaz Sharif's bout with Maleeha Lodhi, the editor of the *Nation*, only exhibited professional solidarity among journalists across the country as he was compelled to withdraw his punitive action. Similarly, political and ethnic parties using coercion against investigative journalists found no favour among readers who have diversified and more open channels of information at their disposal.[32] Daily exposures of seedy operations by intelligence agencies, police torture, molestation of women and the underprivileged in society, ethnic criminalisation and publication of the lists and commentaries on loan defaulters and tax evaders helped the Fourth Estate to emerge as the most powerful instrument of accountability in the country. In the 1990s, the press in Pakistan reached society where parliamentarians and others had failed it, but not without a cost.[33] However, in the longer term more maturity, professional scrupulousness and integrity will be required as well as a determination by the state to ensure that a responsible relationship emerges in the larger interests of the society. The press will certainly remain a barometer of Pakistan's development as a vibrant, forward-looking society.

7 The Politics of Gender in Pakistan

A long-standing legacy of underdevelopment among South Asian Muslims, colonial and post-independence official preferences for a feudal, elitist socio-political structure as well as a retreat to the forces of conservatism have ensured that women in Pakistan remain the most ignored and isolated section of civil society. Since 1979, the increased emphasis on *chaadar* and *chardiwari* and the introduction of restrictive ordinances have increased the marginalisation of this half of the population; consolidated the patriarchal structure; weakened the general struggle for restoration of human rights; promoted the forces of obscurantism and chauvinism; and accelerated the fragmentation and dehumanisation of society at large. By abetting such tendencies, the martial-law regime has been largely responsible for exacerbating serious abuses against women. The identity crisis that permeated every aspect of national life during the previous decade weakened moral values and the brutalisation of women became almost routine. While the military regime sought legitimacy in religious pretensions, so-called Islamisation only multiplied women's ordeal. The replacement of legal traditions with injunctions like *huddood*, law of evidence, *qisas* (revenge) and *diyat* (blood money) together with the policy of prohibiting women's participation in jobs and sports, brought added strains to a fragile civil society. Much more effort and time will be required to escape the morass that has engulfed millions of citizens in a country which, according to its founders, was to be a forward-looking, non-dogmatic welfare society.

THEORETICAL INTRODUCTION

Before discussing gender politics in Pakistan, we will briefly consider the various inter-related theoretical and methodological premises characterising such studies. Most gender-related writings, especially on Muslim societies, until recently have been ahistorical, attempting to see the issues only in a narrow perspective.[1] They have usually interpreted women-related issues in the context of Islam, rather than dealing with the intricate relationship with the state *per se*. Valuable studies in the 1970s saw an inherent conjunction between the teachings and practices of Islam and the

139

predicament of Muslim women, portraying it as an entirely religion-based dilemma.[2] Societal themes and those in the religious arena inadvertently relegated the role of powerful state institutions into a complete 'nothing-ness'. Such analyses acknowledged an intensification and diversification of Muslim attitudes on gender issues with the advent of mercantilist, capi-talist economies underscoring the quest for identity.[3] It is only recently that feminism has begun to attract academic inquiry in the context of its role *vis-à-vis* the colonial and post-colonial state.[4]

Another school of thought representing Muslim apologists justifies the inherent sexual inequality as a divinely-ordained *fait accompli*. In South Asia, this has been the case since the late nineteenth century when a number of Muslims, confronted by the Western socio-political power, adopted a more introspective attitude and demanded the complete seclu-sion of women.[5] Especially since the early 1980s, Muslim feminists have been trying to give a forward-looking and liberal interpretation of the Quran and Hadith, suggesting that women can obtain their due rights within the parameters of Islam. Such views arise from a variety of causes including the dominance of Muslim cultures by a visible religious factor and the presence of powerful ecclesiastic groups, often enjoying official patronage, as in the case of Pakistan under General Zia or Iran under Ayatollah Khomeini. In addition, such views may be rooted in a general disenchantment with Western intellectual and cultural mores (Orientalism) where institutions such as family are perceived to be in decline. Muslim feminism is progressively culture-specific and reactive to being branded as 'Other'.[6] By contrast, smaller groups of Muslim feminists, as do certain Western authors, find Islam patriarchal and inherently non-receptive to women's rights.[7] Yet other groups of edu-cated Muslim women belonging to parties such as the Jama'at i-Islami (JI) or Muslim Brotherhood or individuals from amongst the Muslim expatriate communities in the West are equally disdainful of the idea of feminism in all its manifestations. To them, Islam has already bestowed upon women sufficient rights and it is only necessary to implement them in a comprehensive Islamic setting.

While reinterpreting Muslim women's experiences in an historical per-spective, a number of important facts emerge. First, Islam synthesised early 'Western' and 'Eastern' experiences; women's issues are therefore not so much Muslim specific as cross-cultural and intra-regional.[8] Unlike their successors, women enjoyed an equal or better status in some ancient societies but with urbanisation, growing demands for labour and increased population resulted in patriarchy, eventually relegating women to a 'thing'.[9]

While institutionalising female subordination in Mesopotamia as stipulated by Hammurabi (circa 1752 BC), the most dichotomic and derisive attitude towards women evolved in ancient Greece, where philosophers like Aristotle believed in their inherent physical and mental inferiority. Despite being compassionate, he found them 'more jealous, more quarrelsome ... more void of shame and self-respect, more false of speech, more deceptive' than men.[10] Women during the formative phase of Islam enjoyed wider and more informal interaction with fellow believers, as was the case with the wives of the Prophet. Later interpretations, which generally developed from shadowy circumstances, relegated them to a lower and subsequently derogatory position.[11]

In the case of Pakistan, there is an historical burden in the experience of Muslim women as the upper class *ashra'af* (usually of non-Indian origins) enjoyed a higher and exclusive status while the Muslim laity largely remained localised. The advent of Christian missionaries and the establishment of schools by them and by the government led to a dual Muslim response based on rejection, leading to introversion and acceptance. Rural and tribal societies, augmented by the colonial state structure moulded to provide intermediaries to the imperial edifices, persisted around the small 'island-like' communities of a weak, urban Muslim middle class. The nationalist struggle brought a long-sought respite to Muslim women from their relationship based on subservience,[12] but was soon overpowered by an elitist state seeking legitimacy in Islam, basing itself on the bureaucracy, military and landed aristocracy. The feudalisation of politics, especially under dictatorial regimes,[13] the aversion to land reforms and a static clergy resulted in the serious oppression of women. Women in Pakistan have a long way to go to eradicate injustices and prejudices from the state and from pressure groups. Indeed, the women's movement represents the most crucial contest between state and civil society.

THE GREAT SCHISM

It may not be Islam that is the cause of backwardness and the exploitation of women in Muslim societies, but historical, social, political and regional factors. The legacy has been consolidated by the lack of research on Islam based on *ijtihad* and *ijma* and by the establishment of obscurantist clergy[14] and stifling feudalism. Muslim introversion because of colonialism, unequal relations with a more industrialised West, the absence of intellectual and industrial revolutions in the Muslim world and post-colonial authoritarian state structures have all compounded the dilemmas facing Muslim societies.

Early campaigns in India for women's education, social and electoral reforms such as a universal franchise in India were led by men, largely because women were confined to a traditional role and lacked the educational and organisational qualifications. With the decline in Muslim power, especially after the failed revolt of 1857 when Muslims were the main losers in the colonial set-up,[15] two divergent schools of Muslim modernists and traditionalists emerged to redefine the destiny of the community.[16] While Sir Syed and his followers advocated modern education and rationalism, the traditionalists from amongst the Deobandi and Brelvi *ulama* urged a more introverted communitarian reorientation. This bipolar debate politicised[17] the Muslims to some extent, though it also created a reverberating schism in an already fragmented community. In his evidence before the Education Commission in 1882, Sir Syed explained that poverty was the primary cause of educational backwardness among the Muslim community. He believed that male education was a prerequisite if aristocratic Muslim families were to send their daughters to academic institutions.[18]

By the late nineteenth century some Muslim women had started attending schools initially established by Christian missionaries or by Muslim reform organisations such as the Anjuman-i Himayat-i Islam in Lahore. The Anjuman pioneered the social improvement of Muslims by opening five elementary schools in Lahore in 1885. By then, Muslim women in other British Indian provinces like the UP, Bombay and Madras had acquired an edge in education over their counterparts in the Punjab and adjoining Muslim-majority zones. The traditionalist *ulama* and *mashaikh* seriously questioned the acquisition of modern education by women and in some cases even by Muslim men and urged the seclusion of women by emphasising *purdah* and *chardiwari*. To them, women's education symbolised a complete emancipation leading to the eventual break-up of the strong institution of the family. On his return from the UK in 1892, Sir Mohammad Shafi of Lahore became involved in improving the status of women. He advocated abolition of the dowry and strove for the recognition of women's right to inherit property, which was anathema to the Punjabi feudal classes. His efforts led to the establishment of the Anjuman-i Khawateen-i Islam in 1908 in Lahore to work in education, social reform and the rights of women in the light of Islamic teachings. As early as 1903, Muslim women activists who were engaged in a reform movement, faced verbal abuse from traditionalists.[19]

With the beginning of the twentieth century, women's movements in India gained momentum and more serious organisational and educational efforts were launched from various platforms.[20] An Urdu magazine,

Khatoon, was soon joined by a newspaper, *Haqqooq-i-Naswan*, which was edited by a husband-and-wife team promoting the cause of women's education. Separate schools for girls and more newspapers devoted to women's issues began appearing in the second decade of the twentieth century, although the ratio of educated women remained minimal. These women came from urban upper- and middle-class families and very few of them subsequently opted for a public career. In 1915, the first-ever Muslim Ladies' Conference took place, attended by wives and relatives of leading Muslim professionals. In 1917, the Anjuman-i Khawateen-i Islam passed a resolution against polygamy which 'caused a minor furore in Lahore'.[21]

A delegation of women led by Sarojini Naidu waited on Lord Montagu, the Secretary of State for India, during his visit to the sub-continent in 1917 and demanded improved health and education facilities and equal franchise for women. In the same year the Women's Indian Association was established. In 1918, both the All-India Muslim League (AIML) and the Indian National Congress (INC), passed resolutions in their separate sessions endorsing the demand for women's franchise. Eventually, the government left the matter to individual provinces and Madras granted women the right to vote in 1921. By 1925, all other provinces except Bihar and Orissa had granted similar rights to women. But this was still short of universal votes due to the property qualifications for both male and female voters. In 1932, the AIML supported women's demands for equality regardless of caste, religion, creed and sex. Women activists, enthused by the nationalist movement in India and feminist movements in the West, campaigned for social legislation on issues like child marriage, right to property, outlawing dowry, right to divorce and widows' marriages.[22] The Nawab of Bhopal was one of the few Muslim women who advocated the abolition of *purdah* and emphasised the need to acquire education in the larger interests of the family and community. Contemporary Muslim women activists in politics included Bi Ama – the mother of the Ali Brothers – and Jahan Ara Shahnawaz from Lahore, the latter crusading against *purdah* and taboos on female education.[23]

Muslim leaders like Iqbal[24] and Jinnah, while striving for Muslim betterment in India, spearheaded the case for female education and equal opportunities. Jinnah, in an address at the Muslim University, Aligarh, in 1944, spoke against the perpetuation of women's seclusion: 'It is a crime against humanity that our women are shut up within the four walls of the houses as prisoners. There is no sanction anywhere for the deplorable conditions in which our women have to live. You should take your women along with you as comrades in every sphere of life.'[25] Jinnah took his sister, Fatima Jinnah, with him on his visits and she worked as a faithful and seasoned companion for her brother. As we have seen earlier, she was also a candidate in the presidential election against General Ayub Khan in 1965.

THE BEGINNING OF A NEW ERA

The movement for Pakistan was a success for the millions of Indian Muslim nationalists who built up an articulate programme to steer the Muslims out of their morass.[26] While *ulama* like Hussain Ahmad Madani, Abul Kalam Azad and Syed Maudoodi refuted Pakistani nationalism, the modernists struggled for the emergence of the largest Muslim state in the world. However, their debate on the future programme increased the politicisation of Muslim women and a number of them from urban areas became actively involved. In 1941, the Muslim Girls' Student Federation was formed to muster support for a separate Muslim homeland. The federation generated interest among Muslim families in sending their daughters to schools and colleges and added an influential women's sub-committee to the AIML. In 1943, during the AIML's annual session in Karachi, a number of woman delegates participated in the formation of the Women's National Guard, whose white and green uniform was later adopted by the Pakistan Girl Guides. 'In collecting funds, selling badges and propagating the idea of Pakistan, all the women and girls involved, by appearing in public and interacting with strangers, were violating the unwritten but centuries old rule of *purdah* and confinement for Muslim women.'[27] During the elections of 1946, Muslim women activists campaigned for the AIML and when, despite its majority in the legislature, it was not allowed to form the provincial government, women participated in a widespread strike demanding the dissolution of the Khizr cabinet of the Unionist Party. Activists like Jahan Ara Shahnawaz, Salma Tassaduque Hussain and a number of protesters were put behind bars for violating Section 144. Demonstrations for their acquittal took place both inside and outside Lahore Jail and observers noted with surprise the new roles of a politicised community.

Soon after independence[28] a number of women's organisations aimed at improving of the community at large were founded, in particular the All-Pakistan Women's Association (APWA). The APWA was founded by Begum Raana Liaquat Ali Khan on 22 February 1949, at Karachi. Begun as a voluntary, non-political organisation, APWA was open to all Pakistani women over 16, irrespective of religious or economic background and was committed to the general welfare of women, increased educational and socio-cultural consciousness among them and better job opportunities for them. To this day its membership is mainly from the urban middle and upper classes, and rural women are largely unrepresented. Despite early criticism from the religious elite, the APWA has remained a non-political organisation and has, over the years, managed to open a number of schools, colleges, special industrial homes and meena bazaars in addition to lobbying for socio-legal reforms to improve women's conditions. In 1953, it urged the reservation of ten special women's seats in the national and provincial assemblies. In 1955 the APWA launched a campaign against the second marriage of the prime minister, Mohammad Ali Bogra. Given its influence on the country's ruling elite, it was instrumental in establishing the Family Laws Commission which eventually prepared a draft for the Family Laws Ordinance of 1961. Ayub Khan's apparently liberal attitude to women's issues helped promulgate many of the recommendations of the Family Laws Commission (also known as the Justice Rashid Commission).

The Family Laws Ordinance of 1961 discouraged polygamy by making second marriage conditional upon the consent of the first wife and the decision of a locally-constituted arbitrary council. Instead of a quick verbal divorce, the ordinance stipulated prior written notification by the husband through the local council. The divorce would not materialise for three months, which was originally intended as a 'cooling off' period for a possible reconciliation. All marriages were to be registered with proper provisions on a prescribed *nikah nama*, such as the woman's right to divorce her husband through a notification routed through the local council; determination of woman's right to a specific amount of dowry and, in the case of disputes, arbitration through the local bodies. The ordinance raised the marriageable age of girls to 16 from 14 and of boys from 18 to 21. Despite its weaknesses, it was a milestone in safeguarding women's position in marital relationships and was widely opposed by religious groups, who felt that a major domain of their influence had been taken away from them. Maulana Maudoodi considered the right to second marriage irrevocable on the basis of Islamic tradition, for it might otherwise lead to extra-marital relations. However, the military regime did not budge.

Where the regime under Ayub Khan introduced legislation favourable to women, it denied Pakistan its first woman head of state. Fatima Jinnah's near-victory was outmanoeuvred into defeat through the use of official machinery and manipulation of the limited electoral college. During the 1970s, a number of women activists participated in national and local politics, mostly from the platform of the PPP. The party organised its national, provincial, divisional and local women's wings which operated as important pressure groups. In fact, the 1970s were a period of increased women's mobilisation in universities, mohallas and factories, resulting in a greater demand for more legislation. In 1976, Bhutto was under such pressure and established a 13-member Women's Rights Committee headed by the attorney-general, Yahya Bakhtiar. The Committee had been long demanded by women activists in order to recommend 'law reforms with a view to improve the social, legal and economic conditions of the women of Pakistan and to provide for speedier legal remedies for obtaining relief in matters like maintenance, custody of children'.[29] It submitted its report in July 1976 along with a set of recommendations which were never made public. While the APWA and other organisations largely received its members from the upper classes, women's organisations in the cities like the Women's Front, Shirkat Gah and Aurat presented a new generation of urban, middle-class professional women. It was Shirkat Gah of the 1970s that reemerged as the Women's Action Forum (WAF) of the 1980s and 1990s. These groups spoke for the largest underprivileged section in the Pakistani population, stood against human-rights violations and raised their voice against legal, social and physical discrimination on the basis of gender. They organised rallies, published magazines, sponsored seminars and tried to establish links with international human-rights organisations. They attempted to raise consciousness of the plight of women in general though they themselves were mainly from urban, literate classes with the vast outlying rural and tribal areas staying unrepresented. Here feudalism and religious traditionalism continue to take their toll from women subjected to domestic and field labour of 14 to 16 hours per day with an horrendous rate of illiteracy and serious sociopsychological problems. Pakistani women, both rural and urban, suffer from the unlimited expectations of an extra feminine role – *chiragh i-khana* (light of the house) – and from being an unacknowledged breadwinner. Attitudes towards women are certainly 'blurred and confusing', more often touching on suspicion and hostility.[30]

ZIA'S ISLAMISATION

Zia's military regime coopted elements from the *ulama* and *mashaikh* in the search for legitimacy. With the exception of the JI, which operated as the 'B' team for martial law, other religio-political parties and Shia groups felt disenchanted with his pronouncements for enforcing Sharia law –

Nizam-i Mustafa – in the country. Nevertheless, there was no lack of willing henchmen and with the strong coercive power of the state Zia began to undo a few of the hard-earned achievements of the civil society. Women's rights and other vital national institutions such as the Constitution, political parties, electoral politics, the judiciary, the media and education all suffered. The state became partisan and rather than playing an integrative role it encouraged fissiparous and segmentary forces. In an atmosphere of corruption and coercion, civil rights were a natural casualty and the Islamisation campaign, whose aims were self-preservation and the appeasement of schismatic forces, came to epitomise xenophobia. The weakest elements of society paid the highest cost.

Debates on topics such as whether women should be able to drive a car, attend co-educational institutions or simply go shopping became major issues for the government and its apologists. Plans for a separate women's university, compulsory wearing of the *chaadar*, women's exclusion from sports and advertising, or punishments for sharing a car ride with one's own husband without a marriage certificate were the new barometers of Islamisation. It was officially given out 'that the rights, role and status of women hitherto accepted were not Islamic and that the status, role and rights of women differ from those of men'.[31]

In 1979, in the name of Nizam i-Mustafa, the military regime began to introduce a number of ordinances dealing directly with women's domain. The first in the series is known as the Huddood Ordinance which deals with rape, adultery, fornication, prostitution, false testimony and alcohol consumption, suggesting punishments (*hadd/tazir*) for all these crimes. *Zina* (adultery) was defined as wilful sexual intercourse between a man and a woman 'without being validly married to each other', while *zina-bil-jabr* meant rape and the punishment would entail death for married persons and 100 lashes for unmarried persons. However, to prove the crime, the ordinance required the presence of four Muslim adults of good character (*saleh*) who actually witnessed the intercourse, or a voluntary confession before a court. In the case of women or non-Muslim witnesses, the *hadd* would not be exercised, but the crime could be punishable by *tazir*, which is lesser than *hadd*. The law failed to make any distinction between rape and adultery and the sufferers have of course been women – as in the case of Safia Bibi, a blind maid-servant who became pregnant following multiple rape. She was given a punishment of 15 lashes for *zina-bil-jabr*, while the two criminals involved – father and son – were acquitted, the father because of lack of evidence and the son from the benefit of doubt. Moreover, the ordinance itself is discriminatory as it declares illegitimate birth as evidence of woman's guilt (*zina* not rape) without incriminating the male perpetrator.[32] In a subsequent hearing, the Federal Shariat Court did differentiate between adultery and rape and dismissed Safia Bibi's sentence. Lal Mai from Liaquatpur in Bahawalpur district was the first woman to be publicly whipped on 30 September 1983, on charges of adultery. About 8000 men watched her receive 15 lashes. Another woman in Swat was sentenced to receive 80 lashes while the men involved in both the cases were acquitted.

Women's groups and other civic forums campaigned against the ordinances for being anti-women laws and urged the government to be a signatory of the United Nations Convention on the Elimination of Discrimination against Women. In the tradition of other proposed ordinances governing *qisas* and *diyat*, in 1982 the Council of Islamic Ideology recommended the promulgation of the Law of Evidence (*Qanoon-i Shahadat*), stipulating that in *huddood* cases two male or four female witnesses would be needed to prove a crime. Seeking guidance from the Federal Shariat Court, the government also went ahead with the establishment of *qazi* courts to deal with cases according to Islamic law. The relevant ordinance provided that women could be appointed as *qazis* – which deeply infuriated certain groups in the country. Following litigation, however, the Federal Shariat Court dismissed such objections. During the hearings, the candidacy of Fatima Jinnah by the contemporary *ulama* was presented as a supportive argument by the state in defending the ordinance. Curiously, the *qazi* courts were not empowered to overrule the decisions of the military courts.

Another ordinance, dealing with crimes committed against women, was promulgated on 3 June 1984, after a long campaign by women in Southern Punjab over an incident. In Nawabpur, a carpenter suspected of having an affair with the daughter of a landlord was hacked to death by her father and some accomplices. The women relatives of the deceased were molested, undressed and paraded naked down the street. It was feudal vengeance against the peasantry at its worst. The press and human-rights organisations took up the issue as a typical case of violence against women and demonstrations began all over the country. Just a week after the beginning of the campaign, the Crimes Ordinance was passed stipulating the death penalty or life imprisonment for 'assaulting or using criminal force against a woman, to strip her naked and in that condition expose her to the public'. It was widely welcomed as a great achievement by women's groups and their supporters, though they demanded an overall amelioration of women's status. Moreover, they felt that the ordinance was silent on similar crimes against women inside their homes.

Zia established a commission in 1983 to submit proposals on the form of a proper government arguing that democracy is not an *Islamic* form of government. The commission, headed by Maulana Zafar Ahmad Ansari, submitted its report on 4 August 1983, recommending non-party elections and more powers for the head of state who, in its view, must always be a male. Unlike in the case of men, it raised the minimum age limit for women members of the Shoora to 50. Moreover, it recommended that women candidates must acquire written consent from their husbands before seeking membership of the Shoora. Such recommendations infuriated women as they were premised on a denial of the basic legal and constitutional equality of women. Nine days later, Zia made a speech which incorporated many of these recommendations in his political framework. A year later, he held the referendum making his candidacy for presidency until 1990 mandatory for Islamisation. People did not take it seriously and despite official efforts no more than 10 per cent of the voters turned out to cast their 'yes' for Zia.[33]

Soon after the promulgation of the new ordinances, the courts started giving out judgements on such cases which included for example death by stoning or lashes. These measures raised fears that the Family Ordinance of 1961 was going to be replaced. It also emboldened many religious scholars, with Dr Israr Ahmed heading the list of hardliners. A former member of the JI, Israr Ahmed, had opposed its support for Fatima Jinnah's candidacy in 1965. He was picked up by Zia as a member of the Council of Islamic Ideology and for membership of the hand-picked Majlis i-Shoora. In his regular television appearances, Israr Ahmed forbade women to be present during the recording of his speeches. In an interview with a newspaper, he observed that in an ideal Islamic state all working women should be retired and not be allowed to leave their homes except for emergencies. The APWA, the WAF and a number of other women including Yasmeen Abbasi, the wife of the Governor of Sindh, demonstrated against Israr Ahmed from every possible forum until his weekly programme was taken off the air. Israr had infuriated Shias and Sunnis alike by extending an open invitation to his daughter's marriage on the 8th of Muharram, the month of Muslim mourning. Under public denunciation, he resigned from the Majlis in May 1982, dismissing widespread criticism of his extremist views. The next month, he invited Pakistani Muslims to offer him allegiance (*bait*) to make Pakistan an Islamic society. Thus, Zia's Islamisation encouraged extremists and psychopaths to impose their views on society and created an atmosphere of siege at a time when the country needed to resolve other pressing problems. It added to an existing ambiguity on two major questions that have dogged Muslim societies such as Pakistan: namely, which Islam and whose Islam?

PAKISTAN COMMISSION ON THE STATUS OF WOMEN, 1983

In the history of Pakistan very few efforts have been made to investigate the general malaise afflicting the nation's female population. The report of the Women's Rights Committee instituted by Z. A. Bhutto under the leadership of Yahya Bakhtiar in 1976 never saw the light of day, though women activists persisted with their demand for the establishment of a full-fledged, high-powered investigatory commission empowered to make proper recommendations. It was Zia ul-Haq who finally appointed such a commission, preceded by the establishment of a Women's Division in 1979 under his own supervision. While addressing the National Conference of Muslim Women in October 1980, Zia had made a promise to this effect and the Pakistan Commission on the Status of Women formally came into being on 8 March 1983, with Begum Zari Sarfaraz as its chairperson.[34] It began work in 1984 and was mandated to complete its findings within a year. The Commission aimed at ascertaining the rights and responsibilities of women; safeguarding their rights; advising the government on measures to provide health, education and employment; identifying problems such as social evils, poverty and ignorance; and suggesting ways to integrate women of minority communities in the national life. It consisted of 13 women of socio-academic standing from different regions along with three male professionals representing the law, education and science. Five federal secretaries were also coopted to the commission as ex-officio members. Apart from touring the country, its work included interviews, participant observation, sifting of official and research reports on various women-related issues. Its final report, submitted in 1985, includes a note of dissent by one of its members,[35] and is duly supported by relevant official data. A pioneer of its type, it makes exhaustive and authentic reading on the dilemmas of Pakistani women. It deals with issues such as the status of women in Islam, women and development, demographic statistics, socio-cultural status in reference to various ceremonies and customs, female employment, women's NGOs, health, educational, legal, religious and political status, ratios in jobs. It recommends the establishment of a permanent women's commission as a watch-dog, as well as numerous other tangible measures.

The report begins with an unequivocal acceptance of the fact that women in Pakistan have received a raw deal over the years, because of the specific nature of Pakistani society and the state. Acknowledging the Islamic contribution to the elevation of womanhood at the very outset, it recognises the impact of global movements against colonialism, feudalism and 'other dark forces of exploitation and oppression'. It attacks the contemporary socio-economic scenario which subjects both rural and urban women to continued exploitation:

> The prevailing milieu being still feudal and anachronistic, illiteracy, ill-health, poverty and an iniquitous social dispensation continue to cause deterioration of the condition of deprived and vulnerable sectors, particularly women in the rural areas and the urban slums. Seclusion, segregation and confinement which have limited women's educational and economic opportunities, coupled with early marriages and large families continue to preclude the mass of women from all avenues of advancement.[36]

The report acknowledges Islam's contribution in bringing about equality, justice and harmony between the genders and recognises that the political and military decline of Muslims made women into victims of oppression.[37] While preserving Islamic mores, it was strongly felt that a policy geared towards modernisation (not westernisation) was necessary to help women get rid of the inequities and oppressive socio-political systems that had evolved during the colonial period. Modernisation would cultivate a rational and scientific approach among women after providing them with incentives for the acquisition of knowledge, especially in the realms of science and technology. The authors of the report felt that the affirmation of democracy by women and society at large, accompanied by the preservation of human rights and the dignity of all human beings – the necessary components of the modernisation processes – would result in cultural and social progress. In addition, modernisation would bring about a vigorous and just economic order suited to the entire society. However, this all-encompassing process would require integrated efforts not simply by women but at all official and societal levels. For instance, the so-called green revolution preceded by the colonial-feudal system left one-third of the rural population landless and resourceless, unable even to make a basic living. Rural women are excluded from mainstream development activities. Literacy rates, average life expectancy, access to health, sanitation and education facilities in rural and tribal areas, especially among female members of the population, are starkly low. The report recorded that 'the average rural woman of Pakistan is born in near slavery, leads a life of drudgery and dies invariably in oblivion'.[38]

Problems of Rural/Tribal Women

To a great extent, long-held misperceptions about women, their complete subordination within the roles defined by men over the centuries, together with a lack of educational and economic opportunities have relegated them to a lower status. These realities are more vivid in the case of rural women, as was noted:

> As daughters, sisters, wives and often even as mothers, they have no real voice in the family set up and their usefulness depends largely on how efficiently they serve the family in the humblest possible manner. As a consequence of the low status conferred on them within the family unit, rural women tend to have an extremely low status self image. They believe themselves to have been born inferior, they curse themselves for being deficient and they glorify the males in their lives. Their fathers are often tyrants, their brothers selfish, their husbands uncaring in their attitude towards their women, and yet they dwell in a state of resignation, accepting the myth of male superiority as an important part of their perceptions. It is only as mothers of sons that they experience some fulfilment and the male child is often indulged, to the extent that he grows up with assumptions of his own superiority and obliterates the contribution of women in his life. So the cycle perpetuates itself and becomes a vicious circle of the extreme exploitation of the mental, emotional and physical energies of the rural women by the men of their families and communities.[39]

Rural women were found to be the most hard-pressed in the population. Despite major contributions by them in the rural agrarian economy through long working hours in the fields and demanding household chores varying from food preparation to sewing, matting, quilting and childcare, they are subjected to enormous handicaps. In addition, the following major problems were detected by the commission to have a direct bearing on the lives of women:

1. The sale of girls especially in tribal areas in flagrant violation of the penal code is justified on the basis of *rawaj* (traditions). Numerous young girls are sold/purchased as commodities and subjected to sub-human treatment for their entire life. The marriages of girls frequently take place against their willingness to consummate some other exchange marriage in the family. The age or marital and moral stature of the suitor is never questioned and girls end up in a sort of social imprisonment. Very few escape the enslavement by in-laws and are sheltered in *Darul Aman* (shelters for battered women) only after they have escaped molestation by police or other social miscreants.

2. Denial of inheritance to women in rural, agrarian families is a well-known practice despite Islamic injunctions against it. In certain feudal families of Sindh without a male heir, girls are not allowed to marry so that the ancestral lands will not be transferred to some other family. It is reported that several syed feudal families have arranged marriages of their daughters to the Quran, so keeping them single for fear of losing lands.

3. The oppressive feudal system in rural Sindh, the tribal belt, Balochistan and Southwestern Punjab denies basic human rights to women, with peasant women (*haris*) being the worst sufferers. Many of these women are subjected to multiple crimes of abduction, rape and outright murder by landlords who, in most cases, are not apprehended by collaborative law-enforcment agencies.

4. Girls are pawned as guarantees to settle murder disputes with enemies and during this period they are not allowed to visit their parents.

5. Bride price (*walwar*) is a usual practice among the nomadic tribes in Balochistan and Sindh where the age and physical features of the girl help determine her price.

6. Physical abuse like the cutting of women's noses in areas like Diamer were investigated by the commission. In Baltistan women are sometimes used in place of bullocks. They are even refused medical treatment by their usually uneducated male relatives.

7. Prostitution, despite legal and Islamic prohibitions, does exist in some areas.

8. Marriage of girls abroad through an arranged system is becoming problematic, for example in the case of many British-Pakistani girls who find husbands averse to their expectations and choice. Similarly, Pakistani males settled abroad, despite the apparent attraction of a better material life and immigration, marry Pakistani girls through an arranged system and their inability to develop compatibility makes the women's lives miserable. In both cases the results are disastrous, especially for the girls.

9. Woman abuse, homicide, child marriage and polygamy were widely recorded, especially among uneducated families.

10. Women as bonded labour or hostages are the usual sufferers from incidents of violence. Mostly belonging to *kameen* (village professionals) families, such women are subjected to feudal practices carried on with impunity.

11. Drug addiction was reportedly becoming a major problem among both rural and urban battered women.

12. Old, divorced and widowed women have rough deals like the single working women in cities who, in many cases, reported sexual harassment

by their male superiors. Social intolerance to such women is instrumental in sustaining derogatory attitudes.

13. Female employment is still taboo for most men in Pakistan and in the name of *izzat* (honour) women, both educated and uneducated, are precluded from becoming paid workers. According to the prevalent misperceptions, a working woman

> brings disrepute to her husband because he is thought to be incapable of controlling her and too poor to provide for her. A working woman carries the stigma of poverty and it is generally believed that women work only out of economic necessity. Therefore, men who are well-off see it as a part of their 'honour' to keep their women economically inactive. In villages, the richer farmers tend to have their women observe purdah as a sign of affluence. A daughter in the family is seen as a *bojh*, an economic burden. There is hardly any concept of considering the female infant as a future supporter of the family.[40]

14. Extravagant marriage ceremonies involving lighting, meals, dowry, *salami*, *baraat*, fireworks, *mujra* and currency garlands are the norm in Pakistani society and examples of unnecessary wastage of time, money and energy with serious repercussions for the families and couples themselves. Numerous unnecessary and irrational customs are carried on in the name of *rawaj* and *izzat* even by educated urban families.

15. Violence against women in rural/tribal and urban areas was found to be quite common and unchecked. Remedies such as basic education, awareness of women's rights through the media, strengthening of legal strictures, support for destitute and dependent women by the state, institutionalised help from *zakat* and even training in self-defence were some of the recommendations made by the commission.

Women and the Development Sector

The commission took a serious view of the low rate of female literacy, scarce medical facilities and insufficient number of trained women doctors and nurses. In addition, there were two million children in the mid-1980s in Pakistan with severe disabilities like blindness, deafness or physical and mental disorders, engaging the same number of women to look after them on their own. The state does not provide any help for these two million mothers of handicapped children. Similarly, out of the total 4140 seats in the medical colleges, there were only 721 or 17 per cent reserved seats for women – resulting in one female doctor for more than 40 000 women in the country compared to the international standards of one female doctor per 1000 women. With an astounding increase in population, it was feared that the ratio would become gradually more disproportionate. The government was urged to train more women doctors in surgery since most women still prefer to consult women surgeons. Proper professional and monetary incentives and training facilities for attracting more nurses were strongly recommended in the report. Statistics were provided to show that Pakistan, compared with a number of other developing countries, lagged behind in literacy. The lack of incentives both for the teachers and the taught, especially with insufficient facilities and traditional biases against female education, were found to be taking their toll.

> In summer the children have the choice either to face suffocation or move outside in bright hot sun. During winter they shiver with cold on the damp floor. There are no toilet facilities and no boundary walls. It has been reported that out of about 30 000 primary schools in Punjab, 18 000 have no building. It has also been brought to the notice of the Commission that a large number of primary schools exist only on paper, yet the salaries of teachers of these 'Ghost' schools are drawn regularly.[41]

After a thorough investigation, the commission rejected the concept of a separate federal women's university as unnecessary; rather than developing competitive talents among women it would only intensify their segregation. In addition, being 'a conglomeration of colleges dispersed all over the nation, [it] would suffer from all the ill of a remote control. The usual benefits of a university – good laboratories, a well-stocked library, superior researchers and teachers and vigorous cultural life and intellectual interaction would all be totally lacking.'[42]

The report considered the low proportion of working women in private and public sectors, largely arising from negative attitudes. The largest number were school teachers with 31.9 per cent in primary schools, 30.7 per cent in middle schools, and 29.8 per cent in high schools while 35.9 per cent of intermediate college teachers and 38.2 per cent in degree colleges were women. In medicine, the media, administration, business or other high executive positions men outnumber women. In the mid-1980s there were 21 women in the foreign service compared to 379 male officers, and their postings abroad needed presidential approval. There were no women in official cadres in the police service, though the increasing number of women in areas like the law, banking, research institutes, business schools, airlines, auditing firms and clerical areas were duly noticed. Despite a noticeable number of female telephone operators, the state-owned telephone and typewriter industries (TIP) did not have a single female worker in its labour force of 2000.

Women and Politics

Endorsing efforts by Muslim modernists and nationalists during the colonial era, the commission acknowledged women's contributions in the making of Pakistan but was disturbed by the erosion of their political participation in national and local affairs. Tracing the political and constitutional history of the country, the report took serious note of the opposition to Fatima Jinnah in her presidential campaign. It appreciated the Constitution of 1973 in according better status to women as, through its Article 25, it outlawed any discrimination on the basis of gender. Given all the odds, women's representation in the legislature had to be protected through special reserved seats until there were women candidates to be elected on their own. The report observed candidly that 'Pakistan is the only country in the world where seats have to be reserved for women as otherwise they cannot hope to be represented in the assemblies. Faced with blind prejudice and their dependent status – economically, socially and culturally, they remain politically depressed.'[43] It was felt that women councillors in local bodies could be catalysts of change at the grassroots level. It was urged that all barriers to greater women's participation in national life be removed so that they could be eligible to hold any public office including the highest in the land. Within the category of innovative recommendations, the report urged the political parties to seek maximum enrolment of female membership. 'A political party which does not have at least 20 per cent women membership should not be allowed to contest elections.'[44]

Women's Religious and Legal Status

The commission felt that without a proper appraisal of Islam, distorted notions will continue to suppress women in the name of religion, relegating them to the status of second-class citizens. This has led to legal and social discrimination besides stereotypical attitudes towards women: 'Despite possessing qualities of intelligence, honesty, and hard work, equal to that of man, her integrity and credibility has been challenged by undermining inherent potentials by many laws which have rudely trespassed the constitutional guarantees.' True to Islamic teachings, family must remain significant but not by undermining women's rights. In the words of the report:

> Islam treats a woman as a fitting companion to man and man as a fitting companion of woman. Both are assigned physical, emotional and

spiritual characteristics which enable them to perform all those human obligations without which humanity could not prosper. There are however, fields of common endeavour where points of distinction are available to both. There being no absolute identity in the functions for man and woman absolute comparisons are not possible. If a man on account of his providing the economic needs of the family and protection, is given a position of preference, the same man is asked to seek salvation at the feet of his mother because of what he owes to her.[45]

The commission rejected the general notion of Islam being against family planning, quoting from Quranic verses and Islamic jurisprudence. Such views during the period of General Zia were revolutionary, but the commission did not compromise its integrity. It also provided arguments against child marriage and tried to present a more rational view on polygamy, divorce, *khulla* (a woman's right to seek separation), alimony and remarriage of divorcees and widows. Rather than establishing more *qazi* courts, it was recommended that additional family courts be established and that they be headed by competent judges.

The lack of a clear mandate and specialized training for the performance of their duties as family judges, results in very uneven administration of Law in this field. Decisions change from judge to judge on account of personal predilection and subjective view of the law. The problems are aggravated when the judge consults the medieval anti-feminine interpretations of the law which obscure from his view the pristine teachings of Islam.[46]

The commission laid greater emphasis on legislation to contain the demands for huge dowries resulting in the break-up of numerous marriages or providing simple excuses for coercion by in-laws.

A significant section in the report dealt with the vital ordinances – 'controversial laws' – such as *diyat*, law of evidence and Huddood ordinance. The commission urged that women must be treated as the equals of men and quoted extensively from Islamic literature on the subject to show that, despite various interpretational differences by jurists, Islam remains a just order. While suggesting a new look at the law of evidence equating two women witnesses to a male witness, the commission argued:

There are situations in life where in the nature of things only female testimony would be available, to say that it should be discarded because of the sex of the witness is to make an untenable claim. If four male witnesses claim that they saw a person being killed with hatchets and a female doctor demonstrates that the injuries sustained by the victims were by bullets, should a judge reject her testimony because she is woman! Unfortunately the new Law of Evidence which claims at having been made to reflect Islamic injunctions, succeeds only in over-stepping the Quranic injunctions and passing on the problems it creates to the courts.

Further on, while commenting on the Huddood ordinance, the commission stated that

some parts thereof, particularly those excluding the testimony of women, are contrary to the intendment (*sic*) of Islamic Sharia, as they: (a) do not reflect divine guidance as given in the Holy Quran, and (b) reflect a derogatory view developed during later days under the influence of non-Islamic, socially oppressive alien cultures of con-quered lands. These laws also neglect to take note of modern day intel-lectual and social development of women and impinge on basic human rights enjoyed by women in the contemporary world.

Similarly, the requirement of four Muslim male witnesses to prove a *zina* or *zina-bil-jabr* liable to *hadd* was considered 'an unwarranted addition to the Quranic injunctions in the field'. The commission believed that since the Quranic injunctions usually address the male unless clearly specified they apply equally to both men and women. 'It is no principle of the Islamic law that an act of shamelessness is so, only if committed in pres-ence of the males.'[47] As mentioned earlier, while referring to international conventions on human rights or similar covenants on crimes against women, the commission recommended the establishment of a Permanent Commission on the Status of Women, as a statutory body empowered to recommend legislation for the eradication of socio-legal inequalities and to provide recommendations on the furtherance of education and other essential amenities to women at large. Thus, the report, in a cumulative way, left no area of women's position and rights in Pakistan untouched and by doing so successfully exposed a number of cultural, social, reli-gious and legal biases against women that prevailed due to the feudalist character of Muslim societies, the static nature of Muslim scholarship and a state system reluctant to undertake bold initiatives in this direction.

ZIA'S ISLAMISATION: INTERPRETATIONS

Islamisation under Zia was not without controversy. On the doctrinal front, for example, the Shias felt uneasy with a number of prerogatives and demanded enforcement of *Fiqah-i Jaafria.* The government had to yield to pressure on issues like *zakat* and *ushr*, which was interpreted by Sunni lobbies as a capitulation to the Shia minority, thus unleashing the forces of sectarianism. Even among Sunni *ulama* the Deobandi/Brelvi differences became more prominent. Zia had initially banked on Deobandis (excluding the Jamiat i-Ulema i-Islam) and the JI, but quickly turned to pacifying Brelvis as well. He coopted the *mashaikh* and a number of *ulama* from the Jamiat i-Ulema i-Pakistan so as to create a manageable equilibrium in his second vital 'constituency' after the army. Some individuals from the religio-political parties felt that Zia was not doing enough in terms of Islamisation while others felt that his very presence deterred the secularists, so they tolerated him. The civilian and khaki bureaucracy maintained a strong liberal posture, but compromised with Zia for their own interests. The regime kept the press, the judiciary and other civic groups under tight control, allowing officials a free hand to gain further influence and affluence. In addition, Zia had been able to neutralise the threat from the *maulvis* to his personal advantage and to the larger interests of the state structure. Liberal technocrats like Mahbubul Haq defended the policies and claimed that they had increased women's participation in educational and socio-economic institutions, and that the government was not turning the clock backward.[48]

Some foreign observers felt that Zia's Islamisation policy was intended to appease traditionalists like the JI, preserve the specific (feudal) economy, or that it lacked any appreciation of women's perspective on the issues.[49] Several apologists for Zia felt that he was finally leading Pakistanis towards a meaningful future by combining religion and politics in his own specific manner.[50] Yet others opined that Zia was going along with the tide of Islamic revivalism that was influencing many contemporary Muslim societies.[51] However, Zia took these interpretations seriously and carried pretensions of being the (sole) representative of 950 million Muslims across the world. Ironically, the contemporary pretenders for Islamic revival in Pakistan, Sudan or Libya happened to be military dictators while their other Muslim-Arab counterparts were simply dynastic, autocratic monarchs. Islam was being used the loudest by the most authoritarian regimes in the Muslim world.

Civic groups in Pakistan, although not querying the basic credentials of Islam in the establishment of a moral society, felt critical of the intermixing of religion and state at the expense of a viable, accountable, consensus-based democratic order. They believed that the military regime had widened its base and constituencies by damaging the civil society so vital for national survival, and that using religion in a political and intellectual vacuum would entail further dissension. Without any efforts for larger *ijtihad* or *ijma*, or in the absence of unison on a single, commonly agreed definition of a *Muslim*, state-sponsored religious programmes lacked credibility and smacked of opportunism; without a debate and dispassionate study of these intricate issues in the changed circumstances, the political expediency was apparent. Already, according to such views, there were clear divergences on the comprehension and perception of Islamic injunctions, embodying diversified sectional interests, and any rush to a uniform policy would bring adverse results.

Such intellectuals considered that the early revolutionary spirit of Islam had been compromised with feudalism during the medieval period. Colonisation of the Muslim world by the European powers had helped the emergence of a new form of Islam – the bourgeoisie Islam – by transforming largely pre-industrial, feudal/tribal Muslim societies into mere appendages of the forces of world capitalism. Despite the apparent end of colonialism, the dependency syndrome remains unchanged, it is claimed:

> In such a situation foreign interference, while bolstering authoritarian regimes, has played an important role in perpetuating feudalistic-comprador capitalism. The problems of economic retardation, general poverty and political instability in Pakistan are exacerbated by the blatant manipulation of Islamic/religious ideology. This ideology is based on vague notions and medievalistic categories of thought and is articulated in servile subservience to foreign capital. The basic aim of the 'Islamisation' process ... is to justify the existing economic relationships and the status quo by obfuscating the immediate socio-economic problems of the masses.[52]

Zia's lack of credentials, both intellectual and electoral, in engineering such ordinances had serious ramifications for society at large. The critics viewed it as a crude manifestation of ad-hocism originally intended to perpetuate his personal rule. They felt that Pakistani society in general and women in particular were being seriously affected by new policies which demoted them to second-class citizens, removing the legal, educational and political rights they had struggled long to achieve. Zia, according to such activists, had tilted justice against women.[53]

Objectively speaking, women's rights were seriously compromised by the series of ordinances whereas real issues confronting society as a whole – like the oppressive social system, the high-handedness of the official infrastructure, the dismal rate of literacy (especially among women) and inadequate and inefficient health facilities – remained largely neglected. Discrimination against women in the name of seclusion increased while a

few gains made through the Family Ordinance of 1961 and the mobilisation of the 1970s following the anti-discrimination clauses in the
Constitution of 1973, were lost. At the same time, debate and an awareness of women's issues increased throughout society. For the first time in
the history of Pakistan women and the press emerged as the two major
bastions of civil society. Asma Jahangir, a leading woman activist and
Lahore-based lawyer, observed: 'The women's movement put Pakistan on
the map of the world as a country where women were aware and struggling for rights.'[54] It is too early to say whether this consciousness is widespread enough to result in tangible legislation and social change in the
immediate future. Still, it is largely true that women 'are not accepted as
full human beings',[55] and some believe that they will not be, given the
patriarchal nature of society and the long-held traditions confining women
to the household.[56]

The policies adopted during the 1980s may be merely 'cosmetic',[57] but
their role in reinforcing discriminatory attitudes such as seclusion from
wider society, *purdah*, crimes against women, and in discouraging any
constructive role for women, is acutely visible. These policies added to
the introversion of society and denied women virtually any role in education, family planning, health, the media, the arts, assignments abroad or
business. Obscurantist forces increased and denied intellectual freedom,
individual liberties and world-wide cooperation in human excellence and
arts.[58] The establishment of the Majlis i-Shoora and cooption of elected
members of a partyless house left the feudal families at ease with the
clientele role offered to them by the military regime. Earlier, the Federal
Shariat Court, in a major verdict, had declared the land reforms introduced
by Bhutto to be 'un-Islamic', endearing the regime to the landed aristocracy. By establishing institutions such as the International Islamic
University (largely with Saudi assistance) and the Federal Shariat Court as
well as speaking about 'Islamic' economics, 'Islamic' banking, 'Islamic'
identity and even 'Islamic democracy', the regime appeared to be skirting
the real political and economic issues, preserving feudal and clientele
institutions and avoiding real Quranic injunctions.[59]

BENAZIR BHUTTO: A NEW BEGINNING?

Party-based elections and the acceptance of Benazir Bhutto as prime minister in November–December 1988, became possible only because of the
departure of Zia and his associates from the national scene and by dint of
certain timely decisions by the superior courts. In addition, the press and

other activist groups made the transition unavoidable. Although Bhutto's leadership was more symbolic and less effective given her lack of full authority, the election of a women to the country's highest office, despite all the odds, proved a major boost for the women's struggle. On the other hand, the fact that she is a woman and has a Western education and an assertive temperament did not find any favour among her well-entrenched opponents, many of whom were responsible for her personal miseries including the execution of her father and the unexplained death of a brother. Her mother's ailing health and the continued incarceration and exile of a number of party activists were not happy reminders but she avoided the temptation for revenge. During the electoral campaign, much propaganda was directed against the two Bhutto women, including the suggestion that a woman was not qualified to lead a Muslim country. Once in office, Bhutto adopted a policy of appeasement towards ecclesiastic groups by donning a *dupatta* and avoiding hand-shakes with men. She visited Makkah frequently and, like her father, expressed her affinity with 'popular' Islam by visiting shrines. Many liberal groups including women activists were dismayed by this 'sell-out' but Bhutto, in fact, was trying to establish her credentials. Throughout her 18 months in office, she faced a continual barrage of criticism for being a woman head of a Muslim country, although ordinary Pakistanis were more interested in tangible reforms that would improve their daily existence. It was the traditionalist and pro-Zia forces in the country to whom Bhutto as a woman was totally unacceptable.[60] Bhutto herself appeared dedicated to human rights though the state structure and many of her own colleagues felt no qualms in violating them. She even resisted the army operation in Sindh despite pressure from various directions and allowed Zia's followers in IJT to hold massive rallies at his grave in Islamabad without imposing any official restrictions. She did not curb the freedom of the press though she was in the limelight because of various stories of corruption attributed to her husband, Asif Zardari.

Her successor, Muhammad Nawaz Sharif, began his tenure after a clear electoral majority amidst greater acceptance by the president and army chief – his powerful colleagues in the 'troika'. An uneasy relationship with the opposition dating from the 1980s did not augur well for the nascent, fragile democratic order in the country. Further pulls from his coalition partners like the JI and other religio-political parties did not help Nawaz Sharif at all as they demanded the rapid Islamisation of the country's institutions as promised during election campaigns. Sharif's own Muslim League, a combination of liberal and right but largely dominated by landed groups felt uncomfortable with such pressures. However, despite panicking a number of times, he avoided imposing restrictions on the press.[61] By denouncing allegations of fundamentalism levelled against his government, Sharif avoided carrying on Zia's policies of Islamisation. After the fall of the Najibullah regime in April 1992, he refused to promote Gulbuddin Hikmatyar, the Afghan hardliner and a favourite of the ISI and Zia, and in the process annoyed the JI which left the IJT in protest. He engineered a transfer of power in Afghanistan through a commonly agreed truce. However, to preempt the Shariat bill, waiting since Zia's time, he introduced his own form of the bill. But equally he did not do away with powerful institutions like the Federal Shariat Court, which had been established by Zia and had received constitutional indemnity through the Eighth Amendment under the late president. The Federal Shariat Court took a number of decisions putting the country's financial institutions in a quandary. Such verdicts did not bode well for Pakistan when the Sharif regime pursued privatisation and enticed foreign investments in the country. However, some of Sharif's ministers were openly criticising the religious lobbies for simply rejecting financial institutions without offering any tangible alternatives. Ministers like Assef Ali challenged the JI and others to provide 'Islamic' alternatives to contemporary economic order. At the same time, the government initiated a policy of inclusion of a person's religion in the national identity card, causing quite a protest. Women's groups considered such a policy discriminatory and demanded the resignation of Maulana Sattar Niazi, Sharif's minister for religious affairs and a known critic of women activists including Bhutto. The re-election of Benazir Bhutto in 1993 received a mixed reception by women activists. Largely embattled by polarised politics and ethnic violence, until 1995 Bhutto was unable to introduce any major legislation to improve women's conditions. Despite her symbolic support for a battered wife in 1994 – a victim of her fanatic husband – Bhutto otherwise seemed to have put her plans for social reform on the back-burner. Under both Bhutto and Sharif multiple crimes against women and underdevelopment have persisted, though they have been more widely reported and debated in the media than ever before.

AN ENIGMA IN HUMAN UNDERDEVELOPMENT

Tables 7.1 to 7.3 attempt to highlight the pervasive problems confronted by the civilian populace in Pakistan in terms of male/female basic needs.

It is clear from the statistics in Tables 7.1 to 7.3 that Pakistani women's participation in education, health, labour and politics is lower than in

State and Civil Society in Pakistan

Table 7.1   Comparative Human Development Index, 1992

Country	1	2	3	4	5	6
Iran	66.6	56	3.6	0.56	1.38	4 670
Turkey	66.7	82	3.9	0.82	1.88	4 870
Sri Lanka	71.2	89	7.2	0.89	2.26	2 650
India	59.7	50	2.4	0.50	1.16	1 510
Pakistan	58.3	36	1.9	0.36	0.85	1 970

Notes: 1. Life expectancy at birth; 2. Adult literacy rate; 3. Mean years of schooling; 4. Literacy rate index; 5. Educational attainment; 6. Real GDP per capita, 1991 (US $)
Source: The UNDP, *Human Development Report* (1994).

Table 7.2   Profile of Human Deprivation, 1992

Country	1	2	3	4	5	6	7	8
Iran	8.3	23.8	30	120	4 145	200	13.9	8.6
Turkey	–	4.7	–	122	768	–	6.5	5.0
Sri Lanka	1.8	5.1	7.2	11	762	–	1.3	0.9
India	–	–	750	3 505	69 345	–	271.8	169.3
Pakistan	12.9	55.5	94.9	652	3 725	–	42.3	24.7

Notes: 1. Without access to health services (in millions); 2. Without access to safe water (in millions); 3. Without access to sanitation (in millions); 4. Children dying before age five (in thousands); 5. Malnourished children under five (in thousands); 6. Children missing school (in thousands); 7. Illiterate adults (in millions); 8. Illiterate female (in millions)
Source: UNDP, *Human Development Report* (1994).

many other countries in the region, reflecting a major crisis in civil society. Urgent remedial measures by the state, dependable NGOs and society are required. The underdevelopment of women signifies the backwardness of society at large as it is accompanied by a continuing tradition of multiple crimes against women, especially in poor, rural and tribal backgrounds. This has led some observers to study the problem in a class-based analysis. The existence of commonalities strengthens such a hypothesis but the lack of organisation, given the localised and segmentary nature

Table 7.3   Female–Male Gap, 1992 (Females as per cent of Males)

Country	1	2	3	4	5	6
Iran	101	97	66	92	11	3
Turkey	108	95	79	–	45	2
Sri Lanka	106	99	90	–	49	5
India	101	93	55	–	41	7
Pakistan	100	92	45	–	16	1

Notes: 1. Life expectancy; 2. Population; 3. Literacy; 4. Primary enrolment;
5. Labour force; 6. Parliament
Source: UNDP, *Human Development Report* (1994).

of an otherwise huge underclass, poses a different set of theoretical questions. Urban-based women suffer from sexual harassment, low incomes and social discrimination while in the case of rural women it is a struggle for survival on all fronts. Karachi has a comparatively high ratio of working women with the highest in education, health and factories. Nevertheless, housewives certainly supersede all other groups. Factory workers comprise 41.34 per cent of the entire female work-force in the country.[62] Similarly, the number of women executives is higher in Karachi than anywhere else.

Karachi has also had the largest participation by women (especially from the lower middle class) in politics, as was seen during the heyday of the Muhajir Qaumi Moment (MQM). With a high rate of literacy these young graduates joined women cadres of the party, but were denied any leadership role in electoral and organisational cadres. Subsequently, many of them felt disenchanted with the criminalisation of certain sections of the MQM. The harassment of the media and especially of women editors disillusioned a number of them. After Karachi, Lahore has the highest number of female employees in various categories in addition to a noticeable number of hospital servants (*chowkidars*). For a long time, the number of women phone operators has been steadily increasing, while more and more women are joining travel agencies and computer companies. Urban women are usually less strict on *purdah*, or are totally 'emancipated' from it, and therefore anathema to traditional echelons of society, to whom the unveiling of women means the introduction of decadent, alien traditions in Muslim society. *Purdah* remains a crucial yet unresolved issue, as more and more people are demystifying it as a sociocultural observance rather than a religious injunction.[63]

TORTURE AGAINST WOMEN

Torture against women both in rural and urban areas is commonly practised but gravely under-reported. There are three main channels of violation of women's rights in the country, namely, domestic violence,
organised torture by groups and parties and police abuse of women. In
addition to rape, crimes such as dowry deaths (allegedly attributed to
kerosene stoves accidentally bursting into flames) falling in the domestic
category are gaining more media attention and have been discussed earlier
(see pp. 152–3). The sale of girls in the NWFP, marriages with the Quran
in rural Sindh, gang-rapes in rural and small towns across the country perpetrated by *zamindars, jagirdars,* and *waderas* are daily occurrences. Most
of the victims are families of *haris,* seasonal share-croppers and *kameen.*
The lack of organisation, the illiteracy, superstitions, powerlessness
against the perpetrators, fear of adverse publicity and unsympathetic attitudes facilitate such violations. In most cases *pirs* in Sindh and Punjab
belonging to the landed aristocracy engage in sexual and related exploitation of women of the tenants with complete impunity.

Another major area of women's abuse was found in cities like Karachi
and Hyderabad with the emergence of ethnic organisations such as the
MQM, which undoubtedly caused an unprecedented mobilisation, especially among women. Some leaders are known to have misused their personal status and sexually abused young urban females.[64] In addition,
members of the MQM have routinely harassed its critics, especially those
from the media – the female editors of the *Herald* and *Newsline,* two
respectable Karachi-based monthlies, were forced to seek military
protection.

The third and equally horrific category of abuses on women has been
perpetrated by the police and other official intelligence agencies. Recent
studies have shown that hundreds of women are incarcerated in Pakistani
lock-ups and jails and at least 70 per cent of them are sexually abused by
the police. Prior to the promulgation of Sharia ordinances, only 70 women
had been incarcerated in Pakistan, while by 1991 there were 2000 women
'imprisoned under these laws alone'.[65] Between 60 and 80 per cent of
these women were in the prison under the Huddood ordinance.[66] Another
area of growing concern has been the smuggling of Bangladeshi women
into Pakistan through India for prostitution. They come from poor family
backgrounds and are enticed by organised syndicates with trans-national
connections. Organisations such as Women Against Rapes (WAR) and
others have been documenting violence against women.[67] Pakistan has
apparently found two new catalysts of change and accountability in the

press and women. Both are the emerging, vigorous vigilantes of a nascent civil society in exposing the unsavoury side of society. It was through investigative press reports that abuses against women committed by the police and CIA and FIA officials came into the limelight.[68] The incidents reported make a very small proportion of an otherwise large number as such occurrences are hushed up by the parents so as to protect the *izzat* of the family. In some cases the rape victims are quickly married off or simply disposed of.[69] The press has been raising serious moral and legal questions concerning violence against women by putting the responsibility on the state and an oppressive socio-economic order. For example, 'Instead of moving towards higher levels of respect for human rights, over the past twelve months they have been pushed backwards and denied quite a few basic rights they had hard won not only a couple of decades ago but even in the dark period of colonial bondage.'[70] In addition, the Pakistan Human Rights Commission[71] and other groups of concerned citizens have become active in their roles as watch-dogs, though women have a long way to go to establish a civil society with a restraining influence on the powerful institutions of the state and its coopted intermediaries.

8 Ethnicity, Nationalism and Nation-Building

Despite its liberal protestations, the Pakistani establishment has remained reluctant to accept the plural composition of society and has reduced it to a law-and-order threat, or to the machinations of a few foreign-inspired mavericks. Curiously, the religious elites have frowned upon ethnic diversity in exactly the same way that they were dismissive of the concepts of nationalism and the nation-state – regarding them as transplanted conspiracies to shatter an inter-Muslim, trans-regional unity. It is worth stating here that ethnicity is not merely a fall-out of state-centric politics; it embodies the intricacies of cultural traditions, political economy, modernisation, urbanisation and development, the multi-tiered forces interlinked with both the state and society at large.

Ethnic heterogeneity and cultural pluralism were viewed as threats to the whole country and rhetorical emphasis was placed on religious commonality under the constant supervision of a bureaucratic–military establishment. Not suprisingly, the most serious threat to Pakistan since its inception has been from the ethnic front, which is still in official parlance referred to as 'provincialism' or 'regionalism'. By dismissing ethnic heterogeneity and demands for provincial autonomy, devolution of power, decentralisation and equitable policies governing relations with the centre, the ruling elites have sought refuge in administrative, ad hoc measures and no comprehensive plan has been undertaken to coopt such plural forces through bargaining and appropriate politico-economic measures. The separation of the former eastern wing of the country is the best demonstration of the bankruptcy of this policy.[1] In the 1970s, the lesson to be learned from Bangladesh was lost on the government, which happened to be a *political* set-up – a curious mixture of authoritarian and populist rhetoric. The state assumed an unnecessary, painful and coercive role in Balochistan by resorting to military action and then refused to accept public demands for a devolution of powers until the agitation in 1977 over electoral issues was 'hijacked' by the army.

Since the mid-1980s Sindh, which is the second biggest unit in the federation and formerly the most tranquil province, has witnessed occasional spates of ethnic-based violence.[2] Riots in urban centres like Hyderabad and Karachi between the descendants of the Urdu-speaking refugees from

India (identifying themselves as the Muhajireen) and the native Sindhi-speaking Sindhis, or riots between the settlers from other provinces with either of these two communities exacerbated by police brutalities, have not only made the headlines but also proved to be the main challenge for the fragile post-Zia democracies.[3] Ethnic politics certainly took a nasty turn in the mid-1980s when Pakistan simmered under the longest period of martial law in its history. The new generation of ethnic leaders, especially in urban Sindh, opted for militancy and with easy access to arms – due to the long crisis in Afghanistan – the ethnic strife became increasingly explosive in the absence of political platforms and bargaining processes. Urban guerrillas, supported by the rank and file of their respective ethnic communities, financed by their business or landed cohorts, and sometimes with support coming from across the borders or from the drug mafia, reduced life in Karachi and Hyderabad to a routine of arson, looting, street battles, sniper fire and prolonged curfews. Benazir Bhutto's first government – like her second administration as well – was put under severe strain and the opposition, the IJT under Nawaz Sharif, which enjoyed a clear majority in the national senate, routinely called for the promulgation of an emergency by disbanding the provincial PPP government in Sindh. Even when she directed the army to assist the civilian law-enforcment agencies in Sindh in 1989–90, a number of technical hypotheses regarding the role of the military *vis-à-vis* the civilian authority were invoked. It was premised that the military would demand extra powers, such as the establishment of special military courts issuing summary verdicts in cases of terrorism without recourse to the civilian courts. On the other hand, the army had its own reservations about playing the role of policeman in an inter-ethnic confrontation in the second largest province of the country. The tragic events of 1971 when the armed forces fought the civilian Bengali populace, engagements against Baloch dissidents and the long drawn out struggle for democracy during Zia's martial-law rule, did not augur well for either the military or the political leadership. This state of affairs persisted at a time when both India and Pakistan were on the brink of another showdown over turbulence in Indian-occupied Kashmir and the USA was putting pressure on Pakistan to abandon her nuclear programme.[4]

Eventually the nascent political set-up, based on the results of the elections of November 1988, was disbanded by a presidential decree on 6 August 1990, with the simultaneous dissolution of the PPP-dominated provincial assemblies in Sindh and the NWFP. The interim prime minister, Ghulam Mustafa Jatoi, a native Sindhi landlord and dissenter from the PPP, hoped to become the premier. However, Nawaz Sharif, until recently the chief minister of the Punjab, assumed the office. With support from President Ghulam Ishaque Khan, Jatoi had appointed Jam Sadiq Ali as the chief minister of Sindh, who crafted a coalition with the MQM, pro-IJTS indhi feudals and a few PPP dissenters. Enjoying the support of such diverse ethno-lingual groups, *waders, pirs* and, in particular, the establishment itself, Sadiq Ali set about crushing the PPP, the main opposition group in the provincial assembly. A founder of the PPP and close associate of Z. A. Bhutto, Sadiq Ali had been ignored by Benazir Bhutto during her premiership and carried a personal grudge against the PPP leadership. His hostility towards the Bhuttos and the PPP core in Sindh received encouragement from the IJT, the president and other influential anti-PPP sections in the government. He succeeded in keeping the PPP at bay and, until his death in 1992, ruled Sindh by coercion and favours.

However, Sindh's inter-ethnic dissensions, dacoities in the rural areas and frequent outbursts of urban violence eventually led to military action in the summer of 1992, which largely paralysed the MQM leadership for a while and contained rural disorder. This action continued for over two years, during which time the MQM became divided by internal factionalism and revelations about its torture cells and coercive practices. Its leader, Altaf Hussain, chose to remain in London while the movement in Karachi and Hyderabad saw its popularity plummet temporarily. The Sindhi national leaders suffered from inter-personal rifts given the continued monopoly of the feudals over local and provincial politics. Despite an apparent common cause against Islamabad and 'Punjabi domination', both the Muhajir and Sindhi leaders pursued confrontational politics rather than the real issues faced by their communities. The MQM, led by Altaf Hussain, boycotted the national elections in 1993 but participated in the provincial elections and emerged as the third most powerful party in the country, reaffirming its massive following among Urdu-speakers.[5] It supported the PPP in its presidential campaign for Farooq Leghari but maintained pressure on the government for ministerial positions and an end to the military operation. Sporadic violence in Karachi further polarised relations between the PPP regime and the MQM. The announcement of a new administrative district in Karachi – largely perceived by the MQM as *their* domain – increased the mutual hostilities. The PPP regime refused to withdraw changes of terrorist activities against Altaf Hussain and his close associates and opted for the use of force to curb growing disorder in Karachi. The withdrawal of army troops from Karachi in November 1994, after costing the country more than 800 million rupees, only intensified the violence. The MQM began a new reign of terror in the city to pressurise the government and pursued urban guerrilla activities such as car bombs, rocket attacks and even open armed encounters. It started a discreet campaign in 'ethnic cleansing' against non-Urdu speakers, law-enforcment agencies and its critics from the media and society at large. Its rival Haqiqi faction which had failed to show any electoral strength in 1993 also turned more militant. Like the unsuccessful military operation in the city begun by the army in June 1992, the second PPP administration in the mid-1990s exhibited no tangible policy to combat disorder in Karachi which had succumbed to violence causing daily numerous deaths.

As in the past, Sindhi nationalists were again marginalised in the elections of 1993 with the PPP gaining an absolute majority in rural Sindh, though Nawaz Sharif's Muslim League also obtained a few seats there. However, the urban/rural divide, compounded by a volatile ethnic heterogeneity, remained the prominent feature of Sindh in the mid-1990s. Following the break-down of law and order in Karachi with the MQM pursuing a continuing policy of militancy, Sindhi nationalists began to review their attitudes towards the state. Largely thwarted by an accentuated MQM-led revolt (sometimes mispercieved as *Muhajir* hostility), the Sindhis began to align themselves with the Punjabi and Pushtun communities.[6]

Ethnic politics in Pakistan is a story of ambiguous, often turbulent relations between the centre and the provinces, and also the net result of political, economic and cultural alienation. At another level, it is a saga of majority–minority bickering, exacerbated by rapid demographic changes propelling new economic forces and contestations over census statistics, quotas and jobs. Ethnic politics in Pakistan, despite a shared belief in lingual, territorial and cultural commonalities, is a complex phenomenon with strong prospects for a positive pluralism leading to national integration and acculturation – but only if unevenness in state-led policies is removed and fully empowered democratic institutions are allowed to function in the country. Nevertheless, ethnicity within the Pakistani historical experience (especially after 1971) is not secessionist and tends to be generally integrationist. The question of ethnicity and identity formation in Pakistan will now be considered in depth both theoretically and historically in order to resume discussion of the contemporary situation in Sindh.

ETHNICITY: TODAY'S CHALLENGE

For a long time, ethnicity has been regarded as the sole domain of sociologists and anthropologists, whereas in studies on international relations and intra-regional developments, it has received little attention. Since the dissolution of the Soviet Union, the reassertion of ethnic movements across the globe has forced many political analysts to look at it more closely.[7] Indeed, the greatest challenge to the new world order comes from ethnicity which has largely replaced ideology as the major threshold of political activism.[8] Out of 132 countries in 1992, there were only a dozen which could be considered homogeneous; 25 had a single ethnic group accounting for 90 per cent of the total population while another 25 countries had an ethnic majority of 75 per cent. Thirty-one countries had a single ethnic group accounting for 50 per cent to 75 per cent of the total population whereas in 39 countries no single group exceeded half the total population. In a few European and Latin American cases, one single ethnic group would account for 75 per cent of the total population.[9]

The Greek word 'ethnikos', being the origin of 'ethnic', referred to: (a) non-Christian 'pagans'; (b) major population groups sharing common cultural and (racial) traits; and (c) groups belonging to primitive cultures.[10] Ethnicity denotes the group behaviour of members seeking a common ancestry with inherent individual variations.[11] It is also a reflection of one's own perception of oneself as the member of a particular group.[12] Ethnicity is the subject of much discussion by sociologists who have been unable to agree on a single definition.[13] As Horowitz says, 'Ethnicity has fought and bled and burned its way into public and scholarly consciousness.'[14]

Ethnicity is based on an attachment that brings people together because of similar cultural patterns, so making the group a 'closed network'.[15] The forces of history, language, geography, economics and politics operate as additional factors to push the 'togetherness' toward well-organised and coherent traditions and institutions. A shared belief in a diaspora, as among the Poles of the nineteenth century or the Jews, Kurds, Kashmiris, Tamils, Sikhs, Palestinians and Afghans of the present century, may inculcate strong bonds of common solidarity. Thus, ethnicity would imply more than an experience of migration or sense of insecurity arising from being a minority.

It is interesting that the children of the refugees born in Sindh after 1947 have found it convenient to use the same term – Muhajireen – for themselves, which is literally a misnomer since all of them were born in Sindh. They did not feel comfortable about identifying themselves as 'Sindhis' or 'New Sindhis', the terms that were being used in Pakistan in the early 1970s. Within their large urban communities they trace their origins to a particular area in India, despite the fact that most of them have only heard about it from their families or in textbooks and would undoubtedly never think of returning. They feel that the term 'Muhajireen' does not end with the first generation of refugees but is a permanent identity. Many regional and sub-ethnic groups exist amongst them (such as UP (ites), Hyderabadis, Gujaratis, Madarasis and more recently the Biharis), but politically and psychologically 'Muhajireen' has become an umbrella identity. The external factor has contributed to the popularisation of the term, as the 'locals' began lumping them together as 'Hindustanis' or 'Panahguzeen'. The first term is and was widely used in British Pakistan by the local Muslims to differentiate the Muslims from other British Indian provinces. But the Muhajireen did not feel comfortable with it for the obvious reason that it symbolised a Hindu India and denied them their own roots. Similarly, they did not feel comfortable with the second term as it denoted the temporary nature of their stay in Sindh. Moreover, in the initial stages of their organisation in the mid-1980s, they were hesitant to take on a name that would enable their opponents to brand them as separatists or 'Indian agents' – a term used frequently in Pakistan, though generally not without substance. They had already organised themselves into the MQM though ostensibly they identified themselves as *Haq Parast* (truth worshippers) so as to avoid a last-minute ban by the government, which was under pressure to ban 'regionalist' or 'separatist' organisations.

While ethnicity is intertwined with nationalism it is considered to be less demanding, seeking commonalities in shared origins, culture, historical traditions, language and religion, yet lacking a state.[16] It would be a territorial definition with an inherent concept of sovereignty and authority allowing progression from an ethnic group to nationhood, that might culminate eventually in statehood. The state, as in England, Russia, Prussia, Sardinia or France, could accelerate the process towards nationhood. However, in numerous cases in Africa or Asia the newly independent countries, despite an overdeveloped state, are confronted with the formidable challenge of nation-building. The struggle for independence in such countries, fought on the basis of national self-determination, presupposed the existence of a cross-ethnic nationhood. A process which took Europe so many centuries to develop was expected to be complete within a short span of time in diverse post-colonial societies where the state refurbished itself mostly at the expense of a disparate civil society. In such cases, the ethnic particularism and elitism of the state exacerbated ethnic dissent through an uneasy relationship between the core and peripheries – sometimes referred to as internal colonisation. Interestingly, the same concept of national self-determination used by the anti-colonial elite against the former colonists is now being used by the ethnic elites, causing serious dissension over the extent and definition of the principle.

Ethnicity is never static and at any time a specific identity within the ethnic configuration can be triggered into action. Bengali Muslims stood for a Muslim identity in British India, sharing a common belief with South Asian Muslims at large. After independence, Bengali identity overshadowed Pakistani identity giving rise to Bengali nationalism, which propounded a Bengali majoritarian identity away from a Punjabi–Muhajir-led Pakistani composite identity. A supra-religious Bangladeshi identity eventually gave way to a Muslim Bangladeshi identity, re-establishing links with Muslim communities elsewhere in South Asia. Similarly, the Urdu-speaking Muslim elite redefined themselves as Pakistanis in the 1940s and for the next four decades, until they fell back upon their Muhajir identity which was based on diasporic idealism rather than rooting itself in the UP or the former state of Hyderabad, where the 'pioneers' had come from.[17] The politicisation of ethnicity and its interaction with the given society and state have led to much literature on the subject in recent years. Various approaches have been used including primordialist, cultural pluralist, modernisation and Marxist (inclusive of new-Marxist). The primordialists retain a major emphasis on the historic antiquity and cultural uniformity of a group, taking them as 'given' not 'chosen' traits. Following the primordialists, cultural pluralism[18] accepts the persistent co-existence of various groups based on dominant–subordinate patterns in relationships. But, like the primordialists, such a model presupposes conflictive patterns rather than cooperation.[19] Theorists of modernisation in the 1960s maintained that with accelerated mobility and economic interdependence ethnic differences would eventually disappear. They considered ethnicity to be an obstacle to nation-building which needed to be neutralised through economic planning and social development. However, as seen in contemporary Europe and North America, ethnic separatism continues to defy the processes of diffusion and acculturation. Finally, Marxist theorists regard ethnicity as a false consciousness similar to nationalism and antithetical to class.

Hobsbawm rejects the primordialist theory of ethnicity. He considers that the ethnic activism in post-1989 Europe dates from 1917–18, following the collapse of the Habsburg, Ottoman and Russian empires and the nature of the peace settlements. To him, the contemporary European 'mutation of ethnic politics into nationalist politics' is basically motivated to obtain control of state power and has formulated itself into two forms of 'national separatism and national xenophobia, which means being against foreigners by setting up "our" own states, and being against them by excluding them from "our" already existing state.'[20] Ethnic activism is also a reversal from federal, confederal or national processes when such infrastructures falter due to lack of a coherent ideology or binding authority. In an ideological vacuum, following the demise of the Soviet Union and Yugoslavia people fell back upon their ethnic identities. Ethnic identification, like religious affirmation, provides the next *natural* solace to such societies and countries suffering from fragmentation or segmentation of polity. Ethnicity is certainly a politics of inequality in all the various meanings of the word. Differentiations on the basis of colour, religion and language *invent* ethnic identity, especially amongst the minorities.

NATIONALISM: MYTH OR REALITY?

Like ethnicity, its 'junior' partner, nationalism is an equally evasive term to define. A derivative of the Latin word 'natio' – meaning birth or race – nation initially implied a social collectivity anchored on common birth or race. By the late seventeenth century, it was being used to describe the inhabitants of a country, regardless of their ethnic composition. With Lockean liberalism and the French Revolution, nation would come to imply sovereignty of its people both internally and externally. Thus nation and state merged together with growing emphasis on the right to self-determination. Nationalism, to a great extent, implied concurrently a sense of belonging, sharing and sovereignty with the state rooted in the realities of a nation. Nationalist feelings grow out of commonalities in history, culture and common symbols shared on a particular piece of territory. Along with these factors, a national consciousness is rooted in the quest for a sovereign identity. Nationhood is a recent phenomenon, though with a long history in an ethnic past.[21] Nevertheless, nation, nationality and nationalism are certainly 'notoriously difficult'[22] to encapsulate in a cohesive definition.

It is quite true 'that no "scientific definition" of the nation can be devised; yet the phenomenon has existed and exists'.[23] Kedourie and Kohn see nationalism as a eurocentric (Western and Central European) phenomenon which should operate as the yardstick for non-Western versions of nationalism.[24] Some writers believe that *nation* may be a static and natural phenomenon like family or the human body itself, while others see it as 'a product of strictly modern developments like capitalism, bureaucracy and secular utilitarianism'.[25] With the latter group, there is diversity on the basis of varying emphasis from political to cultural denominators.[26] To Anderson, both nationality and nationalism are 'cultural artifacts of a particular kind. To understand them properly we need to consider carefully how they have come into historical being, in what ways their meanings have changed over time, and why, today they command such profound emotional legitimacy.'[27] To him, nation 'is an imagined political community – and imagined as both inherently limited and sovereign.'[28] Nationalism grows out of national consciousness which may ultimately lead to the creation of a nation itself. German and Italian nationalism preceded the creation of Germany and Italy in the late nineteenth century, with the powerful force of the state led by *nationalist* German and Italian elites. Thus, more than nationalism, nation may be an *invented* tradition. 'Nationalism is not the awakening of nations to self-consciousness, it invents nations where they do not exist.'[29] The essentiality of sovereignty for nationhood evolved because of the relationship of the ideology of nationalism with the Enlightenment in the eighteenth century when revolutionary ideas challenged the political absolutism of divine rights and dynastic orders.

Though an age-old reality, nationalism in its contemporary form emerged with the displacement of lingual (scriptural) uniformity, which helped evolve vernacular languages in Europe and Asia, as the future cores of national identities. Earlier, *sacred* languages had held disparate communities together through a superimposed religious uniformity. Equally, the new mundane concepts about monarchs and their symbolic significance for their communities created territory-based specificities which challenged the previous myths of trans-regional kingdoms. Equally important have been the changing conceptions of time and the evolution of capitalist economies, nurturing *national* needs and ethos. These vital changes led to the development of nationalism in Europe and America, followed by similar evolutionary processes in the former colonies where socio-political and economic transformation, the facilitation of trans-regional and 'print-capitalism' made it possible for the nationalists to spearhead movements for independence.[30] It was in response and reaction to this imperialism that early forms of nationalism emerged in former colonies; in many cases their credentials are now being challenged by the forces of ethnic nationalism.

ETHNICITY, NATIONALISM AND STATE: UNLIKELY BED-FELLOWS

As the sociologists and anthropologists have maintained an academic monopoly over ethnicity, historians have done the same *vis-à-vis* nationalism. To them, a nation without a past is unimaginable, although Ernest Renan, in 1882, in his famous lecture 'What is a Nation?', had observed,

'Forgetting history, or even getting history wrong (*l'erreur historique*) is an essential factor in the formation of a nation which is why the progress of ahistorical studies is often dangerous to a nationality.'[31] According to Hobsbawm, 'a historian who writes about ethnicity or nationalism cannot but make a politically or ideologically explosive intervention'.[32] However, it is a thin line that distinguishes ethnicity from nationalism, though it is also blurring. Nationalism, a comparatively recent development, stands for a political creed that takes formation of a state as a *given* right under the guiding principle of national self-determination. It stipulates the homogeneous (not total) composition of a population with the rights of citizenship enjoying sovereignty. Post-French-Revolution nationalism, as understood by European nationalists and others, aimed at bringing diverse people together by employing cultural symbols and pursuing economic and political programmes. That is why national integration and self-determination became synonymous with nationalism.

> Ethnicity, despite being an important ideological concept, is not programmatic and even less is a political concept. It may acquire political functions in certain circumstances, and may therefore find itself associated with programmes, including nationalist and separatist ones. There are plenty of good reasons why nationalism thirsts for identification with ethnicity, if only because it provides the historical pedigree 'the nation' in the great majority of cases so obviously lacks.[33]

Until 1989, both the Soviet Union and Yugoslavia were considered to be archetypal in resolving the vexing question of ethnic diversity which had remained intractable throughout their history. It was assumed that a language-based territorial definition of nationality bound together with an ideology/pursuing strong economic policies, would develop an interdependence which, instead of religious and 'tribal' affiliations would eventually lead to a new model in pluralism for the rest of the world. The Soviet state under Stalin took it upon itself to implement the formula of nationality-based federalism, which, in its rudimentary form was coercive, strictly unitary and operated only as a temporary safety-valve. It suffered from its own contradictions as, like ethnicity, nationalism itself was viewed with disdain by the Marxists. However, a unilateral emphasis on economic determinism, class-conflict and internationalism – through the authoritarianism of the state – in the twentieth century could not banish ethnicity, nationalism or even religion from the former communist world. Concurrently, the liberal capitalist model presented by Western Europe and consummated through the European Union itself has not been a final solution to the persistence of ethno-national movements in the Community.

A marginalised community may seek its identification in a politicised ethnicity by adopting a separatist/secessionist path and propounding ethnic culturalism. In general, most *nations* are composed of diverse ethnic groups, mutually competitive, collaborative or conflictive – though in each case the state would desire and strive for ethnic homogeneity. A nation could be divided into various states or could be stateless but one cannot imagine a state without a nation. Since state is a political-legal framework, a nation-state, therefore, would imply a nation having political sovereignty. Any democratic, decentralised state would benefit from politicised ethnicity while an authoritarian state would frown at it. A state can obtain national integration by a consensus-based policy without allowing a majority to overrun the minorities or the latter vetoing the former. If a majority turns rebellious, as was the case in former East Pakistan, the state comes under pressure and the processes for national integration suffer. A democratic state, helped by responsive and representative institutions, is geared towards the politics of consensus and is strengthened by a strong, vocal civil society. Ethnicity, in such cases, emerges as the integral part of civil society, rather than being simply an anathema to centrist, monopolistic and particularistic tendencies.

THE POLITICS OF IDENTITY IN MUSLIM SOUTH ASIA

Ethnicity and nationalism are motivated by similar factors, but the latter has a greater emphasis on sovereignty, politics and enormity in numbers. Ethnicity, as seen earlier, is not always political, yet both are 'imagined' culturally partly in reaction to Other(s). Nationalism may be assumed by a specific ethnic group in the name of self-determination, making a case for ethnic nationalism, which may have numerous manifestations.[34] South Asian historiography, for a long time, has wrestled with (a) British activities and achievements in India, (b) the response by Indian nationalists. The recent emphasis on subaltern studies and 'small voices' in history, despite good intentions, does not go beyond a certain period and theoretical timeframe. However, since the 1960s, there has been a growing trend to study the basic changes that took place within Indian societies long before European colonisation. Such an approach largely focuses on identity formation, continuity and changes in regional and social realms, without neglecting the role of the state.[35] In the same vein, for a long time British Indian history has been seen in terms of inter-religious (communal)

conflict which typifies a reductionist approach. This presumes the existence of two major religion-based communities whose often mutually
hostile interaction was patterned largely by their relationship with the
colonial state. Such scholarly interpretations have overlooked the ethnic,
regionalist, lingual, class-based, caste/*qaum*-based diversities and it is only
in recent years that studies embodying such issues have started to appear.[36]

It is important to study the quest for identity among Indian Muslims in
the context of historical and political developments, especially in the post-
1707 decades. A sense of political loss was felt among the ruling elites
particularly and this led to a variety of intellectual activities. The adoption
of Urdu and wider reform movements in the UP took place at a time when
small-town economy had already evolved.[37] The efforts to bridge the
cleavages between the *ashra'af* and *ajla'af* had never been so forceful. To
a great extent this was a reaction to upward mobility among non-Muslims;
it is in non-Muslim majority areas like the UP that the Muslims' sense of
urgency appears more pronounced.[38] While initially Bengal assumed the
mantle of early political leadership under the British East India Company,
it was largely in the UP that the organisational and redefinitional efforts
took place in earnest. Paul Brass finds that Hindus and Muslims pursued
similar revivalist efforts but the Muslims selected separatist symbols while
the Hindus opted for composite symbols. The Muslim elite, to him, 'did
not recognise a common destiny with the Hindus, because they saw themselves in danger of losing their privileges as a dominant community'. The
fears of an imminent loss of economic and political status led to a vigorous identification with region which eventually emerged as Muslim separatism.[39] Although this is a very convincing argument, it reduces the
formation of Muslim identity to a single factor – opportunist politicking
by a pressure group that harboured fears of losing their interests. Equally,
it overlooks the diversity within the Muslim response (even within the UP)
embodying sectarian and hierarchical variations. In addition, it appears
rather superficial to explain the evolution of a superarching identity
through analysis of a single factor based on fear.

Francis Robinson, on the other hand, finds a more logical explanation in
the Muslim quest for identity. To him, Muslims seem to have a tendency
'to organize in politics on the basis of their faith' and this is not merely
confined to the UP or the India of the nineteenth century. Even at present,
a number of political movements such as the Muslim Brotherhood or the
Jama'at i-Islami of Pakistan have tried to synthesise politics with religion,
a point missed by Brass.[40] Without disputing the significance of Brass's
thesis, the role of religion in Muslim political identity is all too obvious in
recent South Asian history.[41] The development of print media, revivalism

and interaction with non-Muslim communities – mutually intertwined developments – led to soul-searching among the Muslims.[42] Muslim identity-formation in India, true to religious ethos, could not remain apolitical. 'The real explanation lies in the very structure of Islam as a religious and political complex', comments a Muslim modernist. 'Whereas the Muslims did not spread their faith through the sword, it is, nevertheless, true that Islam insisted on the assumption of political power since it regarded itself as the respository of the Will of God which had to be worked on earth through a political order'.[43] After the stormy events of 1857, Muslim identity crises peaked as the British interpreted mutiny as a 'Muslim intrigue' and 'a political conspiracy, aimed at the extinction of the British Raj'.[44] The British prime minister, Lord Palmerston, wrote furiously to Lord Canning that as a retaliation every historical Muslim building should be razed to the ground 'without regard to antiquarian veneration or artistic predilection'.[45] However, the Muslims under leaders like Sir Syed and Syed Ameer Ali were able to regain some lost ground and the multifarious efforts to reorganise and reinvigorate the community in the changed circumstances began earnestly. No wonder that the viceroy, Lord Dufferin, writing in November 1888, identified the Indian Muslims as 'a nation of 50 million, with their monotheism, their iconoclastic fanaticism, their animal sacrifices, their social equality and their remembrance of the days when, enthroned at Delhi, they reigned supreme from the Himalayas to Cape Comorin'.[46] The Muslims in British India from the late nineteenth century viewed themselves as a *separate* nation, not just a minority, or part of a supra-religious Indian nation, as was subsequently propounded by the Congress. When Muslim modernists like Sir Syed, Iqbal and Jinnah spoke of South Asian Muslims, they defined them as a *nation* seeking its sovereignty – though they did acknowledge the ethno-regional diversity within the nationhood. Iqbal stretched the argument further by redefining the ideal of *millat*, anchored on a well-knit, inter-dependent community of sovereign nations. As Jinnah concluded in the 1930s and 1940s, the congress wanted to create a 'majority rule as Hindu rule and as a way of making Hindu and Indian into convertible terms'. Like many other concerned Muslims he felt that 'Secularism, socialism, Brahminism marched under the strange ideological device of the *chakra* which Gandhi had emblazoned on the banner of Congress nationalism.'[47]

The intermixing of religion and politics has not been an easy process as Muslim ethno-regional diversities and ideological disagreements were reflected in intra-party politics in Muslim South Asia. Parties like the Jamiat i-Ulama i-Hind supported the Congress for a unitary India and opposed the idea of 'Pakistan', the League's articulation of Muslim nationalism. Simultaneously, for their own reasons, regionalist elites such as the Unionists in the Punjab and the Red Shirts in the NWFP, substituting provincial identities for ethno-national and sub-national causes, tried to block the trans-regional idea of a Muslim state.[48]

The gradual disappearance of Muslim *talukadars* and other influential families in the UP accentuated the quest for identity which was outmatched by majoritarian revivals. From 1920 onwards, it was the UP and Bihar that foreshadowed the Hindu–Muslim relationship. While earlier, Urdu culture had been syncretic and natural even to the Hindus, identification with it became almost a taboo. The early British had found Northern Indian culture to be predominantly Muslim but from the second decade of the twentieth century a backlash began, which gained further momentum in the 1980s with Hindutva becoming the creed of the day. The revival of an assertive Hindu culture intent upon replacing Urdu culture and redefining Indian nationalism has already become an historical cliché.[49] Thus rebellion from below against the 'alien' was not lost on the Muslim intelligentsia whose political programme stipulated Pakistan as an alternative, at least in the Muslim majority areas. Muslim nationalism in India was certainly cultural nationalism incorporating multi-ethnic (then multi-provincial) identities by visualising 'Pakistan' as a super-ordinate identity. Its newness stipulated a positive neutrality which would provide an egalitarian meeting ground for various ethnic identities and lingual, geographical groups, largely Muslim but part of a new composite nationality. It certainly did not envisage a break-up with Muslims in India or expulsion of non-Muslims from the areas now forming Pakistan. *Muslim* meant an historical, neutral yet specific identity which did not negate pluralism and was essentially non-theological. That is why Jinnah and the founders of Pakistan saw in Pakistan a plural society with a large majority of Muslims enjoying equality in citizenship – a prerequisite for nationhood. In his speeches, on more than one occasion, Jinnah was emphatic that Pakistan was to be a predominantly Muslim country based on cultural nationalism and not grounded in religious bigotry.

EVOLUTION OF ETHNIC POLITICS IN PAKISTAN

As seen earlier, the particularistic state structure, authoritarianism and inter-regional imbalances together with uneven development in line with the major demographic changes caused by immigration, led to increased tensions in the polity. The symbiotic relationship between the forces of authority and ideology, while skirting the exigencies of nation-building, deeply politicised ethnicity which was always considered to be a law-and-order question rather than part of a governability crisis. The state has continuously fiddled with ethnicity, and the martial-law regimes of the 1960s and 1980s in particular played a crucial role in ethnic marginalisation. In the 1980s, various intelligence agencies started sponsoring ethnic movements in Sindh in order to erode the popular support for parties like the PPP and the JI.[50] In a very imperial manner, such 'secret' agencies have used temptation, coercion and blackmail to pursue such policies despite open denunciation from various quarters.[51] However, beside these primordial and instrumental reasons lies an entire spectrum of factors engineering ethno-national movements.

The absence of a mass-based trans-regional political dialogue fully exploited by local demagogues, activated the reversal to primordial loyalties in Pakistan, with language and territory providing the bed-rock. Such fragmentation with confrontational connotations was reinvigorated and gradually eroded civil institutions like the independent press, mass-based education, women's rights and the supremacy of political and judicial institutions. The elitist and ethnically discretionary character of the state itself betrayed official efforts for national integration and an added momentum was provided by migration, urbanisation, archaic means of communications, trans-border support, weakening of the civil sector and monopolisation of scarce resources by non-development sectors like defence, leaving little for the rest. The recapitulation of various factors and forces fashioning ever-shifting ethnic identities in Pakistan necessitates a closer review. Regional/territorial identification, provincialisation, historical and cultural postulations, lingual commonalities and economic denominators have, with variations, continued to play a major role in the formation and transformation of ethno-nationalist movements in the country. The initial demand for 'Pushtoonistan' and the evolution of Bangladesh within the first two decades, political dissent during the 1970s in Balochistan and multiple ethnic activism in Sindh during the 1980s have underlined the need to comprehend the static and changing portents of ethnic configuration in the country with reference to various factors.

Territoriality

Like nationalism, ethnicity lays emphasis on roots and territory to establish its nativity. Even in diaspora, as with pre-1948 Zionism and post-1948 Palestinians, regionalisation remains a major determinant. In Pakistan the East Bengalis were the first to assert their territorial distinctness grounded in strong arguments of history and geography.[52] However, since the partition of Bengal in 1905 and South Asian independence, Bengali ethno-nationalism has been structured on a distinct territory, augmented by cultural nationalism and replenished by politico-economic alienation. Historically, religion and borders with India further defined the 'frontiers' of this Muslim Bengali ethnicity which has already evolved into Bangladeshi nationalism. In the case of post-1971 Pakistan, the issue of territorial distinctness is not so simple; on the contrary, it is emblematic of economic, demographic and ecological integration. Earlier, the Pushtoonistan issue remained land-based though its ambiguous attitudes towards a powerful Hindku-speaking urban population and the Hazara and Saraiki regions were exacerbated by irredentist claims by the Kabul regime, which found some useful purpose in politicising Pushtun ethnicity. The multi-ethnic nature of Afghan society and the divergences between settled and tribal areas were overlooked in the way that inter-tribal dissensions were sidelined by early proponents of Pushtun separatism. However, the territorial claims all the way to the Indus and further into Balochistan, justified by a partial interpretation of history and geography, for a long time remained the major attributes of Pushtun ethnicity. This is not to write off the cultural dynamics of Pushtun identity in terms of *Pukhtunwali* but when it came to politicised ethnicity numerous such issues came up and simple territory-based explanations faltered.[53]

Similarly, Balochistan, despite its homogeneous name, is heterogeneous like other provinces in the country, with every third Sindhi and every fifth Punjabi claiming a Baloch descent. Pushtun–Baloch rivalries and inter-tribal dissensions among the two do not allow a well-defined, cogent, distinct Baloch (Balochistani) ethno-nationalism – especially as there are more Balochis in Karachi than in the province itself. The Baloch diaspora cannot overlook the parallel existence of three Balochi *national* identities in three sovereign countries – Pakistan, Iran and Afghanistan. Any irredentist claims on Baloch areas in the NWFP, Sindh or Southwestern Balochistan would therefore entail more problems than solutions.[54] Similarly, Sindh is a single unit territorially, but not demographically, for urban centres maintain overwhelmingly non-Sindhi majorities, some from long before 1947. The Punjab, although a geographic unity, varies on the basis of Pothowari, Saraiki and Central Punjab with three parallel political economies. Saraiki intellectuals seek a language-based, territory-specific identity, yet irredentist claims in Sindh, Southern NWFP and Southwestern Punjab overlook inherent economic integration and interdependence in these regions as well as inherent retaliation to such extra-territoriality. Territorial identification of ethnic plurality in Pakistan is therefore not simple, and unlike superficial generalisations hypothesising secessions, the ongoing intra-regional processes, helped by an inter-dependent economy, a shared ecology and increased mobility, suggest greater prospects for a gradual integration.

Provincialisation

As in many other parts of the world, the colonial state played a crucial role in the early definition and formation of ethnic identity in the areas forming present-day Pakistan. It was purely for administrative reasons that the early presidencies of Bengal, Bombay and Madras were followed by more and 'new' provinces in the nineteenth and early twentieth century. The Punjab included Delhi as well as the trans-Attock region for almost half a century, while Sindh remained part of the Bombay presidency until 1936. Without denigrating Punjabi, Sindhi or other cultural identities, it is an historical fact that the state, from its earliest time, defined its administrative units as provinces (*subahjat*) according to its own imperial preroga-tives. Multan, for a long time, remained part of Sindh under the Arab conquerors, the way Sindh was an integral part of the Qandhar-based dynasties. The NWFP and Jalalabad were part of Punjab (Lahore *subah*/Kabul *subah*) with varying frontiers under the Delhi sultans, Mughals, Sikhs and the British. The British imperial set-up introduced a period of 'consolidation' by rearranging the core areas and peripheral areas within the provinces largely according to cost-effective impera-tives.[55] Sometimes, incongruous areas were intentionally amalgamated into a single province or presidency so as to inter-balance heterogeneous regions. The centrally administered tribal agencies carved out from the western borderlands co-existed with the NWFP, which itself incorporated the settled districts and trans-Indus Hazara region including the Hindku and Saraiki-speaking regions. Sindh, like metropolitan Delhi earlier, remained ceded to the huge Bombay presidency for nearly a century. The provincial demarcations, despite their inherent cultural, religious and econ-omic diversities, were strengthened with the evolution of diarchy when regulated attempts were made to 'provincialise' India-wide politics. The regionalist political parties (pressure groups), largely from the intermedi-aries in 'the Punjab/Indus Valley tradition', operated as safeguards against trans-regional political forces. Even within the respective provinces, the politicisation of region- and religion-based identities operated as efficient internal checks and balances. Thus, an independent South Asia, from its very inception, confronted the issue of multiple and more often conflictive identities which, for a short while during the nationalist period, were sub-merged by supra-regional programmes like *Pakistan* and *India/Bharat*, but began to reemerge once the processes for national integration became weak or simply did not take off because the state itself was pursuing divisive policies. In Pakistan, the state denigrated such identities as mere provincialism or regionalism fostered by nefarious and surrogate elements and failed to coopt them into the mainstream national life.

Cultural Configuration

The adoption of cultural symbols by an ethnic elite is mainly to project a cohesive, legitimate and integrated identity. The emphasis on Muslim cultural symbols varying from religion to dress, language, food and customs was to evoke a *Muslim* response in a plural British South Asia. Simultaneously, the regional/provincial leaders, in their efforts to carve out ethnic identities, advocated cultural mutualities. In Pakistan, the patterns remained the same though region acquired a curious position in the new bi-polar configuration between *nationalists* and *regionalists*. While the ruling groups, centrist state and religious elite would employ religious symbols to claim uniformity, the ethnic elite deemphasised the religious factor. To them, religion was no more an issue, though the latter also used folk cultural symbols in 'creating' ethnic identities. Sindhi nationalists found a common ground with other groups in the writings of Shah Abdul Latif Bhitai, the way the Muhajir, Baloch and Pushtun elite would seek cultural separatism through specific symbols.

Lingual Foundation

Despite being a major rallying point during the Muslim nationalist era, Urdu still had a long way to go in Pakistan before it emerged as the commonly agreed lingua franca. Its monopolisation by the Muhajir–Punjabi oligarchy in the early years led to a backlash by Bengalis and others. Although it eventually became the national language, Urdu was viewed by ethnic dissenters as an *official* instrument to deny them their cultural rights. After the Bengalis, the Sindhis in the 1970s perceived Urdu as a major cultural threat to Sindhi ethnic identity. While Pushtuns and Punjabis largely accepted the lingual multiplicity inclusive of English, Urdu, Pushto and Punjabi, Sindhis, who were already underprivileged both politically and economically in Pakistan, looked at Urdu as a major threat to their cultural identity. The redefinition of Muhajir identity with Urdu as the basis symbolising a non-Sindhi (UP-based?) affiliation added to their resentment. On the one hand, Sindh was given out to be *Babul Islam* (gateway for Islam) with Sindhi as the earliest *Islamic* language in Muslim

South Asia, while on the other hand, the same language and its speakers were being given a raw deal.

Pakistan's vernacular languages have mostly been historical realities in terms of their spoken traditions and written literature. Within a strict regional milieu it has been easy to politicise an ethnic construct by falling back on the lingual commonality. Following Benedict Anderson's print capitalism among competing communities, language in South Asian politics certainly persists as the major rallying point. This is quite explicit in the case of Sindh. While Sindhis could claim a shared history, indigenous roots and a long-held language to build their ethnic nationalism, Urdu-speakers would use language and migration as the two contributory factors in 'inventing' their ethnicity. It is curious to note that the pioneers of the MQM were all born in Pakistan, belonging to the post-1947 generation, without actually experiencing migration. In the same way, Urdu and a shared perception based on 'them against us' cements together otherwise diversified groups – such as the UP (ites), Hyderabadis, Biharis or Madarasis. In Southwestern Punjab, the proponents of Saraiki ethnicity define Saraiki territory in terms of lingual commonality, all the way from Mianwali down to upper Sindh and from Bahawalpur to Dera Ismail Khan in the NWFP. Such a vast and diversified region is claimed for ethnicity on the basis of a common language.[56] However, it would be simplistic to suggest that the situation in Sindh (or for that matter in Pakistan) is perpetual confrontation among the various ethnic or pseudo-ethnic groups. Urdu is already a lingua franca even if this is a major political issue in rural Sindh along with internal migration and the resultant demographic and economic changes in the larger context of Pakistan.

Historicity

As was seen earlier, ethno-nationalism seeks justification in historical tradition. The move from *Muslim* identity to Pakistani nationalism and its interaction with plural forces in the country is itself a historical development. All the ethno-national movements in Pakistan rationalise themselves to varying degrees in the perspective of the past, or interpret historical symbols and traditions to suit their present. While to Pushtuns, illustrious poets like Rahman Baba, Khushal Khan Khattak, Ghani Khan and Ajmal Khattak, belonging to different periods and traditions, represent a *given* Pushtun identity, to Sindhis it would be Sachal Sarmast, Shah Abdul Latif Bhitai, Shaikh Ayaz and G. M. Syed. They see a prehistoric, pre-Muslim past in the Indus Valley Culture as the starting point, the way the Pushtuns seek their origins in antiquity. The Balochis have Gul Khan Nasir and others telling them about their common ancestry with the Kurds, down to great empire-builders like Mir Aziz Khan Kurd. The Punjabis, claiming their Aryan, indigenous or Arab origins, fall back upon Bulleh Shah, Baba Farid, Waris Shah, Shah Hussain, Raja Risalu, Ahmed Khan Kharal, Dulha Bhatti or Ghazi Qutub Shah, depending upon the respective region and preferred symbolism. For the Saraiki-speaking elites, there are numerous historical traditions and personalities to justify their roots, though as mentioned earlier, the language itself is a monument to trans-regional literary creativity in the forms of great writers like Baba Farid or Sultan Bahu.[57] Understandably, the Kashmiris tend to look back to the visit by Syed Ali Hamadani to Baltistan and the Valley which was followed by a golden period under Sultan Haider and a synthesised Rashi humanism. To Chitralis, Kalasha, Ismailis of the Northern Areas and the Kohistanis (Leitner's Dardistan!) there are distinct historical traditions to seek a nostalgic renaissance in the present-day overlapping pluralism that confronts each ethnicity.

Integration

A number of significant factors, both internal and external, have been steadily fashioning and transforming ethnic identities in Pakistan. The state, the political economy, urbanisation, social mobility, new class formation, global and national changes in communication, education and entertainment, as well as expansion of national cultural and related institutions, have already created a state of flux for ethno-national forces across the country. Statism allows a muffled recognition of pluralism in the census records, in its promotion of regional arts and languages, maintenance of provincial boundaries, quota schemes, adoption of regional elites and through powerful provincial legislatures. Zulfikar Ali Bhutto tried to establish working relations with the urban Sindhis without alienating those in rural areas – though G. M. Syed always considered him to be a Punjabi agent. After a major uproar from Urdu-speakers over the Sindhi–Urdu controversy in the 1970s, the two languages were allowed to co-exist as well as the state-led adoption of Sindhi folk culture and cooption of *pirs* and *sajjda nishin*. Zia went a step further. He maintained such alliances with the Jama'at in urban Sindh and sought support from the rural landed elite like the Pir of Pagara and the Soomros. In addition, he kept a liaison with G. M. Syed and exploited the MQM to keep both the Jama'at and PPP on the defensive. Benazir Bhutto tried to establish such an equilibrium but it eventually cast her adrift: the MQM left her in 1989 and joined the IJT. Similar provincial challenges confronted Benazir Bhutto from the

NWFP and Balochistan throughout her 18 months in office, and Nawaz Sharif's government in 1993 remained confined to Islamabad's federal territory. The contenders for power in Pakistan have all used the ethnic (provincial) card in one form or the other.[58]

It is true that economic integration in the wake of migration within the country intensified ethnic dissensions in Sindh. But, as in the NWFP and the Punjab and to some extent in Balochistan, population transfers, the green revolution, migration to the Gulf, wider acceptance of Urdu as a nation-wide medium of communication and education, the emergence of a new powerful, trans-regional intermediary class, political instability in the region around Pakistan, have all reinforced a *national* identity. Emphasis on good education, urban life-styles, consumerism, demands for good government, increasing prosperity and most of all the opening up of society, a freer press, more awareness of human issues and individual rights have all engendered new attitudes among a youthful population which is eager to earn and consume. Market forces are refashioning Pakistani society, which appears more worldly than ever before and, despite plural loyalties, lacks enthusiasm for intermittent spates of ethnic volatility. The monopolisation by a stalemated and discredited leadership, especially in Sindh and Balochistan, has been gradually increasing disenchantment against the ethnic movements. Ethnic elites are locked between their own progressive views and extremely oppressive pressure groups claiming the leadership. Their non-ideological and totally interest-based role in local, provincial and national politics has created serious legitimacy crises for ethnic intellectuals.

Changes in land ownership and the political and constitutional systems are thwarted by the landed aristocracy, usually in league with the state and strengthened by matrimonial alliances. In urban Sindh, despite initial goodwill and unprecedented mobilisation, the MQM has disillusioned many followers because of personality cults, inter-personal rivalries, torture and blackmailing and lack of ideological clarity on fundamental issues. Undefined and often volatile relations with the state and the pursuit of constant confrontational politics with other political forces and all the other major ethnic groups in Karachi and Hyderabad have damaged the movement. In addition, the invention of Muhajir ethnicity on the grounds of simple lingual commonality was unrealistic. Even in terms of that factor, the Urdu-speakers among other regional/ethnic communities exceed the Muhajireen *per se*, and also hold a grudge against the 'system'. This is not to underrate the sense of comradeship amongst Urdu-speakers in urban Sindh, but without a programme of vital political, economic and social changes, hostility to fellow citizens or a frequent resort to violence as seen in 1994–95 can neither guarantee ethnic togetherness nor prevent anomalies and contradictions from damaging the organisational core. Nevertheless, ethnicity is a factor to be reckoned with in Pakistan. Efforts towards achieving democratisation, decentralisation, accountability and a wider consensus must begin at all levels in order to obtain egalitarianism in the country as a whole. Without this a sense of alienation could grow stronger and lead to more frequent spates of ethnic militancy.

9 Sindh: The Politics of Authority and Ethnicity

Attitudes in Pakistan over the decades towards ethnic diversity, factors contributing towards pluralism and the articulation of Sindhi nationalism constitute the salient features of this chapter. By the use of ideological jargon and schemes such as parity, One-Unit, martial law or direct federal rule, the powerful ruling elite has denied heterogeneous communities any participation in national affairs, or has simply manipulated plurality in order to perpetuate its own power. The tensions between centripetal and centrifugal forces and between the centre and federating units have become more pronounced recently in Sindh, where a deep sense of alienation runs through the 'peripheries' against the 'core'. This reflects the dichotomic and strained relationships among the plural forces within the province, characterised by militancy and violence rather than co-existence. Ethnic forces in the province operating in the large vacuum left by a state–civil-society imbalance tend to become involved in conflict rather than collaborative strategies. Administrative high-handedness and official reluctance to strive for a wider consensus while occasionally exploiting inter-ethnic divisiveness for temporary advantage, have dented efforts towards reconciliation and mutual co-existence. A peripheral role in the national/provincial/local political life, burgeoning economic deprivation, problems associated with difficult demographic realities and a lack of communication with other communities have all been instrumental in generating alienation. Indeed, ethnic dissent has retained ideas of turning into social banditry, leaving both rural and urban Sindh at the mercy of local mafia. The dismissal of various governments and deployment of the armed forces to stem violence have remained the main features of discontent in the province. Karachi, since the late 1980s has become the scene of urban chaos and ethnic violence as its inhabitants experienced a Beirut-type scenario. With the presence of more than 3 million Afghan refugees, many armed with the latest weaponry, as well as drug trafficking and the repatriation of hundreds of thousands of Biharis, the situation has been drastic. A strategic redefinition and spasmodic shifts in alignment among the ethnic groups in the country using violent tactics speeded up the process of polarisation and increased the problems of the national economy and security. By dismissing the ethnic question as a movement of surrogates with displaced loyalties, or characterising it as a defeatist cause, the problems have not been eased.

To understand the conflict in Sindh between the forces of authority and ethnicity requires a thorough analysis of its history, political economy and quest for identity among its various communities in the context of the break-down of the traditional mechanics of political control, the politics of cleavages accompanied by vital demographic changes in the province. Such an analysis and interpretation of ethnic politics in Sindh, would help us comprehend the complex relationship between the state and ethnicity and the dialectics of inter-ethnic conflicts.

CRISIS OF POLITICAL CONTROL

The history and politics of Sindh have been moulded by its geography, socio-cultural realities and a system of political control relying on an official policy of patronage which has evolved over the centuries and has been maintained by successive dynasties and regimes with minor variations. The abode of the well-known Indus Valley Civilisation, Sindh (the land of Sindhu or Indus) has given us familiar names like Indus, India, Hindu and Hindustan. The second largest province in Pakistan in terms of population and the largest input into the country's GNP, Sindh is also known as Mehran. Since antiquity its history has been characterised by the River Indus and cross-cultural influences. While the river provided the life-line to the economy, transportation and cultural developments, the hospitable, ingenious and peaceful inhabitants gave the world an extremely developed cultural heritage anchored on rural communities and small townships on both banks of the river. Like the Nile, the Indus valley, both a beneficiary and a casualty of the bounties and vagaries of the river, gradually merged into a vast desert stretching into Rajasthan, Southern Punjab and Eastern Balochistan, while a delta and neighbouring marshes of Katchh demarcated the southern and southeastern frontiers. The inhospitable Thar desert straddling the Katchh and the neighbouring delta made the eastern and southern fringes the frequent abode of pastoral communities. Although it has been largely tribal through most of its history, Sindh was not altogether pastoral (an assumption wrongly made about the tribal societies).[1] Both agriculture and commerce had been established in Sindhi rural communities and ports straddling the banks of the Indus and further south on the Arabian Sea.

Surrounded by desert on all three sides, Sindh did not escape frequent invasions and immigration throughout its known history. The indigenous Dravidians[2] were overtaken by the Aryans from the North who reorganised the society by pioneering various traditions in Hinduism. On the eve of the Arab arrival in Sindh AD 711, Sindhis pursued syncretic traditions of Hinduism and Buddhism, though political power was in the hands of the Hindu rajas. The consolidation of Muslim rule in the area as far as Multan inaugurated a new era of peace and tolerance. Given the emphasis on equality propounded by the Muslim sufis, many members of the under-privileged classes converted to Islam. Both *ulama* and sufis pursued poli-cies of tolerance towards non-Muslims and in the absence of any external political and religious pressures or influences from the rest of India or the Muslim world, Muslim and Hindu communities pursued policies of co-existence. The spiritual form of Islam through *pirs* and *dargahs* held sway over its scriptural counterpart, represented by *ulama* and *maddrassas*.

The establishment of the Muslim Turkic and Baloch dynasties under the Arghuns, Mughals, Tarkhans and Talpurs in subsequent centuries did not alter these socio-religious patterns, though migration from Balochistan and the Punjab into Sindh increased. During this era, acknowledging the geo-graphical isolation of Sindh, a number of Ismaili missionaries activated their evangelising activities. These Shia *ulama* had been expelled from Safwid Persia as a result of the dynasty's discretionary policies in favour of Shias belonging to the As'ana Ash'ara school of thought. The Ismailis were helped by geography as Sindh was largely inaccessible from metro-politan centres like Isfahan, Qandhar and Delhi – as it had been earlier from Damascus and Baghdad during the Ummayyid Caliphate. Long before the British conquest of Sindh in 1843, settled agrarian and commer-cial communities dotted the entire territory with the Turkic, Baloch, Punjabi or Rajput tribes settling to improve their standards of living. Sindh remained largely agrarian throughout its history with migratory, rural and semi-sedentary Muslim and Hindu communities (the former outnumbering the latter by three to one).[3]

As in ancient Mesopotamia, the ecclesiastic class in Sindh enjoyed a prominent socio-economic status. Both the Hindu and Muslim dynasties successively sought cooperation and legitimacy from clerical and spiri-tual groups. Muslim rulers especially sought approval from the sufi *silsi-lahs* and, in return, granted them land. The mystic traditions in Sindh were stronger due to the pioneering role of the saints in the propagation of Islam and minimal external interference. Their descendants institu-tionalised themselves as land-owning *sajjada nishin* families and became regional dynasts.[4] Their economic and spiritual influence was duly acknowledged by the Arghuns and Tarkhans, the Turkic rulers, who sought their loyalty to solidify their own political hold on Sindh. The Mughals followed suit and allowed local chieftains to be incorporated in the Mansabdari system by bestowing upon them estates and local administrative and military powers.[5] The British showed no great eagerness to transform the traditional system of indirect control and continued to rely upon land-owning families of *waderas, pirs, syeds* and *sajjada nishin* as intermediaries between the rulers and the subjects. This collaboration was based on cooption through rewards, land-grants or entitlement to provide influential indigenous channels for imperial control over vast regions in the empire.[6]

Such a relationship of mutual convenience was not all plain sailing, however, as the British had initially manifested an ambiguous cum hostile attitude towards the Muslim elite. Soon after the conquest they described the Sindhis as 'idle, apathetic, notoriously cowardly and dishonourable, addicted to intoxication, unclean and immoral in the extreme'.[7] But imperial prerogatives overcame such inhibitions, as Sir Charles Napier, the first governor of Sindh, decided to reassure the loyal Sindhi *waderas, pirs* and other land-owning *jagirdars* that they could 'rest in peace' as he had no intention of acquiring their holdings.[8] In later years, additional initiatives were undertaken to regulate the *jagirdari* system, which resulted in the complete loyalty of the Sindhi land-owners.[9] The British had been following similar policies elsewhere where such intermediaries were vested with *izzat* and magisterial powers to ease the pressure on the administration and to ensure the uninterrupted supply of revenue.[10] By combing *din* and *dunniya*, the Raj successfully created a cross-regional, largely rural, non-ideological class of faithful who would stand by the regime through thick and thin. In the Punjab, such a process, though considered to be a threshold for modernity and prosperity, came to the assistance of the government during both wars and ensured internal peace when urban activism or peasant revolts occurred. In addition, it operated as a buffer against subsequent trans-regional political forces challenging British rule in India.[11] Many British administrators considered the system to be not only an effective instrument of political control but also a vehicle for social change given the degree of power enjoyed by these 'collaborators' over the grassroots.[12] While this control mechanism guaranteed peace, it also harmed political development, as administration rather than governance remained the official priority. However, the system worked successfully until the 1940s with two major interregnums, both occurring during and after the wars. The Khilafat Movement and the Pakistan Movement put viable strains on this policy of cooption and regional insulation as they were both able to coopt trans-sectional support from within Sindh.[13] Growing political consciousness and massive mobilisation broke the equation between the state and the power elites though it was re-built by the post-1947 regimes and the regional feudal dynasties.

Even after the Khilafat Movement in the early 1920s political activities in Sindh, though largely confined to major towns like Karachi and Hyderabad, continued unabated. Muslim Sindhi leaders like G. M. Syed, Shah Nawaz Bhutto, Abdul Majid Sindhi, Sir Hiayatullah, Ayub Khuro, Seth Abdullah Haroon and others continued to demand the separation of Sindh from the Bombay presidency, which denied the province its own cultural, political and economic distinctness. Sindh had remained a back-yard of Bombay until 1936 and the local *haris*, predominantly Muslim by religion, made the lowest cadres on the socio-economic ladder. The Sindhi *jagirdars* (commonly known as *rais* or *waderas*, *pirs* and *sajjada nishin* (*gaddi nishin*) held complete sway over local political, administrative and economic affairs, while the Hindus overwhelmingly comprised the commercial class. From amongst the Muslims only Memon and Ismaili families held any commercial interests.[14] 'Traditionally, Sindh was a province that the *waderas* owned, the British ruled and the *banias* governed', is how one academic summed up the pre-1947 political economy of the province.[15]

With the separation of Sindh from Bombay in 1936, the emphasis on Muslim identity increased within the young province and Sindh became even more receptive to the idea of Pakistan than neighbouring Punjab or NWFP. It was in 1943 in the Sindh provincial legislature that a forceful resolution supporting the Lahore resolution of 23 March 1940, was passed with a significant majority.[16] In Pakistan, the landed aristocracy saw a guarantee for its own interests against any encroachments, while it was idealised by the *haris* and emerging middle class in Sindh who believed it would be the threshold for long over due economic and political change. As in the Punjab, support for the Muslim League from Sindhi *pirs* and *waderas* broke the age-old tradition of collaboration, with the Raj causing the break-down of its political control through patronage. The powerful class of intermediaries joined their counterparts from other regions within West Pakistan and a new equation of political control resisted land reforms and other such drastic measures. Nothing changed for some time:

Governments over the years have sought legitimacy through their support; either directly, by winning them on to the same political plat-form, or indirectly, by adopting policies towards their shrines which turn them into national religious cultural monuments. The skills which *pirs* perfected during the one hundred years of British rule have equipped them for today's Pakistan. Once again, under Muslim rule, as in the past, they continue, by and large, to prosper, their flexibility still ensuring their survival as one of the most powerful elites in Sindhi society.[17]

Sindh remained tranquil for two decades and it appeared that the political control re-established through mutual convenience and connivance would withstand all the strains which, seen retrospectively, had already set into motion forces of instability. The migration of Hindus across the borders simultaneously with the arrival of many millions of Muslim refugees seeking shelter and jobs, began a new phase in the history of the province. Overnight it became the most plural province in the young country; it received more people than it sent and welcomed them enthusiastically. The vacuum left by urban and commercial Hindus was filled not by Sindhis but by well-educated, mobile Muhajireen whose mother tongue became the national language and who began establishing their own businesses, industries and financial concerns in Karachi, Hyderabad and Sukkur. The allotment of lands, evacuee's property and positions in the new government departments created a better organised, articulate and innovative community which, rather than adapting to indigenous cultural influences, started establishing their own position.

The Sindhis were still recovering from this shock when Punjabis, Pushtuns and Baloch began migrating into the province, many of them being granted lands recently developed with the construction of the barrages at Sukkur and Guddu. Sindh was a coveted territory in a country where competition raged between agrarian and business capitalism. The alliance between non-Sindhi elites on power-sharing and the exclusion of Sindhis and Bengalis generated a sense of alienation which grew with time. While the landed elites sided with the establishment or carried on their matrimonial alliances with the Punjabi and Baloch aristocrats and *sajjada nishin*, in their hearts they felt insecure *vis-à-vis* a growing urban middle class. They were apprehensive of losing their favourable position in the politics of patronage with new economic and political groups, largely based in urban centres, asserting themselves as strong contenders. The Sindhis felt left out of civil and military positions and their intellectuals anticipated the replacement of their culture and language. While Z. A. Bhutto tried to assuage Sindhi feelings through the quota scheme and by the elevation of Sindhi as the second language in the province after Urdu, disenchantment increased (especially after his execution by a Punjab-dominated establishment). On the other hand, the Urdu-speakers, in particular the new, ambitious middle class saw their rights being compromised through a policy of appeasement and, in retaliation, began organising themselves. With a nod from various official agencies operating under different dictates and strategies, angry youths became ethnic militants.

Thus, in a sense, it is the break-down of long-held political control and the inability of the relevant institutions to provide a consensus-based alternative, that largely explains the malady in Sindh. The forces of authority and ethnicity are both in a state of stagnation, looking for a new equilibrium which, if not created, will only increase the problem.

THE POLITICS OF PRIVILEGE AND CLEAVAGES

To a large extent, political militancy in its various manifestations can be explained by the symbiosis between privileged sections and underprivileged strata. It is ironical that Sindh, despite its vanguard role in cultural activities, has attracted very few original studies on identity-formation, inter-ethnic relationships and the role of pressure groups within the province. Apparently, a myth of Sindhi docility has been instrumental in creating stereotypes and when urban and rural turbulence made the headlines few outsiders were prepared to accept that Sindh could be so assertive. To a large extent, the court historians are to be blamed for creating these myths; the politics of patronage encouraged the depiction of Sindhis as uncultured, indolent, irresponsible and listless people who needed to be guided and led. The ruling dynasties as well as the privileged families of *waderas*, *syeds* and *pirs* took pains to identify themselves as *ashra'af*, denying any roots in Sindh. These powerful elites did not consider it a matter of pride to be Sindhi and to identify with the *natives* whom they viewed as sub-human. All the rulers, especially the outsiders, depicted Sindh negatively in order to justify their ventures.

The masses continued to suffer as an underprivileged community under the Arghuns, Tarkhans, Soomros, Sammas and the Mughals – who all claimed their origins in other regions. Mir Yusuf Mirak, an aristocratic intellectual, rose to the occasion and wrote his *Tarikh-i Mazhar-i Shah Jahani* in the early seventeenth century to inform the Mughal emperor, Shah Jahan, about the pitiable conditions of the Sindhi *haris*, who had been suffering at the hands of the privileged classes and the marauding migratory tribes. Unable to bring his work to the notice of the emperor, the manuscript – largely about the state of affairs in Sehwan – remained unknown until Pir Hissam ud-Din Rashdi, a known Sindhi scholar, found and published it.[18] The Kalhoras took over Sindh from a weak Mughal administration yet chose to be called Abbassis, stipulating a non-native identity. Rather than confronting Nadir Shah and Ahmad Shah Abdali, the

Kalhoras chose to surrender by submitting immense riches to the invaders. The Talpurs showered blessings on their Baloch relatives and, except for putting up resistance against the British, two factions joined the Europeans making it easier for them to win the Battle of Miani in 1843 which resulted in the annexation of Sindh. As seen earlier, the landed elite very conveniently switched their loyalties towards the new rulers.

With the ruling dynasties espousing non-Sindhi identities and the landed elite providing the major support to such regimes, ordinary subjects from Bhakkar to Lahri Bandar negotiated a miserable existence. While the rulers and their intermediaries controlled the territory largely unchallenged, the *syeds* and *pirs* exacted privileges from the illiterate masses. At other levels, dacoits either from migratory tribes or from amongst the angry peasants raided rural settlements. Many of these dacoits were linked with *zamindars* or *gaddis* for whom they operated as hatchet men.[19] With the consolidation of the British Raj, the Muslim aristocracy and laity suffered from inertia but the Hindu minority in Sindh undertook dynamic initiatives to reorganise itself. Their interest in commerce, education and official employment brought dividends and soon Karachi, Hyderabad, Mirpur Khas, Nawab Shah, Shikarpur and Sukkur emerged as towns with a prosperous Hindu middle class. The Hindus retained strong links with Bombay and Gujarat and Sindh's integration in the Bombay presidency was a deterrence against a Muslim majority asserting itself. However, many Hindu members of the new middle class identified themselves as Sindhis and supported the separation of Sindh from Bombay. They took pride in their identity and spearheaded a number of efforts to promote the Sindhi language and its mystical literature. In addition to Sindhi–English dictionaries, the well-known *Rasaloo* by Shah Abdul Latif Bhitai was edited and published by Hindu scholars in the nineteenth century. Moreover, the Sindh Historical Society was established to seek the intellectual roots of Sindhi identity in antiquity and began the collection of original source material and publication of a quarterly.

Benefiting from modern schools in Karachi and Bombay, a number of Muslim aristocratic families also began sending their sons for higher education. Among these educated Muslims, two attitudes towards Sindhi identity developed. While a small group espoused the cause of a supra-communal *Sindhi* identity, others advocated closer identification with the Muslim community in other parts of India. Such leaders felt that Sindh should be administratively separated from Bombay but politically and culturally integrated with the rest of the Indian Muslim community.[20] However, there was no pronounced effort to improve the plight of the *haris* through integrated social reformism. In a way ideological bi-polarity on the question of identity persists even today among Sindhi intellectuals. One leading group believes in a supra-religious *qaumi* identity; to them Sindhis, both Hindu and Muslim, are a nation unto themselves seeking a common history from the earliest times of the Indus Valley Civilisation. The other group advocates an Islamic identity within the national framework of Pakistan and a larger trans-territorial Muslim *millat*. Both ideologies regard the Aryan conquest of Sindh and the emergence of Pakistan as focal points.

The creation of Pakistan unleashed dramatic convulsions when the Hindu moneyed classes emigrated to India while the Urdu-speaking Muhajireen moved to Sindh (followed by others). Such demographic changes, as will be seen in a separate section, created varying scenarios for the different classes and communities in the province. The landed elite confronted a challenge from entrepreneurs and powerful urban elites and reorganised their relations with the state and with the Punjabi/Baloch landed interests. In recent years, they have constantly feared the evolution of a *Sindhi* middle class from amongst the *haris* and *murids* challenging their hold. The Sindhi feudal elites have, for quite some time, tried to appease and patronise such a new middle class to neutralise its force by intermittently espousing Sindhi nationalism, which they know is contrary to their own interests. The Sindhi *waderas* are confronted with challenges from outside as well as the forces from within, which they had success-fully contained for such a long period. It is no surprise that a Sindhi *wadera-syed* remained the father-figure for Sindhi nationalism – although not without strong criticism from within nationalist groups. Similarly, pressure from the MQM destabilised the traditional politics of patronage and the state acquired more options and means at its disposal. This sig-nalled the beginning of an end to the long-term stalemate in the province. The Punjabis and Pushtuns, who, until 1994–95 were viewed as the exploiters, were being befriended so as to confront the MQM-led mili-tancy against non-Muhajireen.[21] The forces of change are too strong to be ignored or sidelined and have definite portents for urban and rural, privi-leged and underprivileged sections of the society. Politicised ethnicity occasionally assuming violent options will be the net result of such com-peting forces unless or until a common meeting-ground is formulated through political negotiations in the interest of all.

MIGRATION, ALIENATION AND ETHNIC MOBILISATION

The post-1947 generations of Sindhis and Urdu-speakers have memorised the demographic statistics in order to highlight their feeling of deprivation concerning census figures, quotas and jobs. At junctures, in a reductionist manner, ethnic politics in Sindh appears to be a war of opposing numbers, fought by educated classes. Cataclysmic demographic changes resulted from the migration in 1947 when, as mentioned earlier, Sindh provided a sanctuary to millions of Indian Muslims. Given that there are strong traditions of immigration and ethnicity within the Pakistani national experience, Sindh, which had been a semi-isolated region, was rapidly transformed into an ethnic plurality. The refugees from Eastern Punjab in 1947 were the worst sufferers of the 'ethnic cleansing' of 1947. These Muslims had lost homes, possessions and, in many cases, members of their immediate families. Almost every migrant family from the Indian Punjab was a sad spectacle as many of them had to flee from their ancestral land unprepared. They did not have time to collect their personal valuables including property deeds and for months had to wait in the Walton camp in Lahore for settlement. The abrupt and violent nature of migration from the Indian Punjab into Pakistan left these refugees in a disadvantaged position. By contrast, the refugees from the UP and elsewhere in Northern India escaped the miseries of their Punjabi counterparts. Their migration continued on until 1951 and was comparatively well organised. They had sufficient time to bring their property claims and other documents facilitating early settlement in the new country. Not only were they able to reclaim urban and rural properties across Pakistan they were also absorbed in the newly established official departments. Compared to their ratio in the population, the Urdu-speakers began their new national experience with visible advantages.

Over the years, two kinds of migration have continued to change the demographic realities in Sindh. First, the emigration of people from outside Pakistan since 1947 has not abated. The process began with the partition of the sub-continent, when the worst kind of communal riots, especially in the Punjab, resulted in a holocaust. Around 17 to 18 million people moved in both directions between Pakistan and India, making it the world's largest transfer of population in known history. The number of people who were massacred while emigrating will never be known exactly.[22] The total number of Indian Muslims was around 100 million, out of whom 65 million became Pakistani nationals and the remaining 35 to 40 million remained in India. At the time of independence, Muslims in the provinces of undivided Bengal and Punjab accounted for 55 per cent to 58 per cent of the total population. There were 34 million Muslims in undivided Bengal and 16 to 17 million in the British Punjab. In Sindh, there were more than 3 million Muslims, three-quarters of the local population; in the NWFP around three-quarters of a million accounting for 93 per cent of the total population; whereas in Balochistan, there were around 500 000 Muslims, 88 per cent of the total population. In British India, the United Provinces had a visible Muslim minority of 8 million, accounting for 14 per cent of the total population.[23] These Muslims had been in the vanguard of the Pakistan Movement together with the elites from other Muslim minority provinces of India. When the communal riots and partition took place in 1947, Biharis and Muslims from Calcutta and Madras decided to move to East Pakistan, whereas many emigrants from the UP, Central India, and the former state of Hyderabad decided on Sindh. The Muslims from the Punjab and Delhi generally opted for the Western Punjab.

Thus, urban areas in two provinces became centres of refugee concentration. Lahore and Karachi became huge population centres overnight. Dacca, Rajshahi, Sylhet and Chittagong harboured a number of Bengali and non-Bengali refugees opting for Pakistan. The influx of 'Hindustanis' in both wings was welcomed by the local population who had entertained high hopes of a peaceful co-existence with their Muslim brothers sharing the citizenship of a newly independent state. Soon after independence, the dispute over Kashmir, Junagarh and Hyderabad led a new wave of emigrants to Pakistan – India happily getting rid of 'extra' Muslims from its soil. Independence had led to the emigration of Hindus and Sikhs from Pakistani provinces, which received 2 million more refugees than India in the exchange. According to the census of 1951, 49 per cent of the total population in Karachi were refugees; in Hyderabad, 71 per cent; and, in Lahore, the refugee population was 43 per cent of the total population.[24] In more recent years, Afghans, Iranians, Bangladeshis, Indians, Sri Lankans, Kurds and Africans have also entered the country.

Secondly, and equally crucial, has been the internal immigration or circular immigration which has multiplied in recent years in the wake of rapid urbanisation. In the case of Urdu-speaking Muhajireen, their relative predominance in the civil administration both at the federal and provincial levels, along with their dominant role in business and industry, consolidated them as a strong community which also took advantage of the generous property allotments as compensation. The Muhajireen, with their mobility and ethnic cohesion, high rate of literacy and conducive environment, emerged as the early ruling elite of Pakistan.[25] This was strengthened by the official insistence on Urdu as the national language, which annoyed the educated Bengalis and subsequently the Sindhis. The Punjabi land-owning class, bureaucracy and entrepreneurs joined the Muhajireen and consolidated their position at the national level. Vital national institutions such as the armed forces, the bureaucracy and economic sectors like trade and agriculture showed a long-time Punjabi preponderance. After the loss of East Pakistan the Punjabis, who were favoured by their numerical strength and entrenchment in the 'system', began to replace the Muhajireen (Urdu-speakers) in various sectors of national life.[26]

During the same period a fairly large number of Pushtuns, looking for better opportunities, migrated south and began competing with the blue-collar class in urban Sindh. Many Pushtuns opened 'hotels' to cater for Pushtun labourers and others turned toward transportation. While Pushtuns and Punjabis searched for manual labour, a new class of Pushtun settlers emerged in the rural parts of the province, many of them former army men. There were already many Punjabi and Pushtun military men and policemen in the province and their numbers increased many times after the implementation of the One-Unit scheme. The lack of economic opportunities, introduction of a market economy, concentration of industries and business in Karachi and prospects for better wages, all resulted in an immigration explosion in Sindh. Karachi was the main attraction because of the large number of industries and commerce – which also demonstrated the short-sighted economic policy of the government. To a lesser degree this also happened in the case of Balochistan when many poor Balochis found it hard to make both ends meet and emigrated to Karachi to work as dock-workers or ship-breakers. Over the years, Sindh has received more people than it has sent elsewhere.[27] There are more Balochis in Sindh today than there are in Balochistan which has a total population of 5 million over an area accounting for 43 per cent of the country's territory; more Pushtuns than there are in Peshawar, and undoubtedly a sizeable number of Punjabis, followed by Kashmiris, Afghans, Bangladeshis, Iranians and others who have found their way into Sindh. Karachi, Hyderabad and Sukkur have Urdu-speaking majorities while Karachi has become the biggest Pushtun and Balochi city in the entire country where the population of the Sindhi-speaking Sindhis is around 12 per cent.

The total population of Sindh was 1.2 million in 1847, and no major increase was registered for the next 90 years.[29] Its growing agricultural, industrial and commercial significance with the opening of the Sukkur Barrage in 1932, Karachi's elevation to national capital in 1947 and demarcation as an exclusive federal territory, besides its development as the nation's financial centre, combined to produce an unprecedented spatial mobility. According to the census of 1901, the total population of Sindh stood at 3 071 000 while 30 years later, in 1931, it was 3 336 000 – not a noticeable increase. By 1951, it had doubled totalling 6 128 000 and 30 years later, in 1981, it had trebled to 18 966 000. In 1981, Sindh had a density rate of 134 people per square kilometre with Karachi at the staggering rate of 1538, followed by Hyderabad with 192 per square kilometre. Since the census for 1991 was postponed due to ethnic claims and counter-claims involving disputes over the accuracy of the figures, the statistics showing exact rates of growth in population, urbanisation and density for Sindh remain unknown. However, given the trends, they must certainly be quite high. The urban population, compared to that of rural Sindh in the post-1951 years, has increased noticeably with the Muhajireen making a visible majority in cities like Karachi and Hyderabad. By early 1970, not only language but also statistics had become areas of dispute, as they implied changing socio-ethnic contours which demanded changes in official policies including job allocations.[30]

Economic statistics, like demographic figures, have played a crucial role in generating a deep sense of alienation, ethnic redefinition and polarisation. From the hinterlands of Bombay, Sindh has progressed into a major economic activity zone in Pakistan with the forces of development and modernisation triggering efforts for identity formation and ethnic mobilisation. Sindh, especially the urban areas, accounts for more than half of Pakistan's industrial concerns. It contributes 30 per cent of the GDP and 21.3 per cent of the agricultural GDP with the highest per capita income in the country. It also accounts for 43 per cent of the construction industry. Urban Sindh is the financial capital, housing the headquarters of most of the country's national banks, major branches of international banks, insurance companies and shipping concerns. The province also has the country's largest steel mill, built in the state sector with help from Moscow. Karachi remains the major port and the headquarters for the Navy; it is the main embarkation and disembarkation point for millions of Pakistanis travelling or working abroad and has the largest percentage of female workers in the paid workforce in the country. Such activities have

Table 9.1   Ethnic Percentage in Sindh, 1981[28]

	Total	Urban	Rural
Muhajireen	24.1	54.4	2.2
Sindhis	55.7	20.0	81.5
Punjabis	10.6	14.0	8.2
Pushtuns	3.6	7.9	0.5
Balochis	6.0	3.7	7.6

certainly created a sense of derivation in the hinterland. The high proportion of Urdu speakers and Punjabis in educational institutions, civil and
military departments, factories, banks, offices, hotels, airlines, police, hospitals and in the mills has increased the sense of alienation among a
growing Sindhi middle class as well as the land-owning class who have
their own apprehensions about being marginalised by a powerful class of
businessmen.[31]

Combined with the demographic and economic statistics, linguistic controversy has played an important role in ethnic mobilisation. As mentioned
earlier, the fears of cultural loss due to the replacement of Sindhi by Urdu
(symbolising a new powerful non-Sindhi alliance) politicised Sindhi
ethnic identity. The state, first by promoting Urdu at the expense of traditional languages and then by reversing its policy after 1971, agitated both
Sindhis and Muhajireen. In 1972, soon after the creation of Bangladesh,
there were riots over the Urdu–Sindhi controversy in Sindh (especially in
Karachi). The first PPP government of Sindh under Mumtaz Ali Bhutto
tried to coopt and pacify Sindhi nationalists, but antagonised the
Muhajireen in the process, for they regarded Urdu not merely as
the *national* language but as a symbol of their own *identity*. Eventually,
the regime relented and reverted to the pre-1947 policy of dual languages,
maintaining Urdu and Sindhi side by side. In the meantime, the arrival of
Urdu-speaking Biharis, a decision by Z. A. Bhutto over the strong objections of Sindhi nationalists and his own PPP followers, added a new
element to this polarised situation. Although the Biharis were not able to
enter Pakistan *legally* for the next decade, their back-door migration continued. Naturally, Sindhis felt they were being overwhelmed by Urdu-
speakers who, in extreme cases, were not prepared to be identified as
Sindhis.[32] While Urdu remained the official language, the state used linguistic differences in gathering statistical information in national censuses,
by committing itself to language-based ethnic identities. Mother-tongue in
a household, as is evident from Table 9.2, has remained the criterion in
gathering data.

If the Sindhis felt they were becoming 'American Indians' on their own
soil,[33] the Muhajireen (many of them born in Sindh) felt that, despite their
share in the making of Pakistan and their high literacy rate, they were
being superseded by non-Urdu speakers through quota preferences. The
emergence of the MQM in the mid-1980s during the country's most
oppressive and longest martial-law period, symbolised a shift of politics to
the urban centres and accentuated inter-ethnic tensions. The Sindhis had
already established a number of organisations like Jeeye Sindh and Sindh
National Alliance (SNA) while the Punjabis and Pushtuns established the

Table 9.2   Percentage of Household Languages, 1981

Region/ province	Language							
	Urdu	Punjabi	Pushto	Sindhi	Balochi	Hindko	Saraiki	Others
Pakistan	7.60	48.17	13.15	11.77	3.02	2.43	9.84	2.81
Islamabad	11.23	81.72	4.16	0.18	0.16	0.60	0.10	1.83
Punjab	4.27	78.68	0.76	0.08	0.57	0.04	14.90	0.70
Sindh	22.64	7.69	3.06	52.40	4.51	0.35	2.29	5.97
Balochistan	1.37	2.24	25.0	8.29	36.31	0.13	3.08	2.82
NWFP	0.83	1.10	68.30	0.04	0.04	18.13	3.95	7.59
FATA	0.01	0.10	99.70	0.05	0.01	0.02	0.00	0.90

Source: Population Census Organization, *Statistical Book of Pakistan, 1988.*

Punjabi-Pukhtoon Ittehad (PPI). Another spectre of activism in Sindh – a spill-over from inter-ethnic polarisation – has been organised social ban-ditry which has added to general insecurity throughout the province.

The ethnic situation in Sindh has defied the commonly held perception that economic betterment of two parallel communities could result in an 'integration' of their parallel strata giving way to more inter-ethnic harmony.[34] It has been seen that personal ambitions become synonymous with the ethnic ideals of the whole community and cause a severe sense of insecurity. For instance Urdu-speaking businessmen, long-entrenched in the economic and cultural life of Sukkur, Hyderabad and Karachi, have strong reservations about the Punjabi capitalist class in these cities.[35] Some sections of the Punjabi and Pushtun bureaucracy, business and landed classes may support the PPI; whereas educated unemployed youths from the Urdu-speaking families would support the MQM or similar groups. The Sindhi rural landlords patronise and receive support from the *haris* against 'the settlers' from up-country. The Baloch would naturally turn to their ethnic leadership when their communitarian interests were involved.

Zia's attempts to weaken the PPP in Sindh by making personal visits to G. M. Syed, extending quotas for another decade and trying to build up contacts with the ML and JI alienated the Muhajireen who interpreted it as the appeasement of Sindhi nationalism at their expense and that of the Biharis. Competition from other groups, the high rate of unemployment, urban congestion, violence and 'conspiracy on the part of the state or India factor may have been additional but peripheral factors fuelling ethnic consciousness'.[36] The proposed construction of the Kalabagh Dam was already a serious issue in Sindh and even Ghous Ali Shah, the ML chief minister under Zia, had been vocal against it. Yet the PPP had refused to join the SNA even after the suppression of the MRD struggle in 1983 in which, as seen earlier, the PPP in Sindh bore the brunt of retaliation from the military regime. The MQM's initial emphasis on the issue of nationality alienated a number of opinion groups in the country who generally referred to it as Muhajir chauvinism. Its subsequent demands for a separate Muhajir province equally infuriated non-muhajir communities, to whom it meant expulsion of non-Urdu speakers from Karachi and Hyderabad. Both the federalists and the nationalists held serious reservations about the organisation, its aims and tactics.[37]

FRAGMENTED POLITICAL CULTURE

Ethnic polarisation in Sindh has been a fall-out of Pakistan's political fragility. The widespread problems have been exploited by the administration and ethnic groups who benefited from each other's vulnerabilities. Ethnic militancy grew both as a symptom and an after-effect of the political maladies, exacerbated by demagogues for reasons of self-interest. After the elections in 1993 it seemed that Pakistan was finally heading towards a two-party system at the national level, yet long-standing politics of vendetta, opportunism and temporary prerogatives remained part of the culture. The absence of a national consensus on political and constitutional issues dismayed many citizens who believed that by avoiding the mistakes of the past a new beginning could be made.

Sindhi resentment against settlers started in the 1950s, when they were mainly Muhajireen and, in some cases, Punjabi officials. The separation of Karachi from Sindh in 1948 as a metropolitan territory followed by Liaquat's growing identification with the Muhajireen, sowed the first seeds of disenchantment. Sindhi leaders like G. M. Syed and Haider Bakhsh Jatoi found themselves marginalised by 'new' forces in their own province, while coveted economic prospects created by the departure of moneyed Hindus from the province were disappearing with the influx of Muhajir capital and manpower. Despite the Liaquat–Nehru Pact of 1951, trans-border migration continued unabated, engendering visible demographic configuration. In Pakistan, the official preferences for a unitary, centralist state through the maintenance of the India Act of 1935 and the

One-Unit scheme, created deep feelings of alienation among 'smaller' provinces. Thus, there developed a politics of pervasive friction and polarity between the centre and provinces which, to a large extent, explains Pakistan's continuing difficulties in governance.

Following the dissolution of Nazim ud-Din's cabinet in 1953 and the constituent assembly through executive blandishments, the central government convened a meeting with the provincial chief minister in Karachi in October 1954 to consider the One-Unit scheme. The justification of the scheme was that it would eradicate anomalies between the two wings of the country which were the main hurdle to the formulation of a constitution. It was stipulated that following the abrogation of the provincial boundaries, a single administrative–political unit called West Pakistan would resolve the question of parity once and for all. Pirzada Abdus Sattar, the then chief minister of Sindh, opposed the scheme and held a meeting with other Sindhi leaders like G. M. Syed, Shaikh Abdul Majid Sindhi, Mir Ghulam Ali Talpur and Ghulam Mustafa Bhurguri at the Talpur House. By consensus, they rejected the One-Unit scheme and communicated their decision to the governor of the province, who retaliated by dismissing the Pirzada cabinet and installing Ayub Khuro as chief minister. This move was intended to pilot the scheme through the provincial assembly, though Firoz Khan Noon, the chief minister of Punjab and his counterpart in the NWFP, Sardar Abdul Rashid, had also opposed the merger of the provinces. Overriding such differences the scheme was eventually implemented, which increased the tensions against the centre and produced a generation of politicians who were seen as betraying the cause of their own people. The centrist military regimes of Ayub Khan and Yahya Khan exacerbated bickering between the centre and provinces. The clashes between Bhutto and Mujib, followed by military action and Indian intervention, resulted in the separation of the eastern wing while the pre-1955 provinces were restored by dismantling the superimposed unity. Bhutto's populism, despite its massive appeal, occasionally relapsed into authoritarianism at a time when ethnic redefinition was already taking place in the country. The street agitation which took place in the absence of processes for bargaining and negotiation, only prepared the way for another martial law.

The execution of Z. A. Bhutto in 1979 in shadowy circumstances proved a turning point in the alienation of Sindh which was manifested during the protests by the Movement for the Restoration of Democracy (MRD) in 1983. The emergence of the MQM, its rabble-rousing against the Sindhis and Zia's dissolution of the government of Mohammad Khan Junejo, a native Sindhi, were additional reminders that the establishment and its non-Sindhi cohorts would never allow Sindhis a fair deal in national and provincial affairs. The MQM's actions against the PPP regime in Islamabad at the behest of official agencies and its eventual alliance with the IJI led by Nawaz Sharif, the chief minister of Punjab in 1990, consolidated Sindhi resentment against Islamabad and a deep suspicion towards non-Sindhi ethnic groups. The dismissal of Benazir Bhutto, another Sindhi politician – whom the establishment had accepted reluctantly and then expelled unceremoniously – left a bitter taste in the province. The Sindhi nationalists used such events to show that 'outsiders' made use of surrogate Sindhi politicians for symbolic reasons for a short while, and ditched them when they were no longer useful. Such a double-edged criticism went down well among the educated classes but was not reflected in electoral results, since the state remained powerful enough to carve its own alliances (for example, during the chief ministership of Jam Sadiq Ali). The tussle between the PPP and MQM, dissensions between the IJT and the MQM following the army action in June 1992, the grave political crises in Pakistan in early 1993 resulting in changing alliances in the country and continuous tensions between the MQM and the PPP regime all through 1994 further aggravated the contentious relationship between the centre and the provinces (as will be seen in more detail in the next chapter).

While the PPP wanted its own provincial regime in Sindh as a vindication of its stance against Nawaz Sharif, it simultaneously allowed pro-Ishaque Khan forces to operate in all the provinces, but without trusting them. The premiership of Nawaz Sharif followed a policy of drift. The defiant provincial governments banked on Benazir Bhutto against Sharif but followed directions from the presidency. Because of the discretionary powers enjoyed by the president under the Eighth Amendment, the provincial governments, suffering from severe contradictions and internal fragility, became more dependent on central executive authority. The provinces were in revolt against Nawaz Sharif the way Benazir Bhutto, just three years back, had faced orchestrated defiance against her authority, in particular from the Punjab and Sindh. History had come full circle with an ever-present crisis characterising the relationship between the centre and the provinces exacerbated by president–prime minister rivalries and the opposition intent upon exploiting the weaknesses and cracks in the powerful troika.[38] The army and civil service became divided during the polarisation and pushed Pakistan from one crisis to another, while the superior courts tried to deliver quick verdicts on intricate developments largely emanating from personal ambitions and institutional anomalies.[39] The establishment of the PPP regime in late 1993 both in the centre and in

Sindh heralded a new era of hope as the MQM, despite early confusion, participated in the electoral politics and supported Benazir Bhutto in the presidential campaign of Farooq Leghari. The PPP administration in 1993–94 was stronger, with both the prime minister and president belonging to the same party, and Pakistanis looked towards a new political 'deal' in the country to start an era of peace and stability. But their hopes were short-lived as another intense phase in polarisation between the government and opposition ensued in 1994 followed by complete disorder and chaos in Karachi.

Sindhi ethno-nationalism, based on a separate Sindhi identity, had made inroads among young intellectuals largely due to the efforts of G. M. Syed, the veteran Sindhi politician, who had been a one-time supporter of the demand for Pakistan. He was a charismatic leader with articulate ideas and sufficient economic resourcefulness to support his espousal of what was later known as Sindhi nationalism. He had parted ways with Jinnah and begun his own political movement, which passed through a number of phases and eventually came to be known as the Jeeye Sindh Movement. In the late 1980s he became the unchallenged leader of the Sindh National Alliance (SNA), which brought together various ideological groups.[40]

G. M. Syed (1904–95),[41] the leader of the Sindhi nationalists, managed to remain at the focal point from the early decades of the present century. Born in a family of *sajjada nishin*, land-owning syeds,[42] he began his political career at a comparatively young age by participating in the Khilafat Movement. In the 1930s, along with many other political leaders he campaigned for the separation of Sindh from Bombay. As an astute politician, he manipulated the factional hereditary politics of his province which moved around personalities like Sir Hidayatullah, Allah Bakhsh Soomro, Bandeh Ali Talpur and Abdullah Haroon. He then joined the All-India Muslim League and obtained a prominent position in the party. He was instrumental in introducing a number of vital resolutions on Pakistan in the Sindh assembly, which he later termed 'a mistake'.[43] During the early years of Pakistan, Syed joined the opposition forces and annoyed the military regime led by President Ayub, who imprisoned him. By the late 1960s, he was disillusioned with Pakistan and decided to fight against Punjabi domination. Thus, he established his Jeeye Sindh Mahaz. However, Syed's form of Sindhi nationalism received a crushing defeat at the hands of the PPP in the elections of 1970, when Sindh gave a massive verdict in favour of Z. A. Bhutto.

Under General Zia ul-Haq, Syed received special visits and treatment from the martial-law administrator for the reason that they both hated the PPP. Moreover, Syed was satisfied with Zia's policies which he believed would hasten the dismemberment of Pakistan and the advent of an independent Sindhudesh.[44] He acknowledged that there were ambiguities in his plans for Sindhudesh but put the blame on others, arguing that neither the masses nor the rich understood his views and policies.[45] However, his aversion to land reforms damaged his cause among several younger Sindhi radicals.[46] Many of these turned to Rasul Bakhsh Paleejo, another Sindhi leader who, through his Sindhi Shagird Tehreek, advocated land reforms, abolition of the *jargirdari* system and opposed dictatorship. Zia needed G. M. Syed who, unlike the PPP and Paleejo, had refused to join the MRD which in August 1983 led protests against his martial law. The MRD was established in 1981 under the leadership of Nusrat Bhutto to fight for the re-establishment of democratic institutions in Pakistan under the 1973 Constitution. The PPP therefore remained the major component of the MRD whereas the Muslim League, excluding a few individuals, tended to cooperate with Zia and participated in the partyless elections of 1985 along with Jama'at i-Islami (JI).

The Sindh National Alliance coalition established in 1988 did not win any seat in the elections of 1988, 1990 and 1993, and Syed's dream of establishing a separate Sindhudesh by ousting the non-Sindhis was dashed to the ground. Subsequently, many of his cohorts denounced 'outsiders' and their 'agents' in propaganda that was distributed among Sindhi youths. There have been many factionalist groups and individuals who, off and on, have supported Sindhi nationalism in their own ways. Mumtaz Ali Bhutto, a cousin of Zulfikar Ali Bhutto and a former chief minister of Sindh under the first PPP regime, was one of the co-founders of the Sindhi-Baloch-Pakhtun Front (SBPF) which came into existence in London when Attaullah Mengal, a former chief minister of Balochistan and a tribal chief, and Abdul Hafeez Pirzada, the law minister in Bhutto's government, demanded a decentralised confederation in Pakistan – a redistribution of powers on the basis of nationalities under a very weak centre. However, the SBPF proved abortive and since 1988–89 its leaders have busied themselves in alliances.

With the induction of democracy, Mumtaz Bhutto became chairman of his Sindh National Front and a senior office-bearer in the SNA, whereas Mengal stayed on in London. In the early 1990s, Pirzada tried for a new constitutional consensus within Pakistan, leaving G. M. Syed the largely undisputed leader of the nationalists. Hamida Khuro, the daughter of a former chief minister of Sindh, became a senior office-holder of the SNA and appeared to have inherited the intellectual leadership of the movement. In a rather curious series of interviews in Lahore in November 1991, she 'comforted' the Punjabis by suggesting that she had persuaded Syed to suspend his demand for an independent Sindhudesh, which the latter vehemently denied. In 1993, she contested elections from Larkana on a Muslim League ticket while supporting Nawaz Sharif and lost. Rasul Bakhsh Paleejo, the leftist ideologue who has spent several years in Zia's jails, was disliked by Syed who considered him to have been a collaborator with the military dictatorship since the 1960s. Paleejo himself was the general secretary of the Awami National Party (ANP), organised by Khan Abdul Wali Khan in cooperation with the former members of his National Awami Party (NAP). In 1990, Paleejo left the ANP when the leadership aligned itself with the Muslim League and Jama'at i-Islami in the IDA. He then largely absented himself from political activism. However, he remains popular with Sindhi-speaking youths from middle-income groups and is well known for his progressive, anti-feudal ideas. His setback resulted not only from electoral defeats but also from the mysterious death of his very close associate, Fazil Hussain Rahu. Coming from a humble background both Paleejo and Rahu were strong opponents of the dynastic politics of *mirs*, *pirs*, *syeds* and *sardars* as they organised the Sindhi Shagird Tehreek and Awami Tehreek along revolutionary lines. Paleejo had initially joined the SNA but left it over the lack of an ideological dimension.

The JI was one of the most well-organised parties in Sindh until the 1980s with a vast following among Urdu-speakers and a sizeable number of Sindhi-speaking elites. But its support for General Zia ul-Haq and then the role of its student wing, Islami Jamiat i-Tulaba (IJT), on the campuses in Pakistan damaged its standing. With the emergence of the second generation of Urdu-speakers in Sindh, the loyalties of the old vanguard for the JI were replaced with the desire to have a new, dynamic and responsive organisation based on ehtnic solidarity to 'fight it out' with all the other groups. The JI had considered urban Sindh (and particularly Karachi) to be its main bastion of power since 1947. However, from 1984, the MQM began to claim the same constituency, which put the two parties on a constant course of confrontation in the press, on the streets and on campuses. Each accused the other of kidnap and torture. Interestingly, the two organisations were part and parcel of the IDA, along with the ANP which had previously been a steadfast critic of the JI. Before it splintered into Baloch and Pushtun factions, the ANP claimed to be the guardian of the interests of both communities. Occasionally the leadership used leftist rhetoric including the demand for a nationality-based loose federation in Pakistan. During the 1970s, Khan Wali Khan, the late Abdus Samad Achakzai and the late Mir Ghaus Bakhsh Bizenjo (both from Balochistan) talked of provincial autonomy and not of separatism.[47] In the 1990s the ANP, led by

Wali Khan, aligned itself with the IDA – which included some of its former opponents – and Ajmal Khan Khattak, a firebrand Pushtun critic of Zia, represented the party in Nawaz Sharif's cabinet. The ANP supported Sharif in his ordeal with the president in 1993 and stood by him in the subsequent national and provincial elections. The JI, amongst others, has always criticised both the MQM and ANP for allegedly being anti-Pakistan groups.[48] According to the JI, the MQM is simply a lingual group spreading hatred whereas ANP was viewed as pro-Kabul and pro-Moscow with a soft spot for Delhi. In the event, both the ANP and the JI have lost a number of ardent followers who emphasise the *ideological* factor but feel uncomfortable operating merely as pressure groups to make or break governments.

Both the JI and the PPP retain their support in urban and rural Sindh yet are apprehensive of the MQM which, as manifested in various elections, remains the third largest party in the country. From time to time, despite mutual denunciations, there were rumours of an electoral 'agreement' between the JI and the PPP. Professor Ghafoor Ahmad, the undisputed leader of the JI after its Amir (in this case Qazi Hussain Ahmed, a Pushtun) was the main link in this PPP–JI entente in 1991–92. Any attempt by the JI to move closer to the PPP even for symbolic reasons would produce curious results. For example, during the summer of 1991 the MQM and the JI engaged in internecine street battles in Karachi until tempers cooled off in October when Altaf Hussain and Jam Sadiq Ali left for London for 'medical' check-ups for an extended period. It would suit any government to see its well-organised and volatile partners counterbalancing each other as a trade-off. Such a policy suited the PPP-led opposition known as the Pakistan Democratic Alliance (PDA) which could sit back and watch the two ruling factions at each other's throats. It also provided the PPP and the Sindhi nationalists with an opportunity to discredit the regime led by a Punjabi prime minister. In addition, of course, it demoralised the whole of Pakistan and eventually resulted in a military operation. In the end this polarisation damaged both the JI and the MQM. History repeated itself when in 1994–95 the MQM fought street battles with the police and security agencies operating under orders from the PPP adminstration. The opposition parties such as the ML, the ANP and the JI watched the PPP regime fight it out with MQM militants. Concurrently, street battles between the MQM's factions (Altaf and Haqiqi) were watched gleefully by their political opponents.

The PPP and the ML are the two main national/federal parties as opposed to the ethno-regional organisations espousing narrowly based political ideals. Both parties have a strong belief in Pakistan as one nation and are led by moderate elites. The PPP is a mass-based party which believes in federation and on two occasions it has defeated the nationalists electorally and earned the hatred of those such as G. M. Syed and his cohorts. The reason why Sindh voted massively for the PPP in 1970, 1988 and then in 1993 owes much to the fact that the Sindhis have an over-whelming belief in Pakistan. Its performance in the 1990 elections was also significant in terms of its share as a single party. Although G. M. Syed never gave credit to the mass popularity of the PPP, it is known to every conscious Pakistani voter that the PPP as a major party strengthens a federal Pakistan. The ML, on the other hand, has been well entrenched in Sindh since long before independence, but failed to give enough attention to the serious problems faced by Sindhis and to reach the grassroots. Having a few prominent *sardars* and *mirs* on the roll was not sufficient to gain mass popularity. Its collaborative role with General Zia from 1985 followed by an electoral coalition with the JI to form the IJT further damaged its image. The ML has had its own cadre of very influential leaders in Sindh like Pir Pagara and Mohammad Khan Junejo, who both lost to the PPP in the 1988 and 1990 elections. These leaders judiciously distanced themselves from the nationalists. However, the ML was able to reclaim a number of seats in the 1993 elections.

After the dismissal of Benazir Bhutto's government in August 1990, Ghulam Mustafa Jatoi, one of the biggest *waderas* of Sindh, and an early co-founder of the PPP, was appointed as the caretaker prime minister. During the 1980s, Jatoi had looked after the PPP when the Bhuttos were in exile. His alleged overtures with the martial-law regime and ambition to become prime minister led to his being ousted from the party. He formed his own National People's Party (NPP), which has lacked a distinct party nomenclature, and continued to remain apart from the nationalists even when he was defeated in his own ancestral constituency by the PPP. Jatoi's credentials as an acceptable candidate for the premiership by the Pakistani establishment have frequently caused speculation about his reemergence as the leader of the house.

A faction of the Muslim League continues under the leadership of the legendry Pir of Pagara, a native Sindhi but with strong matrimonial and personal relationships with the Punjab-based ruling families. He is a leading landlord as well as having millions of followers, generally known as Hurs. They are mainly rural/tribal Sindhis with a low rate of literacy and a strong spiritual commitment to the Pir, whose father was executed by the British and so became a martyr. His two sons were sent to England for education in a boarding school and the Pir returned home after inde-pendence with a strong commitment to Pakistan. He is a powerful figure who avoided any political office though both Zia and Junejo sought his blessings. Once he had taken office as premier, Junejo gathered the majority of parliamentarians elected in partyless elections on the platform of the Muslim League. The League is a party of influential families with little mass-based support in Sindh; yet it is these dynastic families in Pakistan that have always mattered. When Junejo, the post-1985 leader of the Muslim League, lost to the PPP in 1988, it was Nawaz Sharif who became the *de facto* leader. His youth, vibrancy, financial resources and Punjabi background, helped along by waywardness in Benazir Bhutto's administration, rejuvenated the League – though the Pir never felt comfortable with this new leadership coming from an industrial/urban background and representing a new generation in the country. However strongly he felt about the new leadership, he nevertheless avoided causing any major disruption.

Nawaz Sharif, with the League behind him, turned to more ambitious ventures and consummated the most curious alliance in Pakistan's history called the IDA/IJT – although perhaps not that surprising given the history of shifting loyalties in the country. Like the PPP and NPP, the League sat on the sidelines watching its two other partners squabbling over leadership in urban Sindh. Meanwhile, the Pir consolidated his personal friendship with Jam Sadiq Ali and through him with Altaf Hussain during their visit to London for medical treatment in October and November 1991. Despite all the manoeuvres and personality-based factionalism in Pakistani politics as well as riots in Karachi, the Pir continues to make occasional comical statements on the situation substantiated by astrological claims. In the elections of 1993, the ML led by Nawaz Sharif came second to the PPP – a development that was hastily interpreted as the beginning of a two-party system in the country.[49]

The religio-political parties like the Jamiat i-Ulama i-Islam (JUI) led by Maulana Fazlur Rahman, son of the late Maulana Mufti Mahmud, has had stronger roots in Balochistan and the NWFP and has a limited constituency in Sindh. The Jamiat represents the Deobandi school of Islamic revivalism emphasising a more puritanical form of Islamic government. On the other hand, the Jamiat i-Ulama i-Pakistan (JUP), which is closer to the masses in terms of its acceptance of a number of folk-based rituals, has a major following in Sindh and the Punjab. Its leader, Maulana Noorani, has been a persistent critic of martial law and judiciously refrained from joining any electoral coalition during the late 1980s. Espousing the Brelvi school of revivalism, this Jamiat has several *mashaikh* and *sajjada nishin* among its members and thus reaches grassroots Pakistan. But Noorani's party generally lost its urban seats in Sindh to the MQM in various local, provincial and national elections, and this allowed the Jamiat i-Mashaikh – a loose group of *sajjada nishin* and *pirs* – to strike direct links with the state. Noorani opposes both the MQM and the nationalists for 'sabotaging' Islam and Pakistan through language-and tribe/territory-based schisms. However, despite his belief in the universality of Islam, Noorani also believes in Pakistani nationhood. During many crucial and volatile months in Pakistan's recent years, Noorani spent his time in Africa propagating Islam, though he came to the forefront during the Gulf crisis in support of Saddam Hussein. Alternatively, the main religio-political parties including the JI, the JUI, Sipah-i Sahaba and Ahle-Hadith have been supportive of Saudi Arabia and its policies in the region, while the Tehreek-i Nifaza-i Fiqh a-Jaafria, representing Pakistan's Shias, has been supportive of Iran.

The entire socio-political scene in Sindh can be summed up as ethno-regional conflict in the absence of a long-overdue democratic system and the inadequacy of certain religio-political parties in responding to the changing situation. Pakistani nationalism has still to prove its credentials *vis-à-vis* the ethnic and regionalist loyalties that have been more conflict-oriented. Perhaps the role of class is being replaced by 'communal' consciousness in the entire South Asian region where language and territorial loyalties have whipped up ethnic awareness and emphasised 'separateness'. The *state* initially exonerated itself from responsibility for the development of civil society and when confronted with severe contradictions it sought refuge in temporary administrative measures. Given its non-democratic characteristics, consolidated over a long period, the demise of civil society has intensified the polarisation. Under the circumstances, any elected government is handicapped by its own flaws and restraints and can do no more than to confront the situation. Negotiations and long-term policy measures have been substituted by short-term administrative decisions and personal choices. Politics and state remain hostages to individuals.

ETHNO-NATIONALISM IN SINDH: SOME INTERPRETATIONS

In order to understand Sindhi ethnic nationalism, and any other ethnicity-based movement in Sindh, three major interpretations must be considered: (1) The intellectual/cultural view; (2) the new left view; and (3) the Islamists' view.

(1) The intellectual interpretation of Sindhi ethno-nationalism has been provided by writers like G. M. Syed, Shaikh Ayaz, Abdulwahid Aresar, G. Allana, Hamida Khuro and Fahmida Riaz among others. Syed emerged

as the focal point due to his long political career and constant defiance of the authorities in Delhi, Karachi and Islamabad. His rise to preeminence owed much to his family background as a land-owning *syed* in rural Sindh and was maintained by his stance on crucial contemporary issues like Khilafat, separation of Sindh, Pakistan, One-Unit, Punjabi–Muhajir domination of Pakistan and his espousal of Sindhudesh by openly defying the populist regime of Benazir Bhutto. His tirades against Jinnah, Sir Shahnawaz Bhutto, Benazir Bhutto, Wali Khan, Paleejo and Altaf Hussain together with his overtures to Indira Gandhi, Rajiv Gandhi and the authorities in Kabul and Moscow, gave him both publicity and notoriety. To the nationalists (separatists), he was the father figure; to the average Pakistani he was a traitor; to many religio-political parties he was a collaborator with the non-Muslims; and to a few foreign observers his Gandhi-like appearance made him 'a rights campaigner for the backward province of Sindh'.[50] It is not surprising that after spending almost all his life in opposition to so many leaders and organisations, G. M. Syed might have reached a point of total frustration with life. His cynical attacks left a bitter taste and his lack of a political and economic programme for his 'Sindhudesh' left his position unclear. However, young unemployed Sindhis, electorally rejected elements and certain vested interests found an outlet in his tirades.

There are many intellectuals who do feel strongly that Sindh has been wronged throughout history and who advocate the resurgence of a strong Sindhi identity – not on the basis of hatred yet sharing a severe sense of alienation and suspicion toward 'settlers'. Fahmida Riaz, the director-general of the National Book Council of the Government of Pakistan in Islamabad during 1989–90, and a known literary figure in Urdu writings, is a good example. While living in self-imposed exile in India during the latter years of martial law, she wrote a commentary on literature in Pakistan and elaborated on themes such as protest and alienation. She stated that in the late 1950s and early 1960s Urdu literature stagnated whereas Sindhi nationalism flourished in its literature:

> During this period, the anti-One-Unit movement in Sindh had gained momentum and young Sindhi writers dedicated themselves to their national cause. Their literature fully reflected the aspirations of Sindhi masses. Many writers who emerged during this era, like Amar Jaleel, Muneer Ahmad and Ali Baba, were later to dominate the literary horizon for a long time. Regional identity, in a way, helped them to separate religion from politics. Unlike West Punjab, where no non-Muslims remained after partition, in Sindh a good sprinkling of Hindus

chose to stay. This had been possible because of the essentially non-hostile relationship between the two communities. There were practically no riots between Sindhi Hindus and Sindhi Muslims. However, the incoming refugees from India tried to spark off disturbances wherever they settled, which was mainly in large cities and towns. The migration of Hindus, accordingly, took place from these places, whereas in the interior of Sindh, peace continued to prevail and thousands of Hindu families were unaffected. The great, unprecedented influx of non-Sindhis, brought the local Muslims closer to local Hindus.[51]

Riaz believes that Muslim Sindhis found much in common with Hindu Sindhis when immigration from outside created 'an alien culture'. This alliance went unnoticed by the authorities as it took place in remote villages, though it constrained the power of the JI in those areas. It was in these villages that riots were organised and Syed's kind of separatist nationalism became popular. On the intellectual background to this nationalism, Riaz gives the major credit to Shaikh Ayaz whose poetry 'is so closely intertwined with the national aspirations of Sindh that it has come to be synonymous with Sindhi nationalism. Its wide appeal, however, is evidence of the fact that its vitality does not rest entirely on the conditions which helped to give it birth.' Ayaz is one of the foremost writer in Sindhi and Urdu who published his first major Sindhi poetry collection in the early 1960s; entitled *Bhanwar Bhre Akass* it challenged the age-old views of mysticism in Sindhi poetry. His poems are a sensuous and earthy celebration of human feelings. He uses non-Arabic, non-Persian words deriving much of his vocabulary and idiom from the works of the celebrated Shah Abdul Latif Bhitai, doyen of Sindh classical poets and mystics. In his fondness for Sindh, Ayaz observed:

> O Sindh! If ever I have come upon a single word, a single phrase of some Talented One, I have snatched it from him. For you, I have robbed the poor and stolen from beggars. Bit by bit, I have made a collection and, like a goldsmith, have scrubbed it clean and sparkling ... I have never been caught, nor have I left footprints anywhere. I confess this to you in confidence; otherwise of my deeds, there is no witness.[52]

Shaikh Ayaz is one of the most prominent writers in present-day Sindhi literature who has tried to portray the plight of the poor and uprooted. Three of his early poetry collections received Pakistan's highest literary awards but were proscribed by the Ayub Khan government which put him in prison for 'seditious' writings. Zulfikar Ali Bhutto appointed him vice-chancellor of the Sindh University – a position he retained for some time under General Zia.[53] It was only after relinquishing the job that Ayaz was able to concentrate on his creative works. In an interview he observed: 'I am not just a political poet. My poetry subsumes everything in the universe – the history of the people of the world, their miseries and anguish, everything I felt. But I have given priority to Sindh, as it is my birthplace. It is my identity in Pakistan and I belong to that nationality.'[54] Shaikh Ayaz today feels enthusiastic about the inclusion of regional vocabularies in Urdu, for it must operate as an integrative medium among the various linguistic communities. In addition, he feels strongly that religion is a personal choice; he condemns dictatorship and espouses democracy. His approach, at present, resembles Fichte's model of cultural nationalism and is not at all rejectionist.

(2) The leftist or liberal approach to the ethnic situation in Sindh takes into account the economic contradictions within the Pakistani, especially Sindhi, socio-economic structure, which are considered responsible for creating class conflicts along the lines of rural versus urban, feudal versus middle class and ruling elites versus have-nots. It also looks at the question of nationalities in a deterministic way, tracing its origin in the Pakistani capitalist economic order which it considers to be a derivative of the neo-colonial world order, carried on by the privileged classes in Pakistan. Such a system was destined to have cracks, which have appeared in the form of strong ethno-national or ethno-regional movements, for example the SNA or the MQM. The leftist school of sociologists and political analysts, while initially bewildered by the character and leadership of these movements, feels sympathetic toward them. With a few exceptions, such an interpretation, like that of the nationalists or separatists, smacks of escapism, taking the 'settlers' to be the major scapegoats. The leftist/liberal school of analysts includes authors like V. Gankovsky, Selig Harrison, Hamza Alavi, Tariq Ali, Feroz Ahmed and others.

Alavi considers that for the last several decades Pakistan has been trying to define its nationhood and its relationship with the aspirants of sub-nationalism, largely because 'Pakistani nationhood' has been the monopoly of the 'Punjabis who dominate the ruling bureaucracy and the military that has effectively been in power in Pakistan since its inception; in partnership, they might say, until the mid-seventies with Muhajirs who were relatively well-represented in the Punjabi dominated state apparatus. Members of the under-privileged have tended to see themselves as subject peoples who have not been given their rightful place in the nation. In their eyes, with a subtle inflection of meaning, the "nation" is transmuted into "country".' However, the 'country' could not be a substitute for 'nation' as the people of Pakistan, according to this authority, are yet to be fused together as a community. Pakistani nationalism has remained a force from above without any long struggle for freedom; it became a country without first becoming a nation, unlike many European or other nation-states. It has been ruled by a pressure group called the *salariat*, which comprises the urban middle class, the bureaucracy and military elites, whose antecedents go back to the nineteenth century.[55]

According to Alavi, the Pakistan Movement was a *salariat*-based and *salariat*-led movement, which catered to its specific interests in the context of the Punjabi–Muhajir oligarchy, since the heart of the movement was based in the UP, with the Punjabis joining it in the 1940s. He believes that the Pakistan Movement was defined by 'a religious ethnic criterion namely, "Muslim". Pakistan was not created, as is ideologically represented by some interests in Pakistan today, to create an "Islamic" state.' In Sindh, according to Alavi's interpretation, an ethnic Sindhi *salariat* did not exist as the Sindhi Muslims were either *waderas* or *haris*, whereas the urban population was overwhelmingly Hindu. Balochistan and the NWFP were similar, having no Muslim *salariat*, unless one confuses the tribal/feudal chieftains in these vast areas with *salariat*. Alavi rightly refers to Jinnah's oft-quoted speech of August 1947 when he made 'a clear declaration of secular citizenship in the new state, a speech that ideological vested interests in Pakistan have a hard time explaining away'. Over the years, with the emergence of the regional *salariats* in the smaller provinces, the Muhajir–Punjabi coalition came under serious criticism as the new *salariats* defined themselves in separate ethnic terms. With the establishment of Bangladesh, these ethno-regional aspirations became more powerful and in the 1980s religious unity would not work as a panacea.

In Sindh the ethnic contradictions appeared rather forcefully, for it has been a multi-ethnic province since the Balochis and Gujaratis emigrated there in the early years and were accepted as Sindhis. After independence, the Urdu-speaking refugees replaced the urban Hindus in Sindh and the Sindhis, to their discomfort, realised that 'they had not only to deal with Punjabi domination of the state but also to compete with the relatively advanced Muhajirs'. The lateral influx of Punjabis, Pushtuns and others further changed the demographic situation to the detriment of the Sindhi *salariat*. Quoting from the census of 1981, Alavi finds that 52 per cent of the population of Sindh consisted of Sindhi-speaking inhabitants, whereas Urdu-speakers made up 22 per cent of the total population and 50 per cent of the population of Karachi, Hyderabad and Sukkur. In Karachi, 54.03 per cent of the population were Urdu speakers, 13.06 per cent were

Punjabis; 8.7 per cent were Pushtuns from the NWFP and the rest were Afghans, Iranians, Sri Lankans, Burmese, Africans and others. The Biharis, Afghans, Iranians and Bangladeshis arrived in Karachi after the statistics for 1981 were published. Alavi is shocked that in the capital of Sindh only 6.3 per cent were Sindhi speakers which was a cause of grievance to Sindhi nationalists. He takes into account the class formation of the Karachi population where 40 per cent of the inhabitants live in slums – *katchi abadis* – and the affluent *salariat* inhabit prosperous areas, causing a severe sense of mutual antagonism.[56]

According to Feroz Ahmed, a leading leftist Sindhi intellectual based in the United States, 'nationality' is a fashionable word in the Pakistani lexicon and it is not clear when it started being applied to Pakistan, though its origin is related to the concept of nationalities in the Soviet Union. Although it may be anathema to Pakistani officials, Ahmed feels that the concept of ethno-linguistic communities, defining themselves as nationalities 'is not based on the mischief of "anti-state" elements'; rather, each one 'evolved into a distinct ethno-linguistic community which, in political terms, should legitimately be called a nationality. Organised and vicious anti-intellectualism of the state of Pakistan and right-wing forces cannot alter this historical and academic fact.' He claims it has involved a process covering thousands of years in the history of these peoples.[57] According to this thesis, Sindhis obtained their community-consciousness way back in history by resisting the foreign invaders. The British faced continuous insurgency in Sindh until they had to impose martial law in 1942 as the Hurs carried on their struggle against the Raj. Such an experience brought the Sindhis together and they supported India-wide movements like the Muslim League.

Unlike Riaz, Ahmed feels that the Hindu money-lenders were a class of exploiters like the Sindhi *waderas*, and the peasantry sought relief in Pakistan. Basing his argument on the statistics provided by Syed, Ahmed asserts that the Hindu money-lenders 'had grabbed nearly 2.5 million acres of land of the peasants as well as of the landlords. The exit of the Hindus, the peasants hoped, would provide them some relief.'[58] Ahmed traces a number of causes, similar to those given by Alavi, for the resurgence of nationality sentiments in Sindh. Along with immigration, he pinpoints the ideological orientation of the power elites as the main reason for Sindhi alienation. 'Islam, integrity of Pakistan and the Urdu language became the code words for national domination. In the name of Pakistan's unity and integrity, the very foundation of unity was eroded.'[59] In addition, he blames the exploitation of Sindhi resources by the Punjabis and feels that Sindh has always suffered because of conspiracies against it. The refugees replaced the Hindu exploitative class and even Karachi was initially taken away from Sindh. In this power politics, some Sindhi surrogates helped the Punjabi–Muhajir oligarchy so that the 'Sindhis would be reduced to the status of the American Indians'.[60] The execution of Zulfikar Ali Bhutto and the use of extensive military power in 1983 during the MRD struggle in Sindh, brought the alienation of the Sindhis to a climax:

> The obverse side of the coin was that the aggregate response from Punjab was extremely limited and of a very low intensity. Failure of the movement to topple Zia ul Haq and the use of the regular army, amid an anti-Sindhi propaganda blitz, to suppress the movement added all the more significance to this differential response and led to the intensification of national feelings in Sind.[61]

(3) The Islamists feel that the solution to Pakistan's problems lies in the enforcement of the Islamic code on the premise that Islam is more than a religion, rather it is a complete guide for life. The JI has been the leading proponent of this view-point and its early opposition to the Pakistan Movement in the 1940s stemmed from its leaders' strong reservations about the Muslim Leaguers, whom it regarded as extremely westernised. Like many other religio-political parties, the JI disagreed with the political creed of the ML but found it judicious to strive for the implementation of Islamic order in Pakistan. The JI, until the early 1980s, remained strong in urban Sindh even though its performance in the elections was dismal. It has dominated the student unions in universities and colleges through its student wing, yet it was not able to develop into a mass-based organisation. The leaders of the JI from the late Maulana Syed Abul Ala'a Maudoodi to Professor Ghafoor Ahmed (one time general secretary of the IDA), Mian Tufail to Qazi Hussain Ahmad (the two Amirs of the JI since Maulana Maudoodi); intellectuals like Syed Assad Gilani, Professor Khurshid Ahmad, Anees Ahmad, Ijaz Shafi Gilani and Tahir Amin; journalists like Altaf Hussain Qureshi and the late Salah ud-Din – the last two representing the monthly *Urdu Digest* in Lahore and weekly *Takbeer* in Karachi – strongly supported and campaigned for an Islamic solution to the ethnic problem in Pakistan. Their support for the Afghan resistance or the Kashmiri activists has largely rested on the same premise which in 1971 aligned them with Yahya's troops against Mujibur Rahman, whom they considered an Indian agent. The JI actively supported military action in Muslim Bengal through organisations like Al-Badr and Al-Shams, which were heavily represented by the Urdu-speaking inhabitants of Bangladesh commonly known as the Biharis. However, though its support for Zia might have helped them both, the JI suffered a credibility gap

among the democratic forces. It feels strongly that a 'foreign hand' is responsible for Pakistan's domestic problems, including Sindh, and believes in a strong stance *vis-à-vis* India. Interestingly, all these leaders, excluding the present Amir, are emigrants from India. We will briefly discuss the views of two JI intellectuals on the ethnic situation in Pakistan. Professor Khurshid Ahmad, a senator and former deputy chairman of the Planning Commission of Pakistan, believes that Islam

> provides a *new basis* for the organization of human society and an equity-based framework for the flourishing of a united yet diversified and genuinely pluralistic society. It establishes its social organization on a faith and ideology that is universal and open to all, ensuring equal opportunities for attaining the most sublime, morally, spiritually and materially and is also tolerant enough to accept those who refuse to join its ideological fold. Within the Islamic community and between the Islamic community and other communities and nationalities it refuses to impose a strategy of forced similarity. Instead it pursues the path of unity in diversity, equality alongside acceptances of differences as genuine and authentic.[62]

He argues that an Islamic democracy based on the concept of *Shoora* representing the Muslim community – *Millat* – can create an all-encompassing ethnic unity among Pakistanis. In an extensive study of ethno-national movements since 1947, Tahir Amin divides the history of Pakistan into specific periods: liberal (1947–70), socialist (1971–77), and Islamic (1977–88). Arguing that the ethno-national movements have their antecedents in pre-partition developments, his study covers the Pushtunistan movement, the Balochistan movement and the Sindhi separatist movement in the context of internal and external factors. According to Amin, economic development alone will not eradicate secessionist movements; rather the consolidation of a participatory democratic system based on Islamic justice can guarantee the enduring integration of the Pakistani nation-state. Tahir Amin considers the founder of Sindhi ethno-nationalism to be G. M. Syed who gave it a socialist framework in 1953 by establishing Sind Awami Mahaz, a coalition of four parties. The Sind Hari Committee, founded by Haider Bakhsh Jatoi was a communist organisation within the Mahaz and its founder coined the term *Jeeye Sind* (Long live Sindh) in opposition to two key institutions of the state – the army and the bureaucracy. Raja Dahir, a Hindu ruler of Sindh at the time of Ibn-i Qasim's invasion in AD 711 was eulogised as a national hero, whereas the Punjabis, Muhajireen and other 'outsiders' were branded as exploiters. The movement gained support among middle-class Sindhis and a few feudal lords until the language issue attained a serious dimension in the early seventies. Mumtaz Ali Bhutto, the PPP chief minister of Sindh and a strong supporter of Sindhi-speakers, successfully put a resolution to the Sindh provincial assembly stipulating the adoption of Sindhi as an official language. The act was toned down by the timely intervention of Bhutto, yet it caused severe resentment among the non-Sindhi speaking communities and further reinforced Sindhi ethno-national feelings. On 18 June 1972, Jeeye Sind Mahaz under the leadership of Syed demanded provincial autonomy, adoption of Sindhi as the national and official language and a one-fourth share in all civil and military services, along with the repatriation of allotted land to the Sindhis.

All these interpretations of Sindhi nationalism highlight the complexity of ethnic politics in Sindh. They equally underline the need for an accountable, decentralised and commonly agreed political system based on distributive justice. While the Sindhi nationalists may be lacking a strong and articulate political platform, their urban counterparts – Muhajireen – have already attempted to spearhead their demands from the platform of the MQM, one of the most complex, well-organised and activist ethnic parties ever to emerge in the country.

10 The Rise of the Muhajir Qaumi Movement and Ethnic Politics in Sindh

The most serious threat to Pakistan's polity since its inception has been from conflictive ethnic militancy. More recently this threat has come in particular from Sindh. The various plural communities in the province in pursuit of self-definition continually antagonise each other, and so add further strains on the federation. In general, both ethnic and pseudo-ethnic protests choose violent means and exacerbate the country's governability crisis. The Sindhis, led by umbrella organisations like the Sindh National Alliance (SNA) or Jeeye Sindh, have complained of economic marginalisation, cultural alienation and political deprivation. Parallel to them, the second generation of Urdu-speaking Muhajireen[1] in Sindh has been responsible for unprecedented organisational work in urban centres through the powerful Muhajir Qaumi Movement (MQM) which, in 1988 and 1990, captured almost all the seats in the national and provincial assembly elections of Hyderabad, Sukkur and Karachi besides an already existing absolute majority in the municipal governments of these cities. In the elections of 1993, once again the MQM won 27 seats in the provincial assembly, reaffirming its stature as the third largest party in Pakistan after the Pakistan People's Party (PPP) and the Muslim League (ML). Both in electoral politics and street agitation, the MQM has superseded all rival parties, and to a great extent replaced the former Karachi-based national political parties such as Jama'at i-Islami (JI), the Awami National Party (ANP) and Jamiat i-Ulama i-Pakistan (JUP). Its emergence on the Pakistani socio-political scene has been so dramatic that sociologists and political analysts have not yet fully understood the process.

THE MQM: A PREVIEW

The MQM is exceptional in the recent history of Pakistan by virtue of its own specific characteristics – its predominantly urban, class-specific, youthful membership, mobilised in the name of an *imagined* ethnicity and motivated by radical ideas. On occasions, it has been portrayed by its numerous opponents as a terrorist organisation working for the Indian RAW and the former KGB to destabilise Pakistan.[2] In the recent past, the MQM organised successful free bazaars and eye-hospitals for the poor but, largely because of its militancy, it has also incurred the wrath of various regimes and other ethnic communities in urban and rural Sindh. Undoubtedly, the MQM has the largest urban representation of all the political parties. Equally, it has been the only middle-class political organisation which without pretending to be secular appeared more mundane than many of its counterparts. It has made use of folk cultural symbols yet its emphasis has remained centred on regional politics. Although it was anticipated that it could become a cross-ethnic and cross-regional party, it has confined itself to a core in urban Sindh. Other than the PPP, the MQM has been the only party to mobilise a large number of women in the country's history, apart from a brief period in 1947 when the Muslim League in Punjab had been able to mobilise women in Lahore against the Unionist government. The MQM has been a party of youths, which reflects recent demographic realities in Pakistan, and all its leaders at the time of formation were in their twenties. In addition, and equally significant, the MQM has had the largest proportion of educated membership of all the national parties except the JI, but in the latter case there is a rigorous selection procedure.

Being an urban, youthful and organisationally well-knit party, the MQM has been able to mobilise some of the largest demonstrations in Karachi and Hyderabad at short notice even when it was not in government. Its ward committees, *mohalla* units, regional sectors and overall provincial structures with international networks in the UK, the USA and the Arabian Gulf have added to its political muscle. According to its manifesto, the MQM is a progressive organisation in favour of land reforms, an end to the quota system, the preservation of cultural heritage, lowering of the age of voting from 21 to 18, the reorganisation of constituencies and other electoral reforms. It has favoured the decentralisation of central and provincial powers by redistributing them among the elected local councillors. In its manifestos and other policy statements, it has promised an egalitarian taxation system, equal opportunities in education and reorganisation of the transport system in urban Sindh. It has demanded strict adherence to domicility, making it either a birthright or contingent upon residency for 25 years – thus ensuring that it is difficult for 'outsiders' to obtain positions in the province. It has promised priority in jobs for local people enjoying Sindhi domicility and demanded more positions for Muhajireen in the municipal, provincial and national services. It has also stipulated strict land allotment for domiciled residents along with the legalisation of *katchi abadis* in Karachi established before 1978, so allowing the provision of necessary civic amenities. On occasions the MQM has defined Muhajireen as the fifth nationality in Pakistan, and urged the 'cessation of *zulm* [cruelty] perpetrated on Muhajir *qaum*' and the repatriation of 'stranded Pakistanis from Bangladesh'.[3]

The founders of the MQM and most of its activists represent the lower middle class who have experienced unemployment and abuse of power by the police, the bureaucracy and the feudal class. The movement was aware of its power-base in terms of demographic realities and virtually *created* an ethnic identity from what had been merely a fleeting ideal to members of the previous generation. Its networking, unending supply of volunteers, funds and mobility helped it create a *Muhajir* identity, though language and *hijrat* to a promised land were the sole determinants to bring together a medley of diversified groups. The leadership has constantly vacillated between different terms in describing the Muhajir identity – such as *qaum* (nation), *qaumaiat* (nationality) and *nassal* (race), which have led to confusion about its ultimate objectives. At different times, the demand for a separation of urban areas from rural Sindh and its designation as *Muhajir subah* (province) would follow the demand for a separate city-state of Karachi [Jinnahpur?], or its internationalisation as 'a new Hong Kong'. This has generated speculation and periodic controversies that have disheartened many moderate Urdu-speakers and alienated other communities from MQM-led Muhajir politics.

The MQM has used propaganda techniques such as mass rallies, strikes, posters, graffiti, printed literature, audio and video cassettes to maintain its 'closed net-work'. Its titular leader, Altaf Hussain – addressed as the *Quaid-i Tehreek* – frequently used trans-continental satellite technology to address rallies in different countries.[4] While spending most of his time in London ostensibly for health reasons and for personal security, the Quaid would speak at length by phone or via satellite to his followers in Karachi, Hyderabad, Chicago, New York and Riyadh. Funds and volunteers would pour in during its heyday and hatchet men displayed the unsavoury side of the MQM through abductions, torture and even the elimination of many critics or 'misled rebels'.[5] The MQM includes unemployed youth, the educated unemployed and underemployed and evolved from the student cadres of Karachi University. It fought against the stereotype of Muhajireen as docile and timid, using militancy and violence bordering on fascism to demolish such humiliating caricatures.

Although unique in certain crucial aspects, the MQM has suffered from problems similar to those of other Pakistani political parties. It experienced a personality cult, with Altaf Hussain assuming the uncontested leadership by means of rhetoric, demagogy, ambiguity and coercion. For a long time Hussain has remained the focal point through a combination of charisma, propaganda, machinations and the fascist structure of the movement. He was made into a cult figure (*pir*); opposition to him was forcefully eliminated, and myths were publicised about his supreme authority and personality. He assumed the authoritarian position of godfather for the Muhajireen and basked in the presence of prime ministers, chief ministers, bureaucrats and parliamentarians who came to his house to pay homage to the *quaid*. The press was blackmailed by strong-arm tactics including physical reprimand, kidnapping and other terrorist acts performed by well-organised groups of armed men. Huge posters of Hussain across Karachi and Hyderabad and his ever-available guidance from London never allowed gullible followers any doubt about the infallibility of *Altaf Bhai*. Like other parties, the MQM attached great importance to staying in the corridors of power of both metropolitan and national politics; it betrayed a deep sense of temporary expediency rather than a commitment to higher and enduring principles. Alliances with the military regime, intelligence agencies and other powerful echelons in the Pakistani establishment proved anathema to many within the Muhajir community and alienated liberal groups across the country who, despite some reservations, had been enthused by the evolution of strong urban-based politics as an alternative to the rural, feudal monopoly. When Hussain himself chose to be considered *Pir Sahib* and to enjoy the company of the landed elites in Sindh, the progressive image of the movement was seriously tarnished.

In 1994–95, the MQM was perceived to be on a war path with the authorities and plural communities in Karachi. Numerous daily deaths because of its increased militancy and organised encounters with the police and the rangers only multiplied serious reservations about its ultimate objectives.[6] Concurrently, the MQM was able to defy the authorities through its frequent massive strikes in Karachi which exposed the inability of officials to maintain law in the city.[7] However, its discreet attacks on the non-Muhajir communities and a stream of body-bags being sent across the country further eroded its image. In 1995, the MQM – officially described as a terrorist organisation – was engaged in a multifaceted campaign. In addition to weekly strikes, its militant groups would engage security forces in urban guerrilla warfare; they would fight street battles against its rival faction, Haqiqi; meanwhile its leadership would express interest in a negotiated settlement. To many observers, Karachi had already become Pakistan's Beirut, largely due to the criminalisation of ethnic dissent attributed to Altaf Hussain. Official mismanagement as exposed through a 30-month-long military operation and the incompetence of the civilian administration played a major role in making Karachi vulnerable to social banditry.

The MQM's persistent tirades and volatile relations with all other ethnic groups in Sindh reflected the absence of a well-considered strategy and an unrealistic dependence on emotional appeal and street violence. By denigrating Sindhis, Punjabis, Balochis and Pushtuns, the MQM entered into a perennial state of war with the parallel ethnic communities who initially sat aloof, watching the movement weaken itself through in-fighting and continuing authoritarianism. Subsequently, they would fall victim to MQM-led militancy. The alliance with the PPP, followed by a dramatic switch-over to the IDA, temporary realignment with the PPP in 1993, followed by another phase in hostilities have been generally viewed as reactionary postures betraying a sense of insecurity on the part of an emotional and confused leadership that has achieved nothing tangible for the community. Although its allies formed governments in the centre and in Sindh, they could not help the MQM in its ordeals with the law-enforcment agencies. A perpetual state of war with the PPP could not wipe out the cross-sectional support for the party; rather it weakened the MQM but strengthened its militant sections. The leadership failed to realise that its authoritarian style would result in in-fighting, and that a constant cold and hot war with other communities and the establishment would serve the anti-MQM coalitions. Manhandling of the press, and even potential challengers within the community were sanctioned by the founders who either stayed on in exile or simply disappeared when the stakes became high.

Indeed, the leadership failed the community when its presence and guidance was most needed. *En masse* resignations by MQM representatives from the assemblies in a haphazard manner in June 1992, followed by the leaders going underground left the movement aimless and leaderless. The other ethnic communities and political parties sat on the sidelines witnessing the disintegration of a movement which could have been a new, vibrant and significant force in Pakistani politics. The MQM was limited by being a junior partner in building a ruling coalition and its dependence on 'signals' from Islamabad largely dented its claims to be a serious, long-term platform to represent middle-class, literate urban groups. As for Altaf Hussain, who was living in London, apart from a few defensive statements he preferred to hibernate for a year while his followers suffered because of the blunders committed by the leadership. Even after announcing his retirement from politics in late 1992, Hussain remained the undisputed leader of the organisation and maintained his contacts with various forces in Islamabad. Nevertheless, he did not return to face trial and answer allegations, but tried to soften the ruling elite who felt comfortable with growing factionalism within the MQM.

In the event, time was the main healer for the MQM, as it gradually came to be perceived as a victim by the Muhajireen. Though it was unable to provide any clear directions in 1992–93, its image as a prosecuted organisation of martyrs during a rather prolonged military operation helped to restore its status. Nevertheless, the inherent weaknesses and contradictions of the movement – its non-democratic structure, personality-centred cultism, intimidatory tactics, confused ideology and, most of all, resort to violence – remain unchanged. This state of affairs has effectively foreclosed the emergence of a second-tier leadership for a smooth transition with the result that the sympathy factor may prove to be temporary. In that sense the MQM, like the ML before it, is still a movement not a party. Its reemergence as the third largest party in Pakistan, however, confirms the inability of the other political parties to fill the vacuum.

The MQM's ambiguity, both intentional and tactical, on vital ideological issues like ethnicity, nationality, federalism and relationships with other ethnic communities while using crucial terms such as *qaum*, nationality and separate statehood or making provocatative statements on issues such as language, quotas and new demarcation of provincial boundaries, have only increased the polarity and produced hostility from various quarters.[8] While the rhetoric was initially attractive for youthful Muhajireen, the reaction to it from the government and other ethnic communities in Sindh was extremely unfriendly. In terms of strategy, the MQM's only policy was one of hostility – even when it joined with country-wide forces such as the PPP or the IJT. The leadership forgot that despite its street and electoral power the MQM would never be in a position to form any provincial or central government on its own but would always be needed as a 'junior' partner for *coalition* arrangements. Although both the PPP and IJT regimes survived without the MQM factor, the MQM nevertheless could have consolidated its position through such a coalition so as to gain a wider, possibly nation-wide, following or could have engineered tactical alliances with other ethnic communities in Sindh to neutralise some of the antagonistic forces. Even the *en masse* resignations in 1992 betrayed a lack of real strategy. The absence of concern for the MQM from any corner of Pakistan or from abroad except for a few, belated muffled statements, confirmed that citizens in general were against the fascist policies that the MQM had allegedly been engaged in. The confrontational campaign and daily violence in Karachi during 1995 irreparably damaged its image among the general populace.[9]

The MQM received steady support from its financiers and patrons and retained its own armed bands engaged in sniping, looting or kidnapping – as was witnessed in Hyderabad in October 1988; in Karachi in February 1990; in both cities in May and August 1990; April–May 1992; and in Karachi in 1994–95. Such internecine strife involving various ethnic groups had cost more than 5000 lives by the middle of 1995. In May 1992, quite a few citizens lost their lives as a result of indiscriminate firing in Hyderabad and Karachi, prompting a new wave of speculation about another period of martial law or governor's rule in Sindh. Such intermittent cases of violence together with an increase in kidnaps for ransom both in urban and rural Sindh, prompted the military action in June 1992. Earlier, as mentioned above, the governments of both M. K. Junejo and Benazir Bhutto were partially the casualties of the fall-out from the Sindhi turmoil. Bhutto tried to contain the Sindhi nationalists (both from within her party and in the SNA) and to maintain a balanced relationship with the MQM. Her efforts to maintain this precarious balance failed as both groups turned against her. History seemed to have come full circle in Pakistan in May 1992, when Nawaz Sharif reluctantly agreed to military action, codenamed 'Operation Clean-Up', to curb the dacoities and kidnappings in Sindh. This state of affairs persisted at a time when India and Pakistan were at odds with each other over turbulence in Indian-occupied Kashmir and America was exerting pressure on Pakistan to abandon her nuclear programme.[10] After a brief cooperation in 1993, the MQM and the PPP reinitiated their polarisation which pushed Karachi into the most violent phase in its history. The ongoing military operation failed to stamp out violence and, despite massive cost and publicity, could not restore order in the city. Following cyclic phases in violence during 1995, Karachi during 1995 had turned into an urban battlefield.

Despite the various convulsions in the MQM's political career, *Muhajir* identity has assumed a cohesive shape. Even within their large rural and urban communities the Urdu-speakers in Sindh trace their origins from a particular area in India – though most of them have only heard about it or read about it in textbooks and have never been there. However, they consider that *Muhajir* identity denoting *hijrat* is a perpetual reality. Not surprisingly, this invites retaliatory attacks from their critics. While the Urdu-speakers include regional and sub-ethnic groups such as UP(ites), Hyderabadis, Gujaratis, Madarasis and more recently Biharis, politically and psychologically *Muhajireen* has assumed an overarching identity thanks to its regional, linguistic and diasporic connotations. Equally important has been the external factor which has indirectly contributed to the popularisation of the term, since the 'locals' lumped together all the

Urdu-speaking immigrants as 'Hindustanis' or 'Panahguzeen'. The former word was and still is used in Pakistan by the local Muslims to identify the Muslims from other British Indian provinces. However, the Muhajireen were not comfortable with it for the obvious reason that it symbolised a Hindu India denying them their own indigenous roots. Moreover, in the initial stages of their organisation in the mid-1980s under General Zia ul-Haq's martial law, they were hesitant to take on a name that would enable their opponents to brand them as separatists or 'the Indian agents' – a term used quite frequently in Pakistan (often with justification). They had already organised themselves into the MQM though ostensibly they addressed themselves as *Haq Parast* (truth worshippers) so as to avoid a last-minute ban by the government which was under pressure from certain quarters to ban 'regionalist', 'separatist' or 'lingual' organisations. More recently they have occasionally used the name Mutahida (united) Qaumi Movement, so far only as a tactical ploy since the MQM in all its incarnations remains confined to urban Sindh with a few weather-beaten branches abroad.

THE EMERGENCE OF THE MQM AND ALTAF HUSSAIN

The Muhajir Qaumi Movement emerged on the Pakistani political scene in March 1984 from amongst the cadres of the former graduates of the University of Karachi, known as the All-Pakistan Muhajir Students' Organisation (APMSO), which was established on 11 June 1978, in reaction to the unilateral policies of the Islami Jamiat i-Tulaba (IJT).[11] The IJT, the student wing of the Jama'at i-Islami, had been providing 'foot soldiers' to its parent organisation for a long time and operated as a coercive force on major campuses across the country. After its successful bout with the PPP regime in the 1970s, the IJT (like the JI) joined hands with Zia ul-Haq and while posing as the vanguards of Islamisation fought long-drawn battles against ethnic and ideological organisations across the country. On the whole, the IJT's new cadres, unlike the previous urban, lower middle-class pioneers, came from the rural areas enthused by religious activism and intent upon using physical violence against any critics. Consequently, the IJT hold on campuses in the late 1980s loosened and a fillip was given to rival student organisations.[12] In the corresponding patterns of political fragmentation of the Pakistani polity and the rise of the centrifugal forces, the APMSO – a former constituent of the IJT itself – led by young student leaders like Altaf Hussain, Farouk Sattar, Abdul Razzak Khan, Imran Farooq and Azeem Tariq decided to expand its activism in the *mohallas* to

defend the rights of the Muhajireen of Karachi and subsequently elsewhere in Sindh. With a youthful spirit, endowed with unlimited energy
and manpower, these student leaders, who had acquired an experience of
militancy from the IJT, began challenging urban issues like the quota
system, unemployment and emigration from up-country.[13]

Altaf Hussain, a Karachi-born 'Muhajir', a former taxi driver in the
United States and a graduate from the Pharmacy Department of Karachi
University, soon emerged as the chief spokesman of the Muhajireen.[14] On
14 August 1979, while leading a procession to the tomb of the Quaid-i
Azam in Karachi, Altaf Hussain was arrested by the martial law authorities who sentenced him to a year in prison in addition to lashes. After his
release, he became the spokesman of the Urdu-speakers in Sindh, and on
18 June 1984, formally launched the MQM. Since independence, the
immigrants had held important positions in the new country and wielded
an enormous influence in business, much greater than their proportion in
the national population. When people from other provincial backgrounds –
initially Punjabis and then Pushtuns – began to outbid the 'Muhajireen',
the latter felt uneasy. With a high rate of literacy in a favourable urban
environment the resentment against Punjabis, Pushtuns and Sindhi-speakers was conveniently turned into a full-fledged movement which began in
Karachi and then spread to Hyderabad and Sukkur.

The enigmatic personality of Altaf Hussain left a deep imprint on the
MQM, though not without opposition.[15] Son to Nazir Hussain, a railway
employee with limited economic means, Altaf Hussain was born in
Karachi on 17 September 1953. After an ordinary childhood, he underwent military training for a year in the National Cadet Corps, a college-
based training programme for civilian youths in Pakistan. It was here that
Hussain developed certain attitudes. He was distressed at the way he was
treated by non-Muhajir cadets – belonging to so-called 'martial races' –
who relished ridiculing Urdu-speakers by taunting them as timid imbe-
ciles. As a sensitive youth, Hussain also imbued himself in the strict disci-
plinary training based on hierarchy, which was later reflected in the
multi-tiered organisation of the MQM. When he commenced his postgrad-
uate career in the Pharmacy department of Karachi University, Hussain
deeply resented ethnic jokes about Muhajireen and suffered physical
torture by IJT activists. The IJT's tough tactics had been instrumental in
alienating a number of Urdu-speaking students in the 1980s.[16] The fragmentation of mainstream politics in the country during martial law and the
stigmatisation of Urdu-speakers by other ethnic groups on campuses, gave
birth to a new sense of *Muhajir* identity. The noticeable growth in Sindhi
nationalist feelings under Mumtaz Ali Bhutto, the former PPP chief minis-

ter in Sindh, language riots and inter-ethnic competition in the socio-
economic sector had already added to *Muhajir* consciousness. The arrival
of the Biharis, some of whom had been exposed to military activities in
East Bengal during 1971, provided a new cadre of young activists ready to
display their combat skills. The easy availability of weapons due to the
Afghan war and the pressure of refugees in Karachi facilitated organisational efforts which received encouragement from the intelligence agencies trying to curtail the influence of the PPP as well as the Sindhi
nationalists (especially after the summer of 1983). Hussain was one of the
founding members of the APMSO at Karachi University which had successfully confronted the unilateral hold of the IJT over the student union.
Seeing the marginalisation of the IJT, other student groups – both
ethnic/regional and ideological – did not challenge the APMSO which in
its new-found glory began to relish supremacy on the campuses and in
colleges in Karachi. In Hyderabad it was not so successful, however, due
to powerful opposition by Sindhi student organisations at the Jamshoro
campus.

After experiencing a leadership role in student politics, Hussain went to
Chicago as a taxi driver. The city of Al Capone and its rough neighbourhood hardened him, and in his leisure time he read literature on the Nazis.
Hitler and his centrist organisation left an undeniable impact on him and
taught him how to manipulate a personality cult.[17] His obsession with
Hitler and personality-centred organisation has been evident throughout
his career as 'the godfather' of the MQM. On his return to Karachi,
Hussain institutionalised his ideas and schemes into the rubric of the
movement. Gathering a team of loyalists from the APMSO, he reincar-
nated himself in the role of a leader who would build a new network with
strong roots in the urban *mohallas* and narrow streets of Azizabad, Orangi,
Baldia, Korangi, Nazimabad and other Muhajir settlements. The pattern
was provided by a faithful reading of *Mein Kampf*, while the volunteers
came in hundreds from urban youths who were catapulted into leadership
roles in the most important city and the only major port of the country. In
addition, there was no scarcity of financiers and helping hands from
various walks of life in Karachi and subsequently Hyderabad, Nawabshah
and Sukkur.

Hussain allowed no criticism and no competition; any flamboyant
speaker other than himself was viewed as a potential threat and would be
chastened.[18] If the challenger still carried on after a hint to 'cool down', he
would be harassed until he was marginalised and silenced. In the shurfa
committee of the movement, Hussain made sure that his loyalists held all
the leading positions. Aamir Khan and Afaq Ahmed who subsequently fell

out with Hussain and went in hiding were initially his close confidantes.[19] Hussain, in the style of his heroes in the West, commanded the organisation from 90 Azizabad, which worked as the headquarters (and his residence) and where dignitaries including prime ministers and governors would be received. To prove the extent of his titular hold over the organisation, Hussain intentionally and sadistically made provincial ministers and parliamentarians belonging to the MQM wait on him and his guests. He presented a curious, enigmatic figure suffering from pshychological inadequacies and a deep sense of personal insecurity.[20] On the one hand he occasionally thundered as a very articulate, self-confident, rhetorical and impassioned speaker exposing the *zulm* against Muhajireen, while on the other hand he remained deeply scared of jails. He would threaten to bring down the government(s) by force, whereas, even at the peak of the MQM's power he chose to stay in London indefinitely simply 'to escape any death threat' on his life.[21] At the height of his popularity he kept a car at the ready near his rallies to whisk him away in case of danger. He wore dark glasses day and night allegedly after advice to protect himself from an evil eye.[22]

After 90 Azizabad, the Abbasi Shaheed Hospital in Karachi became the alternative focal point as he frequently sought admission there for treatment. His ailment would never be made public but his hospital stays were used as major propaganda to elicit sympathy and support from amongst the Muhajireen. Special prayers, vigils, speeches from his hospital bed despite the excruciating pain he was suffering, created the image of an enduring, steadfast and unfailing *quaid*.[23] Although Hussain did have a recurring renal problem largely due to fasting and resultant dehydration in the mid-1980s, there is no doubt that the hospital, in addition to being a predominantly Muhajir domain, was used for various purposes. More than its psychological and symbolical uses, Abbasi Shaheed Hospital provided a sanctuary against law-enforcement authorities and militant rivals.[24] On his arrival in London, Hussain settled in a suburban house in North London, with the local MQM leaders providing the security and hospitality. In 1992–93, he appeared in a few select gatherings in London where he made mild defensive statements; meanwhile his associates sought a sympathetic coverage in the British media. Despite their frantic efforts, such coverage was not forthcoming. However, due to heightened polarisation and violence in Karachi in 1994–95, Hussain received extensive coverage in the British media. After more than 800 deaths in Karachi in the first six months of 1995 alone, the Bhutto government in mid-June issued a demand for Hussain's extradition which was politely refused since no treaty to that effect existed between Britain and Pakistan.[25]

Meanwhile, serious problems existed within the organisation; during Hussain's absence from Pakistan new ideas emerged and 'Young Turks' tried to reorient the MQM. As would be seen subsequently, when any such alternative leader, including its chairman, Azeem Tariq, tried to build a sensible image and pragmatic relationship, they were eliminated. Tariq's assassination in December 1992 created a major dilemma by leaving the organisation virtually leaderless. Tariq himself was a moderate and well-respected leader and after his reappearance in October he had begun to instil a new positive spirit in the organisation. His contracts with the rebels in the Haqiqi faction, the admission of high-handed behaviour by the MQM and public apologies had begun to rally many moderates. His murder, which was attributed to Hussain's loyalists, and a brief resurgence of the politics of *gherao jalao* in July 1993 while the federal government underwent a political crisis further tarnished the credibility that Tariq and other moderates were trying to re-establish during the ongoing military operation.

KARACHI AND THE MQM

Karachi and the MQM have remained intertwined – like Hussain and the MQM – because the organisation had been formed in the country's largest and most significant city in the *mohallas* and *katchi abadis* in order to define a new Muhajir identity. It was in the *mohallas* and *bastis* that MQM fought some of the fiercest battles to gain local control in the Metropolitan Corporation, the Karachi Development Authority, the Sindh Assembly and the Karachi Steel Mills in addition to numerous industries, hospitals and semi-autonomous organisations. The MQM spread like a whirlwind throughout the city and continued with strong organisational work in Hyderabad and Sukkur – though Karachi remained the major arena of its activities including the inter-factional rivalry for the control of a powerful, diverse Muhajir constituency. Karachi is crucial for Muhajireen as well as for Sindhis, Pushtuns, Baloch, Punjabis and Kashmiris, since every tenth Pakistani is a Karachi resident and it is the economic and industrial hub of the country. It is also Pakistan's only opening to the world with a growing significance for Afghanistan and the Central Asian republics. In order to understand present-day Sindh, therefore, a historical and contemporary look at Karachi itself will be useful.

Historically speaking, the city of Karachi started as a humble fishing settlement and received the first European trade ship in 1774, though it remained under the Sindhi Talpur dynasty until the British conquest in

1839. After the First World War, it assumed growing military significance due to its strategic location. Karachi expanded out of all proportion in the post-colonial period when refugees poured in from India. This influx ended in 1951 yet the steady increase in population continued and further increased in the 1970s and 1980s in the aftermath of mechanised farming and the heavy industrialisation in Karachi. 'In Punjab the industrialization developed on account of the historical circumstances, whereas in Sind it took place in spite of them.'[26] Faisalabad, Sialkot, Lahore, Hyderabad and Karachi have remained the traditional centres of industrialisation and urbanisation in Pakistan with a gradual emergence of new centres like Taxila and Nowshera along the Grand Trunk Road. Despite an apparent polarity between the industrial-capital class and the land-owning elite, 'the native bourgeoisie' avoided seeking 'the elimination of the "feudal" landowning class for the purposes of capitalist development.'[27] They remained unsure of their credentials to adapt any outrightly hostile posture towards the landed elite. This alienated the rural agrarian labourers who sought refuge in the cities, though they could not work out any coalition with the urban industrial labourers and identity-formation acquired linguistic and territorial dimensions.

After becoming the metropolis of the young republic, Karachi started expanding to the nearby villages of Malir and Landhi and, with further industrial development, the western side of the Lyari river was developed into the Sind Industrial Trading Estate (SITE). To the east of Landhi, the Landhi Industrial Estate (LITE) was established to allow the setting up of factories. The old buildings in the town gave way to new markets and trading centres whereas the poor sections of the population were pushed out toward low-lying areas in the south and west. Baldia, Orangi, Qasba and Korangi have been the fastest growing areas in the 1970s and 1980s due to a constant stream of migration from up-country, Afghanistan and Bangladesh. Some of these areas lack basic amenities and happen to be quite a distance from the factories and main administrative offices, causing an almost anarchic traffic situation during peak hours. The Defence Colony, Clifton, SITE and Gulshan-i Iqbal are the most affluent areas of the administrative districts of Karachi, while Baldia, Orangi, Qasba, North Karachi and Landhi have the largest concentrations of poor people. There are also a number of semi-independent settlements outside the city called *goths* which have attracted new settlers on an ethnic basis. Similarly, there are a number of *katchi abadis* and slum areas where ethno-linguistic (though not economic) differentiations have played an important role in settlement patterns. Thus, Karachi has emerged as the Pakistani megapolis with a population of about 12 million consisting of every major South

Asian ethnic group, and despite planning attempts by the Karachi municipal authorities it has not been possible to resolve its severe problems.[28]

It is not surprising therefore that ethnic-based movements in Karachi
led by the middle class in the environment of industrial capitalism and
stifled under martial law, have found a ready response among their respective clients. The imagined ethno-regional community was constructed with
auxiliary ingredients such as language and close neighbourhood, building
on a strong antagonism towards 'others'. The MQM, the PPI (Punjabi-
Pukhtan Ittehad), the SNA or the BSO (Baloch Students' Organisation)
found listening ears among their 'respective' communities and, in the aura
of political redefinition in the mid-1980s, ideas about ethnicity and nationality were popular. The Muhajireen, like the Sindhis and Baloch, never
had a large representation in the lower ranks of the armed forces, but there
have been quite a few Muhajir generals including former chief of army
staff, Aslam Beg. The Punjabis, Pushtuns (traditionally) and a small
number of Sindhis since the 1970s have constituted the bulk of the armed
forces and similarly have a better representation in the Karachi metropolitan police. The former two ethnic groups retain their near-monopoly over
urban and inter-provincial transport. In the early years, the Muhajireen
benefited from generous property allotments, easy terms for investment
and the declaration of Urdu as the official language of Pakistan – all the
elements that gradually antagonised the other communities in the country.
For a time, Islam, Urdu and Pakistan became synonymous to the discomfort of many progressive and ethnic opinion groups, who felt a severe
sense of cultural alienation.[29]

In September 1986, a protest march organised by the MQM in Karachi
near the Sohrab Goth was stopped by the police in typical South Asian
brutal manner which resulted in the movement gathering more popularity
among the Muhajireen of urban Sindh irrespective of their age, sex or geographic background. Ghous Ali Shah, the then chief minister, had ordered
a raid on Sohrab Goth, the den of the drug mafia with a heavy Pushtun and
Afghan concentration; they, in retaliation turned the tables on the
Muhajireen in the neighbourhood.[30] Well-armed gangs from the Goth
invaded the Muhajir colonies and mayhem ensued. This proved to be a
turning point in inter-ethnic relations in Karachi with indiscriminate
killings, riots and curfews following in succession. The drug traffickers
and land developers had found a very easy way to get the law-enforcing
authorities off their back by initiating an ethnic riot. The method was
simple: a few hooded hooligans would appear from nowhere on motor
bikes or in stolen cars and engage in indiscriminate firing on the shops or
passers-by and then conveniently disappear in the crowds. Before long it

became common place for the city to be consumed by fire and blood for days. The easy supply of weapons from the Afghans in town and gunrunning by drug barons through the private militia made Karachi a nightmare. Identification of the various ethnic groups by their language, appearance, separate settlements and, most of all, their professions made them easy targets. The situation took a severe turn on 30 September 1988, when a few cars joined the rush-hour traffic and their occupants started firing indiscriminately with automatic weapons leaving more than two hundred people dead. Next day, there was a an angry reaction and an equal number of people died through indiscriminate firing. Such actions and reactions were variously regarded as conspiracies to weaken the federation; to get the elections postponed; or to secure freedom for drug-trafficking. These attacks by unidentified gunmen leading to inter-ethnic backlashes, left enduring scars on the fragile situation in Sindh and made G. M. Syed determined to weaken the Muhajireen. For their part, the Muhajireen insisted on the repatriation of the Biharis; meanwhile the Punjabis and Pushtuns organised themselves into the PPI so as to safeguard the interests of their communities.

In the local elections of 1987, the MQM swept the seats in Karachi and Hyderabad through its organisational acumen and youthful energy. Zia's obsessive desire to weaken the PPP in Sindh by buttering up G. M. Syed and his cohorts by means of personal visits, the extension of the quota for another decade and trying to build up contacts with the ML and the JI, alienated the Muhajireen who interpreted it as the appeasement of Sindhi nationalism at the expense of the Muhajireen and Biharis. Competition from other groups, the high rate of unemployment, urban congestion, violence and 'conspiracy on the part of the state or India factor may have been additional but peripheral factors fuelling ethnic consciousness'.[31] The recent changes such as a new political leadership, volatile university politics, rising unemployment, the kalashnikov culture, the role of the elites including the business community in support of the Muhajireen and the feudal lords on the side of the SNA, with other semi-ethnic conglomerates like the PPI falling in between, all contributed to ethnic volatility. The proposed construction of the Kalabagh Dam was already a serious issue in Sindh and even Ghous Ali Shah, the ML chief minister under Zia, had been vocally against it. Yet the PPP refused to join the SNA even after the suppression of the MRD struggle in 1983 in which, as seen earlier, the PPP in Sindh bore the brunt of the retaliation from the military regime. The MQM, due to its initial emphasis on the issue of nationality, alienated a number of opinion groups in the country who privately referred to it as Muhajir chauvinism. The federalists as well as the nationalists held serious reservations about the organisation and its aims. While referring to Sindhi grievances, even leftist ideologues ended up supporting the Sindhi-speaking organisations and ignoring the MQM.

BENAZIR BHUTTO'S FIRST REGIME AND THE MQM

When the Pakistan People's Party obtained a majority in rural Sindh in the elections of 1988 (also in 1990 and 1993) this was not just a sympathy vote as a result of the execution of the late Z. A. Bhutto, but largely because the Sindhi voters found ethno-regional groupings like the SNA incapable of delivering the goods. Even within the SNA there has been divergence on the extent of autonomy or separation from the federation itself and, unlike the MQM, the leadership has suffered from being heavily represented by feudalists whose role in the past politics of the province and in kidnapping for ransom money, has not earned them a good reputation among the poor or lower middle-class Sindhis. Most of the Sindhi leaders in the SNA have been the beneficiaries of official attention from Karachi and Islamabad, which has caused a severe credibility gap. Even many of their intellectual leaders from amongst the poets, writers and teachers were discredited by having accepted offices in the martial-law regime.

After the victory of the PPP in rural areas and the MQM in urban parts of the province (by winning 11 of 13 constituencies in Karachi and two in Hyderabad), the two parties moved closer through a 58-point agreement signed in December 1988 between Benazir Bhutto and Altaf Hussain, known as the December Agreement.[32] At the same time, the Sindhi nationalists, outvoted by the PPP and the MQM, entered a period of cynical chauvinism with attacks on both parties. The IJT also began its effort to win over the MQM against the PPP as well as offering an olive branch to the SNA so as to embarrass the PPP in its majority province. However, the mutual inter-dependence of the PPP and the MQM, due to their electoral and logistic needs, did not allow any major crack in the first ten months of the Bhutto regime.

The uneasy ethnic situation in Sindh throughout 1989 kept everybody speculating on the role of a number of domestic and regional factors in the entire imbroglio. Scepticism towards the PPP–MQM Accord – between a national party and an ethno-regionalist party – caused people to ask questions. The Sindhi nationalists turned more fiercely against both the MQM and the PPP, particularly the latter since it held power at the federal level. The SNA's agitation in Sindh over the alleged desecration of the Pakistani flag at Sukkur airport in 1989 brought the MQM closer to the federalist parties though the SNA disowned any complicity in the incident. The IJT, however, despite its sporadic denunciation of ethno-nationalist movements, maintained its secret overtures towards the MQM in an attempt to topple Benazir Bhutto's government. The PPP faced difficulties because, despite an overwhelming mandate from rural Sindh, it was nevertheless compelled to cooperate with the MQM for the survival of the national government as well as the smooth running of government in the province. But there is no denying the fact that a strong element within the MQM felt uneasy about the accord and retained pro-IJT sympathies. At the same time, there was an influential section of the PPP from amongst the Sindhi parliamentarians like the Makhdums who remained critical of its collaboration with the MQM.

With 14 members in the plural national assembly, the MQM in 1989 remained a crucial power-broker confident of its role in metropolitan, provincial and national political life. This in turn gave confidence to its leader, Altaf Hussain, who in the summer of 1989 led massive rallies in Hyderabad and Karachi by announcing: 'We are united on a platform and nobody can shake us.'[33] By this time, however, it was quite obvious that the MQM and the PPP had come under severe pressure to ease the ethnic violence in Karachi, which many people had prematurely assumed would wither away quickly once the contenders became partners. Some analysts even predicted that since the MQM could not contain ethnic strife in the cities it was certain to face 'ideological polarisation' within the leadership.[34] Not wanting to appear soft on urban matters, the MQM maintained constant pressure on the PPP in order to squeeze the maximum out of the accord. The usual tactic was that Azeem Ahmed Tariq, chairman of the MQM, and occasionally Altaf Hussain, still the undisputed leader of the movement, would resort to threatening rhetoric, particularly on the eve of the sessions of the national assembly, thus exposing the very vulnerabilities of the nascent democratic set-up, led by a powerful president and characterised by a hostile majority in the senate and an uncertain administrative machinery both in the centre and the provinces. The Punjab under Nawaz Sharif still posed a greater challenge to Benazir Bhutto's authority and an unending series of disputes kept her administration adrift. Notwithstanding such rhetoric, the MQM leadership was anxious to stay in mainstream Muhajir politics and so engaged in a number of public relations activities like the *muft* (free) bazaars for the needy.

The fragile relationship between the PPP and the MQM came under periodic review at times of external strains and sporadic ethnic riots in Hyderabad and Karachi. The Bhutto government was under serious pressure to undertake action against ethnic militants in Sindh whereas its accord with the MQM had been a source of discomfort both for the nationalists and their sympathisers within the PPP. In April 1989, it appeared that the accord would not hold as the provincial government undertook a house-to-house search for arms. At the time Altaf Hussain was trying to pacify extremists within the MQM and had been in Hyderabad where he snubbed Aftab Sheikh, the mayor and former cabinet minister under General Zia, who demanded a stronger stand against the nationalists. On 29 April 1989, policemen surrounded and searched the house where Altaf Hussain had been staying along with other *haq parast* leaders (the original name the MQM used in the elections to avoid a last-minute ban as there was pressure on Ishaque Khan's caretaker government to ban 'separatist' movements). After the incident, the MQM made an appeal to the president and General Aslam Beg, the chief of army staff, to help safeguard the Muhajireen in the interior of Sindh as ethnic clashes had been causing an influx of Muhajireen as well as Punjabis and Pushtuns from rural areas into urban centres. It was generally predicted that Sindh was 'falling apart' and a disruption in the accord would lead to grave ethnic violence resulting in another martial law.

While MQM leaders were redefining their relations with the PPP regime, the Sindhi sections of the PPP began to criticise the central command for its 'soft' policies toward the Muhajireen. A PPP MP, Babul Jakhrani, was reported to have said: 'If the present government continues to rule for another five years, not a single Sindhi will remain in the province.' The PPP government in Sindh led by Qaim Ali Shah registered severe attacks from the Makhdums of Hala, who were believed to want the chief ministership for themselves. Makhdum Khaliq, a leading critic of Bihari repatriation and an influential member of a feudal-spiritual family of rural Sindh, was the former chief of the Sindh PPP and had recently accorded a warm welcome to Jam Sadiq Ali, a fellow *wadera* and PPP stalwart, on his return from exile. None of this augured well for Bhutto who was torn between her party's commitment to a strong Pakistan and the strains from divisive ethnic loyalties. Despite its electoral defeat, the SNA was also on the offensive, adding to volatility in the province to the extent that Benazir Bhutto had to declare the situation a mini-insurgency.[35]

The ethnic fragility within Sindh continued to survive throughout the 18 months of Bhutto's government, at times in the face of daily incidents of kidnapping for ransom and dacoities in urban areas. Issues such as the repatriation of the Biharis or emigration into Sindh continued to fan ethnic discontent.[36] While Zia had pronounced on Islamic brotherhood and solidarity with the Afghan refugees, he had skilfully evaded both these sensi-tive questions. The Bhutto government inherited the legacy of the martial-law regime at a time when ethnic politics had already become extremely polarised. Both the IJT and the MQM, for their own reasons, emphasised the repatriation issue, but the nationalists, Makhdums and a few other PPP legislators resisted it. About 160 000 Biharis had been repatriated to Pakistan in the 1970s by Z. A. Bhutto and, since the 1980s, thousands of them together with other Bangladeshis have been entering Pakistan ille-gally. According to Benazir Bhutto, in 1989 hundreds of illegal immi-grants were entering Pakistan daily from Bangladesh and India.[37] Earlier, during her first official visit to Bangladesh, the issue of repatriation of the 'stranded Pakistanis' was avoided.[38] In the meantime, Karachi in particular was 'stiff with illegal immigrants' where one-third of the population remained illegally (and still do).[39] Parents felt insecure about their children in a city where acute problems in transportation and drug-trafficking had been adding to the ethnic chaos.[40] Still, the efforts of individuals like Abdus Sattar Edhi and Akhtar Hamid Khan in the slums of Karachi on a self-help basis provided some cause for optimism. An emerging consensus on the political resolution of the problems, and particularly the general acceptance of ethnic pluralism in Pakistan with a corresponding politico-economic order and safeguards for the rural and urban communities, are gigantic tasks that require lasting measures. Viewed from the slums of Karachi and Hyderabad it seemed a far-off ideal. It was reported in the Western media that the youthful prime minister was 'fully aware of the great hopes and upsurge of almost physical love she has inspired among the population. She knows that her ability to deal with the monster that Karachi has become will be a decisive test, if not "the" test of her socio-economic policies.' There was a rather optimistic hope that with the equally youthful MQM leader from Karachi, Mayor Farouk Sattar, co-operation would enable them 'to rescue their city from total collapse'.[41] However, it was soon clear that this would not happen.

On 18 September 1989, the MQM formally joined hands with the Combined Opposition Parties (COP) in co-sponsoring a no-confidence motion against Prime Minister Bhutto, taking everybody by surprise.[42] Once again its essential role as a power-broker raised a number of ques-tions and suspicions about the MQM's prospective stratagem in the provincial and the national body-politic. It was revealed that the move-ment had secretly allied with the Nawaz Sharif-led opposition a few weeks earlier and Benazir Bhutto's government had been caught somewhat unawares, though rumours about the no-confidence motion had been in circulation for quite some time.[43] Her government survived but the vulnerability of the regime became apparent, while the COP/IJT/MQM combine prepared for another show-down.

BENAZIR BHUTTO, THE ARMY AND SINDH

In February 1990 when Pakistanis overwhelmingly supported Bhutto on her stance over the Kashmir crisis and the international media reported imminent hostilities between India and Pakistan, the MQM called for a strike which turned into a bloody affair. The confrontation between the administration and MQM protesters produced numerous casualties. (Another strike called by the SNA at the same time was observed in rural Sindh yet passed without any major impact since it was largely confined to the rural areas and had failed to evoke any great interest.) The former allies were at daggers drawn with civilian life coming to a standstill in the entire province.[44] During this spate of ethnic violence organised kidnapping, sniping and lynching in secret torture cells were carried out by both sides. The Bhutto government came under serious attack from various directions, and the opportunity was not missed by the IJT led by Nawaz Sharif, the chief minister of the Punjab and Bhutto's leading opponent. The prime minister replaced Qaim Ali Shah, Sindh's incumbent chief minister with Aftab Mirani, as both capital and industrialists fled from Karachi. The army, which had again moved to centre-stage because of the violent ethnic and inter-factional configuration, reportedly told Bhutto that it 'was not prepared to bail her out every time there was trouble'.[45] Her growing dependence on the army in Sindh, where she enjoyed a clear electoral majority, pinpointed the fragility of the balance of power among the various contenders.

On 27 May 1990, while searching for militants hiding near Pakka Qillah of Hyderabad, the police clashed with predominantly Muhajir groups and this resulted in a massive number of casualties, with the administration and the MQM blaming each other for the bloodshed. The next day snipers retaliated in Karachi, killing people at random and unleashing a chain reaction with the result that the army was called in to patrol the curfewed streets and *mohallas*.[46] The induction of the army for law and order purposes on a large scale raised a number of serious questions including the vulnerability of the political system itself.[47] The prime minister was pressed by the opposition to impose direct central rule on the province (apparently so as to prove that she had failed to administer *her own* province) and it was predicted that she would declare a state of emergency in the province.[48] Sindh made the headlines and Kashmir was pushed onto the back page. Emotional appeals from certain groups and individuals, including Altaf Hussain, were constantly made to the army for a formal take-over though the generals stated that they were not 'interested in imposing martial law in Sind during such time'.[49] These policy postures by the Muhajir leadership strengthened the view held by many Sindhi nationalists and others that the MQM had been brought into being by the ISI on the order of General Zia ul-Haq in order to counteract the PPP and other Sindhi activists and that it would always seek allies outside Sindh. 'Many PPP officials believe there is a conspiracy between the MQM and the army to overthrow the PPP administration in Sind. Such perceptions were likely to make negotiations even more difficult.'[50] Both Bhutto and the army disclaimed such rumours.

However, Benazir Bhutto was put under pressure by the army to let it establish its own military courts. These courts were intended to tackle the terrorists, but would supersede the civilian courts in their jurisdiction as their verdicts would not be challengeable in the country's superior courts.[51] The army leadership publicised its reservations about playing the role of policemen without having the jurisdictional authority through military courts. A leading British daily reported in the early days of June: 'There is increasing pressure on President Ghulam Ishaq Khan to dismiss the Sind government and impose governor's rule or martial law, or to dismiss Ms Bhutto and form a national government without her. But Ms Bhutto has dismissed all three options and has promised to subdue the terrorists.'[52] The army was reported to have 'complained about Ms Bhutto's reluctance to come to a political agreement with the MQM'.[53] On a rather depressing note, one commentator recorded harshly:

> In those circumstances the best service Benazir could render would be to hand over power from one democratically-elected government to another for the first time in the country's history. The question is whether she can survive and whether she wants to bring a measure of enlightenment to the system. She needs time, but it may be denied to her.[54]

However, by the middle of June it appeared that the matter had been sorted out temporarily at the highest level, though belated evidence by General (Retd) Alam Jan Masud, the Lahore corps commander, suggested that the Army Chief, General Beg, had lost patience with Bhutto and wanted to dissolve her government.[55] The arrests of a large number of people across the province by the civilian authorities coincided with the convening of an all-party conference in Karachi under the auspices of the provincial PPP government. Both the MQM and Jeeye Sindh Tehreek boycotted it, yet other parties supported the official policy of a crack-down and taking political measures through negotiations.[56]

NAWAZ SHARIF, JAM SADIQ ALI AND THE MQM

After the dissolution of the PPP government on 6 August 1990 through a presidential proclamation alleging corruption, nepotism and lawlessness, an interim government under Ghulam Mustafa Jatoi, the fourth Sindhi premier in two decades, held elections which returned the IJT with a clear majority. The electoral procedures and results have long been contested by the PPP and other opposition parties who pointed out various cases of planned rigging. Mian Nawaz Sharif rather than Jatoi eventually emerged as the prime minister. He had limited electoral support in Sindh, but counted on continued support from the MQM. Jam Sadiq Ali, the interim chief minister of the troubled province, carried out his responsibilities by forging alliances with the MQM, the ML, nationalists and some PPP dissidents. The Jam was a former PPP stalwart, but after aligning himself with President Ghulam Ishaque Khan he acted harshly towards his former party colleagues. However, his authoritarian rule was also characterised by tactical measures allowing appeasement of various ethnic groups. He proved to be one of the 'most contentious politicians' as, during his tenure of Sindh's chief ministership for 19 months, 'he conducted a reign of terror against his principal political opponents, Benazir Bhutto's Pakistan People's Party (PPP) – a party that he helped create a decade ago'.[57]

Jam Sadiq Ali was born in his ancestral village, Goth Jam Nawaz Ali in 1936 in a *wadera* family and entered politics during the 1960s. He joined Zulfikar Ali Bhutto as a co-founder of the PPP and was appointed provincial senior minister in Sindh in 1972. Through 'wheeling and dealing with *waderas*' he brought over a number of Bhutto's opponents in the province and did not hesitate to use force against some of his critics. With the promulgation of martial law in 1977, Jam left for London and became a close associate and friend of Agha Hassan Abedi, the founder of the BCCI. Abedi provided Jam with a house and largesse to live peacefully in exile.[58] Returning to Pakistan in 1990, Jam expected to be given a major office by Benazir Bhutto, the PPP prime minister, who simply ignored him. True to his nature, he turned against her and aligned himself with Ghulam Ishaque Khan, Pir Pagara and Ghulam Mustafa Jatoi. He played a crucial role in building an anti-Bhutto coalition in Sindh and was rewarded by the chief ministership in August 1990. In the elections of October 1990, Jam was accused by the PPP of widespread rigging which he always denied. With his independent candidates, help from Islamabad and a coalition with the MQM, Jam established a ruling alliance. In the next few months, his harsh actions against PPP activists in Sindh kept both Islamabad and Azizabad happy, though Pakistani and international human-rights organisations as well as the US State Department complained of large-scale human-rights violations under his rule.

With a typical feudal disposition, Jam was extremely repressive towards his detractors and stupendously generous to his favourites. 'He made friends from across the political spectrum and had the uncanny ability to be [sic] humble himself before anyone he wanted to win over.'[59] At the marriage ceremony of his daughter in February 1992 he was confined to a wheelchair by an acute attack of cirrhosis caused by his heavy drinking. Nevertheless, Jam Sadiq Ali entertained more than 30 000 guests including the president, the prime minister, and almost every known politician in Pakistan as well as his friends from London.[60] With his death on 4 March 1992, the PPP heaved a sigh of relief and barely two months later, Operation Clean-Up was initiated by the army in the province. 'Jam Sadiq was loved and hated in the extreme, but as his time came to an end the rancour he had generated in Sind caught up with him', wrote his obituarist in *The Independent*. 'Few ordinary Sindhis will mourn him. He represented an era long gone – when politics would be manipulated by a few to keep the pretence of democracy alive for international consumption.'[61]

Jam Sadiq Ali's personalised manoeuvres using both temptation and coercion maintained a semblance of peace in urban centres though in rural areas the dacoities and kidnapping persisted. In 1991, the MQM suffered an internal setback with a number of provincial MPs fleeing to the USA in mysterious circumstances, on the heel of allegations against Altaf Hussain. Apparently the leadership took the revolt seriously and opted for a safe refuge in London, ostensibly on health reasons. After his arrival in London in 1991, Altaf Hussain was kept in the news through a partisan media both in Karachi and abroad. His long speeches via satellite were exhaustively reported in the Urdu press in London and Karachi, ostensibly under duress. The situation in rural Sindh remained equally insecure, since the dacoits had increased their activities.[62]

There is no doubt that since the MQM took over the Karachi municipal administration there had been comparative calm, yet the inter-*mohalla* and inter-regional migration went on. On the one hand there were reports of a flight of capital from the city, while on the other hand the Karachi stock market picked up favourably. The MQM intimidated dissidents and independent journalists including the correspondents and editors of *Dawn*, the *Daily Jang*, the *Herald* and *Newsline* (in the last case, its woman editor had to seek protection from the security forces). Z. Abbas, the BBC correspondent in Karachi, was manhandled, but several of these journalists showed tenacity and resolution against all the odds and were able to produce the best journalism of its type in the history of Pakistan. The MQM's problems with Salah ud-Din, the pro-JI editor of the weekly *Takbeer* during 1991 also merit special mention. He had been publishing open advisory letters to Altaf Hussain and other MQM leaders on various provocative issues such as the movement's alleged connection with the RAW and the supply of Indian funds and weapons. In addition to sustained personal harassment his office was gutted by MQM activists. Given the importance of the pro-JI press all over the country, the Salah ud-Din issue received unprecedented attention. When offered around 1.5 million rupees in compensation by Nawaz Sharif – who then enjoyed the support of the JI in a coalition – Salah ud-Din politely refused. Although the matter gradually subsided the mutual suspicion persisted. On 4 December 1994, Salah ud-Din was murdered, allegedly by MQM death squads.

For Nawaz Sharif, it had never been easy to carry the mutually antagonistic forces of the JI, the MQM and the ANP. The JI always regarded the MQM as simply a mischief-mongering *lissani* (lingual, in a derogatory sense) group out to destroy Pakistan, even though in the former East Pakistan the Urdu-speakers had largely staffed JI-led, pro-military organisations like Al-Shams and Al-Badr.

After the death of Jam Sadiq Ali his successor, Syed Muzzaffar Shah, banking on the former coalition with the MQM assumed the office initially with the blessings of the PPP and Jatoi's NPP and it appeared that Sindh was entering a unique phase of cooperation and peace. It was at this time that Nawaz Sharif wrote a letter to Benazir Bhutto suggesting a dialogue, something which had been long advocated by political circles in the country for the success of the democratic set-up. However, the effort proved abortive as, a few days later, news of kidnaps made the headlines in the wake of 'revelations' about armed encounters with the alleged members of Al-Zulfikar, an organisation run by Murtaza Bhutto. A number of political activists in Sindh were reported to have been arrested by the provincial government with the PPP hinting at a new wave of suppression. While Pakistanis were experiencing a sense of relief over developments in Afghanistan, Sindh witnessed a new wave of mysterious killings and highway robberies. The military seemed to be losing patience with the rapid deterioration of the law-and-order situation and many observers felt that it might 'be preparing to take the reins of power'.[63] The kidnap of Mashooq Ali, a close associate of the Aga Khan, in mid-May 1992, brought more pressure for a 'clean-up' operation and the army was said to be preparing 'to launch a large scale anti-terrorist drive in the troubled southern province of Sind'.[64]

The crack-down began on 27 May 1992, with mixed reactions from various quarters, though the government and the army chief declared it to be purely an operation against gangsters and not an excuse for political reprisals. Some members of the Sharif administration like Chaudhary Nisar Ali Khan were shocked by the military operation zeroing in on Karachi as they had expected it to concentrate only on rural bandits. To a large extent, the MQM was itself taken by surprise and in confusion its MNAs and MPAs submitted their resignations and went underground. These resignations, including that of the Sindh assembly speaker, haphazardly sent through journalists or by mail, betrayed a sense of panic in the highest echelons. Except for a few mild statements showing concern by the elderly MQM parliamentarian, Senator Ishtiaq Azhar, the MQM whittled away. The return of rebels like Aamir Khan and Afaq Ahmed establishing MQM Haqiqi and promising a new era of peaceful co-existence and renunciation of Hussain's style coincided with the military operation. The army claimed it had not only unearthed several secret torture houses amidst an increasing number of cases of extortion, kidnap, rape and murder registered against Altaf Hussain, Farouk Sattar, Safdar Baqri, Salim Shahzad and others, but it had also arrested and eliminated a number of dacoits in the interior.[65] The army chief, General Asif Janjua, had been deeply involved earlier in assisting the provincial government in law-related activities in Karachi, and was well aware of the syndicates operated by both the MQM and the feudalist interests protecting criminals and prying on civilians.

The operation was widely acclaimed across the country as it brought long-sought peace, while Sharif began whirlwind visits of the province distributing lands among the landless *haris* in the interior. It appears that the military operation had been started at the behest of the army and presidency while Sharif tried to take credit for 'sacrificing' his coalition interests in order to bring stability and peace in the province. Syed Muzzaffar Shah, with a secure chief ministership and Irfanullah Marwat as his adviser on administration, chose to keep a low profile. Corruption, torture and violence remained undiminished in Sindh. As the editor of a leading magazine wrote: 'Nowhere is the unholy link between crime and politics so marked as in Sindh. Political parties in the province have become a haven for criminals, and political power is their shield against the law.'[66]

Political expediency is reported to have reduced the scope of the military operation since, according to many observers, not only the MQM but several other parties and influential families in Sindh had been involved in crimes to different degrees. Leaders of various factions of Jeeye Sindh on the campus of the University of Sindh, Jamshoro, including Qadir Magsi, Bashir Qureshi, Ghulam Haider Shahani, Nawab Leghari, Zulfiqar Mangi and Darya Khan Tunio had been engaged in kidnapping and robbery. Curiously, they worked in league with Hyderabad's deputy mayor and MPA Rashid Ahmed Khan alias Bhaiya and when raided by the police and army, a number of kidnap victims and stolen cars were found with them.[67] The PPI carried on its own criminal activities since it received protection from Irfanullah Marwat.[68] The army operation was certainly not drastic, though several MQM activists were arrested and with the recovery of weapons and disclosures concerning torture cells, the movement found itself in a precarious position. However, even with a nod from the authorities the Haqiqi faction could not fill the vacuum as it was seen by many Muhajireen to be relying on the establishment. The army itself presumably did not want to go too far in searching out militants as it had no wish to create martyrs; it was also hampered by the civilian administration, which refused to divulge the names of important provincial figures wanted by the army. A list of 70 people responsible for gunrunning, theft and other anti-social activities was prepared by military intelligence but never given to the press – though it appears that the army did indeed want to apprehend them.[69] Meanwhile the Muhajireen waited silently for the MQM to reemerge with an improved programme and more coherent politics. The very low turn-out in the by-elections held for vacant urban constituencies gave the impression of a boycott.[70]

Throughout the summer of 1992 questions about the duration of the army action in Sindh, especially in urban areas, and the future of the MQM remained the major topics of debate among political analysts. Belief in a cohesive Muhajir ethnicity was strong, but there were also serious reservations about the continued existence of the MQM given the disappearance of its leadership.[71] While the MQM blamed Islamabad for betraying its allies, some of its supporters thought the army action was simply an exercise to improve its image after two incidents in Sindh. In the first of these, an army officer killed 13 innocent *haris* at Bilawal near Hyderabad; in the second incident, two prominent Sindhi politicians died in a van while being taken to an interrogation centre in the interior. Sindhi groups and human-rights activists took serious note of these occurrences which tarnished the army's image as an honest broker.[72]

Within the civilian establishment, there were mixed feelings about the long-term implications of the clean-up operation. For the president, any continued disorder could trigger disruptive forces or even help the PPP regain its lost ground. For the prime minister, a continued uncertainty and growing alienation in the Muhajir community together with a threatening PPP could mean further instability.[73] It was felt by some observers that the MQM was the result of praetorianism in the Pakistani polity and that the army action, mainly to protect the propertied classes in Sindh, might cause the disintegration of the establishment's own creation without removing the root cause.[74] The army wanted to avoid becoming embroiled in the intricate quagmire for a long period, but pressure from Islamabad prevailed since the superimposed peace suited most people. Also, the army did not want to be seen taking sides in inter-factional dissensions in Muhajir politics.[75] However, the continuation of Operation Clean-Up and the growing dependence of the factionalist Sindh administration on the army, posed a serious dilemma for the military command. A wide variety of groups who had welcomed the operation began to question the strategies as all the major culprits remained at large.[76]

The death of General Asif Nawaz Janjua in November 1992[77] and the selection of General Abdul Waheed as his successor took place at a time of growing crisis between Ishaque Khan and Nawaz Sharif over a wide range of issues such as the controversial Eighth Amendment and the forthcoming presidential elections. There was speculation that Hussain was planning a 'Khomeini-style' come-back to Pakistan to revitalise the campaign for the by-elections. When the stalemate continued for months, intervention by the most powerful member of the troika (the army command) became inevitable. The power struggle in Islamabad involved dissolution of assemblies and polarised antagonism between the president (supported by Benazir Bhutto) and the prime minister (buoyed by judicial restoration of the national assembly yet beleaguered by defiance from the four provincial governments). For a while Sindh went into oblivion though in early July there were signs that the Altaf group of the MQM was regrouping amidst general demands for ending the military operation and releasing the activists. The resignations of the president and the prime minister on 17 July 1993 through an army-brokered formula quickly quietened down the agitation in urban Sindh once again. Apparently some factions in the MQM had begun considering new strategies to cope with the changed political scene in the country.

It appeared that a degenerating process of 'feudalisation' had permeated the movement as its leaders witch-hunted their critics, extorted huge sums from businessmen, were involved in gunrunning and blackmailed factories and banks for the forcible recruitment of MQM sympathisers. Such pressure tactics tarnished the image of the organisation among some Urdu-speakers, though a continuing army operation helped to restore its fledgling support, as was confirmed in the elections.

SINDH SINCE 1993

Some of the Muhajir grievances remain unrectified and the politicisation of Muhajir ethnicity, however 'deficient' or 'imagined' it might look to its critics, remains a reality. This was confirmed in the elections of October 1993, when the MQM took 27 seats in the provincial assembly, showing that in urban Sindh it is still a power to be reckoned with. The MQM supported Benazir Bhutto in her bid for the premiership amidst a growing desire for cooperation to avoid the erstwhile confrontational politics. The organisation also voted for the election of Farooq Leghari, the PPP candidate for the country's presidency. But, soon there was a parting of ways. The MQM accused the PPP of dithering over fulfilling of its promises, especially in allocating ministerial portfolios, and continuously pressed for the recall of the army from enforcing peace in the streets of Karachi. The MQM was enraged when the provincial government led by the PPP suddenly announced the establishment of a new administrative district in Karachi in March 1994. During the same period, followers of both parties engaged in skirmishes and when the army tried to restore order, eight of its members including an officer were brutally killed in a predominantly Urdu-speaking area. Soon after, the MQM sent signals for a possible realignment with the opposition led by Nawaz Sharif and Abdul Wali Khan of the ANP.[78]

However, despite his best efforts, Nawaz Sharif could not win over the sympathies of the MQM leadership. Soon after starting his agitation to destabilise the Bhutto administration, Sharif went to London to woo Altaf Hussain, who refused to meet him. The situation in Karachi took a very violent turn in early December 1994, when the army was withdrawn from the streets of Karachi – apparently, it did not want to be seen as fighting a civil war against the Muhajireen. A joyous Benazir Bhutto interpreted the withdrawal as the restoration of normality in the city after a very long time and hastened to take the credit for it. However, within a few days, hundreds of Karachiites lay dead through sniper fire following ethnic and sectarian clashes. This turned out to be the worst spell of violence and bloodshed ever witnessed in the city. The PPP regime blamed the Indian intelligence, who they said were retaliating against Pakistani support for Kashmiri activists. The squabbles between the Altaf and Haqiqi factions, combined with Shia–Sunni conflict, brought the paramilitary forces back into the city. A superimposed peace in Karachi, with intermittent violence, only exposed the vulnerability of the city. A few Karachi-style hit-and-run incidents took place in Hyderabad and there was renewed criticism of the PPP government in Sindh, led by Abdullah Shah. Nawaz Sharif, who had been unable to secure peace in Karachi, vehemently criticised Benazir Bhutto in the midst of his agitation to topple her government. With more intermittent killings in the month, the tally for 1994 went well above 750 together with stupendous losses in property and national revenue. It was quite demoralising for the country since the regime was trying to attract major foreign investments. Salah ud-Din, the editor of the weekly *Takbeer* – a Muhajir critic of the MQM – was gunned down outside his office on 4 December 1994 while Abdus Sattar Edhi, the well-known philanthropist sought temporary exile in London. In addition to factional fights, the Altaf group engaged itself in regular street battles with the police. The situation was further compounded by the Sunni–Shia conflicts which gained a new momentum and Karachi remained ablaze with anarchy and disorder, with official machinery totally paralysed: 'The violence is the result of four separate conflicts involving rival criminal gangs, Sunni and Shia Muslims, native Sindhis and Urdu-speaking Mohajirs, and rival factions of the Mohajir community' was a contemporary summation.[79]

On 5 February 1995, when the entire country was exhibiting solidarity with the Kashmiris, snipers struck at a mass rally in Karachi and killed 21 people who had been demonstrating against India. Only four days later, ten more were shot down by unknown assailants, as they are officially described. On 8 March, two US diplomats[80] were killed in Karachi by 'unidentified' assailants, resulting in increased global pressure on Bhutto's tenuous administration 'to confront the insidious enemy within before the country explodes'. The Shia–Sunni feuds in the winter of 1994–95, only complemented an enduring ethnic chaos. For instance, during the month of fasting two Shia mosques were attacked leaving more than 26 worshippers dead and an equal number seriously injured. Between 1 December 1994 and 15 March 1995, 542 people were killed in ethnic and sectarian clashes in Karachi.[81] In May 1995, as the sectarian violence subsided, the ethnic turmoil took a new turn. The security forces were confronted with face-to-face clashes with MQM supporters in a type of civil war. In early June, the situation further deteriorated with the first-time application of car-bomb explosives outside the provincial assembly building and a military post. Such a new pattern of violence underlined the inability of the civil and military authorities to curb the violence.

While the MQM demanded the withdrawal of cases against Altaf Hussain and other underground leaders, the PPP refused to negotiate with 'the terrorists'. Altaf Hussain, along with his condemnation of Benazir Bhutto, demanded a separate province for Urdu-speakers and observed: 'They are hunting Mohajirs like birds and animals. They have a license to kill.'[82] Short of criticising the army, he pursued a dual policy of militant assertion and personal expediency as manifested through *nationalist* claims for a stable Pakistan. Benazir Bhutto would hit back at the MQM with a slander. With daily occurrences of violence in the city, the movement was apparently increasing the pressure for acceptance of its growing number of demands, with the regime holding back and the opposition actively seeking support from Altaf Hussain. On 11 June 1995 the PPP government retaliated by instituting 160 cases of corruption and misconduct, including treason, against Nawaz Sharif and it appeared that all avenues of reconciliation and peaceful negotiation among the various parties in the conflict had been closed. Karachi, as in the past, was left to its own ordeal.

Both the PPP and the MQM are engaged in an unending power showdown and are being guided by hawkish elements who veto the politics of negotiations and tolerance. The army itself would not like to be seen as a party in the inter-ethnic and inter-party quagmire yet it is bewildered by its inability to stamp out disorder.[83] The assailants appear with total impunity and select targets of their own choice. The civilian administration remains ineffective and the MQM feels confident of surviving on its own. Such a view allows it to assert itself powerfully on behalf of the urban Sindh. The corrupt civil administration, rent-seeking politicians, intolerant mullahs and unscrupulous mafia bosses trading in guns, narcotics and illegal immigrants pursue their own agendas, apparently unhindered by any restrictions. The country bleeds, with everyone yearning for a deliverer.[84] Pakistani nationalism remains contested and Muslim nationalism stands bruised by sectarian and autonomist forces which impose their own will simply through militancy and violence. Jinnah's dream of a super-ordinate Pakistani nationalism, incorporating ethnic, regional and religious pluralism based on constitutionalism, tolerance and political egalitarianism remains elusive despite numerous incentives.

The situation in Karachi over the past few years has raised a number of issues including the relationship between the state and ethnic communities, Pakistani nationalism and ethnic nationalism and the roles of the army, the bureaucracy and political leadership. Organised violence has become a fact of daily life,[85] and it is quite clear that state-run institutions like the police and other important administrative departments have completely failed in maintaining law and order. Corruption and dishonesty in the local administration, both by the central and provincial governments, often at the expense of justice as in the case of Jam Sadiq Ali and his chief advisor, Irfanullah Marwat,[86] have eroded the credibility and moral weight of office-holders. Moreover, the conflictive roles and interests of various secret agencies have unnecessarily exacerbated the situation. The police force in Karachi is generally regarded as alien and corrupt and, as an abusive arm of the state, it has persistently remained the focus of guerrilla attacks. Senior police officials, while complaining of shortages in logistics and finances, consider politicians and military officials to be indifferent towards their predicament. Many from up-country feel a strong localist/grudge against them. The number of dead bodies being sent back home have also engendered a severe demoralising sentiment. The army, despite its three-year-long operation in Karachi, has failed to stamp out the violence, which appears to have degenerated into a regular urban guerrilla warfare with the militants operating freely without any hindrance. The narrow alleys of Karachi are difficult to patrol and it is not easy to carry out searches for criminals among a general Muhajir populace that is hostile, indifferent or too incapacitated by the militants to combat violence. The Pakistan Army, ostensibly bewildered at the intensity of the violence, is unable to provide or implement any solution that may involve a greater use of force. Its leadership would not care to impose another martial law at least for the moment, as Karachi remains both a major test-case and a liability; neither would the generals like to become too involved in the quagmire as it would lead to soldiers fighting against their fellow citizens.

The Pakistani politicians, national, religious and ethnic, all appear to be lacking the will and imagination to rectify the malady and instead use it against each other in their inter-personal strife. Bhutto would like to talk tough against the MQM so as to appease Sindhis or other anti-MQM elements in her administration. She has refused to open talks with Altaf Hussain until his organisation 'lays down arms, surrenders criminals and condemns terrorism'.[87] Similarly, the opposition has continually reiterated its 'pious' sentiments for a dialogue whereas the religious parties remain totally sidelined or engaged in sectarian rivalries. In the short term, the MQM appears to be benefiting from the volatile situation, with London-based Altaf Hussain speaking with increasing authority and militancy, though his statements would disown any responsibility for violence. But he cannot absolve himself from leading the MQM or at least some of its militant factions along the course of violence and urban guerrilla warfare.[88] The body bags carrying the Punjabi, Pushtun, Sindhi and Balochi citizens who are being killed daily in Karachi have spread gloom, though anti-Muhajir reprisals have not occurred in any part of the country. However, the scheme of a Muhajir separatism cannot be implemented through sheer violence as Karachi is too plural and 'ethnic cleansing' will not bring about a totally Muhajir demography.[89] At the worst, Karachi will remain 'Pakistan's Beirut' for a few more years until a new generation ushers in a fresh beginning. Similarly, Karachi's growing socio-economic problems may cause an eventual revolt from the Urdu-speakers themselves against a continued tradition of violence.

PROGNOSIS

The idea of a separate Muhajir state, as it was mooted in the late 1980s among certain Muhajir sections, is quite impractical given the fact that the Muhajireen are spread all over Pakistan. After initially joining a broad coalition with the PPP and subsequently with the IJT and then again with the PPP the MQM overwhelmingly opted for a democratic/federal Pakistan. More recently, it has been advocating the division of Sindh into two separate provinces, rural and urban respectively. Such an administrative division may not guarantee a resolution of the volatile pluralism in Karachi, rather it may exacerbate ethnic cleansing with the MQM expelling non-Urdu speakers from urban Sindh. Since each province in the country is extremely plural it might prove an impractical and equally explosive precedent. However, a substantial devolution of power with the divisions substituting for existing provinces could alleviate the situation to a great extent.

Sindhi nationalists and other critics see Muhajir identity as an expression of cultural distinctness rather than a complete case of ethnic nationalism. They consider that ethnic identity cannot be a single-factor dispensation brought about by demagogy or sheer coercion. But there is no denying the fact that without a *given* identity, the MQM has transformed a Muhajir consciousness into a full-fledged ethnic identity. Although dissent remains a natural right, its criminalisation in the name of ethnic politics by any group is bound to boomerang. In *real politik*, despite all the assembly seats from urban constituencies, the MQM cannot form any provincial government on its own – it can operate only as a coalition partner or opposition, unless similar urban-based movements emerge in other cities of the country. Such a scenario is impossible as the MQM's appeal remains strictly confined to the core of Urdu-speakers and any country-wide expansion might dilute its impact.

The MQM could absorb other middle-class ethnic activists but it would have to deconstruct its strict Muhajir credentials. If it stays as it is, the hostility or indifferent attitude to the Sindhis, Punjabis, Pushtuns or Balochis would rule out any trans-ethnic sympathies. Its continued territorial and electoral confinement and narrow franchise, besides its occasional relapses into high-handedness, would only add to its contradictions.

Nevertheless, with moderation and cooption it could neutralise its opponents to a large extent, for fundamentally they admire its organisational, urban and demographic dynamics including the mobilisation of women and youths. By challenging traditional organisations like the JI and the JUP, it has proved its supra-religious credentials; but by antagonising Sindhi activists and the PPP, it has not won the sympathies of moderate, liberal and secular elements. By refusing the role of coalition partner, it will have to sit on the opposition benches in the Sindh provincial assembly and this may make it difficult for the MQM to maintain a steady following in the future. In addition, the very presence of a large number of parallel ethnic communities in Karachi and Sindh, demanding co-existence despite an apparent majority of Urdu-speakers, makes any attempt at exclusivity/secession impossible.

It is nonetheless true that the MQM will remain a power to be reckoned with in metropolitan/provincial politics in Sindh while holding a crucial position in the formation/break-up of any federal government in the centre (although such a role would entail a heavy cost for the organisation). Lack of clarity on major issues and long-term objectives could create fissures within the organisation itself. Similarly, the inter-personal feuds which became more apparent in 1991–93, as well as irredentist claims, may have serious ramifications for the movement. Moreover, the MQM has yet to mature from a movement into a full-fledged modern party which is able 'to deliver the goods'. Many people are already questioning the rationale of an ever confrontational politicking from pre-1947 Hindus to Bengalis in former East Pakistan to Sindhis, Punjabis and Pushtuns in present-day Sindh, not to mention various shifting political alignments. Such a persistent antagonism drummed up by a hollow personality cult cannot be a long-term binding force for the heterogeneous groups within the MQM. Technically, mere lingual commonality may prove an insufficient base to guarantee ethnic cohesion.

To most Pakistanis, the Muhajireen are still disproportionately the most privileged of all the ethnic groups in urban Sindh, and the idea of being outnumbered, outmanoeuvred and outrun by the MQM raises strong reservations among non-Muhajir communities. The MQM may feel confident that no one can rule Pakistan peacefully while it is on the offensive; but it must not ignore the demographic realities of the 1990s, where Karachi has become the largest Pushtun city in the country. Equally, it needs to be remembered that there are more Balochis in Karachi alone than in the entire province of Balochistan and that Karachi has already become the sixth largest Punjabi town. Thus the new imperatives demand more inter-dependence among these diversified communities. Similarly, civil society in Pakistan is becoming increasingly vocal and by coercing the press, labour unions or student unions the MQM will only acquire more critics. The inexplicable absence of a charismatic leader like Altaf Hussain from Pakistan on the grounds of his own personal security, has already seriously compromised the status of the MQM among its supporters. Questions about corruption, misuse of unaccounted funds, malpractice, torture and scandals still largely remain unanswered. By dallying with the very institutions earlier accused of exploitation and the turn-about on issues like land reforms, the movement has exposed a bleak absence of ideological commitment. It also shows the limitations of a lingual/cultural nationalism in competition with strong parallel ethnic movements. Unless the MQM reorients itself radically, a new phase in Pakistani politics – the emergence of urban-based, mundane, middle-class-led politics – might be doomed.

Epilogue

The establishment of the PPP regime led by Benazir Bhutto in 1993 following the national and provincial elections in October, appeared to be the beginning of a long-sought era of political stability. The election of Farooq Khan Leghari as the country's president further secured the government and removed fears of another executive order rooted in the controversial Eighth Amendment. (Earlier, the Amendment – originally incorporated by General Zia ul-Haq in the Constitution of 1973 – had helped Ghulam Ishaque Khan accomplish a 'hat-trick' with three dissolutions in as many years.) It was the second time that the PPP, founded by Zulfikar Ali Bhutto in 1967, had been able to hold simultaneously the two highest offices in the country and it was only the second time in 44 years of the country's history that a politician had become the head of state. Pakistan's youthful leadership, both in the government and opposition since the departure of 'the old guard', brought hope and anxiety to the country. The 'troika' of power shared by the president (usually a bureaucrat or general), the chief of army staff and the prime minister – with the last being the weakest of the three – had moved more in favour of the political duo. Such a major shift boded well for the political forces in the country. In late 1993, the country was enjoying a most favourable geopolitical environment following the dissolution of the Soviet Union, the emergence of friendly Muslim Central Asian republics with a supportive Afghanistan, and India (confronted with a massive revolt from within Kashmir) agreeing to hold talks with Pakistan. But this optimism was short-lived as the country tumbled into another abysmal phase of an ever-haunting governability crisis.

Barely a few weeks after the installation of the PPP administration, the government and the opposition began to destabilise each other. While long-term politico-constitutional anomalies waited for tangible solutions, the country entered a new phase of instability. The opposition-led provincial government of Sabir Shah in the NWFP was replaced by a new coalition, precariously anchored on bribes and cabinet positions. The PPP failed to establish a sought-after provincial government in the Punjab where Manzoor Wattoo continued by forming a multi-party coalition through official patronage. After trying for several months and increasing the number of its adversaries, the PPP reluctantly accepted the Wattoo ministry in Lahore. The coalition government in Balochistan led by Zulfikar Magsi managed to survive by keeping Islamabad happy. Sindh,

257

however, presented the worst scenario where the PPP established its own provincial administration headed by Abdullah Shah yet refused to share power with the MQM. Long-time hostilities between the MQM and the PPP resurfaced over contentious issues including the quota, demarcation of administrative districts and, most significantly, the ongoing army operation in Karachi. The MQM demanded the withdrawal of troops from Karachi, the restoration of local government and annulment of cases against its leaders.

At a time when Benazir Bhutto and Murtaza, her brother, were engaged in an acrimonious dispute over the PPP leadership, the MQM revitalised itself. In 1994, the PPP administration was fighting on many fronts. The regime came under severe attack after a financial scandal (known as Mehrangate) involving the president and other notables became public. The shadowy land deals, revelations of corruption at the highest level including generals, senior bureaucrats and politicians prompted the opposition to mount a campaign to remove the PPP regime. Although nation-wide demonstrations led by Nawaz Sharif failed to topple the government they exposed the fragility of the entire system. The PPP, which had itself been a victim of the strong presidency, now started defending the Eighth Amendment. It reneged on its electoral campaign to streamline the national political system by restoring viable constitutionalism. It pursued a policy of drift and showed no interest in building a new consensus in the country. The government, rather than strengthening political and civil institutions, became dependent upon the bureaucracy and intelligence agencies. While the country waited for a break-through, the prime minister spent most of her time undertaking highly-publicised foreign tours. Rather than establishing new traditions in civic attitudes, the regime instituted 160 cases against the opposition leader including treason.

With a political deadlock in the country the ideological tensions resurfaced. In late 1994 Malakand and Swat turned into battlefields as the security forces fought the local fundamentalists who were demanding promulgation of Sharia law. Eventually the administration had to yield as it agreed to some of the demands presented by the *ulama* and sought refuge in temporary respite. Following a multiple increase in sectarian tensions, the Shia–Sunni conflict in Jhang, Lahore and Karachi became volatile and caused several deaths. Encouraged by sectarian militancy, certain extremist groups in Central Punjab started their anti-blasphemy campaign against minorities. The case of Salamat Masih, a 14-year-old, illiterate Christian boy in early 1995 became a major challenge for the civil society. His death sentence was commuted by the High Court only after a great commotion but the entire episode highlighted the fragility of the civil society in the country. Forces of ideology – with all their contentions and prevarications – remained unharnessed, proving vulnerable to a rhetoric and exploitation at the expense of civil rights.

More than sectarianism and religious intolerance, it is the defiant pluralism and a stubborn administrative machinery that have continued to rock Pakistani polity for so long. Seeing the regime vulnerable and lacking any policy initiative on strife-torn Karachi, the MQM intensified its militancy. By early 1995, Karachi had become ungovernable; with a daily toll of 10 to 15 deaths largely due to ethnic violence, the unrest had gradually turned into a civil war between the security forces and the MQM. Benazir Bhutto and Altaf Hussain, supported by hawkish elements in their organisations, confronted each other in the worst show-down in the city's history. Within the first six months of 1995, more than 800 citizens lay dead. Such a polarisation presented the most serious threat to Pakistani state and civil society, but both the contenders seemed to be disinterested in breaking the logjam. Karachi bled while the country waited for a new Jinnah to steer it towards a consensus. Pakistan, in its short history, had suffered at the hands of elitist bureaucrats, arrogant generals, opportunist feudalists, bigoted *mullahs* and a regionalised intermediate class. Both the state and civil society needed a new relationship rooted in the humaneness of the society and supremacy of political culture.

Throughout its turbulent and uncertain history Pakistan has been unable to develop a consensus-based political culture facilitating national integration. However, its strides forward in the economic and social arena, largely due to the efforts of its people, are quite noteworthy. From the backwaters of the British empire, Pakistan has not only succeeded in repudiating apprehensions and expectations to the contrary but has also reached the threshold of a middle-income status. The loss of its former eastern wing was largely caused by political alienation exploited by foreign intervention, yet it quickly moved to repair the socio-psychological and military damage. Pakistanis withstood a radical shift in the South Asian balance of power, especially in the 1970s following the military defeat and explosion of India's nuclear device in 1974. In the 1980s, Pakistan was in the throes of a critical governability crisis but nevertheless felt strong enough to resist temptation and coercion from a global power and reestablish its credibility, resilience and regional preeminence. The cost to Pakistan was immense but the country came of age. The development of Urdu as a lingua franca, unprecedented mobility both within and outside the country and progress in scientific areas including nuclear technology, sped up the emergence of an intermediate class imbued with the desire for a stable, tolerant and forward-looking political system. Vital demographic changes such as urbanisation and an overwhelmingly youthful and aware population in an environment of *attainable* prosperity persuaded people to strengthen mundane forces. Pakistanis, quite conscious of their *Muslim* identity, have always supported and voted for 'worldly' parties in a pragmatic manner and, if left to them, the country would certainly avoid the politics of extremism that has produced an imbalanced relationship between the state and civil society. All these positive developments can be harnessed to establish a new covenant between these two major areas so as to evolve a consensus in the country, which is ready for a break-through.

Despite all these positive and no less singular achievements, the country remains bedevilled by a series of unresolved problems. One cannot overlook the very weak nature of political institutions, which are still vulnerable to personality-centred manipulation. On the one hand, Pakistan in early 1994 appeared to be heading towards a desired two-party system; on the other hand it retained serious deficiencies within *national* party politics in terms of second-tier leadership, political programmes and clear policies on domestic and regional issues. Relationships between the ruling party and opposition are still governed by attempts to annihilate each other rather than a spirit of acceptance. Constitutional lacunae, including the drift between a parliamentary and presidential form of government, anomalies like the Eighth Amendment, the relationship between the centre and the provinces, the guarantee of a judiciary independent of administrative monopoly and incentives for the enfranchisement of women and minorities are some of the major issues still awaiting solutions. Corruption as manifested in changing loyalties and horse-trading and institutionalised through plots and remission of loans, is deeply engrained in the political culture and must be eliminated. The lack of ideological commitment and the emphasis on the politics of patronage keep political forces fragmented and the masses and intellectuals lose confidence in parliamentarians.

The state and its functionaries remain unilaterally powerful and are ready to accept only a docile political structure. The bureaucracy has become well-entrenched over the decades while vital sectors in civil society remain fragile and vulnerable to its machinations. Generals play a crucial role in the formation and dissolution of governments and allow 'irresponsible' politicians to earn the nation's displeasure. Intelligence agencies are frequently stretched beyond their ambiguous mandate, and torture and harassment of the weakest in society both by feudalists and the powerful state functionaries have been routine. The judiciary remains under the strong vetoing thumb of an elitist oligarchy where administration rather than governance patterns the narrowly based prerogatives. Education, health, social welfare, empowerment of women and minorities, a free press, autonomous socio-cultural groups and think-tanks all remain non-priority areas within a largely ignored peripheralised development sector. Loan servicing, defence allocations and maintenance of a major administrative set-up are consuming the nation's scarce resources and sapping its vitality. The country's politico-administrative structure, with its outdated, cumbersome provincial boundaries, encourages fissiparous forces and has failed to grasp changing realities and challenges within Pakistan. Huge constituencies allow resourceful feudal participation and the monopolisation of electoral politics while the middle class is kept at bay.

Ideological groups have failed miserably to provide any intellectual leadership but, on the contrary, have merely given muffled or open support to authoritarian regimes seeking legitimacy. The intermingling of religion and politics for limited partisan gains has betrayed the path chosen by the founders of Pakistan and dented the process of national integration. Centralist tendencies have exacerbated the centripetal forces whereby, in place of negotiations and political bargaining, coercion and opportunism set the rules. Ideology and ethnicity, instead of being bound in a mutually acceptable relationship with the forces of authority, have only shown themselves to be volatile without presenting any positive alternatives. The need for decentralisation of power, massive empowerment of the general population through a new political consensus obtained by means of debate and democratisation, and prioritisation of the development sector through widespread domestic and regional dialogue has never been so great. It may be a gigantic task but it is not impossible since such reform is in the larger interests of the country. The power elites from the bureaucracy, the military and their counterparts from religious and ethnic groups have to be reminded of their collective responsibility towards a just order. A weak, disorderly, underdeveloped, militarised and war-torn Pakistan is in nobody's interests. The break-up of Pakistan through internal turmoil and external intervention will signal disaster for the whole of South Asia, leading to the worst kind of ethnic cleansing and communalisation. The necessary ingredients and resources to develop a tolerant, forward-looking and peaceful society exist, despite its location in a volatile region. Pakistan needs to undertake bold initiatives in order to achieve a new equilibrium between state and civil society based on mutual co-existence rather than negation, and thus redefine the relationship between the tri-polar forces of authority, ideology and ethnicity. It is a test-case for Pakistani leaders of all hues and views.

Notes

INTRODUCTION

1. Iftikhar H. Malik, 'Pakistan's Security Imperatives and Relations with the United States' in K. Matinuddin and L. Rose (eds), *Beyond Afghanistan: The Emerging U.S.–Pakistan Relations*, Berkeley, 1989, pp. 60–93.
2. Louis D. Hayes, *The Struggle for Pakistan*, Lahore, 1982, p. 3.
3. Zbigniew Brzenzinski, representing a section of opinion in the West in 1988, stated that: 'The Pakistanis should not be pressured by outsiders to move precipitously toward "democracy", for that could actually intensify domestic tensions given the ethnic and political hatreds inherent in Pakistan ... If the younger surviving senior officers should move to create a transitional regime, Pakistan deserves the West's sympathetic encouragement, not strident lectures.' *The Times* (London), 26 August 1988. British conservative opinion was equally sceptical of the PPP, as was observed in a leading comment: 'It is to be hoped that Pakistan's new economic well-being will rally support behind conservatives like Mr. Junejo. There is, however, a risk that General Zia's political excesses will deliver victory to Miss Benazir Bhutto.' *The Daily Telegraph* (London), 19 August 1988.
4. Christina Lamb, a British journalist in Islamabad, reported an attempted military coup which was denied by Benazir Bhutto, General Beg and Pakistan's foreign office. See *The Financial Times* (London), 8 September 1989; *The Daily Jang* (London) 9, 10, 11 and 12 September 1989. But Christina Lamb insists that her report was not based on hearsay as she had been informed by a very reliable source. See Christina Lamb, *Waiting For Allah: Pakistan's Struggle for Democracy*, London, 1991, pp. 16–17.
5. For instance, see G. W. Choudhury, *Constitutional Developments in Pakistan*, New York, 1959.
6. Many prominent studies, several referred to in the subsequent chapters, have dealt in detail with political developments in Pakistan. In addition to quite a few research papers in scholarly journals, see Khalid B. Sayeed, The Political System of Pakistan, Boston, 1967; Lawrence Ziring, *The Enigma of Political Development*, Durham, 1980; K. K. Aziz, *Party Politics in Pakistan, 1947–58*, Islamabad, 1976; M. Rafique Afzal, *Political Parties in Pakistan, 1958–1969*, Islamabad, 1987; S. J. Burki, *Pakistan Under Bhutto, 1971–1977*, London, 1988 (reprint); Omar Noman, *Pakistan: Political and Economic History since 1947*, London, 1990 (reprint); Craig Baxter, *et al.* (eds), *Pakistan Under the Military: Eleven Years of Zia-ul-Haq*, Boulder, 1991.
7. See A. H. Syed, *Islam, Politics and National Solidarity*, New York, 1983.
8. Asaf Hussain, *Elite Politics in an Ideological State*, London, 1979.
9. For an early useful study, see Lawrence Ziring, *The Ayub Khan Era*, New York, 1971; and Herbert Feldman, *Revolution in Pakistan*, London, 1967. For an official perspective, see M. Ayub Khan, *Friends Not Masters*,

London, 1967; and Altaf Gauhar, *Ayub Khan: Pakistan's First Military Ruler*, Lahore, 1993.

10. See Rounaq Jahan, *Pakistan: Failure in National Integration*, New York, 1972; G. W. Choudhury, *Last Days of United Pakistan*, London, 1974; and Ayesha Jalal, *Democracy and Authoritarianism in South Asia: A Comparative and Historical Perspective*, Cambridge, 1995.

11. From a host of writings, referred to throughout this book, see G. W. Choudhury, *Pakistan: Transition from Military to Civilian Rule*, London, 1988; and Paula R. Newberg, Judging the State: *Courts and Constitutional Politics in Pakistan*, Cambridge, 1995.

12. Ralph Braibanti, *Research on the Bureaucracy of Pakistan*, Durham, 1966; and Charles H, Kennedy, *Bureaucracy in Pakistan*, Karachi, 1987.

13. Stephen Cohen, *The Pakistan Army*, Berkeley, 1984. For a useful study on the military's role *vis-à-vis* politics in the country, see Hasan-Askari Rizvi, *The Military and Politics in Pakistan, 1947–86*, Lahore, 1988.

14. Leo E. Rose and Richard Sisson, *War and Secession. Pakistan, India, and the Creation of Bangladesh*, Berkeley, 1990; and Hasan Zaheer, *The Separation of East Pakistan*, Karachi, 1994.

15. For useful works on Z. A. Bhutto, see Salman Taseer, *Bhutto: A Political Biography*, London, 1979: Stanley Wolpert, *Zulfi Bhutto of Pakistan. His Life and Times*, Karachi, 1993; and Anwar H. Syed, *The Discourse and Politics of Zulfikar Ali Bhutto*, London, 1992.

16. For an overview, see S. J. Burki, 'Economic Policy after Zia ul-Haq', in Charles H. Kennedy, *Pakistan 1992*, Boulder, 1993. Also S. J. Burki and Robert LaPorte Jr. (eds), *Pakistan's Development Priorities: Choices for the Future*, Karachi, 1985.

17. See Hasan-Askari Rizvi, *Pakistan and the Geostrategic Environment*, London, 1993; and Hafeez Malik (ed.), *Dilemmas of National Security and Cooperation in India and Pakistan*, New York, 1993.

18. Pakistan's defence policy is a comparatively new subject. See, P. I. Cheema, *Pakistan's Defence Policy, 1947–58*, London, 1990.

19. S. M. Burke and Lawrence Ziring, *Pakistan's Foreign Policy: An Historical Analysis*, Karachi, 1990. The Afghanistan issue in the 1980s generated quite a lot of academic interest in Pakistan-related subjects. See Noor A. Hussein and Leo E. Rose (eds), *Pakistan–U.S. Relations*, Berkeley, 1988; and Rasul B. Rais 'Afghanistan and the Regional Powers', *Asian Survey*, XXXIII (9), 1993, pp. 902–22.

20. See Iftikhar H. Malik, *Continuing Conflict in Kashmir: Regional Détente in Jeopardy*, London, 1993; Robert G. Wirsing, *India, Pakistan and the Kashmir Boundary Dispute. The Search for Settlement*, New York, 1993. For a pertinent study, see Alastair Lamb, *Kashmir: A Disputed Legacy, 1846–1990*, Hertingfordbury, 1991.

21. T. Ali, *Can Pakistan Survive? The Death of a State*, Harmondsworth, 1983.

22. Without underrating Harrison's academic work, it may be suggested that his specific interpretation evolved during a specific time-frame characterised by the cold war, presuming a powerful external factor from the northwest. Selig Harrison, *In Afghanistan's Shadow: Baloch Nationalism and Soviet Temptations*, New York, 1981.

23. Inayatullah Baloch, *Greater Balochistan: A study of Baloch nationalism*, Stuttgart, 1987.

24.	Lawrence Ziring, *Pakistan: The Enigma of Political Development*, Folkstone, 1980.

25.	Hamza Alavi, 'Nationhood and Nationalities in Pakistan', *Economic and Political Weekly*, XXIV, 8 July 1989.

26.	Anwar H. Syed, 'Political Parties and the Nationality Question in Pakistan', *Journal of South Asian and Middle Eastern Studies*, XII (1), Fall 1988, pp. 42–75.

27.	Akbar S. Ahmed, *Pakistan Society: Islam, Ethnicity, and Leadership in South Asia*, Karachi, 1986.

28.	Tahir Amin, *Ethno-National Movements of Pakistan: Domestic and International Factors*, Islamabad, 1988.

29.	Mumtaz Ahmad, 'Class, Religion and Power: Some Aspects of Islamic Revivalism in Pakistan', Ph.D. Thesis, University of Chicago, 1990.

30.	There is a huge amount of literature available dealing with the historical and theoretical dimensions of state, its evolution and policies *vis-à-vis* national institution-building. In the case of Pakistan, one finds a growing collection of useful works on the subject. For instance, see M. Asghar Khan (ed.), *Islam, Politics and the State: The Pakistan Experience*, London, 1985; William Richter, 'Persistent Praetorianism: Pakistan's Third Military Regime', *Pacific Affairs*, 51 (3), 1978, pp. 406–26; Ayesha Jalal, *The State of Martial Rule in Pakistan: The Origins of Pakistan's Political Economy of Defence*, Cambridge, 1990; and Zamir Niazi, *The Press in Chains*, Karachi, 1987 (reprint).

31.	More recently, there has been an interest in investigating the kind of system and traditions that Pakistan inherited so as to understand its present predicament. For a noteworthy study, see D. A. Low (ed.), *The Political Inheritance of Pakistan*, London, 1991.

32.	In recent years, a few revealing works that do not specifically fall into the realm of serious research but are exposés by nature, have tried to record issues such as monopolisation of power by the military, trans-regional feudalism and criminalisation of state-led institutions like intelligence agencies. See Benazir Bhutto, *Daughter of the East*, London, 1988; Emma Duncan, *Breaking the Curfew. A Political Journey Through Pakistan*, London, 1989; Tehmina Durrani, *My Feudal Lord*, Lahore, 1991; Lamb, *Waiting for Allah*; Wakeel Anjum, *Siyasat Kay Firoan* (Pharaohs of Politics), Urdu, Lahore, 1992; and Muneer Ahmed, *Pakistan Mein Intelligence Agencion Ka Siyasi Kirdar* (The Political Role of Intelligence Agencies in Pakistan), Urdu, Lahore, 1993.

33.	Keith Tester, *Civil Society*, London, 1992, p. 5.

34.	John Locke, *Two Treatises of Civil Government*, London, 1924.

35.	Adam Ferguson, *An Essay on the History of Civil Society*, New Brunswick, 1980 (reprint).

36.	Jean Jacques Rousseau, *The Social Contract*, trans. Maurice Cranston, Harmondsworth, 1968.

37.	Lewis White Beck (ed.), *Kant. Selections*, New York, 1988.

38.	D. D. Raphael and A. L. Macfie (eds), *The Theory of Moral Sentiments*, Oxford, 1976.

39.	Karl Marx, *Early Texts*, trans. by David McLellan, Oxford, 1971.

40.	Antonio Gramsci, *Selections from the Prison Notebooks*, ed. and trans, by Quintin Hoare and Geoffrey N. Smith, London, 1971, pp. 208–9.

41. Tester, op. cit., p. 8.

42. For further discussion, see Benedict Anderson, *Imagined Communities*, London, 1990 (reprint).

43. 'The South Asian disciples of Gramsci need urgently to be liberated from the historical context of the *Prison Notebooks* and look at the state–society dialectic from within the historical and cultural traditions of South Asia.' Subrata K. Mitra and Gowher Rizvi, 'The State and Civil Society in South Asia', a paper presented at South Asia Conference, Nuffield College, Oxford, 27–8 June, 1992, p. 6.

44. In fact, all the major theories of social change since the nineteenth century considered the 'Indian' model to be irrelevant. Following Marx, Weber and Tawney, the inter-war constitutionalism and post-war models of development have been based on specific environments, not particularly germane to South Asia.

45. Subrata K. Mitra and Gowher Rizvi, 'The State and Civil Society', p. 3.

46. See Harold D. Laswell and Abraham Kaplan, *Power and Society: A Framework for Political Inquiry*, New Haven, 1950.

47. Robert LaPorte, Jr., *Power and Privilege. Influence and Decision-Making in Pakistan*, Berkeley, 1975, p. 3.

1 DILEMMA OF POLITICAL CULTURE, NATIONAL INTEGRATION AND CONSTITUTIONALISM

1. 'Pakistan's Chance', (editorial) *The Financial Times*, London, 20 July 1993.

2. Rupert Emerson, *From Empire to Nation*, Cambridge, Mass. 1960, p. 94.

3. Clifford Geertz, 'The Integrative Revolution', in *Old Societies and New States*, New York, 1963, p. 109.

4. For more on this subject, see David Easton, *A Systems Analysis of Political Life*, New York, 1965; and John H. Kautsky (ed.), *Political Change in Underdeveloped Countries: Nationalism and Communism*, New York, 1962.

5. See, Home Affairs Division, *Population Census of Pakistan*, 1961, vol. 1, part IV.

6. In the areas constituting present-day Pakistan, Urdu had been largely adopted as an official language in the late-nineteenth century. Hindustani, a variant of Urdu, was commonly understood in the British Indian Army and was emerging as the popular language. During the nationalist era, languages emerged as the bed-rock of ethnic differentiation defining *communities*.

7. The interplay of Indian, Bengali, Muslim, Hindu and Bangladeshi identities to varying degrees since the nineteenth century has still not resolved the quest for identity on *both* sides.

8. Jahan's timely book appeared when Bangladesh had already come into being, largely validating her theses. But more recent studies point to a number of 'immediate' factors as well, though dwelling on such themes and counter-arguments might not be relevant to the present study. See Rounaq Jahan, *Pakistan: Failure in National Integration*, New York, 1972. For a more recent study, see Richard Sisson and Leo E. Rose, *War and Secession. Pakistan, India, and the Creation of Bangladesh*, Berkeley, 1990.

9. In a sense Balochistan may appear to be less of a problem, but at another crucial level this is not the case. The sense of being outnumbered both in Balochistan by Pushtuns and 'others' while being ignored by Islamabad exacerbates the sense of insecurity among the Baloch intelligentsia, who, in some cases, receive support from tribal chieftains for their own purposes.

10. For additional information on Baloch history, see, A. W. Hughes, *The Country of Baluchistan: Its Geography, Topography, Ethnology and History*, London, 1877; Raj Bahadur H. Ram, *Sandeman in Baluchistan*, Calcutta, 1916; Charles Masson, *Narratives of Various Journeys in Baluchistan, Afghanistan and the Punjab*, 3 vols. Karachi, 1974; Mohammad Sardar Khan Baluch, *History of Baluch Race and Baluchistan*, Lahore, 1976; Sylvia A. Matheson, *The Tigers of Baluchistan*, Karachi, 1975; and, Mir Ahmad Yar Khan Baluch, *Inside Baluchistan*, Karachi, 1975.

11. For a rather alarmist study on this subject, see Selig S. Harrison, *In Afghanistan's Shadow: Baluch Nationalism and Soviet Temptations*, New York, 1981.

12. For more on this, see Mir Gul Khan Nasir, *Tarikh-i-Mastung*, Kalat, 1979.

13. For a good historical analysis from a nationalist viewpoint, see Inayatullah Baloch, *The Problem of 'Greater Baluchistan:' A Study of Baluch Nationalism*, Stuttgart, 1987.

14. For a detailed Balochi perspective, see Mir Khuda Bakhsh Marri, *Searchlight on the Baluchis and Baluchistan*, Karachi, 1974.

15. For an interesting thesis, see Imran Ali, *Punjab Under Imperialism*, London, 1989.

16. See P. H. M. van den Dungen, *The Punjab Tradition*, London, 1972; and Iftikhar H. Malik, *Sikandar Hayat Khan: A Political Biography*, Islamabad, 1985.

17. See David Gilmartin, *Empire and Islam. Punjab and the Making of Pakistan*, London, 1988.

18. For a first-hand account of these families, see L. H. Griffin and C. F. Massy, *Chiefs and Families of Note in the Punjab*, 2 vols, Lahore, 1940; also, Wakeel Anjum, *Siyasat Kay Phiroan* (Pharaohs of Politics), Urdu, Lahore, 1992.

19. See Ian Talbot, 'The Unionist Party and Punjabi Politics, 1937–1947', in D. A. Low (ed.), *The Political Inheritance of Pakistan*, London, 1991.

20. For a pertinent viewpoint on the divisiveness of the Bengali Muslim intelligentsia, see Tazeen M. Murshid, 'A House Divided: The Muslim Intelligentsia of Bengal', in Low, *Political Inheritance*.

21. Sarah Ansari, 'Political Legacies of Pre-1947 Sind', in Low, *Political Inheritance*.

22. Farzana Shaikh, *Community and Consensus in Islam. Muslim Representation in Colonial India, 1860–1947*, Cambridge, 1989, pp. 186–93.

23. See Ian Talbot, 'The Growth of the Muslim League in the Punjab', *Journal of Commonwealth and Comparative Politics*, XX (1), 1982, pp. 5–24.

24. Apart from political expediency, many Punjabi intellectuals in recent years have felt that the province has surrendered much of its culture and history. There are serious efforts to promote Punjabi as a medium of instruction

along with idealisation of past Punjabi heroes. See for example Hanif Ramay, *Punjab Ka Siyasi Muqqidamma*, Lahore, 1987.

25. To many observers, the rural–urban chasm in Pakistan became apparent in the elections of October 1993.
26. For more on Sindh, see H. T. Lambrick, *Sind: A General Introduction*, Hyderabad, 1975 (2nd ed); M. A. Khuro, *A Story of the Sufferings of Sind: A Case for the Separation of Sind from the Bombay Presidency*, Karachi, 1930; and Hamida Khuro, *The Making of Modern Sind: British Policy and Social Change in the Nineteenth Century*, Karachi, 1978.
27. Sarah F. D. Ansari, *Sufi Saints and State Power. The Pirs of Sind, 1843–1947*, Cambridge, 1992, p. 13.
28. See G. M. Syed, *Struggle for a new Sind (1937–1947)*, Karachi, 1949.
29. For more on this, see Stephen A. Rittenberg, *Ethnicity, Nationalism and the Pakhtuns. The Independence Movement in India's North-West Frontier Province*, Durham, 1988; also, Erland Jansson, *India, Pakistan or Pakhtunistan? The Nationalist Movement in the North-West Frontier Province 1937–47*, Stockholm, 1981.
30. Erland Jansson, 'The Frontier Province: Khudai Khidmatgar and The Muslim League', in Low, *Political Inheritance*.
31. 'The Nawab of Hoti, a somewhat erratic personality but the leading *khan* of the province, chose to resign from the Muslim League {in 1946} and the seat he held in the Assembly. He told the governor that it had always been the policy of his family to support the government of the day and that he intended to uphold that tradition' (ibid., p. 209).
32. The Pushtunistan issue 'was originally raised by the Frontier Congress for bargaining purposes. Subsequently the cause was adopted by Afghanistan as well as a variety of *maliks* in tribal territory. However, "Pukhtunistan" meant different things to different people' (ibid., p. 215).
33. This view is rejected by a number of authors who feel that the Muhajir dominance is a myth, concocted to suit certain nefarious claims. See Mushtaqur Rahman, *Land and Life in Sindh, Pakistan*, Lahore, 1993; and Hamza Alavi, 'Nation and Nationalities in Pakistan', in Hastings Dounan and Pnina Werbner (eds), *Economy & Culture in Pakistan. Migrants and Cities in Pakistan*, London, 1991, pp. 182–3.
34. See Shahid Javed Burki, 'Economic Policy After Zia ul-Haq', in Charles H. Kennedy (ed.), *Pakistan 1992*, Boulder, 1993.
35. For more on this see Gustav F. Papanek, *Pakistan's Development: Social Goals and Private Incentives*, Cambridge, 1967.
36. For instance see Gunnar Myrdal, *Asian Drama: An Inquiry into the Poverty of Nations*, 3 vols., New York, 1968.
37. Haq himself turned against what he had been propounding earlier. For his views see his *A Strategy of Economic Planning: A Case Study of Pakistan*, Karachi, 1968.
38. For further details see Omar Noman, *Pakistan: A Political and Economic History Since 1947*, London, 1990.
39. For a useful critical study see Ayesha Jalal, *The State of Martial Rule: The Origins of Pakistan's Political Economy of Defence*, Cambridge, 1990.
40. Liaquat's assassination was reported to London on the same day through a number of telegraphic messages sent from the British High Commission.

Even today, his murder remains an unresolved mystery. See UK High Commissioner (Karachi) to Commonwealth Relations Office (London), nos. 1139, 1140 and 1141, 16 October 1951, *DO 35/3188*, Public Record Office (hereafter PRO) Kew, London. The next day it was reported that 'there was nothing yet to show what lay behind assassination which may conceivably have been act of a fanatic, but there are suggestions that Khaksars may have been responsible', (UK HC to CRO, London, no. 1143, 17 October 1951, PRO).

41. Nazim ud-Din was described in British confidential papers as a man 'of Mughal aristocratic origin' who had studied at Cambridge and had a political feud with H. Suhrawardy. 'He is very fat, with a pleasant smile and unassuming manner. He was something of an athlete when young and still plays good tennis and shoots well. He is pious and has a reputation for honesty. He is not a strong personality but he is reasonably shrewd, well-balanced and though slow to make decisions, will not shirk responsibility, though he finds it constitutionally difficult to say "no"' (Folio no. 14, in *DO 35/3188*, PRO).

42. In the cabinet meeting headed by Ghulam Muhammad himself, he told 'them that they could see the state of the country and that he must now call on them to resign at once. Prime Minister had replied that they had just got budget through and must decline to resign. Governor-General could dismiss them if he liked' (UK High Commissioner to CRO, 17 April 1953, no. 663, *DO 35/5106*, PRO).

43. 'My assessment is that Governor-General has about gauged public reaction accurately and that his dramatic and certainly very courageous decision will have strong public support. All the indications are that he took no-one in confidence over this (except possibly Iskander Mirza) up to last moment. The New Prime Minster declares that he was given no warning' (UK HC to CRO, 18 April 1953, no. 669, ibid.).

44. For an eyewitness account, see Qudratullah Shahab, *Shahab Nama* (an autobiography), Islamabad/Lahore, 1988. Shahab was a senior civil servant who served all the successive governments until his retirement in the 1980s. It is interesting to note that in his closing years of life, Shahab became a sufi-saint for his contemporaries.

45. Zafrullah Khan told the British High Commissioner that the decision to dismiss the Nazim ud-Din Ministry was taken in the meeting of governors and service chiefs. General Ayub Khan had pushed for 'immediate action to remedy position if confidence of Army was to be maintained. New A. I. G. Baluchistan (Qurban Ali) had drawn telling comparison' between the British and Nazim ud-Din governments. The new cabinet was to be anti-mullahs as Fazlur Rahman, 'the evil genius and responsible for advising' Nazim ud-Din, the former prime minister, had become ineffective. See UK HC to CRO, 19 April 1953, no. 679, *DO 35/5106*, PRO.

46. For further details see Government of the Punjab, *Report of the Court of Inquiry Constituted under the Punjab Act II of 1954 to Enquire into the Punjab Disturbances of 1953* (also known as Justice Munir Report), Lahore, 1954.

47. To some authors, the role of the judiciary in Pakistan has been rather assertive. See Paula R. Newberg, *Judging the State: Courts and Constitutional Politics in Pakistan*, Cambridge, 1995.

48. For a recent study of the early years of Pakistan, see A. Yunas Samad, 'South Asian Muslim Politics, 1937–1958', D. Phil. dissertation, University of Oxford, 1991.

49. Mohammad Ayub Khan, *Friends Not Masters: A Political Biography*, New York, 1967, p. 206, and quoted in *The Pakistan Times*, 29 March 1959.

50. For a contemporary official record, see Altaf Gauhar, *Twenty Years of Pakistan*, Lahore, 1968.

51. 'From the beginning bureaucracy got a substantial share in the power structure at the higher level, and monopolized it at the lower levels. Aziz Ahmad and Fida Hasan, two senior civil servants, even held the assignments of Deputy CMLA and Deputy MLA of West Pakistan respectively. Civil servants composed the civilian advisory council of the CMLA and the advisory committees of the provincial governors, enjoying powers previously exercised by cabinets. When cabinets were appointed, the powers of the civil servants were not curtailed. They received their share even in the cabinets. Ayub Khan's first eleven-member cabinet had three Lieutenant-Generals and three civil servants who held key portfolios' M. Rafique Afzal, *Political Parties in Pakistan 1958–1969*, vol. II, Islamabad, 1986, p. 3.

52. Noman, *Pakistan: A Political and Economic History*, pp. 101–11. Also, Anwar H. Syed, *The Discourse and Politics of Zulfikar Ali Bhutto*, London, 1992.

53. For a very useful study, see Shahid Javed Burki, *Pakistan Under Bhutto, 1971–77*, London, 1988 (2nd edn)

54. After dissolving the national assembly in August 1990, Ghulam Ishaque Khan instituted special references against dismissed prime minister, Benazir Bhutto, and her associates. A group of retired bureaucrats worked in the presidency for several years on end, costing *crores* of rupees to the national exchequer, to substantiate presidential allegations against her. The cases eventually died their death.

55. M. Rafique Afzal, op. cit., p. 79.

56. Khalid Bin Sayeed, 'Collapse of Parliamentary Democracy in Pakistan', *The Middle East Journal*, XIII, 1959, p. 389.

57. Ibid.

58. For details, see Begum Shaista Suhrawardy Ikramullah, *Huseyn Shaheed Suhrawardy: A Biography*, Karachi, 1991.

59. 'Fatima Jinnah had once declared that there was a hidden hand which guided Pakistan's politics; her reference was clearly to the role of President Mirza' (ibid., p. 399). A leading contemporary British magazine agreed with the viewpoint that most Pakistani politicians deserved to be stoned but it must not be Mirza's prerogative. See *The Statesman* (London), 18 October 1958.

60. Maleeha Lodhi, 'Pakistan People's Party and Pakistan's Democracy', *Journal of South Asian and Middle Eastern Studies*, VI, Spring 1983, p. 29.

61. For an early note, see Charles J. Adams, 'The Ideology of Mawlana Mawdudui', in Donald E. Smith (ed.), *South Asian Religions and Politics*, Princeton, 1966.

62. Zafaryab Ahmed, 'Maudoodi's Islamic State', in M. Asghar Khan (ed.), *Islam, Politics and the State: The Pakistan Experience*, London, 1985, pp. 95–113.

270Notes

63. Campus violence involving the IJT cost the lives of 80 students in the years 1982–8 and violence was interpreted as endemic to the student wing of the JI. Despite efforts by the parent body, the militancy could not be stopped. See Zahid Hussain, 'The Campus Mafias', *The Herald* (Karachi), October 1988, p. 52.

64. Seyyed Vali Reza Nasr, 'Students, Islam, and Politics: Islami Jami'al-i-Tulaba in Pakistan', *Middle East Journal*, XXXXVI (1), 1992, p. 75.

65. Ibid.

66. For details on different political parties, see Afzal, *Political Parties*, pp. 53–119.

67. This phenomenon is not confined to Pakistan; even in Europe and North America this polarisation has been accentuated by the external patronage of Muslims (both Sunni and Shia). Iranian influence came after the Iranian revolution in 1979 and the Gulf wars. The Salman Rushdie affair provided the Iranian regime with a cross-ethnic constituency in countries like the United Kingdom. Over the years, the Saudis have been funding more than 800 mosques in Britain alone and their influence restrained pro-Iraq sentiments among Muslim expatriates during 1990–91. Similarly, the Sunni–Shia conflict increased in the 1980s, largely due to Middle Eastern political rivalries as well as the domestic rhetoric on Islam under the patronage of General Zia ul-Haq. Earlier, Libya had tried to cultivate such a constituency in countries like Pakistan or among the Muslim expatriates in Europe. In Pakistan, such extra-regional affiliations and connections continue, largely due to financial patronage or simply confused ideas on nationalism and supra-nationalist identities among the South Asian Muslim religious leaders.

68. For a detailed analysis of the constitutional history of Pakistan, see G. W. Choudhury, *Constitutional Developments in Pakistan*, London, 1969.

69. Kamal Azfar, 'Constitutional Dilemmas in Pakistan', in Shahid Javed Burki and Craig Baxter (eds), *Pakistan Under the Military. Eleven Years of Zia ul-Haq*, Boulder/Oxford, 1991.

70. Lawrence Ziring, 'Public Policy Dilemmas and Pakistan's Nationality Problems. The Legacy of Zia ul-Haq', *Asian Survey*, XXVIII (8), 1988, pp. 795–812.

71. For further details on contemporary political issues, see Rasul B. Rais, 'Pakistan in 1988', *Asian Survey*, XXXI (2), 1990, pp. 199–206.

72. Lawrence Ziring, 'Pakistan in 1990: Fall of Benazir Bhutto', *Asian Survey*, XXXI (2), February 1991, p. 121. Ever since, the PDA has contested the electoral results and published a number of studies to substantiate its claims. Ghulam Mustafa Jatoi, the interim prime minister and a hopeful for prime-ministerial position in 1990, was reported to have admitted malpractice in certain constituencies though he soon denied his own assertions.

73. Pakistanis felt a deep sense of betrayal due to the constant irresponsible behaviour by politicians in the wake of a consolidated elitism in the country. The leadership had been avoiding the basic issues facing the country. 'Hope has given way to apprehension' wrote a scholar on the contemporary state of demoralisation among his countrymen. Rais A. Khan, 'Pakistan in 1992', *Asian Survey*, XXXIII (2), February 1993, pp. 129–40.

2   ELITE FORMATION, POLITICS OF IDEOLOGY AND COOPTION

1.   The best example is Emperor Babur who, in his will, preferred to be buried in Kabul, close to his native Farghana in present-day Uzbekistan. In his Turkish memoirs, *Tuzk-i Baburi*, Babur very emphatically decried everything *Indian* except for the wealth and riches of his new empire. His warfare with the Pushtun tribals and dislike of the Indian way of life stemmed from his Chughtai Turkish background mixed with imperious pride. Many centuries later, Mirza Ghalib, the famous Urdu–Persian poet attached to the last Mughal emperor in Delhi, Bahadur Shah Zafar, in the mid-nineteenth century, celebrated his Turkish origins with an undiminished sense of pride.

2.   Earlier, Shah Wali Allah and his descendants and disciples sought closer cultural and political affinity with the Muslims across the sub-continent, and this continued in the nineteenth and twentieth centuries.

3.   Babur's secret will to his heir, Prince Humayun, largely underlines the inter-religious harmony and supra-communal nomenclature of the imperial policy. It observed: 'O son, in the continent of India, people of diverse religions live. Thanks be to God who has given the kingship of this country to thee! It is for thee to keep thy heart from religious bias and creed. To everyone render justice in keeping with his religion. Particularly abstain from the slaughter of cows and it be the reason for the conquest of Indian hearts. Let gratitude make the people of the country bear goodwill to the king. Never let the temples and places of worship of all the people which lie in thy dominion be spoilt, and in these matters always be just, so that the king be happy and satisfied with the people and the people with the king. The advancement of Islam is better with the sword of gratitude than with the sword of oppression. Thou must stop the conflict between Shias and Sunnis. In the conflict lies that weakness which is injurious to Islam. Treat the people of the empire like the four elements, so that the body of the empire may defend itself against diseases. And lastly, always remember the achievements of Hazrat Taimur, Saheb-e-Quran' (Syed Mahmud, *The India of Yesterday*, Hyderabad, India, 1957, p. xv).

4.   'The Mughals used Islam to legitimate the feudal state and the faithful South Asian minority strongly supported them. But the Muslim rulers never attempted to Islamicize India, and the Islamic politico-economic system was never enforced. The reason was primarily the dependence of the imperial treasury for its surplus wealth on taxation of the Hindu majority and the collection of land revenues and tributes from conquered princely states. All this maintained the status quo of the ruling dynasty' (Asaf Hussain, *Elite Politics in an Ideological State. The Case of Pakistan*, Folkstone, 1979, p. 21).

5.   Shah Wali Allah 'did succeed remarkably in kindling a flame that lighted the way of many who came after him and worked for the preservation of the religious beliefs and the ideological entity of the Muslim community. And this success was more lasting than any castles that could have been built with the shifting and loose sands of politics' (Ishtiaq Husain Qureshi, *Ulema in Politics*, Karachi, 1974 (2nd edn), p. 126).

6. While considering Shah Wali Allah as the founder of 'modern Islam in India', a noted Muslim intellectual considers Sir Syed and Iqbal as 'progressive' Muslim reformers. To him, Iqbal and Shariati are the two greatest progressive Islamic reformers of the twentieth century. He further observes: 'There are of course other varieties of political Islam. Islam may be used with the explicit expedient goal of keeping unrepresentative regimes in power, or, in some cases with some quantum of conviction and self-righteousness, for delegating absolute governmental authority to hereditary monarchies. In such instances, the majority of *ulama* have invariably supported those in power, from either conviction, sheer opportunism, or a mixture of both. Then there is the purely secular approach to politics, as for example in Turkey, where religion is confined to the personal realm and spared from being dragged into politics by a plethora of competing "Islamists" wielding the magic wand of *fatwa* (religious decree) for warding off their political opponents by branding them "un-Islamic", "deviants", "hypocrites", or "communists"' (Suroosh Irfani, 'The Progressive Islamic Movement', in M. Asghar Khan (ed.), *Islam, Politics and the State. The Pakistan Experience*, London, 1985, pp. 32, 38.

7. For a more recent account by a former well-known ICS, see Penderel Moon, *The British Conquest and Dominion of India*, London, 1990.

8. From Lord Macaulay's 1835 Minute of Education in A. Maddison, *Class Structure and Economic Growth: India and Pakistan since the Mughals*, New York, 1971, p. 41.

9. 'The British in India perceived and projected Muslims as a unified community. This was so because of their inadequate understanding of the ideological schism in Indian Islam. They were dimly aware of the acute differences, say, between the Deobandis and the Barelwis and only superficially conscious of the Shia–Sunni divide.' But the same author acknowledges that when 'Pakistan' provided a superordinate identity, such sectarian or ideological differences were submerged: 'In the end, "Muslim nationalism" overwhelmed sectarian allegiances' (Mushirul Hasan, 'Sectarianism in Indian Islam: The Shia–Sunni divide in the United Provinces', *The Indian Economic and Social History Review*, 27, 2, 1990, pp. 210, 227.)

10. Hamza Alavi, 'Pakistan and Islam: Ethnicity and Ideology', in Fred Halliday and Hamza Alavi (eds), *State and Ideology in the Middle East and Pakistan*, London, 1987, p. 79. One may use terms like 'secular', 'fundamentalist' or 'modernist' to comprehend the Muslim experience and even if this categorisation is considered controversial, it does help in understanding the ideological diversity within the Muslim elites in British India. Alavi accepts the fact that there was a very small, almost indiscernbible Muslim middle class, but it was largely apolitical and non-ideological. He coins his own term of *Salariat* to describe the class of state-related elites whose own politico-economic ambitions led to a new elite configuration in British India.

    Professor Anwar Syed divided the Muslim ideological leadership in British India into two broader groups – Muslim nationalists like Iqbal and Jinnah and their ideological opponents like Maulana Maudoodi. See Anwar Syed, *Pakistan: Islam, Politics and National Solidarity*, Lahore, 1984, pp. 30–73.

11. Some Deobandi *ulama* like Maulana Shabbir Ahmad Usmani and Zafar Ahmed Ansari supported the movement for Pakistan along with *pirs* like the Pir of Pagaro in Sindh and the Pir of Manki Sharif in the NWFP. Both the *gaddis* espoused defiant anti-colonial and pro-AIML policies.

12. Maulana Maudoodi, *Te-rik-i Azadi-i Hind aur Mussalman*, Lahore, 1974 (reprint), pp. 329–40.

13. Syed, op. cit.

14. He further said rather unequivocally: 'In the sight of God Muslim nationalism is just as cursed as Indian nationalism' (Quoted in Syed, op. cit., p. 41).

15. 'According to Maududi, there is always a person (*Mizaj Shanas-i-Rasool*) who alone is competent to decide what the Holy Prophet would have done in a given situation if he were alive.... And his chief lieutenant, Maulana Islahi declared before the Punjab Disturbances Inquiry Committee that he wholeheartedly and unreservedly accepted Maudadi as the Mizaj Shanas-i-Rasool', (K. K. Aziz, *Party Politics in Pakistan 1947–58*, Islamabad, 1976, pp. 143–4).

16. Government of Pakistan, *Quaid-e Azam Mahomed Ali Jinnah: Speeches as Governor-General, 1947–1948*, Karachi, n.d., pp. 8–9.

17. Jamil ud-Din Ahmad (ed.), *Speeches and Writings of Mr. Jinnah*, vol. II, Lahore, 1960, p. 563.

18. *Speeches as Governor-General of Pakistan*, p. 9.

19. Ibid., p. 58. He did not reject Islam as a guiding force and envisioned Pakistan as a democratic country not 'to be ruled by priests with divine mission', p. 65.

20. For instance, Maulana Maudoodi believed that 90 per cent of Pakistani Muslims were illiterate, followed a blind faith in Islam and were vulnerable to exploitation. Five per cent of the elites were westernised and only 5 per cent were enlightened. Khalid B. Sayeed, 'The Jamaat-i-Islami Movement in Pakistan', *Pacific Affairs*, XXX, 2, 1957, p. 64.

21. *The Pakistan Observer*, (Dacca), 3 October 1964.

22. According to a number of observers, Benazir Bhutto strongly believes in *pirs* and seeks regular guidance from them.

23. 'Pakistan Banks Contest Usury Ruling in Court', *The Guardian*, 22 January 1992.

24. 'Enemies and More Enemies', *Newsweek*, 13 January 1992.

25. *International Herald Tribune*, 5 February 1992.

26. 'He has distanced himself from the conservative Muslim party that helped bring him to power, the Jamaat-i-Islami, and he has opposed the Army's hawkish policy on the Afghan war by pressing for a negotiated settlement. With 3 million Afghan refugees languishing in Pakistan, Sharif can't afford to stand on principle. Aides say he has even made conciliatory overtures toward the PPP', (Ibid.).

27. 'During the martial law rule of General Zia, the army became the custodian of the country's Islamic values and identity. Now, the new liberal elements within the army are signalling that they are willing to back the Nawaz Sharif government in any effort to moderate fundamentalist influence in foreign and domestic policies' (Kathy Evans, 'Pakistan Puts Pressure on Mojahedin', *The Guardian*, 28 January 1992).

28. The idea of a coalition government in Kabul was flouted by some of the Mujahideen leaders leaving no room for Pakistan to manoeuvre. The closure of Pakistani embassy in the city in early 1994 came as a great shock to Pakistanis who had suffered so much for the neighbouring Afghans in their long ordeal.

29. Iftikhar H. Malik, 'Pakistan's National Security and Regional Issues: Politics of Mutualities with the Muslim World', *Asian Survey*, XXXIV, 2 December 1994.

30. In the mid-1980s, Allama Sajjad Zaheer, a Sunni pro-Saudi *alim* and leader of Ahl-i Hadith, while addressing a public rally in Lahore, was mysteriously killed. A few months later, the assassination of a pro-Iran Shia *alim*, Allama Husaini, in early 1988 in Peshawar, allegedly led to the eventual murder of General (retd.) Fazl-e-Haq, a former strongman of the NFWP in 1991. Since then a number of Shia–Sunni conflicts have been reported from cities like Jhang, Lahore and Sahiwal, resulting in frequent assassinations on both sides as well as the imposition of a curfew. Many *ulama* have been murdered on both sides. The Tehrik-i Nifaz-i Fiqah-i Jaafria, the strongest Shia political party, has been demonstrating through protest rallies for the implementation of Jaafria Fiqah since Zia began the Islamisation process. Similarly, the Tehrik-i Sipah-i Sahaba, has been campaigning to declare Pakistan a Sunni state. Such polarisation multiplied in Pakistan when the *state* under Zia introduced its version of Islamisation (presumably for legitimacy) from above without any consensus from below. Inter-sectarian and inter-doctrinal dissensions, like the inter-ethnic mistrust registered a major increase in Pakistan's troubled history when the *state* took refuge in religion to escape ad-hocism. Time has proven again and again that any theocratic (or ethnic) particularism in a plural Pakistani society would naturally lead to chain reactions. For more details, see Afak Hayder, 'The Politicisation of the Shias and the Development of the Tehrik-e-Nifaz-e-Figh-e-Jafaria in Pakistan', in Charles H. Kennedy (ed.), *Pakistan 1992*, Oxford, 1993. The most volatile phase in Shia–Sunni conflict in Pakistan occurred during the month of fasting in 1995, when a number of bomb explosions killed scores of worshippers in mosques in Karachi. *The Financial Times*, 28 February, 1995; and 'Confronting the Enemy Within' (editorial), *The Guardian*, 9 March 1995. Both denied attacking each other's mosques and blamed 'unknown saboteurs' or 'Indian agents' for inflaming sectarianism.

31. One cannot absolve the *ulama* of their major role in fanning anti-Christian feelings among Pakistani Muslims. The existing blasphemy law in the country allows the death sentence for 'insults by imputation or innuendo against Islam' and for 'derogatory remarks in respect of the Holy Prophet'. Many human-rights activists would like it to be amended or totally removed but a staunch opposition from the religio-political parties through street agitation has not allowed any regime to do so. The application of such a law against Christians and other religious minorities in Pakistan has always been a contentious issue, as was observed in the case of Salamat Masih, a 14-year-old illiterate Christian Punjabi who was accused of blasphemy by a local *alim*. His case became a national issue due to the arguments on both sides, and attracted considerable global attention due to his tender age and the stipulated death sentence. The local courts had sentenced him to death

but the High Court in Lahore acquitted Salamat despite major pressure from the *ulama*. Fearful of retaliation, the entire Christian community of Ratta Dohtran fled the village for personal safety, whereas Salamat was given asylum in Germany. The case amply highlighted the threat of religious extremism to the country's civic institutions. 'Most disconcerting of all was the hysteria which the case provoked in the more extreme sections of Pakistani society' ('Salamat's Safety' (editorial), *The Times*, 25 February, 1995). See also Roy Hattersley, 'Sadness and Shock will not Save the Child', *The Guardian*, 20 February, 1995.

32. Qureshi, *Ulema in Politics*, p. 16.

33. William Pfaff, in an article on Islam, outlined three main problems confronted by the world of Islam: first, the absence of an historical Muslim Enlightenment-cum-industrial revolution, secondly, the colonial legacy and, finally, the consolidation of the repressive orders throughout the Muslim world. These have all compounded the Muslims' dilemma in the late-twentieth century. Such a view was offered during the recent Gulf crisis. See *International Herald Tribune*, 11 July 1990.

34. One cannot absolve the westernised ruling elite of dallying with clerical groups in Pakistan. Their appeasement, political expendiency and opportunism only encourage religious intolerance. Benazir Bhutto, despite her modernist outlook, has also been criticised for her 'double standards'. See Paula R. Newberg, 'One of these Benazir Bhuttos isn't Nice', *International Herald Tribune*, 13 February, 1995.

35. For further details, see Iftikhar H. Malik, 'Identity Formation and Muslim Party Politics in the Punjab, 1897–1936: A Retrospective Analysis', *Modern Asian Studies*, 29, 2, May 1995.

3 THE SUPREMACY OF THE BUREAUCRACY AND THE MILITARY IN PAKISTAN

1. After defence and the servicing of foreign loans, the major portion of the budgetary allocation in Pakistan goes to the salaries and emoluments of the bureaucrats. While Pakistan was halved in 1971, its bureaucracy in the subsequent two decades has multiplied five times, both in manpower and costs. For instance, in 1970, within the ministry of the interior headed by a federal secretary, a section looked after Kashmir and tribal affairs. Twenty years later, the same section has four divisions, each under a secretary with a retinue of additional, joint and deputy secretaries. Simultaneously, a separate ministry for Kashmir, Northern and Tribal Areas has been in operation for a long time. Since the additional expansion in both personnel and expenses did not give rise to a corresponding increase in efficiency, a separate division of federal ombudsman with its own secretariat was created in the 1980s. How far the ombudsman and attached departments have been effective in safeguarding civil rights or curtailing the maintenance cost of *naukarshahi* is a separate subject in itself. In 1992, the country's administration was costing Pakistan 1080 *crores* (1 *crore* = 10 million) of rupees per annum more than it needed to maintain the pre-1971 bureaucracy. Certain official departments

cost 50 to 60 *crores* of rupees to the national exchequer just in maintenance, yet are left with either a paltry sum or, in some cases, no money at all to carry out development work. In the time of Zulfikar Ali Bhutto, a special post was created in the secretariat to advise on former East Pakistan, which existed even in 1992, costing taxpayers Rs. 850 million over 20 years. Examples abound of such huge expenditure being in some cases allowances for tenancy and house rent. For further details see *The Daily Jang* (London), 11 March 1992. There is no doubt that substantial resources in Pakistan are being spent on maintaining a huge non-development sector with no money left for development. Even to maintain the non-development sector (defence, loans and services) further new loans with higher and compound interests are borrowed from various foreign banks and monetary agencies.

2.   When Ghulam Ishaque Khan dismissed the eighth National Assembly and the government of Benazir Bhutto on 6 August 1990, he appointed four retired bureaucrats to prepare references and material against the deposed prime minister. After three years and millions of rupees, the committee could not come up with any tangible proofs to substantiate these charges. (Interestingly, the same bureaucrats were engaged by Benazir Bhutto to establish similar charges against her predecessor, Nawaz Sharif.) This and many other examples speak of the professional inadequacies and waywardness in priorities among the country's leading administrators.

At times, it appears that both the state and politicians have tried to excel each other by inducements for corruption. For instance, during the conflict between a short-lived 'rebellious' Punjab government led by Manzoor Wattoo and Prime Minister Nawaz Sharif, the bureaucrats were lavished with temptations to curry favour. For details, see *The Daily Awaz International* (London), 11 August 1993. Also, in Sindh, Jam Sadiq Ali in the 1970s and then in 1990–92, showered his favourites with favours varying from money to expensive urban property.

3.   Ghulam Muhammad, a bureaucrat who sent Prime Minister Nazim ud-Din home in April 1953, had advisers like Iskander Mirza and Chaudhary Muhammad Ali, senior civil servants with unbounded political ambitions. General Ayub Khan represented the hawkish breed of generals. Iskander Mirza, originally from the political department of the Raj and without any military training, became a major-general and eventually manoeuvred the country's presidency for himself. Chaudhary Muhammad Ali obtained the post of secretary-general or the chief civil servant in the country and eventually became the prime minister of Pakistan. General Ayub Khan rose to become the president of the country until his abdication in March 1969, when General Yahya Khan imposed martial law which eventually led to the break-up of the country.

Fifty years after the dissolution of Pakistan's first elected government, President Ghulam Ishaque Khan, in April 1993, dissolved the ninth National Assembly of Pakistan and dismissed the government of Prime Minister Nawaz Sharif. Earlier, on 6 August 1990, he had dissolved the elected government of Benazir Bhutto. In July 1993, Ghulam Ishaque Khan completed his 'hat-trick' by dissolving the assemblies and governments once again, followed by his resignation. After a modest career beginning as a revenue official in the 1940s he became the acting president in August 1988 following the Bahawalpur air crash which killed General Zia who had promoted him. Zia himself had been selected by Z. A. Bhutto to the coveted position of army chief of staff. Following public agitation against Bhutto in 1977, Zia had imposed his martial law and assumed the country's presidency. He secured a five-year presidential term through a fraudulent referendum in 1984 and never forsook his military office. He dismissed M. K. Junejo and the assemblies in May 1988 when he felt that they were causing some opposition to his dichotomic position as the army chief and the country's chief executive.

4. See Philip Woodruff, *The Men Who Ruled India: The Guardians*, London, 1954, p. 197.

5. Khalid Bin Sayeed, 'The Political Role of Pakistan's Civil Service', *Pacific Affairs*, XXXI, 2, 1958, p. 131.

6. The controversial Eighth Amendment of the Constitution of 1973, allowing indemnity to martial law and allocating vital discretionary powers to the president remains a major block in the evolution of a viable parliamentary system in Pakistan. Introduced by General Zia in a partyless house in 1985, the Amendment has already caused four dismissals of elected assemblies and governments within five years. Article 58–2 (Section B) allowing such a power to dissolve government is, in a way, a rewording of Section 93 of the India Act of 1935.

7. Ralph Braibanti, 'Public Bureaucracy and Judiciary in Pakistan', in Joseph La Palombara (ed.), *Bureaucracy and Political Development*, Princeton, 1963, pp. 365–7.

8. According to one estimate, only one ICS official belonged to East Pakistan. See Minister Shahab ud-Din's statement in *Dawn*, 27 June 1965.

9. However, this changed and today customs, taxation and excise have assumed top priority, given the endemic corruption and monetary benefits to be gained.

10. H. F. Goodnow, *The Civil Service of Pakistan*, New Haven, 1964, p. 173.

11. Criticism of the elitist training came, off and on, from the legislators. See National Assembly of Pakistan, *Parliamentary Debates*, 15 February 1957, quoted in Asaf Hussain, *Elite Politics in an Ideological State. The Case of Pakistan*, Folkestone, 1979, p. 64.

12. Ralph Braibanti, 'The Higher Bureaucracy in Pakistan', in R. Braibanti (ed.), *Asian Bureaucratic Traditions Emergent from the British Imperial Tradition*, Durham, N. C., 1966, p. 327. The Pakistani bureaucracy has maintained all along that it knows what is 'good for the nation'. Lawrence Ziring, *The Ayub Khan Era: Politics in Pakistan 1958–1969*, New York, 1971, p. 121.

13. See Jamil ud-Din Ahmad (ed.), *Speeches and Statements of Mr. Jinnah*, vol. II, Lahore, 1964, pp. 501–2.

14. Charles H. Kennedy, *Bureaucracy in Pakistan*, Karachi, 1987, p. 1.

15. Ibid., pp. 4–5.

16. Robert LaPorte, Jr, 'Administrative Restructuring During the Zia Period', in S. J. Burki and C. Baxter (eds), *Pakistan Under the Military. Eleven Years of Zia ul-Haq*, Oxford, 1991, p. 128.

17. Ibid.

18. See Sayeed, 'Political Role', p. 131.

19. *Dawn*, 20 September 1950, quoted in ibid., p. 133.
20. 'It appears very probable that these men came to an agreement among themselves about the composition of the succeeding government' (Imdad Husain, *'The Failure of Parliamentary Politics in Pakistan, 1953–1958'*, D. Phil. dissertation, University of Oxford, 1966, p. 58.
21. The term was used in a debate by a legislator in the West Pakistan Legislative Assembly. See *The Pakistan Times*, 14 March 1957.
22. *Constituent Assembly of Pakistan Debates*, I (4), 19 March 1956, p. 216.
23. *The Pakistan Times*, 20 October 1957.
24. *Dawn*, 31 October 1957. H. S. Suhrawardy had himself earlier acknowledged the helplessness of the political sector *vis-à-vis* the bureaucracy in Pakistan. In an assembly debate, he had stated: 'Sir, to be the Prime Minister of Pakistan which has been held by certain honourable gentlemen who have been turned out, taken by the ears and thrown out as it suited the ruling coterie is not a matter of very great honour' (Quoted in Sayeed, 'Political Rule' pp. 137–8).
25. Both Professors Rowland Egger and Bernard Gladieux, the two foreign experts, had found serious flaws in the Pakistani administrative system, which was still firmly anchored in its colonial roots and tendencies. To them, law and order and not national development remained the main objectives for the bureaucrats seeking further centralisation. See R. Egger, *The Development of Public Administration in Pakistan*, Karachi, 1953, and, Bernard L. Gladieux, *Reorientation of Pakistan Government for National Development*, Karachi, 1955.
26. As well as bureaucrats, the team framing the constitution included Z. A. Bhutto and Manzur Qadir. A number of politicians from West Pakistan, like Zafrullah Khan and Pir Ali Rashdi encouraged Ayub to promulgate a presidential form of centralised government. On the other hand, the Bengali members of his cabinet cautioned him against such preferences, which might ultimately accentuate bi-polarity between the two wings of the country. For further details, see Altaf Gauhar, *Ayub Khan. Pakistan's First Military Ruler* Lahore, 1993, pp. 189–92.
27. *The Pakistan Times*, 1 April 1973.
28. Hussain, 'Failure of Parliamentary Politics', p. 77. However, to Hussain, along with the 'decolonisation' of the bureaucratic elites, Pakistan's guarantee for an egalitarian system averse to vested interests 'can only be implemented through the institutionalization of the Islamic order in the society' (ibid., p. 78).
29. Initially, Bhutto did want to break the monopolist and elitist hold of the bureaucracy over Pakistan. His rebukes and reforms only earned him hostility from the powerful echelons of state. Zia, on the other hand, restored the *de facto* power of the bureaucracy and solidified the viceregal system. For a retrospective analysis, see LaPorte, Jr, 'Administrative Restructuring'.
30. See Rounaq Jahan, *Pakistan: Failure in National Integration*, New York, 1972, pp. 26, 107. And Hussain, *Elite Politics*, p. 65.
31. Khalid B. Sayeed, *Pakistan: The Formative Phase*, Karachi, 1960, p. 392.
32. It was duly acknowledged by certain civil servants. See Muneer Ahmed, *The Civil Servant in Pakistan*, Karachi, 1964, pp. 112–13.

33. These language groups are scattered all over the country, especially in major cities, and are no longer confined to traditional provincial boundaries. It is equally interesting to note that many urban, literate Punjabis and Pushtuns teach Urdu and English to their children. Urdu has undoubtedly emerged as the lingua franca in the country, though in terms of strict mother tongue it appears to be confined to a small section in society – predominantly the Muhajireen.
34. Kennedy, *Bureaucracy in Pakistan*, p. 186.
35. In 1966 there were 23 divisions and 2 agencies, while in 1983 they were 40 and 6 respectively. Ten years on, the number must have multiplied. Ibid., p. 6.
36. See Charles H. Kennedy, 'The Politics of Ethnicity in Sindh', *Asian Survey*, XXXI (10), 1992, p. 943.
37. For details see Stanley Kochanek, *Interest Groups and Development: Business and Politics in Pakistan*, Karachi, 1983, pp. 93–7.
38. In 1993, there was growing pressure from the World Bank and other international financial institutions on Pakistan to increase the tax base generally. The interim regime of Moeen Qureshi obliged, but with the installation of the *political* government there was a reluctance in official circles given the PPP regime's dependence on feudal votes in the assemblies.
39. Many of these deals involve personal 'perks' through palm greasing. In June 1992, during investigations into the false deals of Ferranti in London, it was revealed that its executive had obtained fictitious deals involving millions of rupees from Pakistani officials. General Talat Masood, a leading Pakistani general heading the Pakistan Ordnance Factories at Wah, was reported in the British media to have readily provided such a bogus order from the Pakistan government involving more than £500 million so that the executive could be bailed out.
40. Several examples may be given. The most recent one involved an expensive advertisement in the spring of 1992 in Western newspapers inviting Pakistani expatriates and foreign investors to buy bearers' certificates in foreign currency from national banks. The advertisement naively promised complete secrecy as to the origin of such money and its future use, causing a serious official reaction in the United States. In the aftermath of the BCCI fiasco, American officials and many bankers felt that the State Bank of Pakistan was providing excuses to entice black money. The government of Pakistan had to withdraw the offer.
41. Some investigative and credible press reports did surface as early as 1991, though the demands for the publication of such lists had been made for over a decade. Pakistanis were horrified to see almost every notable industrial and feudal family as well as former bureaucrats and generals defaulting on loans to the tune of billions of rupees. The lists, amongst others, included groups or 'families' like the Saigols, Saifullahs, General (retd.) Habibullah and associates, Mians, Karims, Mazaris, Noons, Sheikhs, Fancys, Hyesons and Parachas. Just to give one case-study, the feudal family of the Mazaris led by former senior bureaucrat, Ashiq Mazari, dismissed over corruption charges and later a PPP MNA, owed 49, 742 million rupees to the national exchequer. The defaulters in the family included Ms Shireen Mazari (a former academic), Shaukat Mazari (politician) and Durr e-Shahwar Mazari,

the wife of Ashiq Mazari. Such a family-based expropriation of national resources and tax-payers' money only confirms the mutually intertwined tentacles of feudalism, bureaucracy and professionalism aligned together to consolidate dynastic elitism. For details on the groups and outstanding amounts, see M. Sahibuddin Ghausi, 'The Lone Rangers', *The Herald*, February 1991. Also see, 'Confessions of a Banker', in ibid.

42. Moeen Qureshi was widely praised for exposing the names of the defaulters and the outstanding loans, running into billions. His government also made public all the names and business concerns engaged in tax evasions. Every newspaper and magazine in Pakistan published the lists and widely commented on these defaulters, who, in many cases, were able to manoeuvre their way back into the assemblies following the elections of 1993. While the lists included politicians of all factions as well as businessmen, curiously, they excluded the names of serving/former bureaucrats and senior military officials owing millions to the nation. Despite all the commotion, by early 1994 not more than 10 per cent of the loans and taxes were paid back to the national exchequer.

43. In the early 1990s, three former ambassadors to the USA dealt in real estate in the Washington area, while during their tenure they exhorted Pakistanis to go back and serve their country. A former air marshal in the 1980s was known for his personal use of C–130s to fly his horses and one of his colleagues managed to import banned expensive foreign duty-free cars to sell them to the highest bidders in the country. He subsequently represented Pakistan in a very sensitive diplomatic post.

Even Nawaz Sharif is on record as saying that the majority of the police in Sindh were corrupt, to the extent that former criminals had been put in charge of police stations. In 1991, quite a few revelations about the involvement of the CIA (Criminal Investigation Agency) in Karachi in torture, kidnap, extortion and similar crimes that appeared in the responsible press, shocked the nation. Mr Irfanullah Marwat, the son-in-law of Ghulam Ishaque Khan, responsible to the late Jam Sadiq Ali for Sindh's administrative machinery, was discussed in the press at home and abroad but was never investigated. In 1994, Benazir Bhutto quietly forgave him despite numerous serious cases pending against him.

In June–July 1992, the federal police and the Capital Development Authority (CDA) mounted an operation against encroachments on federal territory in Islamabad. The list included figures of great national importance such as the Pir of Pagara, Syed Iftikhar Gilani and Dr A. Q. Khan and eventually the case was hushed up.

44. In 1994, allegations of corruption against Farooq Leghari, the president of the country, appeared in the press. Yunus Habib, the executive of the Mehran Bank, made revelations of paying millions of rupees to Leghari in 1993 on a land deal in Southwestern Punjab. Otherwise an arid piece of land, its purchase was conducted through Habib to bribe Leghari to curry political favour. Known as the 'Mehrangate Scandal', despite an initial embarrassment the PPP regime was able to suppress its coverage in the media. The opposition led by Nawaz Sharif, itself tainted with numerous cases of financial scandals, could not press for further judicial investigation.

Yunus Habib is also on record for allegedly providing Rs. 140 million to General (retd) Aslam Beg who reportedly opened an ISI account at the Mehran Bank. Similar bribes were made to Aftab Sherpao, the PPP chief minister of the NWFP, a few cabinet members and several MQM leaders including Altaf Hussain. For more details on sums and personalities involved, see *The Herald*, April 1994.

45. Gowher Rizvi, 'Riding the Tiger: Institutionalising the Military Regimes in Pakistan and Bangladesh', in Christopher Clapham and George Philip (eds), *The Political Dilemmas of Military Regimes*, London, 1985, pp. 201–37.

46. Hasan Askari-Rizvi, *The Military and Politics in Pakistan*, Lahore, 1974, p. 111. A British newspaper put the figures of such 'disqualified' persons at 5000. See *The Guardian*, 18 February 1960.

47. Jahan, *Pakistan: Failure in National Integration*, p. 111; also, Altaf Gauhar, *Ayub Khan*, pp. 191–2. Ayub believed that the country was 'behaving like a wild horse that had been captured but not yet tamed'. Ayub Khan, *Friends Not Masters*, London, 1967, p. 217.

48. Gowher Rizvi, op. cit., p. 217.

49. Ibid., p. 220.

50. Ibid., p. 223.

51. See Francis Robinson, 'Origins' in William E. James and Subroto Roy (eds.), *Foundations of Pakistan's Political Economy*, New Delhi, 1992.

52. For details see Ainslie T. Embree (ed.), *Pakistan's Western Borderland. The Transformation of a Political Order*, Durham, N.C., 1977.

53. This has been substantiated by the revelations made by Christopher Beaumont, the former secretary to Sir Cyril Radcliffe, the chairman of the Boundary Commission. See *The Daily Telegraph* (London), 24 February 1992. Beaumont's own statement is preserved at All Souls College, Oxford. Beaumont's claim was confirmed by Alastair Lamb in a rejoinder in the same paper, the next day. Ibid., 25 February 1992.

54. For details, see Alastair Lamb, *Kashmir: A Disputed Legacy, 1846–1990*, Hertingfordbury, 1991.

55. P. I. Cheema, *Pakistan's Defence Policy, 1947–58*, London, 1990, p. 164.

56. Ibid., p. 160.

57. Stephen Cohen, *The Pakistan Army*, London, 1984, p. 133.

58. Ibid., p. 48.

59. Eqbal Ahmed felt that there were two 'classes' in the Pakistan Army: first, the pre-Second World War generation, basically greedy, conservative but religiously moderate from an upper-class background, who led the forces until 1971. Secondly, the recent generation who received incomplete training during the War and came from the petit bourgeoisie, were extremely conservative, religiously intolerant and politically ambitious. Eqbal Ahmed, 'Pakistan: Signposts to What?' *Outlook* (Lahore), 18 May 1974. Cohen agrees with K. B. Sayeed's analysis that the officers were lately coming from rural areas or belonged to the lower middle class, and were ideologically ambivalent, unintellectual and not from 'political' families. See Cohen, op. cit., p. 53.

60. See Gerald Heeger, 'Politics in the Post-Military State: Some Reflections on the Pakistani Experience', *World Politics*, 29 (2) January 1977, pp. 242–62.

Richter felt that weak political parties, the avoidance of elections and mass agitation followed by military take-over make the 'praetorian tradition' in Pakistan, where no ruler ever relinquished power on a voluntary basis. William E. Richter, 'Persistent Praetorianism: Pakistan's Third Military Regime', *Pacific Affairs*, 51 (3), Fall 1978, pp. 406–26.

61.   Hussain, *Elite Politics*, p. 133.
62.   Even some former colleagues of Zia such as Chishti have been trying to put the blame for martial law on the late Zia ul-Haq, absolving themselves from responsibility. See Lt. General (Retd) Faiz Ali Chishti, *Betrayals of Another Kind*, London, 1989. Also his *Zia, Bhutto Aur Mein* (Urdu), Lahore, 1992. General Aslam Beg, the former army chief of staff, in a number of speeches has tried to take credit for allowing 'civilianisation' of the polity, and despite denunciatory statements against the politicians, would not allow a military take-over. A number of books by retired generals, including Rao Farman Ali and K. M. Arif, are conscious efforts to 'set the record straight' by extricating themselves from blame for the abortion of the political process in Pakistan in successive decades. It is interesting to note that all such studies have appeared since the death of General Zia.

A person writing a letter to the editor in an Urdu paper lamented his 'home being robbed intermittently by thieves'. See Mr Naeemullah's letter, *The Daily Jang* (London), 20 March 1992.

63.   Cohen, op. cit., p. 34.
64.   For further details see Samina Ahmed, 'Civil-military Relations in India', *Regional Studies*, X (3), 1992, pp. 3–52.
65.   For an interesting study see Clive Dewey, 'The Rural Roots of Pakistani Militarism', in D. A. Low (ed.), *The Political Inheritance of Pakistan*, London, 1991, pp. 255–83.
66.   This is clear in Pothowar, which is on the whole a rain-fed area with small, fragmented land-holdings, but has witnessed the growth of a very mobile middle (intermediate) class. The inception and consolidation of this class is largely due to military service subsequent upon the growth of a *mandi*-based economy with a good business in cash crops like peanuts, channa and oil seeds. In addition, the development of Islamabad and industrialisation around the Grand Trunk Road has helped transform the Pothowar and Hazara regions from outlying, rural, *barani* economies into semi-urban, middle-level and extremely mobile societies, well integrated in the economy of the country. To a large extent, Pothowar and Hazara, no wonder, have escaped the vagaries of the feudal set-up seen in Southwestern Punjab or rural Sindh.
67.   For an early background see Ayesha Jalal, 'State-Building in the Post-War World: Britain's Colonial Legacy, American Futures and Pakistan', in Sugata Bose (ed.), *South Asia and the World Capitalism*, Delhi, 1990, pp. 282–93.
68.   For instance see various chapters in H. Gardezi and J. Rashid (eds), *Pakistan: The Roots of Dictatorship*, London, 1983.
69.   Cohen, *Pakistan Army*, p. 115.
70.   Ibid.

4 FEUDALISTS IN POLITICS: TRANS-REGIONAL ELITIST ALLIANCE

1. Historians remain divided on the evolution of capitalist economies in early modern South Asia. For a long time, urbanisation and the growth of bourgeois nomenclature were attributed to Western influences until in the 1980s new research produced convincing alternative explanations. The growth of small towns in the sub-continent was highlighted as a *region-specific* development. The eurocentric view was challenged by an emphasis on indigenous evolution without exaggerating the development. For an interesting dialogue on related issues raised by Immanuel Wallerstein, David Washbrook and Chris Bailey, see Sugata Bose (ed.), *South Asia and World Capitalism*, Delhi, 1990.

2. For details, see Thomas R. Metcalf, *Land, Landlords, and the British Raj: Northern India in the Nineteenth Century*, Berkeley, 1979.

3. More than any other region in the world, South Asia has experienced unbridled inter-regional population transfers, unleashing inter-state and intra-state forces of instability. Such migrations are mainly motivated by economic and political factors, occasionally spurred by religious and ethnic volatility in the region. Upheavals in the neighbouring regions in more recent years have also encouraged mass movements of political and economic refugees into South Asia.

4. 'The feudals have always survived the game because, largely due to their own deliberate suppression of education, no leading politician has ever emerged from the lower or even middle classes. While politics remains the preserve of the rich, living insulated lives from the country's myriad problems and educated in an alien context, it is hard to see how the needs of ordinary people can be truly represented. Ironically, in his social background, General Zia was perhaps the most representative if least legitimate of all Pakistan's rulers. The only election to have been fought (and won) on economic slogans was that of 1970, and the man calling "*roti, kapra aur makan*" was a wealthy *zamindar*' (Christina Lamb, *Waiting for Allah. Pakistan's Struggle for Democracy*, London, 1991, p. 291).

5. In the formation of *ashra'af* traditions, land and caste were the main determinants and both were inter-related, though in some exceptional cases intellectual excellence could also prove decisive. Traditionally, the Turkish, Persian or Rajput nobility in the Muslim court in Delhi was hereditary and land-based. Nearness to the court determined the social stature of such elites and land grants (*jagirs*) were used to extract loyalty. The British solidified the tradition.

6. The ruling dynasties of Pakistan have been simply land-based. It is not uncommon to meet former graduates of prominent Western universities belonging to aristocratic families unabashedly bragging about their land possessions. An Oxford-educated Benazir Bhutto went to great lengths to describe the ancestral land-holdings in her autobiography: 'Before the first land reforms in 1958, the Bhuttos were among the largest employers of agricultural workers in the province. Our lands like those of other landowners in Sindh were measured in square miles, not acres. As children we loved to

hear the story of the amazement of Charles Napier, the British conqueror of Sindh in 1843. "Whose lands are these?" he reportedly asked his driver as he toured the province. "Bhutto's lands", came the inevitable response. "Wake me up when we are off Bhutto's lands", he ordered. He was surprised when some time later he woke up on his own. "Who owns this land?" he asked. "Bhutto," the driver repeated. Napier became famous for his dispatch in Latin to the British military command after he conquered the province: "*Peccavi* – I have sinned." As children we thought it a confession, not a pun' (Benazir Bhutto, *Daughter of the East*, London, 1988, p. 26).

7.   There are frequent commentaries in the Pakistani vernacular press on such cross-regional alliances. More recently, many Pakistani and foreign analysts have begun studying matrimonial linkages among the 'provincial' landed elites. For example, see Craig Baxter, 'Union or Partition: Some Aspects of Politics in the Punjab, 1936–1945', in Lawrence Ziring, *et al.* (eds), *Pakistan: The Long View*, Durham, 1977; and, Wakeel Anjum, *Siyasat Kay Firoan* (literally, 'The Pharoahs of Politics'), Lahore, 1993. The latter volume, a well-researched study in Urdu, is a useful treatise on the evolution of dynastic feudal interests since the nineteenth century and their growing hold on local and national politics. It also documents the matrimonial relationship among the ruling elites of Pakistan and is thus a revealing 'Who's Who' of Pakistan.

8.   'When the tiny world of the upper classes has such a large hand in running the country, genealogy becomes politics. A foreigner I know who is interested principally in government has taken up family trees as a sideline. He showed me his masterpiece – Pakistan on a single sheet of paper in the 1960s. Ayub Khan, the president, is at the centre ... From Ayub Khan, it is two steps to the Haroons, the country's most prominent newspaper-owning family, one of whom is a minister of Zia's; one step away is General Yacoub Khan, Zia's brilliant foreign minister and a member of one of the old Indian princely families. Starting again from Ayub, it is two steps to the Qureshis, and they are directly, linked to the families of Abida Hussein and Fakr Imam: that bit of web ties up three of the most important political forces in Punjab' (Emma Duncan, *Breaking The Curfew. A Political Journey Through Pakistan*, London, 1989, p. 52).

9.   For example, Ayub Khan married his sons into industrial families of the NWFP and his daughter wedded the son of the Wali of Swat, whose daughter was married off to a senior bureaucrat. The bureaucrat, despite his non-Pushtun origins, eventually married off his own daughter to the son of a Punjabi landlord – a one-time minister. Feudal dynasties like the Hayats would venture into non-feudal yet industrial or services' magnates such as the Durranis. Brigadier (retd) Assad Durrani accumulated wealth and held important positions after his military retirement. One of his daughters, while still married, flirted with Ghulam Mustafa Khar and eventually married him. Khar, a landlord from Muzzaffargarh, Southwestern Punjab, eventually left her for younger women. In her autobiography, where she narrates the excesses of her former husband, she also notes various opinions about her father working for the CIA in the early 1970s. Brigadier Durrani was then heading the state-owned Pakistan International Airlines (PIA) and allowed American intelligence agents to use its aircraft for espionage over China.

For details, see Tehmina Durrani, *My Feudal Lord*, Lahore, 1991.

10.   Benazir Bhutto selected Asif Zardari, an aristocrat with strong tribal links, as her husband. Similarly, the Khattaks of the NWFP have matrimonial relations with the Saifullahs who have similar bonds with Ghulam Ishaque Khan, the former president of Pakistan. One of the Khan's daughters is married to Irfanullah Khan Marwat, a chieftain of the Marwat Pushtun tribe and a political figure in the Sindh's provincial politics. Marwat won notoriety in Sindh during his days as a non-elected but all-powerful adviser on administration to the late Jam Sadiq Ali and was implicated in a number of scandals. He lost in the provincial elections of 1993. Syeda Abida Hussain, a leading politician from an influential *pir* family of Jhang, an articulate parliamentarian and a former Pakistani ambassador to the United States, is married to Syed Fakhr-i Imam, a former speaker of Pakistan's National Assembly and a minister in various governments. Syed Imam, beside being a fellow Syed like his wife, who is also his cousin, comes from an aristocratic family of Khanewal in Multan division. Similar cross-regional marital patterns are common among the Baloch chieftains of Southern Punjab, rural Sindh and Balochistan.

11.   There may be some rare exceptions but, in such cases, the extent of land-holding and political clout could compensate for *zat* distinctions. For instance, Abida Hussain's cousin, Bokhari, a political rival, is married into the Qureshis of Multan who are not Syeds yet trace their origins from the Quresh of the Hejaz. The Qureshis are the *sajjada nishin* of Baha ud-Din Zakariya, the saint buried in Multan, and are also known as Makhdooms. Nawab Sadiq Qureshi was governor and chief minister of the Punjab under Zulfikar Ali Bhutto, while Sajjad Hussain Qureshi, with millions of followers in the Punjab and Sindh, remained the governor of the Punjab under General Zia ul-Haq while his son, Mahmood Qureshi, a graduate of Aitchison and Cambridge, has been an aspirant for the provincial chief ministership. In more recent years, both the Qureshis, true to their tradition of changing loyalties with every regime, maintained close links with Mian Nawaz Sharif and supported him in provincial and national politics. Mahmood Qureshi was the finance minister under Nawaz Sharif and his successor in the Punjab, Ghulam Haider Wyne, until the dissolution of the regime in April 1993. The Qureshis switched over to the PPP on the eve of the elections of October 1993 like the Gardezis and Gilanis and other feudal dynasties of Southwestern Punjab. It was hard for these aristocrats with immense local powers to 'follow' an urban industrialist. True to their traditions, they changed their loyalties overnight to Benazir Bhutto, whom they had 'detested' until a few weeks earlier. However, some of the feudal *gaddi nishin* families like the Makhdooms of Hala are exceptions as they have steadfastly supported the PPP since its inception despite persuasions and dissuasions from doing so. After Z. A. Bhutto, the Makhdooms have stood by Benazir Bhutto throughout her tumultuous career.

12.   Despite the fact that Mohammad Hayat Tamman was the chief political adviser to Zulfikar Ali Bhutto, he triumphantly resisted the upgrading of Tamman's women's school from middle to secondary level. His private argument was that once they were educated the women would not be willing to work at his home and other *havelis* (huge family houses). Even the then

PPP chief minister, Hanif Ramay, an otherwise urbane ideologue, could not make any headway. (This information is based on an interview with a source who was himself involved in the campaign and was personally confided to him by the chief minister.)

13. There are a number of case-studies to illustrate the point. A constituency of the Attock district in Punjab has been hereditary for the Pir of Makhad, Lal Shah, a loyal British subject. His disciples, thanks to illiteracy and superstition, guaranteed his election to the Punjab Legislative Assembly. After his death, his playboy son and heir, Safi ud-Din, cashed in on his father's constituency exploiting his 'spiritual' constituencies. Throughout his career in the various assemblies, he is known to have uttered no single word except for 'yes' to support any given government of the time. On the eve of elections, he would simply call the local notables and 'touts' to his native Makhad, shower them with money and jeeps, and ask them to tell his *murids* who to vote for. Most of the voters would never see the candidate and there was no need to do so. On some occasions, the rural illiterate folk would be seen kissing the jeeps of the Pir out of reverence. The Pir lived in cities pursuing his favourite pastimes and there was no scarcity of official patronage. Pakistan's tribalism served both the suitors and the supporters. The story of the Pir of Pagara, the most powerful *pir* in Pakistan is not very different. See Sarah F. D. Ansari, *Sufi Saints and State Power. The Pirs of Sind, 1843–1947*, Cambridge, 1992; and H. T. Lambrick, *The Terrorist*, London, 1972.

14. With a few exceptions, these feudalists are alleged to have double standards. Their agents and local intermediaries intimidate the peasants and artisans. During the course of the present study, many instances of repression, kidnap and forcible ejection from property were reported in various rural constituencies of Mansoor Hayat Tamman. In Sindh, Southwestern Punjab and tribal-rural areas of the NWFP and Balochistan the conditions of sharecroppers and tenants are extremely sub-human. For instance, the months-long feuds between the Bugtis and Raisanis in Balochistan had already cost scores of lives in 1994–95. In addition to old-time tribal rivalries, their chieftains have been disputing over electoral contests and results. 'In the labyrinthine world of Balochistan's tribal politics, it is sometimes hard to tell the reasons behind a particular incident of bloodletting ... at the back of it all is a ruthless race for power and the ego of countless chieftains, big and small, trying to hold on to their domains in an increasingly fragmenting social order' (Massoud Ansari, 'The Politics of Vendetta', *The Herald* September 1994, p. 52).

15. Even under martial law, with its apparently strict laws and summary military courts, there were frequent reports of molestations of peasant and *hari* women across the country, and in some cases they were marched nude in public.

16. No observer, local or foreign, misses out on the ever-increasing, unchecked influence of the *jagirdars*: 'There are probably only 5000 or so Pakistani landed families that matter, but their political influence is disproportionate to their numbers or even their wealth. Any slice of Pakistani history has the big names playing their part: the Qureshis, Gardezis, Noons, Tiwanas, Soomros, Khuros, Bhuttos, Jatois are a social and political Who's Who of

families. The landowners have dominated any sort of parliament in the area, even before Pakistan was created: they have held on to a fat slice of every cabinet, and have provided the last two prime ministers of Pakistan, Zulfikar Ali Bhutto and Mohammed Khan Junejo. In this Pakistan is quite different to India. Important Hindus have been businessmen more than landlords: and the Congress party has been dominated by Brahmins who, by tradition, do not own land. Land reforms since partition have helped wipe out large estates.' According to the author, the foundations of Pakistani landed estates were laid long before the Raj. Duncan, *Breaking the Curfew*, p. 100.

17. 'To contest the election one had to be rich, and many workers saw the campaign as their way to effect the redistribution of wealth that they had little hope of the politicians bringing in. So while the official limit on spending was 500 000 rupees (about $25 000), many candidates were spending more than that each day – much slipping into the pockets of everyone from the man distributing the posters to the rickshaw driver and cigarette vendor paid to display them. Chaudry Shujaat's house in Gujrat, the headquarters for the family's election campaign of four seats, resembled the feeding of the five thousand throughout the thirty-eight-day campaign, with huge marquees erected in the garden to serve up unimaginable quantities of lentil curry and rice' (Lamb, *Waiting for Allah*, pp. 63–4).

18. *The Guardian*, 30 September 1993.

19. The electoral campaigns in 1990 and 1993 were largely lacklustre. In some constituencies, the constituents had put out banners disallowing any entry to the candidates since they would default on their promises. For instance, a village on a main road near Chakwal had large banners demanding: '*Bijly Do, Vote Lo*' (You bring us electricity, we vote for you). Banners outside another village in Pothowar region near Gujar Khan, echoed the disenchantment of their fellow peasants as they demanded schools and roads from the candidates.

20. It is interesting to see how many of these ruling dynasties are national defaulters to the tune of many billions of rupees from the national exchequer. Besides evading taxes, payment of electricity charges and phone bills (in many cases) through collaboration with the local officials, they have taken immense loans from nationalised banks and cooperative societies. A list of these defaulters was published only by the caretaker government of Moeen Qureshi in 1993 since all other governments feared losing support.

21. The best example is of Wali Khan Kukikhel, a known Afridi chieftain, who extracted favours from both the Kabul regime and Pakistan during the 1980s.

22. For an inside and rare view, see Durrani, *My Feudal Lord*.

23. For details see ibid., pp. 133–5. Mr Khar was given exceptionally prominent coverage by a leading British weekly, when he published a four-page critique of Pakistani domestic and foreign policies. See Ghulam Mustafa Khar, 'Four Choices Facing Front-line Pakistan', *The Economist*, 21 October 1981, pp. 21–4.

24. In the by-elections of 1993, Khar's son was also elected from their 'ancestral' constituency.

25. For details see, M. Rafique Afzal, *Party Politics in Pakistan, 1947–1958*, vol. I, Islamabad, 1986 (reprint); also Khalid B. Sayeed, 'Collapse of Parliamentary Democracy in Pakistan', *The Middle East Journal*, 13 (4), 1959, p. 393.
26. Feroz Khan Noon, *From Memory*, Lahore, 1966, as quoted in Asaf Hussain, *Elite Politics in an Ideological State. The Case of Pakistan*, Folkestone, Kent, 1979, p. 53.
27. *The Civil and Military Gazette*, Lahore, 29 June 1962.
28. Rasul B. Rais, 'Elections in Pakistan: Is Democracy Winning?', *Asian Survey*, 12, December 1985, pp. 43–61.
29. Khalid Bin Sayeed, 'The Three Worlds of Democracy in Pakistan', *Contemporary South Asia*, 1 (1), 1992, p. 56.
30. Quoted in Mohammed Noman, *Our Struggle*, Karachi, n.d., p. 27.
31. Malcolm Lyall Darling, *Rustious Loquitur*, London, 1930, p. 214.
32. M. Masud, *Hari Report – Note of Dissent*, Karachi, 1948, p. 2.
33. *Report of the Government Hari Enquiry Committee*, p. 7. Some peasants might be self-sufficient by virtue of a land-holding or other means of income. But, in general, 'villages in Pakistan are not really subject to the law of the land'. See H. H. Kizilbash, 'Local Government: Democracy at the Capital and Autocracy in the Villages', *Pakistan Economic and Social Review*, XI (1), Spring 1973, pp. 104–24. For more studies on rural communities, see, Z. Eglar, *A Punjabi Village in Pakistan*, New York, 1960; and Saghir Ahmed, *Class and Power in a Punjab Village*, New York, 1977.
34. Government of Pakistan, *Report of the Land Reforms Commission for West Pakistan 1959*, Lahore, 1959, p. 14.
35. Herbert Feldman, *Revolution in Pakistan*, London, 1967, p. 59.
36. Khalid B. Sayeed, 'Pakistan's Constitutional Autocracy', *Pacific Affairs*, XXVI (4) Winter 1963–64, p. 365.
37. Quoted in Tariq Ali, *Pakistan: Military Rule or People's Power*, London, 1970, pp. 95–6.
38. Asaf Hussain, *Elite Politics*, p. 57.
39. M.G. Weinbaum, 'The March 1977 Elections in Pakistan: Where Everyone Lost', *Asian Survey*, XXII (7), July 1977, p. 604.

5 UNILATERALISM OF THE STATE: 'INVISIBLE GOVERNMENT' AT WORK

1. Such a judicial verdict came after the martial-law regime, confronted with a petition from Nusrat Bhutto, pledged before the court to hold the promised elections within the stipulated period.
2. Zia's policies were eulogised in the official media which was controlled by Mujibur Rehman, an active military general and close Punjabi confidant of Zia. Like General Sher Ali, the information minister under General Yahya Khan, General Mujib masterminded a persistent campaign in favour of Zia. Anti-Bhutto forces were coopted and, through a string of right-wing protagonists, Zia was projected as the *Islamic* leader. Concurrently, the Afghan crisis proved equally helpful for the regime. Many conferences and semi-

nars were held on the nature of Islamisation and Zia's strong East Punjab credentials worked to establish his authority over a shocked nation. Some went to the extent of finding his Punjabi Arain roots to prove that, true to the tradition of Mughal Emperor Aurengzeb, Zia was a frugal, unassuming but extremely religious and hard-working model Pakistani Muslim, unlike a partying, brash Dara Shikoh, personified by Z. A. Bhutto. For an interesting sociological extrapolation, see Akbar S. Ahmed, *Pakistan Society: Islam, Ethnicity and Leadership in South Asia*, Karachi, 1986.

3. For further details, see Abbas Nasir, 'Pakistan's Intelligence Agencies: The Inside Story', *The Herald*, January 1991.

4. This is not to suggest that it was only with General Zia ul-Haq that sycophancy and repression became the order of the day in Pakistan, since the process began soon after the death of the Quaid i-Azam in 1948. The politics of patronage at the behest of a growingly strong state anchored on the pillars of bureaucracy and the military ensured that efforts to empower the masses were unsuccessful. In the process, depoliticisation and irreverence towards Jinnah's constitutionalism became the order of the day. 'The palace conspiracies' were epitomised under General Ayub Khan, whose regime set the pattern for future military regimes. Despite its liberal espousals, his regime remained elitist and monopolistic, with the field marshal assuming a supreme position. For an insider's viewpoint, see Altaf Gauhar, *Ayub Khan. Pakistan's First Military Ruler*, Lahore, 1993. (Mr Gauhar was one of the trusted few who had closer access to the General and as a rare exception assumes responsibility for various non-democratic decisions taken by the regime. He was subsequently jailed by Z. A. Bhutto and released under international pressure. During his 'exile' in London, financed by Agha Hasan Abedi's BCCI, Gauhar became a well-known journalist and publisher before writing his account of the Ayub regime. According to one reliable source in London, the BCCI financed *South* and *Third World Quarterly* – Gauhar's London-based magazines – to the tune of £22 million.

5. 'Today he acts as Prime Minister Nawaz Sharif's eyes and ears while the IB, under him, is said to run Pakistan's invisible government. As a cabinet minister put it: "The Prime Minister takes key decisions not in the cabinet but somewhere else. That somewhere else is when he is closeted with the IB chief". Says a senior bureaucrat: "Imtiaz is the most important member of the Sharif's mini kitchen cabinet. His influence is not limited to giving just advice; he plans the Prime Minister's political moves and ensures their implementation". He has been one of the most influential men in the history of Pakistan's intelligence agencies and was nick-named James Bond. He retired during the first tenure of Benazir Bhutto but was re-hired by her successor.' See Maleeha Lodhi and Zahid Hussain, 'The Invisible Government' in *The Daily Jang* (London), 31 October to 1 November 1992. Following the dissolution of the Sharif government, he resigned and was, for a while in 1994, tried by the PPP regime.

6. For the CIA, it was not the first time they had collaborated with another intelligence agency, but for the ISI it was certainly new. Bypassing the political facade under Junejo, the ISI's cell on Afghanistan, headed by a brigadier, funnelled weapons into Afghanistan and operated as a conduit for the CIA in the region. The story has been brought to light recently by the

brigadier himself. For details, see Brigadier (Retd) Mohammad Yusuf and Mark Adkin, *The Bear Trap; Afghanistan's Untold Story*, London, 1992.

7. Bob Woodward, *Veil: The Secret Wars of the CIA, 1981–1987*, London, 1987, p. 311.

8. For details, see Lawrence Lifschultz, 'Islamabad was Conduit for Israeli Arms to Iran. The Contra Sideshow', *Far Eastern Economic Review*, 19 December 1991.

9. It is widely believed that intelligence agencies are unable to differentiate between political opposition and subversion. Any kind of dissent from any quarter is taken to be seditious activity against 'national interests'. It is noteworthy that the surveillance of politicians and other opinion-makers began earnestly under Iskander Mirza and was promoted by Ayub Khan. See Lodhi and Hussain, op. cit.

10. For more details, see Brigadier (Retd) Mohammad Yusuf, *Silent Soldier: The Man Behind the Afghan Jehad, General Akhtar Abdur Rahman Shaheed*, Lahore, 1991.

11. Ibid. Many generals and civilian officials are known to have made millions of dollars during the Afghan war. Given Islamabad's significance as the largest CIA operation centre outside the USA, various foreign agencies cultivated influential Pakistanis and Afghans. Even some of the officials working for the rehabilitation and subsequent repatriation of the Afghan refugees have privately acknowledged receiving special favours.

    In a row between the sons of the late General Zia ul-Haq and General Rahman during the summer of 1993, each was reported to have claimed that their own father left many more millions than the other.

12. After the dissolution of the Soviet Union Pakistan was no longer relevant to US global interests. It renewed its criticism of Pakistan's nuclear programme and alleged support to the Kashmiri militants: the 'most allied friend' joined Syria, Libya, North Korea, Iraq and Iran as sponsors of international terrorism.'"Pakistan, as far as the United States is concerned, would become a non-country", a diplomat said yesterday' (Gerald Bourke, 'Washington Ready to Brand Pakistan a Terrorist State', *The Guardian*, 14 December 1992). Pakistan was under severe pressure all through the first six months of the Clinton administration until US officials confirmed that it was not involved in international terrorist activities.

13. Junejo was unceremoniously removed a few weeks after the Ojhri ammunition dump explosion on 10 April 1988, costing numerous lives and loss of expensive property in Rawalpindi and Islamabad when rockets and grenades rained on both the towns. The dump, under the supervision of the ISI, stored ammunition earmarked for Afghan mujahideen. After an inquiry – whose report has never been made public to date – when Junejo hinted at possible reprimand of army officials, he was eased out of office.

14. Gul was asked by the army chief, General Beg, to mastermind an anti-PPP coalition. It was also admitted by a former insider who observed: 'No civilian was involved in the making of the IJT; this was done entirely by the ISI.' Brigadier Imtiaz then worked for the ISI as the head of internal security operations and is reported to have invented the slogans in Punjabi widely used during Nawaz Sharif's campaign. Salamat Ali, 'Tarnished Brass: Scandal over Soldiers Playing Politics', *Far Eastern Economic Review*, 15 October 1992.

15. Ibid.
16. "'The COAS, General Mirza Aslam Beg took the decision in principle but left the nuts and bolts to Hamid Gul, who speedily completed the job within weeks of the polls", said a knowledgeable source' (quoted in ibid.).
17. In any democratic country, it would have been a major crime, but given the powers of the military establishment in Pakistan, it was not pursued. In 1993, even long after Beg's retirement, the Supreme Court refused to reprimand Beg retrospectively.
18. Chalking on the walls in Lahore and other cities of Punjab read: 'jaag Punjabi, jaag' (wake up Punjabi! wake up!).
19. Such views were clandestinely given out to PPP or pro-PPP parliamentarians to gain support for a no-confidence motion against Benazir Bhutto. She became aware of such attempts and pro-PPP sleuths in the IB began monitoring ISI officials like Brigadier Imtiaz and Major Aamer. Cassette recordings of their secret talks with the MNAs were released to the public by the PPP leaders but without much impact on the agencies themselves. For the transcripts, see Munir Ahmed, *Pakistan Mein Intelligence Agencion Ka Siyasi Kirdar* (The Political Role of Intelligence Agencies in Pakistan) (Urdu), Lahore, 1993, pp. 117–234.
20. During the election campaign, personal insinuations against Nusrat Bhutto and Benazir Bhutto were not uncommon – they were portrayed as extremely liberal and socially uninhibited so as to malign them.
21. As seen earlier, Nawaz Sharif, her successor (and predecessor) in Islamabad, also lost favour with the 'establishment' as his government was dissolved through the application of the Eighth Amendment. Benazir Bhutto's installation as the prime minister for the second time on 19 October 1993, was the fifth government of the year.
22. For details, see Zahid Hussain and Hasan Mujtaba, 'Crime and Politics', *Newsline* (Karachi), August 1992.
23. The amount of Pakistani losses in human lives and property due to counter-attacks by the Afghan/KGB secret agents will never be known. In the 1980s, bomb blasts across Pakistan took their toll and a number of citizens were bludgeoned to death while asleep. There has been much speculation on the involvement of some Pakistani agencies in incidents of violence in urban centres, presumably by *hathora* group(s). In any case, the military regime of General Zia certainly took advantage of the atmosphere of insecurity, and growing hatred towards the communists and the Indian government.
24. See Tehmina Durrani, *My Feudal Lord*, Lahore, 1991, p. 146.
25. After her installation as prime minister in November 1993, Benazir Bhutto, for a time, reportedly considered implementing the Commission's recommendations.
26. 'General Beg personally "delivered the MQM to IJT", according to the IJT leader Chaudhry Nisar Ali. An IJT insider says that Beg in fact hosted a meeting at his own house between opposition leader Mustafa Jatoi and the MQM's Imran Farooq' (Lodhi and Hussain, 'Invisible Government'). In August 1992, the PPP released the audio-tapes of Operation Midnight Jackals, confirming that the two ousted military officials were collaborating with the commerce minister, Mohammad Naeem Khan, in luring the PPP MNAs to defect. 'At the time of the affair, Naeem was regarded as a princi-

pal troubleshooter for Nawaz Sharif ... and his response to the PPP's allegations was delayed until 25 September, when he denied in a press interview
having offered inducements to PPP MPs to vote against their party leader.
However, Naeem added that he might have mentioned something like that
as a bluff which was "a necessary part of practical politics".

'The Defence Ministry's rather low key reaction to these revelations
came a day before Naeem's clarification. It cautioned the local press that
there was a law against defaming or ridiculing the armed forces' (Ali,
'Tarnished Brass').

27. Ibid.
28. In a press conference, Ahmed Saeed Awan, a former PPP minister for information, disclosed that after the dissolution on 6 August 1990, the PPP leadership had received a message from 'a sensitive agency containing a deal'.
Accordingly, a possible restoration of the assemblies was made conditional
upon the Bhuttos' withdrawal from politics. It was also conveyed that
should they decide to participate in the forthcoming elections, only 40 to 45
seats 'would be allowed to the PPP'. Though Mr Awan did not divulge the
identity of the 'agency', it was assumed that the message came from
General Beg. For more details, see *The Daily Awaz International* (London),
2 April 1993.
29. 'A former MI official described measures that were tantamount to a coup in
civilian disguise as "normal protective steps". But he did not deny that the
Presidential act of dismissal was effectively by a military intelligence
agency' Lodhi and Hussain, 'Invisible Government'.
30. General Beg is known for making public his views on national and regional
issues irrespective of their ramifications. On the eve of elections in 1988, he
had deputed Senator Wasim Sajjad to sound out the judges of the Supreme
Court of Pakistan against the restoration of the Junejo government and the
assemblies dissolved by the late Zia. The Supreme Court, following a petition by Haji Saifullah, a former parliamentarian and minister in the Junejo
government, is reported to have reached a decision for the restoration but
was stopped by Beg, the contemporary army chief of staff. The matter
would have remained outside public knowledge if it wasn't for Beg's own
statement in a press conference on 4 February 1993. Justice Zullah, the chief
justice of Pakistan, took notice of Beg's 'confession' and began a hearing.
Given contemporary press reports and video-tapes of Beg's mentioned press
conference, a verdict could have been reached. However, nothing came out
of the case initiated by the Supreme Court. For further details, see *The Jang*,
10 February 1993.
31. During the Gulf crisis in 1990, General Beg gave statements that ran contrary to the country's foreign policy and caused severe embarrassment to
the government, which was supporting Kuwait, Saudi Arabia and the USA.
32. 'Beg's rejoinder to Mahsud's allegations was widely seen as lacking in conviction. In particular, Beg ignored some of Mahsud's disclosures about his
role in destabilising the Bhutto government. According to Mahsud, the army
commanders were shown a list of charges against Bhutto while she was
prime minister that later became the basis of her dismissal by Ishaq Khan in
August 1990' (Ali, 'Tarnished Brass').
33. Lodhi and Hussain, 'Invisible Government'.

34. The world media carried written and visual coverage of the protest marches and the crack-down by the security forces. See 'Bhutto held after Day of Farce and Fury', *The Guardian*, 19 November 1992; and 'Bhutto beaten, banished', *The Times*, 19 November 1992.

35. 'Populism in Pakistan. Bhutto deserves no support in her undemocratic bid for power' (editorial), *The Times*, 19 November 1992.

36. Christopher Thomas, 'Pakistan Police Brutality gives Bhutto Propaganda Victory', ibid., 19 November 1992; and 'Reunited Bhuttos Remain Defiant', *The Independent*, 21 November 1992.

37. Ahmed Rashid, 'Feud Worsens as Bhutto Returns to the Fray', *The Sunday Times* (London), 22 November 1992.

38. For details, see Ayesha Jalal, 'State-Building in the Post-War World: Britain's Colonial Legacy, American Futures and Pakistan', in Sugata Bose (ed.), *South Asia and World Capitalism*, New Delhi, 1990, pp. 271–72.

39. It is interesting to note that the disinformation campaign on the nuclear issue has served many purposes. It has helped to promote as well as demote individuals while maintaining an aura of secrecy about the entire episode. There is certainly a consensus among Pakistanis to have a nuclear capability as it deals with basic questions like sovereignty and national security. However, a debate on the issue which is so crucial to Pakistan's existence has not been allowed in the media.

40. For example, General Umar, a close associate of General Yahya Khan, and N. A. Rizvi, the director of IB, embezzled millions of rupees from the large sums earmarked from secret funds for the manipulation of elections in 1970. For details, see Ahmed, *Pakistan Mein Intelligence*, pp. 20–21. It is curious that General Umar subsequently headed the prestigious Pakistan Institute of International Affairs, Karachi, during the 1980s. However, Rizvi was made to pay back some of the money he had made when Z. A. Bhutto tried him in court.

41. During election campaigns, the intelligence agencies generally have their own favourites whom they support by any means. Ayub Khan's presidential elections from a limited electoral college of 80 000 were largely manipulated by the administration and intelligence agencies. During the elections of 1970, N. A. Rizvi gave generous sums to politicians like Maulana Bhashani in former East Pakistan and Abdul Qayyum Khan in the western wing to gain more seats. The generals used IB, MI, ISI and Special Branch to obtain mixed results which would give them a vetoing power over politicians to stay on in power. The results dismayed the junta immensely.

42. Idrees Bakhtiar, 'Trial by Torture', *The Herald* (Karachi), November 1992, p. 32.

43. A stream of such names have maintained covert contacts with foreign agencies like the CIA, KHAD and RAW. Many political figures, while trying to oust existing regimes, have attempted armed revolts by manoeuvring links with Indian intelligence. For a contemporary record of collaboration between individuals like Ghulam Mustafa Khar and Jam Sadiq Ali and Indian intelligence, see Tehmina Durrani *My Feudal Lord*, pp. 133–55.

It is interesting to note, however that the father of the aforementioned author, Shakirullah Durrani, a former military official turned banker, developed links with the international world of finance and banking. In the late

1960s, benefiting from his close association with Generals Ayub Khan and Yahya Khan, Durrani became the head of Pakistan International Airlines (PIA). Durrani, as his daughter recorded, is alleged to have allowed Pakistani civilian aircraft to be used by the American CIA to carry on espionage and surveillance of Chinese installations during the years of the cold war. Z. A. Bhutto eventually put Durrani behind bars but he was soon rehabilitated in the banking world and lived peacefully on the Mediterranean riviera. See ibid., pp. 166–7.

44. 'Bombings Increase Tension', *The Independent*, 15 March 1993.
45. Many of the agents have been on these campuses for years and are well known to everybody. Their lack of proper education and incomprehension of academic life certainly have not been helpful to anybody. At Quaid-i University, the premier federal university, Sheikh Imtiaz Ali, a former pro-martial law vice-chancellor used to boast before senior teachers of the daily presence of seven different agencies on his campus. On the same campus, some of these agents would stand outside the classrooms during the 1980s asking questions from the drivers of the buses about the 'affiliations' and views of the teachers.
46. Quite a few leading journalists and writers in Pakistan have been 'on the payroll' of security agencies, the Press Information Department, unofficial interest groups or similar outfits. For details, see Zamir Niazi, *The Press in Chains*, Karachi, 1987 (2nd edn); and Ahmed, *Pakistan Mein Intelligence*.
47. The press had not named the Maulana initially, but when he rang the newspapers to deny involvement, his denial was given pronounced coverage. Calling himself 'a soldier of Islam', the Maulana accused both the government and the press of blackmail. Given his strong views on women's segregation, women activists demanded a trial under Islamic law stipulating death by stoning. 'Bed-time Stories', *The Economist*, 9 November 1991.
48. Kathy Evans, 'Sex Scandal Shocks Pakistani Elite', *The Guardian*, 4 November 1991; also, *The Times*, 4 November 1991.
49. 'One theory is that the government "doctored" the brothel keeper's confession because the Maulana had been attacking the government for dragging its feet over implementing Islamic laws. The government, grateful for the distraction from stories of its corruption, sensibly declines to comment' (*The Economist*, 9 November 1992).
50. All the way from the governors to the local petty functionary in *thana* or *tahsil*, efforts were made to defeat Miss Jinnah, the sister of the founder of the country. A disinformation campaign, bribes and coercion were used to manipulate the limited electoral college, together with a lot of rigging. In addition, wherever she travelled to campaign for her candidacy local magistrates and deputy commissioners would impose Section 144, denying people the right to assemble. Her supporters, at both national and local levels, were rounded up so that they could not cast their votes. The entire government machinery was lined up against a woman contender although, in the absence of universal suffrage, only 80 000 members constituted the electoral college.
51. Many people in Pakistan are still baffled by Bhutto's u-turn on making public the Hamoodur Rahman Commission Report, which reportedly contains information on the extent of involvement of the military regime and its policies in the former eastern wing leading to the break-up of the country. It

is assumed that the military leadership and intelligence agencies persuaded him against publication.

52. Quoted in Bakhtiar, 'Trial by Torture'.

53. 'There is substance too, in the PPP's allegation that the MQM, its nemesis in Sind, was sustained by the ISI under Zia' (editorial, *The Friday Times* [Lahore], 12–18 July 1990).

54. According to one report 'more than five million farmers in Pakistan's Southern province work as bonded slaves for landlords, who torture them and rape their wives and daughters ...' (see *The Daily Telegraph*, 1 January 1993).

55. The plight of poor *haris*, like the share-croppers and peasants in Southwestern Punjab and Balochistan, has largely remained unchanged over the centuries. The emphasis on traditionalism by a self-perpetuating feudal system refurbished the localist influence of *wadera*, *pir* and Syeds, who, in league with the local administration, zealously resist encroachments on their interests. Marriages with the Quran and other archaic practices take their toll from the weakest, the most disorganised and illiterate in the society including women who make 51 per cent of Sindh's population.

56. Quoted in Bakhtiar, op. cit.

57. They were: Ghulam Mohiyudddin, Yusuf Jakhrani, Ali Haider Shah and Mujeeb Jatoi.

58. Benazir Bhutto, during her second administration, appointed a number of judges, who, in some cases, did not even qualify for the positions.

59. The decision by the Lahore High Court in the blasphemy case of Salamat Masih in February 1995 commuting his death sentence to an acquittal is another landmark verdict by the country's superior courts in defence of civic rights, especially those of the minorities. However, such examples are very rare and one cannot be oblivious of the societal and official pressures on judiciary. 'Blasphemy Boy's Family Flees Rage of Mullahs', *The Independent* 25 February 1995.

60. *International Herald Tribune*, 15 November 1992. (It may be interesting to know that Asif Zardari has quite often invited criticism of his financial deals and links with shadowy characters. See Ahmed Rashid, 'Wheeler-Dealer', *Far Eastern Economic Review*, 28 April, 1994.)

61. For reactions from Pakistani human rights groups, lawyers and judges, see *The Daily Jang* (London), 16 November 1992.

62. For further details, see Aziz Siddiqui, 'Children of a Lesser God', *The Herald* April 1991; Sohail Warraich, 'Striking Terror', ibid., January 1991.

63. Asia Watch, *Double Jeopardy: Police Abuse of Women in Pakistan*, New York, 1992.

64. It was reported that out of 50 interviewed adolescents in custody, only 16 had been presented before the court within the judicial time-limit. In District Jail, Lahore, out of 2709 inmates, 1559 were on drugs. A survey of three jails in the Punjab revealed that 44 out of 200 interviewed children had been sexually molested and, in the District Jail, in Lahore, out of 116 children under 14 interviewed by the human rights groups, 19 had been subjected to sexual assaults. All these figures are based on various reports investigated and published by human rights groups in Pakistan. For the press coverage, see Irshad Ahmed Haqqani, 'Yey Galla Sarra Nizam' (This rotten system!), *The Jang*, 30 December 1992.

65.   Salim Tahir, 'Inside the CIA', *The Herald*, October 1991.
66.   Ibid.

6   STATE AND SOCIETY IN CONFLICT

1.   United Nations, *Human Development Report 1992*, Oxford, 1992, p. 176.
2.   World Bank, *World Development Report 1990*, Oxford, 1990, p. 26.
3.   For more details, see M. Irfan and Rashid Amjad, 'Poverty in Rural Pakistan', in Mahbubul Haq and Moin Baqai (eds), *Employment, Distribution and Basic Needs in Pakistan*, Lahore, 1986, pp. 206–32.
4.   Omar Noman, *Child Labour In Pakistan*, Lahore, 1990, p. 2.
5.   Omar Noman, *Pakistan: A Political and Economic History Since 1947*, London, 1990, p. 75.
6.   The interim government of Moeen Qureshi in 1993 imposed an agricultural tax through an ordinance. Although widely hailed across the country, soon after the installation of the political regime the landed aristocracy started finding fault with it.
7.   Asian Development Bank, *Strategies for Economic Growth and Development: The Bank's Role in Pakistan*, Manilla, 1985, p. 117.
8.   United Nations, *Human Development Report, 1992*, Oxford, 1992, p. 171.
9.   In spite of his apology, pressure on Khan continued unabated until he was arrested in early October 1992. It was only after external pressure that Khan was finally released, yet cases of blasphemy against him were instituted across the country.
10.   See 'Keti Jamshoro', *Newsline*, August 1992.
11.   This was observed during personal visits to the university in 1992 and 1995.
12.   In Pakistani folk vocabulary the term *Qabza group* means that a group of hooligans, either through coercion or by cooption, captures an examination centre and then manipulates the entire test through extortion. The proceeds are subsequently shared by all. Like some 'resourceful' police stations, certain examination centres have turned out to be lucrative. Even the prestigious competitive examinations to select civil servants for both provincial and federal services suffer from a credibility crisis given incidents of such malpractice.
13.   Based on extensive interviews at Mayo Hospital, Lahore.
14.   It is very common to mix up vital laboratory test results. Due to an absence of proper management and accountability, the results of crucial tests on blood and urine samples carried out in hospitals are misplaced. Proper connections are required at every stage to receive a correct diagnosis and relevant treatment.
15.   Exorbitant consultation fees, high-cost hospitalisation and non-existent physiotherapy, mean that many orthopaedic patients end up with local masseurs whose manipulation of bones and muscles can exacerbate the problem.
16.   Based on first-hand information gathered in Rawalpindi and Islamabad.
17.   In some cases, doctors make a perfunctory examination and then suggest a quick operation in some private hospital irrespective of the necessity or the

financial situation of the patient. Many patients with minor back-pains have undergone unnecessary surgery by specialists eager to make a quick lump sum.

18. After questions from the opposition in the national assembly of Pakistan in October–November 1992, the government released a long list of such individuals whose treatment abroad had been incurred by the national exchequer. The list included an overwhelming majority of bureaucrats – some even retired – and their relatives, but did not include anybody from academia, the media, the law, the arts or literature. Many cases of foreign treatment have been 'bogus' and are merely alibis for visits to meet relatives or for shopping purposes. Fictitious claims, consultation fees and charges for medicines and hospitalisation are shown to consume the funding expressly provided for complicated health problems not curable within Pakistan. Largely uninvestigated, this realm of corruption at the highest levels remains outside public knowledge and scrutiny.

19. For further details, see Iftikhar H. Malik, *US–South Asia Relations, 1784–1940: A Historical Perspective*, Islamabad, 1988, pp. 261–87.

20. Eventually, both organisations met their demise. For further details, see Government of Pakistan, *Report of the Press Commission*, Karachi, 1954, p. 181.

21. Qasimi was later won over by Ayub Khan through Qudratullah Shahab, the founder of the Writers' Guild and the Information Secretary under Ayub Khan. Shahab was in the forefront of winning support for the military regime among writers and journalists. Eventually, Qasimi was awarded a Pride of Performance by Ayub Khan in 1968 for his 'services' – an award which Sibte Hasan and a few other independent writers refused to accept.

22. Faiz undoubtedly remains the most famous twentieth-century Urdu poet after Allama Iqbal. His poetry is consciously against economic and social exploitation of the down-trodden in society. In the 1980s, during the Lebanese civil war, Faiz edited and published *Lotus* from war-torn Beirut.

23. Though a son of a feudal lord, Mazhar Ali Khan, until his death in 1993, devoted his life as a journalist to exposing human misery. He owned and published the weekly *Viewpoint* (Lahore) until his death. His son, Tariq Ali, a journalist, television writer and novelist rose to fame in the 1960s while leading peace marches in Oxford and London. He chose to settle in London.

24. After a long career in bureaucracy, Shahab turned to mysticism during his retirement and gathered a number of former favourites around him. He also published a 1300-page autobiography just before his death which is actually a defence of his long career as a powerful bureaucrat at the helm of national affairs. Shahab was deeply aware of opinions about him as the linchpin of various authoritarian regimes in the country. In his book, he does not take responsibility for the draconian policies to coerce or tempt Pakistani intellectuals; nor for introducing 'black laws' to muzzle the press. For his view, see *Shahabnama*, Urdu, Lahore, 1988.

25. Khushwant Singh, a reputed Indian journalist, had once written about Altaf Husain: 'Altaf Husain, editor of *Dawn*, is one of the most powerful editors in the Indo–Pak subcontinent' (quoted in Zamir Niazi, *Press in Chains*, Karachi, 1987, p. 84). Husain died on 26 May 1968, a few months before General Yahya Khan took over from Ayub Khan.

26.   Gauhar was tried by Z. A. Bhutto and allowed to proceed to London, where he established his Third World Foundation with help from Agha Hasan Abedi, the founder of the BCCI. After the fall of BCCI, Gauhar, by then a known journalist because of his magazine, *South*, and a champion of freedom of expression, went back to Pakistan and become the editor of *Daily Muslim* (Islamabad). On occasions, he has defended both himself and Ayub Khan. For his own version, see *Ayub Khan: Pakistan's First Military Ruler*, Lahore, 1993.

27.   Niazi, op. cit., p. 7.

28.   Ibid., p. 47.

29.   *Dawn*, 3 September 1963, quoted in Niazi, op. cit., pp. 98–9.

30.   Quoted in ibid., p. 3.

31.   Many journalists were rewarded with expensive property by the regime for advocating its case. Executive positions were offered to such apologists in the so-called autonomous Television Corporation. For instance, amongst a number of cases, is that of *Hurmat*, a magazine brought out by Zahid Malik, a pro-Zia journalist with a PPP past. For his unflinching support to the dictator he was given a very expensive property in Islamabad to build a commercial plaza.

        The authorities depend on journalists in a number of ways. When, in 1987, Pakistan feared an attack from India, a journalist was asked by a security agency to arrange an interview between Dr Qadeer Khan, supposedly the brain behind Pakistan's nuclear research and Kuldip Nayyar, a known Indian journalist. The interview was meant to warn India that Pakistan had the nuclear capability to ward off any attack on its soil. The publication of the interview cost the journalist his editorship but had the desired impact in the relevant quarters.

        During the Benazir Bhutto–Nawaz Sharif fracas from early 1989 to 1993 both sides hired journalists to lead propaganda and 'disinformation' campaigns. For more on this, see 'Politics of Husseins', *The Herald*, June 1993.

32.   The journalists bravely recorded and exposed the intermittent cases of organised crimes against media at the behest of the authorities, student groups and ethnic parties. See Idrees Bakhtiar, 'The Press Under Fire', *The Herald*, April 1991; and Zaffar Abbas, 'Burning Issues', ibid. (The second report carries a catalogue of crimes committed against the press from 1969 to 1991.)

33.   The journalists did complain of official harassment during the mid-1990s, especially after their disclosures of financial scandals involving the president, senior cabinet ministers and the husband of the prime minister herself. Several journalists incurred fury over the exposures of child labour in the carpet industry and brick kilns. Concurrently, during 1994–95, the MQM intensified its campaign to terrorise independent journalists in Karachi. In late 1994, Salah ud-Din, the editor of the Urdu weekly, *Takbeer*, was gunned down outside his office, apparently by MQM hitmen.

7   THE POLITICS OF GENDER IN PAKISTAN

1.   For more on this see Deniz Kandiyoti (ed.), *Women, Islam and the State*, London, 1991. Some recent historical studies, while dealing with the

modern phase, turn out to be country-specific given the vast and diversified
areas of the discipline. For instance, see Leila Ahmed, *Women and Gender
in Islam*, New Haven, 1992.

2.   The institutionalisation of traditions such as *purdah* or similar latter-day
attitudes in Muslim societies, largely canonised on the basis of diversified
Quranic injunctions, have resulted in their perpetuation. 'Probably because
of the religious associations it took on, it has been harder to discard veiling
in Muslim countries than it has been to get rid of it or parallel customs in
non-Muslim countries ... What is special about Islam in regard to women is
the degree to which matters relating to women's status have either been leg-
islated by the Quran, which believing Muslims regard as the literal word of
God as revealed to the Prophet, or by subsequent legislation derived from
interpretation of the Quran and the traditional sayings of the Prophet. Thus,
innovators in this, as in many other matters, have to deal not merely with
some customary belief that may be relatively easily replaced by another,
once the newer one becomes more functional, but with the heart of religion,
which is the holy law or sharia' ('Introduction', Lois Beck and Nikki
Keddie (eds), *Women in the Muslim World*, Cambridge, Mass., 1978, p. 25).

3.   For instance, attitudinal changes amongst rural women who henceforth
began imitating the urban petty bourgeoisie (*bazaari*) in donning the veil for
status purposes, while earlier only women from upper Muslim classes
(*ashra'af*) would observe *purdah*. Also, some of the urban compatriots of
these rural women began to face more segregation and isolation in the towns
as their menfolk pursued a busy sedentary life and kept their wives in the
domestic sphere largely because of their rural origins.

4.   In many former colonies, early feminism demanding better educational
facilities and wider participation in the socio-political set-up embodied a
strong strand in contemporary nationalist movements. See K. Jayawardena,
Feminism and Nationalism in the Third World, London, 1988.

5.   One may include the novels by Deputy Nazir Ahmad, satirical poems by
Nazir Akbarabadi, or posthumous writings by the *ulama* from both the
Brelvi and Deobandi schools upholding such views, where women's role is
strictly domestic. An early religious education imparted by female teachers
within the *chardiwari* is recommended by such schools. In Pakistan, the
Jama'at i-Islami, various sections of the Jamiat and individual scholars like
Dr Israr Ahmed, in their speeches and writings, have raised serious objections to co-education and female participation in public life, besides criticising women professionals. *Bahishti Zaiwar* (Urdu), a comprehensive book
on the role and duties of an *Islamic woman* by Maulana Ashraf Thanawi,
has remained a best-seller since its publication in 1926. Similarly, Maulana
Maudoodi's *Purdah* (Urdu), a critique of feminism, has remained an
influential work decrying the mores and norms of Western *liberated woman*,
since its publication many decades ago.

6.   The best example is Fatima Mernissi, a Moroccan sociologist who, through a
reinterpretation of the Quran, Hadith and early primary Arabic sources on
Islamic thought and history, has attempted to present a different portrait of the
status of women in early Islam. 'Ample historical evidence portrays women in
the Prophet's Medina raising their heads from slavery and violence to claim
their right to join, as equal participants, in the making of their Arab history.

Women fled aristocratic tribal Mecca by the thousands to enter Medina, the Prophet's city in the seventh century, because Islam promised equality and dignity for all, for men and women, masters and servants. Every woman who came to Medina when the Prophet was the political leader of Muslims could gain access to full citizenship, the status of *sahabi*, Companion of the Prophet. Muslims can take pride in their language that they have the feminine of that word, *sahabiyat*, women who enjoyed the right to enter into the councils of the Muslim *umma*, to speak freely to its Prophet-leader, to dispute with the men, to fight for their happiness, and to be involved in the management of military and political affairs. The evidence is there in the works of religious history, in the biographical details of *sahabiyat* by, the thousand who built Muslim society side by side with their male counterparts' (Fatima Mernissi, *Women and Islam. An Historical and Theological Enquiry*, translated by Mary Jo Lakeland, Oxford, 1992, p. viii).

7. For instance, see F. A. Sabbah, *Women in the Muslim Unconscious*, New York, 1984.

8. Leila Ahmed brings out this point very convincingly. See *Women and Gender in Islam*, pp. 36–7.

9. Gerda Lerner, *The Creation of Patriarchy*, New York, 1986, quoted in Ahmed *Women and Gender in Islam*, p. 13.

10. Quoted in ibid., p. 29. Aristotelian views were widely and readily accepted by peoples in the Near East and West.

11. Mernissi goes to great lengths in deciphering the origin of commonly held but 'false' traditions such as the following: 'Those who entrust their affairs to a woman will never know prosperity'. See *Women and Islam*, pp. 3, 49–61.

12. Ayesha Jalal, 'The Convenience of Subservience: Women and the State of Pakistan', in *Women, Islam and the State*.

13. Alavi finds a diversity in women's experience, with lower middle-class urban women in the vanguard, especially since the 1980s. The battle for women's rights is certainly being fought in cities. Hamza Alavi, 'Pakistani Women in Changing Society', in Hastings Donnan and Pnina Werbener (eds), *Economy and Culture in Pakistan*, London, 1991.

14. Fazlur Rahman, *Islam*, London, 1966, p. 5.

15. Embodying a widespread contemporary antagonism towards the Muslims, Lord Ellenborough is quoted as saying. 'I cannot close my eyes to the belief that the race (Mohammadans) is fundamentally hostile to us and our true policy is to reconciliate the Hindus' (quoted in A. R. Desai, *Social Background of Indian Nationalism*, Bombay, 1966, p. 393).

16. Even the so-called Muslim *ashra'af* were impoverished and fallen from grace. The famous contemporary Urdu poet, Mirza Ghalib, in his post-1857 testimony, gave elaborate examples of Muslim socio-economic bankruptcy. See R. Russell and Khurshidul Islam, *Ghalib: Life and Letters*, vol. I, Cambridge, Mass. 1969, p. 205.

17. Peter Hardy, *The Muslims of British India*, Cambridge, 1972, p. 61.

18. Quoted in Sarfaraz Hussain Mirza, *Muslim Women's Role in the Pakistan Movement*, Lahore, 1981 (2nd edn), p. 7.

19. See statement to this effect by Chand Begum of Madras at the Mohammedan Educational Congress in Bombay in 1903, in ibid., p. 12.

20. For more on this, see Gail Minault (ed.), *The Extended Family: Women and Political Participation in India and Pakistan*, New Delhi, 1981.
21. Khawar Mumtaz and Farida Shaheed (eds), *Women of Pakistan. Two Steps Forward, One Step Back?* London, 1987, p. 42.
22. For further details, see Shahida Lateef, *Muslim Women in India. Political & Private Realities: 1890s–1980s*, London, 1990.
23. Bi Ama was active when the Ali Brothers were incarcerated over the Khilafat issue. Jahan Ara Shahnawaz, the daughter of Sir Mohammad Shafi, the well-known Muslim jurist, came from a Lahore-based aristocratic family who pioneered the tradition of sending their women for higher education and allowed them to participate in public life including politics. See Jahan Ara Shahnawaz, *Father and Daughter*, Lahore, 1971.
24. Iqbal did have certain reservations about contemporary women suffragists in the West. See Javed Iqbal (ed.), *Stray Reflections: A Note-Book of Allama Iqbal*, Lahore, 1961, pp. 64–5.
25. Quoted in Mumtaz and Shaheed, op, cit., p. 7.
26. 'In spite of the most acrimonious debate on all aspects of the demand for Pakistan, the Muslim League leaders had nowhere referred to Pakistan as the future Islamic State. They were trying to prove that Muslims in India constituted a separate nation and they therefore had a right to self-determination. Further that the separate homeland was needed to protect the Muslims from the domination of Hindus ... The substance of what they said was that since the majority of the population of Pakistan would be Muslims, the polity would be profoundly influenced by Islam' (Kalim Bahadur, 'Problems of Secularism in Pakistan', in Pandav Nayak (ed.), *Pakistan: Dilemmas of a Developing State*, Jaipur, 1985, p. 31).
27. Mumtaz and Shaheed, op. cit., p. 45.
28. Begum Shahnawaz and Shaista Ikramullah were the only women members in the first Constituent Assembly of Pakistan. Ghulam Muhammad, the contemporary minister for finance and later governor-general of Pakistan, even refused to sit with the female members of the assembly by arguing that only *burqa*-wearing women above 50 be allowed to become members of the assembly. In September 1954, when Jahan Ara Shahnawaz presented a Charter of Women's Rights in the Assembly demanding more seats for women, equal economic and legal opportunities and safeguards of women's rights under Islamic Personal Law of Sharia, it was surprisingly resisted by Sir Zafrullah Khan. After some lobbying, the Constitution of 1956 accepted the principle of universal suffrage for women.
29. *Dawn*, 19 July 1976.
30. Khalid Ishaque, 'Introduction', in Sabeeha Hafeez, *The Metropolitan Women in Pakistan: Studies*, Karachi, 1981, p. viii.
31. Mumtaz and Shaheed, op. cit., p. 73.
32. See *The Muslim* (Islamabad), 21 February 1983.
33. To attract more voters, officials visited homes to fetch the people; loudspeakers in the mosques urged people to go to referendum booths; the prerequisite of the national identity card was done away with and, given the very low turn-out, even the polling time was extended, yet to no avail. Politicians and independent observers considered it Zia's joke in the name

of Islam, with the country and the people staying indoors. People in
Pakistan nick-named the whole exercise 'rigrandom'.

34. Begum Zari Sarfaraz had also served in the Committee established by Z. A.
     Bhutto in 1976.

35. The note of dissent in Urdu was submitted by Mrs Nisar Fatima who felt
     that Islam had already provided solutions to the various problems faced by
     women and that their role must mainly be within the confines of the home.

36. Zari Sarfaraz, et al., *Report of the Pakistan Commission on the Status of
     Women* (hereafter *Report on Women*), Islamabad, 1985, p. 2.

37. 'The exploitation and discriminatory practices prevalent in these societies
     today have nothing to do with Islam as these are clearly contrary to Quranic
     injunctions and the spirit of Islam. Both men and women belonging to the
     weaker and oppressed sections of society suffer from such inequities, more
     so the women as prevailing laws and customs keep them deprived and dis-
     possessed of their human rights granted by Islam' (ibid., p. 2).

38. Ibid., p. 31.

39. Ibid., pp. 29–30.

40. Ibid., p. 37.

41. In secondary schools girls' enrolment was only 25 per cent of the total, with
     rural and tribal areas having a particularly low share. Out of a total of 278
     degree colleges in 1983, there were around 75 girls' colleges, with very low
     enrolment in the *Katchi abadis*, rural and tribal areas. In the 20 universities
     there were 7866 female students compared with 47 587 male students.
     Similarly, in vocational and training colleges, the number of female students
     was negligible. For details, see ibid., pp. 71–83.

42. It dismissed the view that co-education in the universities encouraged moral
     laxity since women's role in such institutions over the previous four decades
     was known to have been 'above reproach'. Ibid., pp. 78–9.

43. Ibid., p. 119.

44. It was also recommended that in each local council there should be at least
     two women members, and that government, along with the NGOs, must
     campaign to create consciousness as well as demand for wider participa-
     tion. Ibid., pp. 126, 127.

45. Ibid., pp. 128–30.

46. Ibid., p. 137.

47. 'It has been brought to the Commission's notice that women are convicted
     and punished for *zina*, including whipping, even in cases where the male
     accused goes free. This is a crime which can only be committed by two
     persons and punishment can only be awarded to a couple. In this behalf note
     has to be taken of the fact that under the law as drafted women complainants
     of rape have been convicted for *zina*. The Ordinance is making it dangerous
     for the victim and her family to file a complaint. In fact, there should be sep-
     arate laws for *zina* and *zina-bil-jabr*' (ibid., see pp. 140–9).

48. *The Muslim*, 17 May 1983.

49. Anita M. Weiss, 'Implications of the Islamization Program for Women' in
     Anita M. Weiss (ed.), *Islamic Reassertion in Pakistan*, Lahore, 1987,
     pp. 108–9.

50. See G. W. Choudhury, *Pakistan: Transition from Military to Civilian Rule*,
     London, 1988.

51. See Shahid Javed Burki and Craig Baxter (eds), *Pakistan Under the Military. Eleven Years of Zia-ul-Haq*, Oxford, 1991.
52. It was felt that without economic independence cultural, political and intellectual sovereignty will remain meaningless and religion will continue to be used both as a coercive force and a smoke-screen for larger-than-life forces. Ziaul Haque, 'Islamisation of Society in Pakistan', in M. Asghar Khan (ed.), *Islam, Politics and the State: The Pakistan Experience*, London, 1985, pp. 114, 122.
53. 'Interview with Asma Jahangir', *Viewpoint*, (Lahore), 5 December 1991.
54. Ibid.
55. Interview with Farida Shaheed in ibid.
56. For such a viewpoint, see Fareeha Zafar (ed.), *Finding Our Way. Readings on Women in Pakistan*, Karachi, 1991.
57. Weiss, op. cit., p. 104.
58. Contemporary journalistic accounts observed a dwindling of recreational and artistic values in the society. For example, see Richard Reeves, *Journey to Peshawar*, New York, 1983; and Emma Duncan, *Breaking the Curfew*, London, 1989.
59. Haque, op. cit., pp. 121–2.
60. Many Muslim intellectuals believed that, from a religious viewpoint, her being a woman did not veto her right to lead the country. See Asghar Ali Engineer, *Trial of Benazir Bhutto: An Insight into the Status of Women in Islam*, Bombay, 1990.
61. In the summer of 1992, in retaliation for the publication of a poem exposing the huge embezzlement of public money by the cooperative societies, the Sharif government began a treason case against Maleeha Lodhi, the editor of *The News*, an English daily. When confronted with a widespread strike he backed down.
62. See Hafeez, *Metropolitan Women*.
63. See Mazhar ul-Haq Khan, *Purdah and Polygamy: A Study in Social Pathology of the Muslim Society*, Peshawar, 1972.
64. Altaf Hussain, the founder of the MQM, chose to be called *Pir Sahib* and retained an ever-present posse of young women around him. See *The Observer*, 4 April 1990.
65. 'Reported abuses include beating and slapping; suspension in mid-air by hands tied behind victim's back; the insertion of foreign objects, including police batons and chili peppers, into the vagina and rectum; and gang rape. Yet despite the alarming reports, to our knowledge not a single officer has suffered criminal penalties for such abuse, even in cases in which incontrovertible evidence of custodial rapes exists. One senior police official (DIG Maqbool of Lahore) told a delegation of local human rights activists that "in 95 percent of the cases the women themselves are at fault"' (Asia Watch, *Double Jeopardy. Police Abuse of Women in Pakistan*, New York, 1993, p. 2).
66. Ibid., p. 3.
67. For instance, see Asma Jahangir and Hina Jilani, *The Huddood Ordinances: A Divine Sanction?* Lahore, 1990.
68. The following case-studies, described briefly, will illustrate the point:

    Aasia Ayoub, a housewife, was picked up by police in Rawalpindi on an allegation of stealing her neighbour's purse. Without any FIR or warrant she had been arrested and put in the lock-up at the police station on 3 September 1991 along with her husband and 14-year-old son. The SHO pulled her hair, while his constables brought chillies and threatened to spray her vagina. She had already been subjected to policemen kissing and fondling her body. She was released the next day and warned not to disclose her ordeal to anybody. She ended up in hospital with a nervous break-down. Under public pressure the case was registered in a magistrate's court following an inquiry which established that the police had sexually tortured Aasia. Under police pressure the magistrate was transferred and, despite Nawaz Sharif's personal intervention, the court dismissed the allegations against the police for lack of evidence.

Bushra Bibi and Anwari, the latter a deaf mute, were sexually assaulted by the police in Sheikhupura jail on 25 August 1990. Medical reports confirmed the charges of rape, and under special directive from the Lahore Court the case was registered. But the women, under police pressure, withdrew their complaints and the case was dropped.

Raheela Tiwana, a 26-year-old PPP activist was taken into custody by the CIA in Karachi on 26 December 1990, and was hung from the ceiling in an investigation cell. She was beaten up and abused and had to be sent to hospital. She was not raped, apparently because she came from an influential family. Other cases of torture of PPP activists under the orders of the then Sindh administration were widely reported by the *Herald*, which was, in retaliation, removed from the news-stands by CIA officials. The October issue of the monthly was reprinted a number of times, given its exposure of torture under Jam Sadiq Ali and Irfanullah Khan Marwat.

Veena Hayat, a close friend of Benazir Bhutto and the daughter of Shaukat Hayat, a leading freedom fighter, was raped at her home in Karachi on 27 November 1991 by five men acting under official orders. Her case attracted immediate attention as she accused Irfanullah Marwat, the son-in-law of the president, of masterminding the assault. The family expressed lack of trust in the official commission of inquiry and refused to give evidence before it; instead, they decided to take the case to a tribal *jirga*. In its verdict on 24 December 1991, the inquiry found Marwat innocent, while the *jirga* pronounced death for the accused. For details see Rehana Hakim, 'The Politics of Rape', *Newsline*, December 1991; Hidayat Shah, 'Cry in the Wilderness', ibid., January 1992; and *The Herald*, January 1992.

69. Table 7.4 (p. 305) records reported events from August to November, mainly in the Central Punjab and in Karachi; many such occurrences in rural and tribal areas would remain unreported: for details, see *Viewpoint*, 5 December 1991.
70. 'Editorial', ibid.
71. In a report on human rights violations in 1992 alone, the Commission recorded 75 major cases of rape including 33 gang-rapes in interior Sindh. Most of the victims were girls under 26. In just three months in the Punjab 457 cases of sexual abuse against women were recorded. In addition to smuggling children to the Gulf states as camel jockeys, numerous cases of police torture against ordinary citizens were recorded in the report. In addition, 60 cases of harassment of journalists were recorded in the report, which expressed its concern about growing violations of human rights both

Table 7.4 Crimes Against Women in 1991

Date	Place	Nature of the crime
August	Lahore	32 women were burnt alive and were victims of stove explosions
10 October	Muzz'garh	A medical officer sedated and raped a woman health visitor
13 October	Faisalabad	A bailiff recovered four teenage girls from a police station
21 October	Alipur	A private medicine practitioner dosed and raped a woman
28 October	Faisalabad	The chief justice of Lahore High Court ordered city police to register a case against three persons for raping a poor girl
1 November	Lahore	Two young girls burnt to death A mother of four died of stove explosion
2 November	Lahore	A man raped a 6-year old girl A mother burnt by stove
	Multan	Eight men raped a woman and cut her nose
	Karachi	100–150 Bangladeshi women were being smuggled into Pakistan each month
7 November	B'Pur	Five men abducted, raped and murdered a 16-year-old girl
	Sh'garh	A woman burnt by stove
8 November	Sh'pura	A brother suspecting his sister of an affair hanged her
10 November	Karachi	A woman killed with 64 stab wounds
11 November	Karachi	A young lady doctor murdered
	Lahore	A woman torched alive by robbers
	Karachi	A woman assaulted near her home
12 November	Sang'hill	A man with help from a sister and two friends raped a girl
	Lahore	A man stabbed a girl as she refused sex
	Lahore	A woman died of stove-explosion
14 November	Jhang	Three persons made a woman walk naked in the village of Wadan Qadipur
15 November	Kotri	A woman kidnapped
17 November	Lahore	A man attempted to rape a 6-year-old girl
20 November	Lahore	Two women robbed of their belongings
21 November	Sh'pura	A 14-year-old girl kidnapped
22 November	Lahore	A 17-year-old-girl stabbed
	Sh'pura	A brother hanged his sister as she had run away with her lover
4 November	Lahore	A man threw acid on a girl who refused to marry him
27 November	Lahore	A man burnt his wife on suspicion of an affair

by the official agencies and local influential people during the regime of the IJT. For further details, see *The Awaz International* (London), 26 April 1993.

8   ETHNICITY, NATIONALISM AND NATION-BUILDING

1. For a very useful study, see Leo Rose and Richard Sisson, *War and Secession. Pakistan, India, and the Creation of Bangladesh*, Berkeley, 1990.
2. Salamat Ali, 'Sindh Erupts on Wave of Ethnic Killings', *Far Eastern Economic Review*, 7 June 1990; *The Times*, 28 May 1990; and, *Newsweek*, 11 June 1990.
    In 1992, the army began its 'clean-up' operation in Sindh to curb ethnic violence in Karachi and banditry in rural Sindh. While the dacoities subsided, ethnic militancy in Karachi during 1994–5, grew out of proportion. Both the PPP regime and the MQM leadership pursued a policy of active, militarist confrontation resulting in numerous deaths in the city. Karachi, to many observers, had become Pakistan's Beirut with law-enforcing agencies unable to control violence. See *Newsline* (Karachi Special) March 1995; 'The Enemy Within' (editorial), *The Friday Times*, 18–24 May, 1995.
3. Ethnic volatility entered a critical phase in 1994–95 with daily occurrences of violence. The death figures just for the first six months of 1995 for Karachi stood at 1000. Based on the BBCWM Radio Report, monitored in Birmingham (UK), 11 July 1995.
4. Pakistan's nuclear programme made the headlines in the world press in the 1980s and early 1990s. For instance, see James Adams, 'Pakistan–nuclear war threat', *The Sunday Times*, 27 May 1990; 'The Demolition Man', *Time*, 5 September 1994. Because of strong reservations on the nuclear issue, the US Government stopped its economic and military assistance to Pakistan in October 1990. In early 1993, the Americans were pressurising Pakistan to roll back its nuclear programme, withdraw its support for the Kashmiris or be prepared to be declared a terror-sponsoring state. In December 1993, there was a growing American recognition of Pakistani security imperatives when efforts to substitute the Pressler Amendment were afoot in the US Congress. The Pressler Amendment singled out Pakistan for allegedly carrying out a nuclear development programme and stipulated a ban on military and economic assistance to the country.
    Even during Benazir Bhutto's visit to the US in April 1994, there was media reportage of Pakistan's nuclear activities. See 'Pakistani Nuclear Reactor, Nearly Done, Unsettles U.S.', *International Herald Tribune*, 10 April, 1995.
5. Earlier in the summer, the MQM successfully called for a complete boycott of the by-elections for the seats vacated by it in protest against the military operation in 1992. Its rival group, MQM (Haqiqi), led by Afaq Ahmed and Aamer Khan, failed to provide any alternative to the MQM. The MQM, again, boycotted the elections to the National Assembly in October 1993 but decided to participate in the provincial elections and achieved an overall majority from Karachi. In 1995, the militants belonging to the movement

were engaging security forces in regular gun battles and selected their civilian and official targets with impunity.

6. Despite serious resentment against the MQM-led offensives against the non-Muhajir Karachiites and arrival of body-bags from the strife-torn city attributed to 'Muhajir chauvinism', there was no noticeable anti-Muhajir feeling in the whole of Pakistan.

7. A number of scholars had been suggesting that the ethnic factor within the former Soviet Union and Eastern Europe could eventually disintegrate the Communist bloc as such. US Senator Daniel P. Moynihan reaffirmed his early statements on ethnic volatility in his Cyril Foster Lecture on the subject at Oxford on 29 November 1991.

8. President Bush, in a speech at the US Naval Academy, Annapolis, emphasised this great shift in global politics. See *The Boston Globe*, 15 April 1991.

9. For further details, see Myron Weiner, 'Peoples and States in the New World Order', *Third World Quarterly*, XIII (2), 1992, p. 320.

10. *The Harper Dictionary of Modern Thought*, New York, 1988, p. 285.

11. Frederick Barth, 'Introduction', in F. Barth (ed.), *Ethnic Groups and Boundaries*, Boston, 1969, p. 14.

12. George DeVos, 'Ethnic Pluralism: Conflict and Accommodation', in George DeVos and L. Romanucci-Ross (eds), *Ethnic Identity and Change*, Palo Alto, 1975, p. 17.

13. 'It is no accident that ethnicity as a subject has tended to be slighted, if not ignored', wrote Moynihan in his recent work. 'At the onset of the twentieth century, there were two large ideas abroad, curiously congruent, which predicted a steady or even precipitous decline of ethnic attachments.' He then proceeds to define both the liberal and communist interpretations, which took the issue rather lightly until it came full circle in recent times. Daniel P. Moynihan, *Pandaemonium*, Oxford, 1993, pp. 27–9.

14. Donald L. Horowitz, *Ethnic Groups in Conflict*, Berkeley, 1985, p. ix.

15. John Rex, *Race and Ethnicity*, Milton Keynes, 1986, p. 16. Also, Fred W. Riggs, *Help for Social Scientists. A New Kind of Reference Process*, Paris, 1986, pp. 43–8.

16. E. J. Hobsbawm, *Nations and Nationalism Since 1780: Programme, Myth, Reality*, Cambridge, 1990, p. 63.

17. One could extend this argument to the Afghans in the 1980s, the Kurds in the 1990s, Yugoslavia and the former Southern and Western Soviet Union since 1989 or, for that matter, the Irish in Northern Ireland for the past several decades.

18. For more on the subject, see Anthony D. Smith, *The Ethnic Origins of Nations*, Oxford, 1987.

19. For further details, see Urmilla Phadnis, *Ethnicity and Nation-building in South Asia*, New Delhi, 1991, pp. 16–17.

20. 'Electoral democracy produces a ready-made machine for minority groups to fight effectively for a share of central resources, once they learn to act as a group and are sufficiently concentrated for electoral purposes. This gives ghettoised groups a lot of potential leverage. At the same time, for reasons both of politics and ideology, and also of changing economic organisation, the mechanism for defusing inter-ethnic tensions by assigning separate

niches to different groups, atrophies. They now compete, not for comparable resources ("separate but equal" as the phrase went) but for the *same*
resources in the same labour or housing or educational or other markets.
And, in this competition, at least for the disadvantaged, group pressure for
special favours ("affirmative action") is the most powerful weapon available' (Hobsbawm, op. cit., p. 25).

21. See Anthony D. Smith, op. cit.
22. Benedict Anderson, *Imagined Communities*, London, 1991 (revised edn),
    p. 3.
23. Hugh Seton-Watson, *Nations and States. An Enquiry into the Origins of
    Nations and the Politics of Nationalism*, Boulder, 1977, p. 5.
24. For a classical treatment of this subject, see E. Kedourie, *Nationalism*,
    London, 1961 (2nd edn); and Hans Kohn, *The Idea of Nationalism*, New
    York, 1967.
25. Smith, op. cit., p. 10. Smith finds ethnicity to be the driving force behind
    nationalism and thus differs with the 'modernists', to whom nationalism is a
    more recent development.
26. Ernest Gellner takes nationalism as an integral part of the process of 'mod-
    ernisation'. For a good commentary on his views, see Anthony D. Smith,
    Theories of Nationalism, London, 1983 (reprint).
27. Anderson, op. cit., p. 4.
28. 'It is *imagined* because the members of even the smallest nation will never
    know most of their fellow-members, meet them, or even hear of them, yet in
    the minds of each lives the image of their communion ... The nation is
    imagined as *limited* because even the largest of them, encompassing perhaps
    a billion living human beings, has finite, if elastic, boundaries, beyond
    which lie other nations. No nation imagines itself coterminous with
    mankind. The most messianic nationalists do not dream of a day when all
    the members of the human race will join their nation in the way that it was
    possible, in certain epochs, for Christians to dream of a wholly Christian
    planet' (ibid., pp. 6–7).
29. Ernest Gellner, *Thought and Change*, London, 1964, p. 169. To many other
    sociologists and historians 'the national phenomenon cannot be adequately
    investigated without careful attention to the "invention of tradition"'. See
    Terence Ranger and Eric Hobsbawm (eds), *The Invention of Tradition*,
    Cambridge, 1984, p. 14. To them, tradition itself is a space between custom
    and modernity and between an invariant and changing world. Ibid., p. 2.
30. 'The convergence of capitalism and print technology on the fatal diversity
    of a new form of human language created the possibility of a new form of
    imagined community, which in its basic morphology set the stage for the
    modern nation' (Anderson, op.cit., p. 46).
31. Quoted in Hobsbawm, 'Whose Fault-line is it Anyway?', *New Statesman
    and Society*, 24 April 1992, p. 23.
32. 'Historians are to nationalism what poppy-growers in Pakistan are to heroin-
    addicts: we supply the essential raw material for the market' (ibid.).
33. Ibid., p. 24.
34. These may be enumerated as follows: Irredentism, Secession, Autonomy,
    Interest group claims, Ethnic corporatism, Nativism, Hegemonic claims, and
    Fundamentalism. For further details, see Weiner, 'Peoples and States'.

35. For an early study see P. H. M. van den Dungen, 'Changes in Status And Occupation in Nineteenth Century Punjab', in D. A. Low (ed.), *Soundings in Modern South Asian History*, Berkeley, 1968. For a more recent study though largely in the realm of political history, see Ian Talbot, 'The Role of Crowd in the Muslim League Struggle for Pakistan', *The Journal of Imperial and Commonwealth History*, XXI (2), 1993, pp. 307–33.

36. This argument has been made very capably in a study on pre-1947 politics in the NWFP. See Stephen A. Rittenberg, *Ethnicity, Nationalism and the Pakhtuns: The Independence Movement in India's North-West Frontier Province*, Durham, 1988.

37. See C. A. Bayly, *Rulers, Townsmen and Bazaars. North Indian Society in the Age of British Expansion, 1770–1870*, Cambridge, 1983.

38. For a pertinent study, see Francis Robinson, *Separatism Among Indian Muslims: The Politics of the United Provinces' Muslims, 1860–1923*, Cambridge, 1974; and Mushirul Hasan, *Nationalism and Communal Politics in India, 1916–1928*, Delhi, 1978.

39. Paul R. Brass, *Language, Religion and Politics in North India*, London, 1974, p. 124.

40. Francis Robinson, 'Islam in Muslim Separatism', in David Taylor and Malcolm Yapp (eds), *Political Identity in South Asia*, London, 1979, pp. 78–112.

41. Farzana Shaikh, *Community and Consensus in Islam. Muslim Representation in Colonial India, 1860–1947*, Cambridge, 1989, p. 5.

42. Francis Robinson, 'Technology and Religious Change. Islam and the Impact of Print', *Modern Asian Studies*, XXVII, part 1, 1993, pp. 229–51.

43. Fazlur Rahman, *Islam*, London, 1966, p. 2.

44. Thomas R. Metcalf, *The Aftermath of Revolt: India 1857–1870*, Princeton, 1965, p. 298. Some senior British officials like John Lawrence found among them a 'more active, vindictive and fanatic spirit than Hindoos' while the Collector of Agra viewed the Muslims as inherently anti-British: 'The green flag of Mahomed too had been unfurled, the mass of the followers of the false prophet rejoicing to believe that under the auspices of the Great Mogal of Delhi their lost ascendancy was to be recovered, their deep hatred to the Christians got vent, and they rushed forth to kill and destroy' (quoted in Peter Hardy, *The Muslims of British India*, Cambridge, 1972, p. 63).

45. Letter dated 9 October 1857, quoted in ibid., p. 71 However, there were some sane voices counselling restraint. See Sir G. Campbell, *Memoirs of My Indian Career*, London, 1893, pp. 397–9.

46. Quoted from *The Papers of the First Viscount Cross*, India Office Records and Library (London) in ibid., p. 1.

47. Ainslee T. Embree, 'Indian Civilization and Regional Cultures: The Two Realities', in Paul Wallace (ed.), *Region and Nation in India*, New Delhi, 1985, pp. 35–6.

48. See Ayesha Jalal, *The Sole Spokesman: Jinnah, the Muslim League and the Demand for Pakistan*, Cambridge, 1985; David Page, *Prelude to Partition: The Indian Muslims and the Imperial System of Control 1920–1932*, Delhi, 1982.

49. 'It must be stressed, however, that what is coming up in U.P. is not just rural discontent. Nothing is more central to twentieth-century U.P. history

than the upsurge of the formerly long-subordinated Hindu culture of the mass of population. After seven centuries of Muslim dominance, as we have seen, Hindu dominance has taken over. The consequences are not all immediately apparent. It can be no coincidence, however, that U.P. should be so aggressively minded in the attachment to Hindi: Urdu has been triumphantly overthrown, and in the circumstances it is hardly surprising that there is little truck with that other alien-based tongue, English. Whether the two great stirrings from below will coalesce or conflict remains to be seen. Both, however, are plainly of singular importance' (D. A. Low, 'Introduction' in Low, *Soundings*, p. 17.

50.   For the misuse of state authority see Salim Tahir, 'Inside the CIA', *The Herald* (Karachi), October 1991, pp. 22–34.

51.   Professor Abdul Ghafoor, the General Secretary of the JI, in a statement in Karachi, warned concerned citizens about the persistent involvement of the intelligence agencies in exacerbating inter-ethnic relationships in Sindh. Like many other observers, he believed that such official bodies were engaged in a constant internecine warfare. Quoted in *The Awaz International* (London), 23 June 1993.

52.   See Rafiuddin Ahmed, *The Bengal Muslims, 1871–1906: A Quest for Identity*, Delhi, 1981.

53.   An interesting example can be found in the debate on renaming the NWFP as Pukhtoonkhwa – the land of the Pushtuns. The strongest resistance came from the non-Pushto speakers of Hazara, Kohistan, Chitral and Dera Ismail Khan. The resolution in the provincial assembly in the 1990s failed to gain a majority vote. The NWFP is as pluralist as any other province in the country. The Pushtun leaders of Balochistan were not in a position to integrate their region into a proposed Pukhtoonkhwa, largely controlled by the Pushtuns of the NWFP. Even Khan Abdul Wali Khan, the son of the late Khan Abdul Ghaffar Khan, has not been enthusiastic about a transprovincial Pukhtoonkhwa.

54.   It should not be forgotten that economically and politically these areas are integrated into their provincial set-ups, given that such administrative definitions took place decades ago. Just as Saraiki- and Sindhi-speakers would not like to cede their territories to Balochistan, the Baloch would resist any claims by Pushtu- or Hindku-speakers on their northern territories. The Pushtuns would be equally reluctant to let go of Hazara/Kohistan territory. In the case of former East Pakistan, being a distinct geographic and cultural unit, 'separation' was easier, but in the case of an existing Pakistani federating unit or ethnic community such a proposition is not only unlikely but also impractical. That is a major reason for the deflation of the question of nationalities soon after its espousal in the mid-1980s – long before the dissolution of the Soviet Union. The idea was circulated by certain disgruntled Sindhi and Baloch political leaders like Mumtaz Bhutto, Abdul Hafeez Pirzada and Ataullah Mengal, when they established the Sindh–Baloch National Front (SBNF) in London in 1984. Even the frequent vacillations by MQM between nationality, nationhood and ethnicity have been merely for symbolic and bargaining reasons rather than reflecting a well-planned and feasible political creed.

55.   For instance, the sale of Kashmir Valley and adjoining territories to Maharajah Gulab Singh was rationalised by Lord Hardinge to recover the

losses incurred in the war with the Sikhs in Punjab. Irrespective of the morality and technicality of the sale for a paltry sum, the transaction carried out under the Amritsar Treaty (1846), by a stroke of the pen 'created' a state *per se*. (See Hardinge's letter to Queen Victoria, 18 February 1846, in A. C. Benson and Viscount Esher (eds), *The Letters of Queen Victoria. A Selection of Her Majesty's Correspondence between the Years 1837 and 1861*, vol. II, London, 1908, pp. 73–4.)

56. In a sense, Saraiki is the lingua franca of Punjab, southern NWFP and upper Sindh, as it is the language of folk culture, sufi traditions and written literature. It is the majority language and to confine it to a single *subah* or state may be belittling a trans-regional literary heritage.

57. In a wider sense, people belonging to all the lingual traditions in the Punjab, Hindku- Pothowari- or Saraiki-speaking regions have equal claims on Bulleh Shah, Waris Shah, Baba Farid, Mian Bakhsh or Shah Muhammad, the famous sufi-poets in the classical period. Many of these Muslim poets are equally venerated by the Sikhs.

58. *The Guardian*, 30 June 1990. In 1994–95, Benazir Bhutto maintained uneasy relations with the coalition governments in the Punjab and Balochistan. She manoeuvred to establish the PPP government in the NWFP in 1994, but was confronted by a defiant MQM in her home province during the mid-1990s.

9 SINDH: THE POLITICS OF AUTHORITY AND ETHNICITY

1. This point has been made in a study. See Richard Tapper (ed.), *The Conflict of Tribe and State in Iran and Afghanistan*, London, 1983, p. 6.

2. The Dravidians might have lost to the Aryans but a number of their cultural traditions were adopted. It is no coincidence that Baruhi – still the only Dravidian language – surrounded by its numerous Indo-Aryan counterparts, survives as a major language both in central Sindh and the adjacent areas of Balochistan. See V. Y. Gankovsky, 'Sindhi Ethnic Community at the End of the Colonial Era', in Hamida Khuro (ed.), *Sind Through the Centuries*, Karachi, 1987, pp. 180–87.

3. For more on Sindh's geography, see H. T. Lambrick, *Sind: A General Introduction*, Hyderabad, 1975 (2nd edn).

4. A. M. Schimmel, *Islam in the Indian Subcontinent*, Leiden, 1980. The sufi-saints like Shah Abdul Latif Bhitai and Sachal Sarmast had their followers among both Muslims and Hindus. Similarly, the *sajjada nishin* of Baha ud-Din Zakariya in Multan and Ucch Sharif have had millions of followers across Sindh and Punjab.

5. Sindh did not figure that significantly in the Mughal imperial structure despite the fact that Humayun had sought refuge in Sindh on his way to exile in Persia and his son, Akbar, was born in the historic town of Umarkot. A few decades later, Shah Jahan also came to Thatta and made it his capital during his period of distress. But the Mughals usually appointed insignificant regional officials from places like Sehwan or Bhukkar as their *mansabdars*, who lacked both vision and administrative acumen. For

details, see Ansar Zahid Khan, *History and Culture of Sind*, Karachi, 1980, p. 71.

6. For a very useful study on this subject, see Sarah F. D. Ansari, *Sufi Saints and State Power. The Pirs of Sind, 1843–1947*, Cambridge, 1992.

7. R. F. Burton, 'Notes Relative to the Population of Sind and the Customs, Language and the Literature of the People', in *Selection from the Records of the Government of Bombay*, Bombay, 1947, p. 639.

8. For more on Sir Charles Napier, see H. T. Lambrick, *Sir Charles Napier and Sind*, Oxford, 1952.

9. For further details, see David Cheesman, 'Rural Power in Sind', unpublished Ph.D. dissertation, University of London, 1980.

10. In the Punjab a similar tradition had been initiated, which with the development of canal colonies proved of immense economic, social and political significance. See David Gilmartin, *Empire and Islam. Punjab and the Making of Pakistan*, London, 1988.

11. Imran Ali, *Punjab Under Imperialism*, London, 1988.

12. For further details, see Hamida Khuro, *The Making of Modern Sind: British Policy and Social Change in the Nineteenth Century*, Karachi, 1978.

13. The Hur rebellions of the 1890s and 1940s proved formidable challenges to this bi-partisan relationship. The British brutally suppressed the Hur rebellion in the 1930s and 1940s led by Pir Sibghatullah Shah, the Pir of Pagara. Martial law was imposed on the area; the Pir, along with many of his followers, was executed in 1943 and his two sons were sent to a private school in England. For further details, see Ansari, op. cit., pp. 50–1, and 129–49; also, H. T. Lambrick, *The Terrorist*, London, 1972.

14. For details see, Ansari, op. cit., p. 13.

15. Mushtaqur Rahman, *Land and Life in Sindh, Pakistan*, Lahore, 1993, p. 199.

16. For details on this subject, see M. Q. Soomro, *Muslim Politics in Sind (1938–47)*, Jamshoro, 1989.

17. Ansari, op. cit., p. 160.

18. See Yusuf Mirak, *Tarikh-i Mazhar-i Shah Jahani*, edited by Pir H. Rashdi, Hyderabad, 1962.

19. For an interesting study on such social cleavages, see Mubarik Ali, *Sindh: Khammoshi Ki Awaz* (Urdu), Lahore, 1992.

20. Many liberal intellectuals believe that leaders like G. M. Syed who belonged to the landed elite, wanted extra-territorial links, both to neutralise Hindus and to maintain their hold on the ordinary Sindhi Muslims. See ibid., pp. 254–5.

21. Such a dramatic change in attitude was noticeable in 1995 following the frequent massacres in Karachi largely attributed to the MQM.

22. O. H. K. Spate, *India and Pakistan: A General and Regional Geography*, London, 1954, p. 119.

23. For details, see *Census of India, 1941*, Command No. 6479, Tables II and VI.

24. A. Tayyab, *Pakistan: A Political Geography*, Oxford, 1966, pp. 171–2.

25. Many would contest the view that the Muhajireen are a privileged community. See Mushtaqur Rahman, op. cit., p. 9.

26. For a convincing account on this subject, see S. J. Burki, *Pakistan Under Bhutto, 1971–1977*, London, 1980, pp. 12–48.

27. In more recent times, 200 000 inhabitants per annum have been settling in Karachi alone.

28. Charles H. Kennedy, 'The Politics of Ethnicity in Sindh', *Asian Survey*, XXXI (10), 1991. (It is interesting to note that ethnicity in the census of 1981 was based on 'language most often used in household'. The census for 1991 was postponed due to various pressures.)

29. Quoted in Mushtaqur Rahman, op. cit., p. 89.

30. It was given out that rural Sindh would be the loser in terms of the quota allocation of jobs, admissions into higher institutions and the demarcation of electoral constituencies necessitating drastic changes in the mechanics. Following the 1971 census, Z. A. Bhutto was accused of having ordered that 'Karachi's urban population be reduced by 12.5 percent and rural population increased by 12.5 percent. One of Karachi's leaders, Mirza Jawad Beg, challenged the figures and was sent to jail on May 16, 1973, on orders of the federal government.' It is held 'that the 1972 census was inflated in favor of rural Sindh' (ibid., pp. 92–3).

31. It is no surprise that Karachi and Hyderabad exhibited the loudest reaction against the dismissal of Nawaz Sharif on 18 April 1993, and similarly pronounced rejoicing was noticed on his restoration 39 days later. It was not merely his Punjabi identity but also his representation of Pakistan's powerful industrial class which gave him such a following.

32. During the 1970s, apparently non-controversial terms like *new* Sindhis and *old* Sindhis also backfired. Ethnic polarity in Sindh had already been too intensified.

33. Feroz Ahmed, 'Pakistan's Problem of National Integration', in M. Asghar Khan (ed.), *Islam, Politics and the State. The Pakistan Experience*, London, 1985, pp. 229–30; and Zaffar Abbas, 'G. M. Syed: Personality Interview', *The Herald* (Karachi), August 1989.

34. See John Rex, *Race and Ethnicity*, Milton Keynes, 1986, pp. 75–7.

35. It does not mean that ethnic solidarity may preclude the possibility of any extortion or crime against the members of the same ethnic group. For instance in early 1995, the MQM, in a kidnap case, allegedly extracted more than 3 *crores* of rupees (30 millions) from the Sumars – a Muhajir industrialist family in Karachi. The Altaf and Haqiqi factions of the MQM have been involved in several cases of abduction and extortion.

36. Tahir Amin, *Ethno-National Movements of Pakistan*, Islamabad, 1988, p. 281.

37. In 1995, a number of Pakistanis believed that Altaf Hussain and his associates in London were being financed and manipulated by the Indian intelligence. To some, Hussain lacked a proper strategy and a viable political programme to steer Karachi out of a debilitating morass and simply pursued confrontational politics with a personal vendetta against Benazir Bhutto. To them, the official policies were equally not helping the moderate forces from amongst the MQM to begin a meaningful dialogue. Based on extensive interviews in the UK during May to August 1995.

38. For details, see *The Times*, 7 July 1993.

39. When President Ishaque Khan dismissed Nawaz Sharif's government and the national assembly on 18 April 1993, the Supreme Court, in an historic verdict, restored them on the plea that the president had overstepped his

constitutional authority. The interim government, largely comprising anti-Sharif politicians with a PPP majority, had to give way to a Sharif government which was to confront changed loyalties in provinces like the Punjab and NWFP. Anti-Sharif coalitions in these two crucial provinces, added to Sharif's reluctance in calling fresh elections, fearing that the four provincial governments would influence votes against him. Benazir Bhutto, despite initial goodwill following the court verdict, joined the president and provincial coalitions against Sharif with threats of long marches. While many people welcomed the verdict by the Supreme Court in reinstating the national assembly and the cabinet, several critics from Sindh raised pertinent questions as to why similar dissolutions in 1988 and 1990 were allowed to proceed.

40. For his views, see G. M. Syed, *Struggle for a New Sind. A Brief Narrative of Working of Provincial Autonomy in Sind During the Decade (1937–1947)*, Karachi, 1949; *Sindhi Culture*, Karachi, 1972; and *Diyar-i Dil va Dastan-i Mohabat*, Bombay, 1973.

41. For more on him, see Zaffar Abbas, 'G. M. Syed. Saint or Sinner?', *The Herald*, February 1992, pp. 22–6.

42. Syed, like Bhutto and Zia, happened to elicit extreme love and hostility among the people. 'He seems to have developed an undisputed reputation of one who defied harmony and order. Anything others wanted to do, he rejected. Anyone who dared his authority, he scorned. He believed only in the old institution of authority and his submission' (Mushtaqur Rahman, *Land and Life*, p. 79, fn. For Syed's own views, see G. M. Syed, *Struggle for a New Sind*.

43. Zaffar Abbas, 'G. M. Syed: Personality Interview', *The Herald*, August 1989, p. 170.

44. When asked in an interview about his hostility towards Jinnah and Bhutto and his alleged support for Zia and Jam Sadiq Ali, he simply observed: 'I refuse to reply to such questions' (Adil Rashdi, 'Interview', *The Herald*, February 1992, p. 27).

45. Ibid.

46. The observation attributed to Dodo Mehri is widely shared by many other critics of Syed's silence on land reforms. Ibid., p. 31.

47. The ANP Pakhtoonkhwa is a splinter group of the ANP in Balochistan which aims at safeguarding the interests of Pushtuns living in the province. Since the deflation of demand for 'Pushtunistan', Pushtun leaders like Wali Khan from the NWFP and Mahmood Khan Achakzai from Balochistan have joined the mainstream *national* politics.

48. The pro-JI press in Pakistan, and especially Karachi, have vehemently criticised the MQM, which has never relented in its coercive pressure on them. Salah ud-Din, a very vocal critic of the MQM and the proprietor and editor of the Urdu weekly, *Takbeer* (Karachi), was quite often molested by MQM activists until, on 4 December 1994, he was shot down by 'unknown' assailants.

49. A faction of the ML led by Hamid Nasir Chhatha, a former associate of Junejo and Sharif, supported the president in his confrontation with the prime minister. Eventually, the Chhatha group, sometimes referred to as the Junejo League, became coalition partners with Benazir Bhutto's PPP.

50. Christina Lamb, 'Bhutto detains Sindhi activist', *The Financial Times* (London), 12 October 1989.
51. Fahmida Riaz, *Pakistan. Literature and Society*, New Delhi, 1986, p. 31. Amar Jaleel, another leading Sindhi literary figure, headed the Pakistan Council of Arts in Islamabad during Benazir Bhutto's first regime.
52. Quoted in ibid., p. 45.
53. Ibid., p. 39. The appointment led to severe criticism against him from certain ultra-nationalist quarters in Sindh. He relinquished the position long after the imposition of martial law by General Zia ul-Haq. Another Sindhi nationalist writer, G. Allana, was made vice-chancellor of Allama Iqbal Open University in Islamabad by General Zia. Allana had earlier headed the Institute of Sindhology in Hyderabad.
54. Sheikh Aziz, 'Shaikh Ayaz: Personality Interview', *The Herald*, May 1989, pp. 151–2.
55. Hamza Alavi, 'Nationhood and the Nationalities in Pakistan', *Economic and Political Weekly* (Bombay), XXIV, 8 July 1989, pp. 1527–9. However, this analysis lacks lateral ideological orientation – both pro-IDA and pro-PPP – within the *salariat* besides the emergence of a strong industrial class from the urban areas and small business class from rural areas. See, Akmal Hussain, 'Pakistan: The Crisis of the State', in Khan, *Islam, Politics and the State*, pp. 208–10. Also Alavi, 'Class and State in Pakistan', in Hassan Gardezi and Jamil Rashid (eds), *Pakistan: The Roots of Dictatorship*, London, 1983. Tariq Ali believes that foreign aid to ethno-national movements will ultimately destroy Pakistan. See Tariq Ali, *Can Pakistan Survive?* London, 1983, p. 10.
56. Alavi, op. cit., pp. 1530–1. However, it is curious to note that the riots take place among the lower classes living in *bastis* or *katchi abadis*. It is only dacoities or kidnaps for ransom that are directed against the *salariat*.
57. Feroz Ahmed, 'Pakistan's Problem of National Integration', in Khan, *Islam, Politics and the State*, pp. 229–30. It is a very persuasive argument to suggest that Pakistan's persistent trauma in building up a national consensus and integration has been due to its failure to establish a democratic system. For a comparative study, see M. Nazrul Islam, *Pakistan and Malaysia. A Comparative Study in National Integration*, New Delhi, 1989, pp. 233–6.
58. G. M. Syed, *Sindhudesh Chho ain Chha Lai*, Ulhasnagar, 1974, p. 125, quoted in Ahmed, op. cit., p. 232.
59. Ibid., p. 234.
60. Ibid., p. 243.
61. Ibid., p. 245.
62. Khurshid Ahmad, 'Foreword', in Tahir Amin, *Ethno-National Movements of Pakistan: Domestic and International Factors*, Islamabad, 1988, p. xvi.

10 THE RISE OF THE MUHAJIR QAUMI MOVEMENT AND ETHNIC POLITICS IN SINDH

1. Literally 'Muhajireen' means migrants – persons who undertook *hijrat* in the tradition of the Holy Prophet when he shifted from Mecca to Medina in

the early years of Islam. A Muhajir is a refugee in a sense, though the Muhajireen in Karachi avoid using this term believing it betrays a temporary, mundane reflection on an otherwise more complex yet noble experience. Equally, in a literal sense, most of the members of MQM are not Muhajireen as they were all born in Pakistan, but *hijrat* remains a sublime and more acceptable identity. Born in Sindh, most of them refuse to be identified as Sindhis, which increasingly denotes Sindhi-speaking population. Many Sindhis would apply the term *panahguzeen* to Muhajireen, which literally means shelter-seekers – a derogatory term in present-day Sindh. Surprisingly, in the NWFP and Punjab the terms do not have any negative or positive connotations, though in many cases mutual cooperation and co-existence have precluded the antagonistic patterns of ethnic tensions. Equally, it is curious to note that in Pakistan, the concept of *hyphenated* ethnic identity (Muhajir-Punjabi, Pushtun-Muhajir or Punjabi-Sindhi) has not yet evolved, though one sees a growing receptivity to terms like Pakistani Punjabi, Sindhi Muslim or Pushtun Pakistani.

2. The founder of the MQM, Altaf Hussain, though critical of the PPP (Sindh), occasionally champions the case for a united Pakistan. While remembering the carnage in Hyderabad on 30 September 1988, which caused more than two hundred deaths from indiscriminate firing, he came out with strong pro-federation statements. At a reception of G. M. Syed in Sukkur, his followers desecrated the Pakistani flag and hoisted the Sindhudesh flag instead on 1 October 1989, but Altaf Hussain issued a strong rebuke, demanding the prosecution of such 'anti-Pakistan' elements. See *The Jang* (London), 3, 4 October 1989. According to the SNA, the movement for Sindhudesh will result in a military action, presumably inviting Indian intervention to help 'liberate' Sindh. See G. M. Syed's statement in ibid., 3 October 1989. Benazir Bhutto, during her premiership, described the situation in Sindh as a 'mini insurgency' and gradually became more dependent on the security forces for maintaining order.

3. For details on the manifesto and common charter, see Ahmed Saleem, *Sulugta Hooa Sindh* (Urdu), Lahore, 1990, pp. 210–13.

4. Many Pakistani politicians have found it necessary and tempting to use the symbolic term *quaid* to establish their credentials; the Quaid-i Azam, the founder of Pakistan, remains the ideal evoking respect and bestowing legitimacy on populist leaders.

5. Such practices subsequently became the main reason for its downfall and cases were installed in the summer of 1992 against a number of MQM leaders and members for 'running a parallel state within the state' and unleashing 'a reign of terror' in urban centres.

6. For instance, within the first two weeks of July 1995, the death toll in Karachi had reached 156. The BBC World Service monitored in Oxford, 16 July 1995.

7. Its hitmen selected civilian and para-military targets in Karachi and used rockets, car bombs and machine guns to kill the maximum number of persons. It is amazing to note that despite its persistent campaign of terror, there was no anti-Muhajir retaliation in the NWFP, Punjab or Balochistan. During visits to such places in 1994–95, there was a greatest sense of sadness and shock among the general population.

8. The Muhajireen in Sindh, under the leadership of the MQM, did not openly declare themselves to be a nation as such, although before the elections of 1988 there were occasional demands for the 'fifth nationality'. Similarly, the Sindhi nationalists, despite a rhetorical emphasis on 'separateness' have been using terms like nationality/sub-nationality, nation and ethnicity interchangeably. Occasionally, the MQM leadership would speak of dying for Pakistan and sacrificing everything for the motherland at a time when the Sindhi nationalists were speaking of breaking the Punjabi Muhajir-dominated federation, or vice versa.

9. A number of Urdu speakers privately were indignant of the high-handedness and distanced themselves from the organisation. While being equally critical of official stubbornness, such elements would eagerly differentiate between the MQM and the general Muhajir grievances.

10. Pakistan's nuclear programme was often in the headlines of the world press in the 1980s and early 1990s. See James Adams, 'Pakistan – nuclear war threat', *The Sunday Times*, 27 May 1990 and 'Official Reveals Extent of Pakistan's Bomb-making Program', *International Herald Tribune*, 8–9 February 1992.

11. According to a number of informed sources, the MQM enjoyed official patronage of the Zia regime through state-led intelligence agencies. Based on interviews in Karachi, January 1992.

12. 'Jami'at's confrontation with APMSO in 1988 turned Karachi University into a war zone, leading the military to occupy and close the university. As a result of Jami'at's fighting simultaneously against religious, ethnic, and secular student organisations, great confusion permeated its ranks with delirious consequences,' Seyyed Vali Reza Nasr, 'Students, Islam and Politics: Islami Jamiat-i Tulaba in Pakistan', *Middle East Journal*, XXXXVI (1), 1992, p. 75.

13. For a detailed analysis, see Anwar A. Syed, 'Political Parties and the Nationality Question in Pakistan', *Journal of South Asian and Middle Eastern Studies*, XII (1), Fall 1988, pp. 42–75.

14. 'A former New York taxi driver, newly dubbed a saint, is upsetting the political establishment of Pakistan as he languishes in bed here, surrounded by a posse of young virginal protectresses ... [He] lies muffled up in bed in a humble house in Azizabad, a middle-class area of Karachi, Pakistan's largest and best-armed city. Outside, in the cordoned-off roads leading to his house, hundreds wait, some joining him in his fast. In his bedroom, a group of girls, some no more than 14, clasp hands round the leader's bed, holding back the mob of women who come to kiss his gold-slippered feet. His fast has earned this former pharmacist and taxi driver a new title among his followers – Pir Sahib, or Saint. For the last three days, he has been on a glucose drip to prevent damage to his kidneys.' See *The Observer* (London), 4 April 1990. For more on his life and ideas, see Altaf Hussain's statement given in London to the local Urdu press while residing there during May to June 1990. *The Jang* (London), 14 June 1990. Altaf Hussain has been once again in London since October 1991 for medical treatment and was frequently visited by the Pir of Pagara and the late Jam Sadiq Ali who were also in London for medical treatment. It is curious that all three spent most of their time together making press appearances and attending special

parties hosted for them. *The Jang*, a very pro-MQM newspaper, gave extensive coverage to Altaf Hussain's speeches and messages, many of them
based on his extended telephonic statements to his camp followers across
Britain, Europe and North America. Given the reports of rebellion within
the MQM in the previous summer, Altaf Hussain is reluctant to go back to
Pakistan, ostensibly for personal security reasons, a fact borne out by many
American and British correspondents in South Asia.

15.   For further details see I. Bakhtiar, 'The Altaf Factor', *The Herald*, January
      1993, pp. 59–62.

16.   Campus violence with the IJT as a major factor took the lives of 80 students
      between 1982 and 1988. For details see Zahid Hussain, 'The Campus
      Mafias', *The Herald*, October 1988, p. 52. Also, *The Friday Times* (Lahore),
      14 September 1989, p. 11.

17.   Younis Ahmed, 'The Rise and Fall of Altaf Hussain', *The Herald*, October
      1988, pp. 62–4.

18.   'It was not until Altaf Hussain began to speak to his 50 000 delirious fol-
      lowers in Hyderi Market that one could see why half of Karachi regards
      him as a saint and the other half remembers Germany in the 1930s. The
      37-year old leader of Mohajor Qaumi Movement had the tinted shades,
      droopy moustache and podgy good looks the sub-continent favours in its
      films stars, but graffiti-writers call him "Altaf Killer"' Raymond Whitaker,
      'Pakistan's Top Orator Divides Karachi Voters', *The Independent*, 22
      October 1990.

19.   'No politician in Pakistan can match him for oratory, nor is that the only
      reason they fear him. The MQM has violent ways with the opponents and
      dissidents' (ibid.).

20.   There have been stories of his 'sexual appetite', which reveal his own com-
      plexes multiplied due to the immense amount of power he came to hold
      over so many obedient, simple and 'raw' people. Visiting Urdu-speaking
      areas in Karachi in the late 1980s and early 1990s, multi-storey portraits of
      Hussain with a raised hand looked down on the passers-by. They disap-
      peared however during the military operation.

21.   This was borne out by many Pakistani and foreign correspondents in a
      number of interviews in London and Karachi. Despite numerous attempts at
      various levels, it remained impossible for the present author to see Hussain
      in person. In response to calls and personal encounters with his hosts in
      London – the local MQM leaders – reluctance was constantly shown. Even
      after two years, when pressed for an interview, Manzoor Yazdani, observed:
      'Doctor Sahib, we would let you know when Altaf Bhai would agree to see
      you, but do bring around a Western correspondent.' Their motive was
      clearly to gain publicity and not a generous gesture towards a fellow
      Pakistani academic.

22.   Someone was reported to have said to a credulous Hussain: 'Aapki khub-
      surat ankho ko nazar lag jai gi' (your beautiful eyes will come under some
      alien influence) and so he began wearing dark glasses.

23.   Among many other complexes, Hussain has always been apprehensive of
      pain. For details see Bakhtiar, 'The Altaf Factor'.

24.   Even in 1990, *The Daily Jang*, under the direction of its late editor-owner,
      Mir Khalilur Rahman, gave exaggerated details on Hussain's 'medical
      check-ups' in Harley Street clinics. With a major Muhajir component, the

Jang publications in Pakistan and London repeatedly printed pictures of Hussain in hospital bed or being administered intravenous medicines. Hussain's speeches occasionally made the headlines and were reprinted in all the papers of the *Jang* publications in Karachi. The moment was eclipsed by the military action in 1992, as such generous coverage stopped forthwith. However, a year later, small press-releases and appeals began to resurface complaining of the *zulm* against the Muhajireen.

In the press coverage until June 1992, Hussain would be shown speaking to usually 'huge' groups of followers in Baden-Powell Hall in London and more so to the local women's chapter. Special press notes issued from Manzoor Yazdani's residence, operating as the MQM's overseas headquarters in the Mill Hill area, would appeal to the *qaum* to pray for the health and safety of the Quaid and to send donations for the 'great cause'. In 1991–92, appeals were made by mail and in the press for the hides of sacrificial animals 'to carry out good work in Sindh'. Special newsletters reprinted Hussain's speeches and messages in addition to reports on charity work done under the auspices of MQM in Karachi and Hyderabad. These were meant to elicit wider support for Hussain and MQM, though many in London believed that he did not need any money as 'he was being looked after and provided-for *properly by his friends*'. The information is based on press-clippings of the Pakistani press, MQM's propaganda literature and personal interviews in Karachi, Islamabad and London between 1989 and 1995.

25.   Tim McGirk, 'Bhutto Gags Press as Killers Run Amok', *The Independent*, 30 June 1995.
26.   R. A. Specht *et al.*, *Urbanization in Pakistan. The Case of Karachi*, Copenhagen, 1983, p. 45.
27.   Hamza Alavi, 'The State in Post-Colonial Societies: Pakistan and Bangladesh', in K. Gough and R. Sharma (eds), *Imperialism and Revolution in South Asia*, New Delhi, 1973, p. 162.
28.   For details, see F. Selier and M. Karim (eds), *Migration in Pakistan*, Lahore, 1986.
29.   See Hamza Alavi, 'Pakistan and Islam: Ethnicity and Ideology', Fred Halliday and Hamza Alavi (eds), *State and Ideology in the Middle East and Pakistan*, London, 1987, pp. 64–112.
30.   There are different versions of the sequence of events. The MQM had been active since 1984 organising protest marches to the Tomb of the Quaid-i Azam, and frequently triggered incidents of violence against Pushtun rickshaw drivers.
31.   Tahir Amin, *Ethno-National Movements of Pakistan: Domestic and International Factors*, Islamabad, 1988, p. 281.
32.   For the text see Saleem, *Sulugta Hooa Sindh*, pp. 213–18.
33.   *Dawn*, 16 May 1989.
34.   Anwar Iqbal, 'Is the tide turning against the MQM?', *The Muslim*, 17 May 1989.
35.   See Zaffar Abbas, 'Sindh: Falling Apart?', *The Herald*, May 1989, pp. 27–31.
36.   See *The Pakistan Profile* (London), no. 20, 22 September 1989. Also see Ben Whitaker *et al.*, *The Biharis in Bangladesh*, MRG report no. 111, London, 1982.

37. For details on her press conference in Malaysia, see *The Jang*, 21–2 October 1989.
38. *Dawn*, 2 October 1989.
39. Emma Duncan, *Breaking the Curfew. A Political Journey Through Pakistan*, London, 1989, pp. 168–70; and Christina Lamb, *Waiting For Allah*, London, 1991, pp. 138–66.
40. Zubeida Mustafa, 'Having Daughters: Dilemma of a Mother' and Muhammad Ali Siddiqui, 'Having Sons: Dilemma of a Father', *Dawn*, reproduced in *The Jang*, 29 September 1989.
41. Jean-Pierre Peroncel-Hugoz, 'Eyesore City is a Major Test for Bhutto', *Le Monde*, in *The Guardian*, 30 July 1989.
42. The government of Benazir Bhutto survived the no-confidence motion tabled by the COP in the National Assembly on 1 November by a margin of 12 votes and the immediate dent in her coalition due to the defection of the MQM seemed to have recovered, but this parting of ways was to have its own implications in the future for all concerned. It was then rightly feared that the 'MQM's defection to the opposition might be taken as betrayal to the Sindhis' (*The Times*, 25 October 1989). Another British paper characterised the MQM as the representative of 'an embattled immigrant community in Sind province'. *The Daily Telegraph*, 25 October 1989. Also, Kathy Evans, 'Bhutto Facing "Crisis" Vote', *The Guardian*, 24 October 1989; Christina Lamb, 'Pakistani Premier Faces Battle for her Political Life', *The Financial Times*, 26 October 1989; 'Confidence in Miss Bhutto' (editorial), *The Times*, 26 October 1989. See *The Economist*, 21 and 29 October 1989; and *The Independent*, 1 and 2 November 1989.
43. It was subsequently revealed by Chaudhary Nisar Ali, an IJT minister, 'that it was General Aslam Beg who brought the MQM to the IJT fold. The ISI and military intelligence were also reportedly used to pressurise PPP MNAs to vote against Ms. Bhutto. A videotape was later produced by the PPP government showing two senior ISI officials, Brigadier Imtiaz and Major Aamer, trying to persuade MNAs to switch sides. Brigadier Imtiaz told the MNAs that the army fully backed the opposition's move against Ms. Bhutto' Zahid Hussain, 'The Ides of August', *Newsline*, August 1992, pp. 69–70.
     However, in an interview in London, General Aslam Beg refuted the claim that he ever was involved in aligning MQM with the IJT. For his detailed statement, see *The Daily Jang* (London), 25 July 1993.
44. 'The fighting came during a strike day in the cities of Sind called by the Mohajir Qami [sic] Movement, which represents the families of Muslims who migrated from India at partition, in protest at the detention of mohajir activists … The mohajirs and Miss Bhutto's People's party accuse each other of kidnapping and killing each other's members. The mohajirs say that Miss Bhutto's promises of more money and recognition for the community have not been fulfilled. Karachi is Pakistan's largest city, one of the world's great drug entry points and home to large numbers of armed Pathans from Afghanistan. The mix is often deadly' (*The Daily Telegraph*, 8 February 1990). See also *The Independent*, 8 February 1990.
45. 'Pakistan's worsening political crisis will continue as long as there is no real trust between the PPP and the opposition. PPP leaders admit that Ms Bhutto lacks the vision to seek reconciliation with the opposition, but it is

equally true that the opposition is determined to topple her, even if it means the return of the martial law. Although the army is unlikely to oust her for the moment, it has now returned fully to centre-stage, running Pakistan's foreign policy, negotiating hostage exchanges in Karachi, enforcing curfews and keeping the peace in the recent by-election. It looks less and less likely that Ms Bhutto or democracy will regain the political initiative' (*The Independent*, 26 February 1990).

46. *International Herald Tribune*, 28 May 1990. 'A spokesman for Ms Bhutto in Islamabad claimed that gunmen were concealed among the protesting women in Hyderabad and said the government was in a no-win situation. "When the Sind police did not act everybody hit them over the head and when they do they get accused of rape and pillage", he said. There is speculation that the Prime Minister is considering putting the province under direct rule from Islamabad. However such is the level of public frustration that many are demanding martial law. Yesterday's deployment of troops marked the second time Ms Bhutto has resorted to the army to maintain order. The army has been reluctant to get involved in policing Sind at a time of growing tension with India over Kashmir. The higher echelons of the army have also complained about Ms Bhutto's reluctance to come to a political agreement with the MQM' (*The Guardian*, 28 May 1990; and *The Independent*, 25 May 1990).

47. *The Times*, 4 June 1990. It has been suggested that General Beg and the ISI conspired to destabilise the Bhutto government and that the MQM was used as a pawn in the chess game. 'The police operation against the MQM in Hyderabad in the last week of May [1990] was used to prepare the ground for Bhutto's overthrow' (Hussain, 'The Ides of August', p. 70).

48. *The Guardian*, 28 May 1990.

49. 'Most observers believe that in the aftermath of the killings, a renewal of the discussions would be almost impossible' (Kathy Evans, 'Bhutto Deploys Army in Cities', *The Guardian*, 30 May 1990).

50. 'A senior Sind official claimed that there was an orchestrated campaign by the army to run down the Sind administration, the police, and the judiciary so that pressure for martial law was increased' (*The Guardian*, 29 May 1990).

51. Ibid.

52. 'Any crackdown needs the cooperation of the army, which is demanding that it should be aimed even-handedly at terrorists from the PPP and the MQM. Ms Bhutto is balking at this because it would erode her support among her fellow Sindhis who back the PPP' (*The Independent*, 5 June 1990).

53. 'Rising Tide of Ethnic Unrest in Sind', *The Pakistan Profile*, no. 36, 1–14 June 1990, p. 2.

54. Raymond Whitaker, 'Bhutto has yet to Usher in Age of Enlightenment', *The Independent*, 30 May 1990. The tension between the army and Benazir Bhutto was reportedly centred on the extent of authority the military was to enjoy in case of a crack-down over the militants and outlaws. The army insisted that the operation should be against terrorists both within MQM and the ruling PPP, and those arrested should be tried in special military courts.

55. 'The generals met again on July 22 to finalise their strategy. Bhutto had to be removed and a contingency plan was formulated. The President was told

to remove the government by August 14 or else the army would step in directly. This time round President Ghulam Ishaq was only too willing to oblige as relations between him and Bhutto had hit an all-time low. The opposition had already been taken into confidence and the stage was set for the return of a shadow military government' (Hussain, 'The Ides of August', p. 70.

56. 'Pressure from the military coincides with growing signs of discontent within Bhutto's own party. Opposition circles suggest that meaningful national reconciliation can be achieved only under a new leadership of the PPP. Ms. Bhutto appears increasingly isolated, protected by a circle of fanatically loyal aides from the storm of criticism emerging in the ranks of her party. Resentment is also growing about the influence her husband, Asif exerts over her' (Kathy Evans, 'Bhutto Party Splits over Sind Policy', *The Guardian*, 14 June 1990.

57. Ahmed Rashid, 'Jam Sadeq Ali' (obituary), *The Independent*, 6 March 1992. Also Syed Ghulam Mustafa Shah, *Jam Sadiq Ali*, Karachi, 1993.

58. Jam returned that favour in 1991–92, when BCCI was closed and international pressure mounted on Pakistan to hand over Abedi for trial. Jam, the then chief minister, refused to submit. He provided full protection to his former benefactor in Karachi.

59. Ahmed Rashid, op. cit.

60. His wide circles of friends, including quite a few British, admired his generosity and were prepared to overlook his harshness towards the PPP. Based on interviews in London and Karachi in 1992–93.

61. Ahmed Rashid, op. cit.

62. In a report in 1992 it was revealed that there were at least a hundred organised groups of dacoits active in Sindh. Each group commanded the loyalty of scores of followers. Furthermore, 5000 influentials – *patharidars* – provided protection to such miscreants across the province. From 1984 to 1990, 6000 individuals were released by the dacoits after exacting ransom and 1000 were killed. In another report, the total number of dacoits in Sindh was estimated to be 17 000 with open enticements by some notorious dacoits for new recruits. For details, see 'Sind mein Dacoan Ka Masalla' (Dacoits in Sindh) (editorial), *The Daily Jang*, London, 1 May 1991.

63. Kathy Evans, 'Top Military Officials Want Early Election in Pakistan', *The Guardian*, 14 May 1992.

64. Derek Brown, 'Pakistani Army to Stamp on Sind Gangsters', *The Guardian*, 20 May 1992.

65. For details of crimes committed by MQM hit squads in the torture houses, see *Weekly Takbeer*, (Karachi), 1 July 1992. Without underestimating the extent of violence, one needs to be careful given the dissensions between the magazine and the MQM leadership.

66. Razia Bhatti, 'Editor's Note', *Newsline*, August 1992, p. 11.

67. 'After a successful kidnap operation the urban gangs would pass the victims to their rural Sindhi counterparts for "safe keeping". Crime, it appears, unlike almost everything else is not necessarily divided on ethnic lines.' (Hasan Mujtaba, 'Keti Jamshoro', ibid., p. 25).

68. 'During a recent tour of Karachi, a visibly concerned Nawaz Sharif asked an official of the Citizens–Police Liaison Committee (CPLC) why the authori-

ties had failed to curb the rising incidence of car theft in the city. The CPLC official promptly replied, "How can crime be controlled when car snatchers enjoy the blessings and patronage of powerful advisers in the government?" To substantiate his statement, the official requested the Prime Minister to issue on-the-spot orders to raid the house of a provincial adviser. "There are at least four stolen cars parked at the adviser's house", he informed the Prime Minster. Perhaps aware of the adverse political fallout the raid could have on his government, Mr. Sharif advised the CPLC official to bring the issue to the Sindh chief minister's notice in writing. But before the official could write to the chief minister the adviser was tipped off, and the cars had disappeared from his house within a few hours.' For further details on orchestrated crime enjoying the support of influential people in the Sindh government, see Zahid Hussain and Hasan Mujtaba, 'Crime and Politics' (cover story), *Newsline*, August 1992, pp. 2–22.

Marwat was named as a major patron of car thieves operating in Balochistan and Sindh by some officials of the Field Investigation Team (FIT) in early 1993. His contacts included provincial ministers and sons of senior bureaucrats who had been caught red-handed. The inquiry was about to begin 'when a message was received from a very important political personality, who reportedly asked the investigators not to proceed any further'. For details see Mazhar Abbas, 'Operation Cover-up', *The Herald*, April 1993, p. 57.

69. The list included 60 names from the MQM, a few names from the Al-Zulfiqar Organisation (AZO) and some Sindhi *patharidars*, some of whom like the minister Sher Jan Mazari held important positions in the government. Those from the MQM, included Dr Imran Farooq, Salim Shahzad, Suhail Mashadi, Javed Langra, Maqsood and Safdar Baqri. In the case of the AZO, other than its top leaders, it included Ghulam Rasool Hingoro, Ghulam Mustafa Korai and Ali Sunnara (the last reputedly being the AZO commander for Sindh). Certain members of the government like Syed Qabool Shah, Ghulam Hussain Unnar and Anwer Nizamani were listed for harbouring the criminals. Other *patharidars* included PPP MNAs like Syed Parvez Ali Shah, Sattar Bachani and Zafar Ali Leghari, Senator Amir Magsi and regional influentials like Malik Asad Sikander, Agha Tariq Pathan, Imdad Mohammd Shah, Syed Shabbir Ahmed Shah, Mohammed Thebo, Tahrani, Saif Otho, Haji Ramzan Chandio, Diriani Mal, Waseem Ahmed, Mureed Shah, Gul Mugheri, Ayub Junejo, Wazir Kalhoro, Amir Ali Goddar, Mumtaz Shah, Abdullah Chandio, Ejaz Hussain Shah, Haji Rehmatullah, Zafar Ali Leghari. All of them were allegedly involved in harbouring dacoits, thieves and other dangerous criminals. For further details, see Mazhar Abbas, 'And Now for the Most Wanted List ...', *The Herald*, September 1992, pp. 20–1.

70. Various versions have been given of the nature, timing and rationale for Operation Clean-up, but it appears that in Hyderabad the MQM leadership found itself well prepared in advance. Though last-minute efforts persisted for some deal through Ishtiaq Azhar and Islam Nabi, the federal minster, to avert the operation, the MQM had forewarned its cadres to prepare for the worst. Hussain is reported to have told his close aides long in advance: 'My life is in danger. If I am assassinated, no one from the other community

should be held responsible but those who wear the *baray baray phool* (the big, big stars) on their shoulders' (quoted in Hasan Mujtaba, 'A Party in Hiding', *Newsline*, August 1992, p. 49).

71.　A letter, written to the editor of a monthly, concluded: 'It would suffice to say that the MQM seems to have outlived its utility as the establishment's political filibuster and so, for the MQM, toll the bells of doom' (Arif Ali (Sukkur), 'End of Empire', *The Herald*, August 1992, p. 13).

72.　In one case the officer was court-martialled while in the other case it was given out that the prisoners died of heart attack and not by suffocation or heat.

73.　'The army's unilateral actions predictably sparked tensions with the civilian components of troika. The president and the prime minister were now said to be on one side, and the army brass firmly on the other. These differences came into public view when two of the prime minister's most trusted lieutenants, Chaudhry Nisar Ali and Ghulam Hyder Wyne, spoke out against the way the operation was being conducted in the urban areas of Sindh' (Idrees Bakhtiar, 'Is the Army Here To Stay?' (cover story), ibid., August 1992, p. 26).

74.　S. Akbar Zaidi, 'The Roots of the Crisis', ibid., pp. 32–5.

75.　Ayaz Amir, 'Strategic Withdrawal?' *The Herald*, October 1992, pp. 37–8.

76.　It was felt that the MQM had been created, used and punished by the same forces, and most of the people wanted as criminals, until a few weeks earlier, had been ministers, parliamentarians and partners in coalitions. The chickens were coming home to roost, as was bluntly noted in an editorial comment: 'The MQM has been nurtured by the civil and military establishments since the Zia days, and the perils of supporting groups for political ends should be very obvious now. The MQM became a byword for terror but it was only when it threatened the army's self-respect that the need to break its might was felt.

'Stymied by the inaccessibility of its erstwhile allies and desperate to produce results, the army is now using methods that would have done the MQM proud. Nothing the MQM did justifies the illegal detention of innocent people or the horrifying incidents of torture that are now the order of the day among the mohajir population of Karachi' (*Newsline*, November 1992, p. 13).

77.　A few days later, Azeem Tariq, the chairman of the MQM, was killed while asleep in his home. Tariq, a close confidante of Hussain, had recently resurfaced from his hiding and apologised to all and sundry for excesses committed in the name of the organisation. As a moderate voice, he was trying to patch up the differences with the Haqiqi rebels and was in the process of revamping the entire movement. It took the authorities to trace down his assassin, Inam ul Haq, whom they came upon by chance while carrying out searches in the neighbourhood. In an identity parade, he was duly recognised as the murderer by the widow and brother-in-law of the deceased MQM leader. Under interrogation, Haq, the former personal guard to Altaf Hussain, confessed. He acknowledged his continued contacts with Hussain and supplied details of the other accomplices. According to his statement, read out by the DIG Karachi police, the plan to murder Tariq was planned by Dr Khalid Maqbool Siddiqui, chairman of the APMSO, in collaboration with other Altaf loyalists. Further revelations about the murder case would certainly damage the MQM and Hussain to a significant extent. For details, see *The Daily Awaz International*, London, 13, 14 July 1993.

Regardless of who ordered the assassination, the differences between Tariq and Hussain had been wide-ranging. Hussain suspected Tariq of building contacts with the establishment over and above the former's authority. Hussain also felt that Tariq, who had been *de facto* in charge of the MQM's finances, had not given him sufficient funds and was angry over rumours about his flight to London along with two *crores* (20 million) of rupees. It is noteworthy that details of the MQM accounts have remained a well-guarded secret through the history of the organisation. See, Idreess Bakhtiar, 'The Acid Test', *The Herald*, March 1993, pp. 61–3.

78. For such and other, related, in-depth analyses, see *Newsline* (Karachi Special), March 1995.

79. Christopher Thomas, 'Snipers get Upper Hand in Karachi Violence', *The Times*, 21 December 1994.

80. 'Confronting an Enemy Within' (editorial), *The Guardian*, 9 March 1995.

81 By 29 June 1995, 800 people had been killed in ethnic violence since the beginning of the year. *The Independent*, 30 June 1995.

82. Quoted in ibid.

83. According to the figures revealed to the national assembly in February 1995, the army's clean-up operation in Karachi had cost the nation 750 million rupees in less than 30 months. It was further revealed that from June 1992 until early 1995, 4091 murders had been reported in the city due to ethnic and sectarian clashes in addition to 3505 dacoities. See *The Jang*, 11 February 1995. Two years earlier, a press report had suggested that the operation was costing 10 million rupees per day. *The Daily Awaz*, 15 July 1993.

84. Disorder in Karachi has seriously damaged Pakistan's economy, with national and foreign investors avoiding the city. Within a year the Karachi Stock Exchange Index plummeted from 2600 to 1400. *The Financial Times*, 29 June 1995.

85. For instance, in just the first two weeks of June more than one hundred people were killed by 'unknown' assailants. The miscreants, riding taxis or stolen cars, would barge into public places, including civil offices, and start their killing sprees. The BBC World Service, monitored in Oxford, 17 June 1995.

86. Marwat, a former leader of the PPI and son-in-law of Ishaque Khan, the former Pakistani president, headed the civil administration in Sindh. He appointed his own favourite, Samiullah Marwat, as the head of the Federal Investigation Agency (FIA) and manipulated his powers to maximum advantage. He has been involved in publicly recorded kidnaps, car thefts, rapes and numerous cases of extortion. His cases were made public by investigative journalism, with *The Herald* leading the team. In its October 1991 issue, the Karachi-based monthly carried all the details of Marwat's reign of terror and, following massive public demand, ran 15 editions until S. Rahman, its woman editor, could not meet any more demands. Marwat allegedly tortured a number of PPP activists besides allegedly ordering the rape of V. Hayat, one of Ms Bhutto's closest friends. But, when Benazir

Bhutto came into power, for some unknown reason, cases against Marwat were quietly withdrawn by the PPP government.

87. *The Independent*, 26 June 1995. The talks at the lower-tier level between the PPP and the MQM in July 1995 took place amidst uncertainty and mutual recrimination with each side pressurising the other with a long list of demands.

88. The murder of the MQM's chairman, Azeem Tariq, only served to marginalise moderate elements from within the MQM. Hussain, through his network of the faithful and avowed militants, has been able to re-establish his control over the movement unilaterally, though people had initially hoped that, with the lapse of time, the party would change its tactics of ever-confrontational politics.

89. It was being widely suggested in Pakistan and abroad that the militants would mainly target non-Urdu speakers except when the two factions of the MQM were fighting each other. Based on interviews in Pakistan and the United Kingdom, 1994–5.

Bibliography

Special Collections

Lord Attlee Papers, The Bodleian Library, University of Oxford.
Christopher Beaumont Papers, All Souls College, University of Oxford.
Professor Reginald Coupland Papers, The Rhodes House Library, Oxford.
Sir George Cunningham Papers, India Office Records & Library (IOR & L), London.
Sir Malcolm L. Darling Papers, The Centre of South Asian Studies, University of Cambridge.
Sir Percival Griffiths' Papers, IOR & L, London.
Sir Francis Mudie Collection, IOR & L, London.
Ian M. Stephens Papers, The Centre of South Asian Studies, University of Cambridge.
Professor Edward Thompson Papers, The Bodleian Library, University of Oxford.

Official Collections/Correspondence/Documents

Government of Pakistan, *Quaid-e-Azam Mohamed Ali Jinnah: Speeches and Governor-General, 1947–1948*, Karachi, 1948.
——, *Constituent Assembly of Pakistan Debates, 1949*, vol. V, Karachi, 1949.
——, *Report of the Press Commission*, Karachi, 1954.
——, *Constituent Assembly of Pakistan Debates, 1956*, vol. I, Karachi, 1956.
——, *Report of the Land Reforms Commission for West Pakistan*, 1959, Lahore, 1959.
——, *Population Census of Pakistan*, Karachi, 1961.
——, *White Paper on the Performance of the Bhutto Regime*, Islamabad, 1979.
——, *Population Census of 1981*, Islamabad, 1981.
——, *Report of the Pakistan Commission on the Status of Women*, Islamabad, 1985.
Government of the Punjab, *Report of the Court of the Inquiry Constituted under the Punjab Act II of 1954 to enquire into the Punjab Disturbances of 1953* (Munir Report), Lahore, 1954.
HM Government, *Pakistan: Iskander Mirza's Visit to the United Kingdom (1957)*, DO/35–6520, PRO.
——, *Pakistan, Liaquat Ali Khan's Assassination*, DO/35–2981, 2983, 2985, 2987 and 3188, PRO.
——, *Pakistan: Nazim-ud Din's Dismissal*, DO/35–5106, 5107A, 5107B, PRO.
——, *N.W.F.P.*, DO/35–5329 and 5330, PRO.
——, *The Punjab Boundary Award*, DO/35–3054, PRO.
——, *PRODA*, DO/35–5111, 5112, 5114, 5115 and 5118, PRO.
——, *Jama'at-i-Islami*, DO/35–5154, PRO.
——, *Report on Sind*, DO/35–5322, PRO.
——, *U.S. Aid to Pakistan*, DO/35–5564 and 5565, PRO
——, *Pakistan: Treausry Papers*, T236/–1331, 2170 and 2620, PRO.
——, *Fortnightly Governor's Reports*, L/P & J/5/249, IOR & L, London.

——, *Report on the Situation in the Punjab*, L/P & J/5/247, IOR & L, London.
——, *Fortnightly Reports from Pakistan*, L/P & S/13/1845, IOR & L, London.
US Government, Department of State, *Security Decision-Making in Pakistan* (authored by Stephen Cohen), Washington, DC, 1984.
Mansergh, N., Moon, Penderel, *et al.* (eds), *The Transfer of Power 1942–47*, vol. IX, London, 1980.

Special Reports and Seminar Papers

The Asian Bank, *Strategies for Economic Growth and Development: The Bank's Role in Pakistan*, Manilla, 1985.
Damodaran, V. 'Violence in Countryside. Agrarian Unrest and Communal Rioting in the Villages of Bihar, November 1946', a paper presented in South Asian History Seminar Series, St Antony's College, Oxford, 8 May 1990.
Human Rights Watch, *Double Jeopardy: Police Abuse of Women in Pakistan* (An Asia Watch Report), New York, 1992.
Ife, Douglas Stanton, 'Sunset of the Raj: A View by the ICS', a paper presented in Commonwealth Seminar Series, Nuffield College, Oxford, 2 February 1990.
International Commission of Jurists, *The Events in East Pakistan*, Geneva, 1971.
International Institute for Strategic Studies, *Military Balance, 1992–1993*, London, 1992.
Kapur, Harish, 'India's Foreign Policy', a paper presented in Contemporary South Asia Seminar Series, Queen Elizabeth House, 30 January 1992.
Rizvi, Gowher and Mitra, Subrata K., 'The State and Civil Society in South Asia', a paper presented at South Asia Conference, Nuffield College, Oxford, 27–28 June 1992.
Rhodes House, *The Rhodes Trust and Rhodes House*, Oxford, 1992.
——, *A Register of Rhodes Scholars, 1903–1981*, Oxford, 1981.
United Nations Development Programme, *Human Development Report*, (1990–95), Oxford, 1990–95.
Whitaker, Ben, *et al.*, *The Biharis in Bangladesh*, MRG Report No. 111, London, 1982.
The World Bank, *World Development Report* (1990–95), Oxford, 1990–95.

Books

Afzal, M. Rafique, *Political Parties in Pakistan, 1947–1958*, vol. I, Islamabad, 1986 (reprint).
Ahmad, Aziz, *Islamic Modernism in India and Pakistan, 1857–1964*, Oxford, 1967.
Ahmad, Jamil-ud Din, (ed.), *Speeches and Writings of Mr. Jinnah*, vol. II, Lahore, 1964.
Ahmad, Riaz, *Constitutional and Political Developments in Pakistan, 1951–54*, Rawalpindi, 1981.
Ahmad, Saghir, *Class and Power in Punjab Village*, New York, 1977.
Ahmad, Syed Nur, *Mian Fazl-i-Husain. A Review of His Life and Work*, Lahore, 1936.

——, *Martial Law Say Martial Law Tak*, translated by Mahmud Ali and edited by Craig Baxter, Boulder, 1988.

Ahmed, Akbar S., *Pakistan Society: Islam, Ethnicity and Leadership in South Asia*, Karachi, 1986.

Ahmed, Leila, *Women and Gender in Islam*, New Haven, 1992.

Ahmed, Muneer, *Pakistan Mein Intelligence Agencion Ka Siyasi Kirdar* (Urdu), Lahore, 1993.

Ahmed, Rafiuddin, *The Bengal Muslims, 1871–1906: A Quest for Identity*, Delhi, 1981.

Akbar, M. J., *Nehru: The Making of India*, London, 1988.

Alavi, Hamza and Halliday, Fred (eds), *State and Ideology in the Middle East and Pakistan*, London, 1987.

Ali, Chaudhri Muhammad, *The Emergence of Pakistan*, New York, 1967.

Ali, Imran, *Punjab Under Imperialism, 1885–1947*, London, 1989.

Ali, Mubarik, *Sindh: Khammoshi Ki Awaz* (Urdu), Lahore, 1992.

Ali, Tariq, *Can Pakistan Survive? The Death of a State*, Harmondsworth, 1983.

Amin, Tahir, *Ethno-National Movements of Pakistan: Domestic and International Factors*, Islamabad, 1988.

Anderson, Benedict, *Imagined Communities*, London, 1990 (reprint).

Anjum, Wakeel, *Siyasat Kay Firoan* (Urdu), Lahore, 1992.

Ansari, Sarah F. D., *Sufi Saints and State Power. The Pirs of Sind, 1843–1947*, Cambridge, 1992.

Aziz, K. K., *Party Politics in Pakistan, 1947–58*, Islamabad, 1976.

Baloch, Inayatullah, *Greater Baluchistan: A Study of Baluch Nationalism*, Stuttgart, 1987.

Baluch, Mir Ahmad Yar Khan, *Inside Baluchistan*, Karachi, 1975.

Baqai, Moin and Haq, Mahbub-ul (eds), *Employment, Distribution and Basic Needs in Pakistan*, Lahore, 1986.

Barth, Frederick, *Leadership Among the Swat Pathans*, London, 1972.

Baxter, Craig, *et al.*, *Pakistan Under the Military. Eleven Years of Zia-ul-Haq*, Boulder 1991.

Bayly, C. A., *Rulers, Townsmen and Bazaars. North Indian Society in the Age of British Expansion, 1770–1870*, Cambridge, 1983.

Beck, Lewis White (ed.), *Kant. Selections*, New York, 1988.

Bhutto, Benazir, *Daughter of the East*, London, 1988.

Binder, Leonard, *Religion and Politics in Pakistan*, Berkeley, 1961.

Bose, Sugata, (ed.), *South Asia and World Capitalism*, Delhi, 1990.

Braibanti, Ralph, *Research on the Bureaucracy of Pakistan*, Durham, 1966.

Brass, Paul, *Language, Religion and Politics in North India*, Cambridge, 1974.

Burki, Shahid Javed, *Pakistan Under Bhutto, 1971–1977*, London, 1988 (reprint).

Burki, Shahid Javed and LaPorte, Robert Jr, (eds), *Pakistan's Development Priorities: Choices for the Future*, Karachi, 1985.

Callard, Keith, *Pakistan: A Political Study*, London, 1957.

Campbell-Johnson, A., *Mission with Mountbatten*, London, 1951.

Cheema, P. I., *Pakistan's Defence Policy, 1947–58*, London, 1990.

Chishti, Faiz Ali, *Betrayals of Another Kind*, London, 1989.

——, *Zia, Bhutto Aur Mein* (Urdu), Lahore, 1992.

Choudhury, G. W., *Constitutional Developments in Pakistan*, New York, 1959 (reprinted 1969).

——, *Last Days of United Pakistan*, London, 1974.
——, *Pakistan: Transition from Military to Civilian Rule*, London, 1988.
Clapham, Christopher and Philip, George (eds), *The Political Dilemmas of Military Regimes*, London, 1985.
Cohen, Stephen, *The Pakistan Army*, Berkeley, 1984.
Corson, J. Henry, *et al.* (eds), *Contemporary Problems of Pakistan*, Leiden, 1974.
Darling, Malcolm Lyall, *Rusious Loquitur*, London, 1930.
Desai, A. R., *Social Background of Indian Nationalism*, Bombay, 1966.
DeVos, George and Romanucci-Ross, L. (eds), *Ethnic Identity and Change*, Palo Alto, 1975.
Duncan, Emma, *Breaking the Curfew. A Political Journey Through Pakistan*, London, 1989.
Durrani, Tehmina, *My Feudal Lord*, Lahore, 1991.
Easton, David, *A Systems Analysis of Political Life*, New York, 1965.
Egger, R., *The Development of Public Administration in Pakistan*, Karachi, 1953.
Eglar, Z., *A Punjabi Village in Pakistan*, New York, 1960.
Embree, Ainslee T. (ed.), *Pakistan's Western Borderland. The Transformation of a Political Order*, Durham, 1977.
Emerson, Rupert, *From Empire to Nation*, Cambridge, Mass., 1960.
Engineer, Asghar Ali, *Trial of Benazir Bhutto: An Insight into the Status of Women in Islam*, Bombay, 1990.
Feldman, Herbert, *From Crisis to Crisis*, London, 1972.
Ferguson, Adam, *An Essay on the History of Civil Society*, New Brunswick, 1980 (reprint).
Gardezi, H., and Rashid, J. (eds), *Pakistan: The Roots of Dictatorship*, London, 1983.
Gauhar, Altaf, *Ayub Khan: Pakistan's First Military Ruler*, Lahore, 1993.
Geertz, Clifford, *Old Societies and New States. The Quest for Modernity in Asia and Africa*, New York, 1963.
Gilmartin, David, *Empire and Islam. Punjab and the Making of Pakistan*, London, 1988.
Goodnow, H. F., *The Civil Service of Pakistan*, New Haven, 1964.
Gough, K. and Sharma, R. (eds.), *Imperialism and Revolution in South Asia*, New Delhi, 1973.
Gramsci, Antonio, *Selections from the Prison Notebooks*, translated and edited by Quinton Hoare and Geoffrey N. Smith, London, 1971.
Griffin, L. H. and Massy, C. F., *Chiefs and Families of Note in the Punjab*, 2 vols, Lahore, 1940.
Hafeez, Sabiha, *The Metropolitan Women in Pakistan: Studies*, Karachi, 1981.
Haq, Mahbubul, *A Strategy of Economic Planning: A Case Study of Pakistan*, Karachi, 1968.
Hardy, Peter, *The Muslims of British India*, Cambridge, 1972.
Harrison, Selig S., *In Afghanistan's Shadow: Baluch Nationalism and Soviet Temptations*, New York, 1981.
Hasan, Mushirul, *Nationalism and Communal Politics in India, 1916–1928*, Delhi, 1978.
Hobsbawm, E. J., *Nations and Nationalism since 1780: Programme, Myth, Reality*, Cambridge, 1990.

Horowitz, Donald L., *Ethnic Groups in Conflict*, Berkeley, 1985.

Hughes, A. W., *The Country of Baluchistan: Its Geography, Topography, Ethnology and History*, London, 1877.

Huntington, Samuel P., *Political Order in Changing Societies*, New Haven, 1968.

Husain, Azim, *Fazl-i-Husain. A Political Biography*, Bombay, 1946.

Hussain, Asaf, *Elite Politics in an Ideological State*, London, 1979.

Ikramullah, Begum Shaista Suhrawardy, *Huseyn Shaheed Suhrawardy: A Biography*, Karachi, 1991.

Inden, Ronald B., *Imagining India*, Oxford, 1990.

Iqbal, Javed (ed.), *Stray Reflections: A Note-Book of Allama Iqbal*, Lahore, 1961.

Islam, M. Nazrul, *Pakistan and Malaysia. A Comparative Study in National Integration*, New Delhi, 1989.

Jahan, Rounaq, *Pakistan: Failure in National Integration*, New York, 1972.

Jalal, Ayesha, *The Sole Spokesman: Jinnah, the Muslim League and the Demand for Pakistan*, Cambridge, 1985.

——, *The State of Martial Rule in Pakistan: The Origins of Pakistan's Political Economy of Defence*, Cambridge, 1990.

James, Maurice, *Pakistan Chronicle*, London, 1992.

James, William E. and Roy Subroto (eds), *Foundations of Pakistan's Political Economy. Towards an Agenda for the 1990s*, New Delhi, 1992.

Jansson, Erland, *India, Pakistan, or Pakhtunistan? The Nationalist Movement in the North-West West Frontier Province 1937–47*, Stockholm, 1981.

Jayawardena, K., *Feminism and Nationalism in the Third World*, London, 1988.

Kalia, Barkat Ram, *A History of the Development of the Police in the Punjab, 1849–1905*, Lahore, 1929.

Kandiyoti, Deniz (ed.), *Women, Islam and the State*, London, 1991.

Keay, John, *The Gilgit Game. The Explorers of the Western Himalayas 1865–95*, London, 1979.

Keddie, Nikki and Beck, Lois (eds), *Women in the Muslim World*, Cambridge, Mass., 1978.

Kedourie, E., *Nationalism*, London, 1961.

Kennedy, Charles H. *Bureaucracy in Pakistan*, Karachi, 1987.

——, (ed.), *Pakistan 1992*, Oxford, 1993.

Khan, Ansar Zahid, *History and Culture of Sind*, Karachi, 1980.

Khan, M. Asghar (ed.), *Islam, Politics and the State. The Pakistan Experience*, London, 1985.

Khan, Mazhar ul Haq, *Purdah and Polygamy: A Study in Social Pathology of the Muslim Society*, Peshawar, 1972.

Khuro, Hamida, *The Making of Modern Sindh: British Policy and Social change in the Nineteenth Century*, Karachi, 1978.

——, (ed.), *Sind Through the Centuries*, Karachi, 1987.

Khuro, M. Ayub, *A Story of the Sufferings of Sind: A Case for the Separation of Sind from the Bombay Presidency*, Karachi, 1930.

Kochanek, Stanley, *Interest Groups and Development Business and Politics in Pakistan*, Karachi, 1983.

Kohn, Hans, *The Idea of Nationalism*, New York, 1967.

Kool, Maarten L. *et al.*, *Squatter Settlements in Pakistan*, Lahore, 1988.

Lamb, Christina, *Waiting for Allah. Pakistan's Struggle for Democracy*, London, 1991.

Lambrick, H. T., *The Terrorist*, London, 1972.
——, *Sind: A General Introduction*, Hyderabad, 1975.
——, *Sind: A General Introduction*, Hyderabad, 1975 (reprint).
LaPorte, Robert Jr, *Power and Privilege. Influence and Decision-Making in Pakistan*, Berkeley, 1975.
Laswell, Harold D. and Kaplan, Abraham, *Power and Society: A Framework for Political Inquiry*, New Haven, 1950.
Lateef, Shahida, *Muslim Women in India. Political & Private Realities: 1890s–1980s*, London, 1990.
Leitner, G. W., *The Languages and Races of Dardistan*, Lahore, 1977.
Lerner, Gerda, *The Creation of Patriarchy*, New York, 1986.
Locke, John, *Two Treatises of Civil Government*, London, 1924.
Low, D. A. (ed.), *Soundings in Modern South Asian History*, Berkeley, 1968.
——(ed.), *The Political Inheritance of Pakistan*, Cambridge, 1990.
Mahmud, Safdar, *A Political Study of Pakistan*, Lahore, 1984.
Malik, Hafeez (ed.), *Dilemmas of National Security and Cooperation in India and Pakistan*, New York, 1993.
Malik, Iftikhar H., *Sikandar Hayat Khan: A Political Biography*, Islamabad, 1985.
——, *US–South Asian Relations, 1940–47. American Attitude towards the Pakistan Movement*, London, 1991.
Marri, Mir Khuda Bakhsh, *Searchlight on the Baluchis and Baluchistan*, Karachi, 1974.
Marx, Karl, *Early Texts*, translated by David McLellan, Oxford, 1971.
Masson, Charles, *Narratives of Various Journeys in Baluchistan, Afghanistan and the Punjab*, 3 vols, Karachi, 1974.
Masud, M., *Hari Report: Note of Dissent*, Karachi, 1948.
Matheson, Sylvia A., *The Tigers of Baluchistan*, Karachi, 1975.
Maudoodi, Maulana, *Mussalman aur Maujuda Siyasi Kashmakash* (Urdu), vol. III, Pathankot, 1942.
——, *Purdah* (Urdu), Lahore, 1964.
——, *Tehrik-i-Azadi-i-Hind and Mussalman* (Urdu), Lahore, 1974 (reprint).
Mernissi, Fatima, *Women and Islam. An Historical and Theological Enquiry*, translated by Mary Jo Lakeland, Oxford, 1992.
Metcalf, Thomas R., *Land, Landlords, and the British Raj: Northern India in the Nineteenth Century*, Berkeley, 1979.
Minault, Gail (ed.), *The Extended Family: Women and Political Participation in India and Pakistan*, New Delhi, 1981.
Mirak, Mir Yusuf, *Tarikh i Mazhar i Shah Jahani*, edited by Pir H. Rashdi, Hyderabad, 1962.
Mirza, Sarfaraz Hussain, *Muslim Women's Role in the Pakistan Movement*, Lahore, 1981 (reprint).
Moon, Penderel, *The British Conquest and Dominion of India*, London, 1990.
Moynihan, Daniel P., *Pandaemonium*, Oxford, 1993.
Mumtaz, Khawar and Shaheed, Farida, *Women of Pakistan. Two Steps Forward. One Step Back?* London, 1987.
Myrdal, Gunnar, *Asian Drama: An Inquiry into the Poverty of Nations*, 3 vols, New York, 1968.
Nasir, Mir Gul Khan, *Tarikh-i-Mastung*, Kalat, 1979.

Nayak, Pandav (ed.), *Pakistan: Dilemmas of a Developing State*, New Jaipur, 1985.

Newberg, Paula, *Judging the State: Cowts and Constitutional Politics in Pakistan*, Cambridge, 1995.

Niazi, Zamir, *The Press in Chains*, Karachi, 1987 (reprint).

Noman, Omar, *Pakistan: Political and Economic History Since 1947*, London, 1990 (reprint).

Noon, Firoz Khan, *From Memory*, Lahore, 1966.

Page, David, *Prelude to Partition. The Indian Muslims and the Imperial System of Control 1920–1932*, Delhi, 1987 (reprint).

Phadnis, Urmila, *Ethnicity and Nation-building in South Asia*, New Delhi, 1990.

Powell, A. A., *Muslims and Missionaries in Pre-Mutiny India*, London, 1992.

Qureshi, Ishtiaq Husain, *Ulema in Politics*, Karachi, 1974 (2nd edn).

Rahman, Fazlur, *Islam*, London, 1966.

Rahman, Mushtaqur, *Land and Life in Sindh, Pakistan*, Lahore, 1993.

Ram, Raj Bahadur H., *Sandeman in Baluchistan*, Calcutta, 1916.

Ramay, Hanif, *Punjab Ka Siyasi Muqqidamma*, Lahore, 1987.

Ranger, Terence and Hobsbawm, Eric (eds), *The Invention of Tradition*, Cambridge, 1984.

Rex, John, *Race and Ethnicity*, Milton Keynes, 1986.

Riaz, Fahmida, *Pakistan. Literature and Society*, New Delhi, 1986.

Rittenberg, Stephen A., *Ethnicity, Nationalism and the Pakhtuns. The Independence Movement in India's North-West Frontier Province*, Durham, 1988.

Rizvi, Hasan-Askari, *The Military and Politics in Pakistan, 1947–86*, Lahore, 1988 (2nd edn).

Robinson, Francis, *Separatism Among Indian Muslims. The Politics of the United Provinces' Muslims 1860–1923*, Cambridge, 1974.

Rousseau, Jean Jacques, *The Social Contract*, translated by Maurice Cranston, Harmondsworth, 1968.

Russell, R. and Islam, Khurshidul, *Ghalib: Life and Letters*, vol. I, Cambridge, Mass., 1969.

Sabbah, F. A., *Women in the Muslim Unconscious*, New York, 1984.

Saleem, Ahmed, *Sulugta Hooa Sindh* (Urdu), Lahore, 1990.

Samad, Yunas, *A Nation in Turmoil*, Delhi, 1995.

Sayeed, Khalid B., *The Political System of Pakistan*, Boston, 1967.

——, *Pakistan: The Formative Phase 1857–1948*, Karachi, 1968.

Schimmel, A. M., *Islam in the Indian Subcontinent*, Leiden, 1980.

Selier, F., *Rural–Urban Migration in Pakistan: The Case of Karachi*, Lahore, 1988.

Selier, F. and Karim, M. (eds), *Migration in Pakistan*, Lahore, 1986.

Seton-Watson, Hugh, *Nations and States. An Enquiry into the Origins of Nations and the Politics of Nationalism*, Boulder, 1977.

Shah, Sayid Ghulam Mustafa, *Jam: The Man and His Politics*, Karachi, 1993.

Shahab, Qudratullah, *Shahab Nama* (Urdu), Lahore, 1988.

Shahnawaz, Jahan Ara, *Father and Daughter*, Lahore, 1971.

Shaikh, Farzana, *Community and Consensus in Islam. Muslim Representation in Colonial India, 1860–1947*, Cambridge, 1989.

Singh, Anita Inder, *The Origins of the Partition of India, 1936–1947*, Delhi, 1987.

——, *The Limits of British Influence. South Asia and the Anglo-American Relationship, 1947–56*, London, 1993.

Sisson, Richard and Rose, Leo E., *War and Secession. Pakistan, India, and the Creation of Bangladesh*, Berkeley, 1990.

Smith, Anthony D., *The Ethnic Origins of Nations*, Oxford, 1987.

——, *Theories of Nationalism*, London 1983 (reprint).

Smith, Donald E. (ed.), *South Asian Religions and Politics*, Princeton, 1966.

Soomro, M. Q., *Muslim Politics in Sind (1938–47)*, Jamshoro, 1989.

Spate, O. H. K., *India and Pakistan: A General and Regional Geography*, London, 1954.

Specht, R. A. *et al.*, *Urbanization in Pakistan. The Case of Karachi*, Copenhagen, 1983

Stephens, Ian, *Pakistan*, London, 1963.

Syed, Anwar H., *Pakistan: Islam, Politics and National Solidarity*, Lahore, 1984.

Syed, G. M., *Struggle for a New Sind. A Brief Narrative of the Working of Provincial Autonomy in Sind during the Decade 1937–1947*, Karachi, 1947.

——, *Sindhi Culture*, Karachi, 1972.

——, *Diyar-i Dil va Dastan-i Mohababt*, Bombay, 1973.

Symonds, John Richard, *The Making of Pakistan*. London, 1950.

Talbot, Ian, *Punjab and the Raj, 1849–1947*, Delhi, 1988.

Taseer, Salman, *Bhutto: A Political Biography*, London, 1979.

Tapper, Richard (ed.), *The Conflict of Tribe and State in Iran and Afghanistan*, London, 1983.

Taylor, David and Yapp, Malcolm (eds), *Political Identity in South Asia*, London, 1979.

Tester, Keith, *Civil Society*, London, 1992.

Thanawi, Maulana Ashraf, *Bahishti Zaiwar*, Lahore, 1972 (reprint).

Wallace, Paul (ed.), *Religion and Nation in India*, New Delhi, 1985.

Weiss, Anita M. (ed.), *Islamic Reassertion in Pakistan*, Lahore, 1987.

Williams, L. F. Rushbrook, *The State of Pakistan*, London, 1962.

Wolpert, Stanley, *Jinnah of Pakistan*, New York, 1984.

——, *Zulfi Bhutto of Pakistan. His Life and Times*, Karachi, 1993.

Woodruff, Philip, *The Men Who Ruled India: The Guardians*, London, 1954.

Woodward, Bob, *Veil: The Secret Wars of the CIA, 1981–1987*, London, 1987.

Yusuf, Mohammad, *Silent Soldier: The Man Behind the Afghan Jehad, General Akhtar Abdur Rahman Shaheed*, Lahore, 1991.

Yusuf, Mohammad and Adkin, Mark, *The Bear Trap: Afghanistan's Untold Story*, London, 1992.

Zafar, Fareeha (ed.), *Finding Our Way. Readings on Women in Pakistan*, Karachi, 1991.

Ziring, Lawrence, *Pakistan: The Enigma of Political Development*, Durham, 1980.

——, *The Ayub Khan Era. Politics in Pakistan, 1958–1969*, New York, 1971.

—— *et al.* (eds), *Pakistan: The Long View*, Durham, 1977.

Articles and Research Papers

Abedin, Najmul, 'The Politics of Separatism. Some Reflections and Questions', *The Round Table*, 310, April 1989.

Alavi, Hamza, 'Nationhood and Nationalities in Pakistan', *Economic and Political Weekly,* XXIV, 8 July 1989.

Etzioni, Amitai, 'The Evils of self-determination', *Foreign Policy,* 89, 1993.

Hasan, Mushirul, 'Sectarianism in India Islam: The Shia–Sunni divide in the United Provinces', *The Indian Economic and Social History Review,* 27 (2), 1990.

Heeger, G. A., 'Bureaucracy, Political Parties and Political Developments', *World Politics,* XXV (4), 1973.

——, 'Politics in the Post-Military State: Some Reflections on the Pakistani Experience', *World Politics,* XXIX (2), 1977.

Hobsbawm, Eric, 'Whose Fault-Line is it Anyway?' *New Statesman and Society,* 24 April 1992.

Kampelman, Max M., 'Secession and the Right of Self-Determination. An Urgent Need to Harmonize Principle with Pragmatism', *The Washington Quarterly,* XVI (3), 1993.

Kennedy, Charles H., 'The Politics of Ethnicity in Sindh', *Asian Survey,* XXXI (10), 1991.

Khan, M. Ayub, 'The Pakistan–American Alliance. Strains and Stresses', *Foreign Affairs,* 42 (2), January 1964.

Khan, Rais, A., 'Pakistan in 1992', *Asian Survey,* XXXIII (2), 1993.

Kizilbash, H. H., 'Local Government: Democracy at the Capital and Autocracy in the Villages', *Pakistan Economic and Social Review,* XI (1), 1973.

Lodhi, Maleeha, 'Pakistan People's Party and Pakistan's Democracy', *Journal of South Asian and Middle Eastern Studies,* VI (1), 1983.

Malik, Iftikhar H., 'Islam, State and Ethno-Nationalism; Contemporary South Asian and Central Asian Politics', *Asian Survey,* XXXII (10), 1992.

——, 'Indo-Pakistan Relations: A Historical Reappraisal. A Lost Case or a Turning Point?' *Contemporary South Asia,* 1 (1), 1992.

——, 'Ethnicity and Contemporary South Asian Politics. The Kashmir Conflict as a Case Study', *The Round Table,* 322, April 1992.

——, 'Islam, the West and Ethno-Nationalism', *The American Journal of Islamic Social Sciences,* IX (1), 1992.

——, 'Ethno-Nationalism in Pakistan: A Commentary on MQM in Sindh', *South Asia,* XVIII, 2, December 1995.

——, 'Identify Formation and Muslim Politics in the Punjab, 1897–1936: A Retrospective Analysis', *Modern Asian Studies,* 29, 2, May 1995.

Morris-Jones, W. H., 'The Transfer of Power, 1947', *Modern Asian Studies,* XVI, 1982.

Mortimer, Edward, 'Christianity and Islam', *International Affairs,* 67 (I), 1991.

Nasr, Seyyed Vali Reza, 'Students, Islam, and Politics: Islami Jami'at-i Tulaba in Pakistan', *The Middle East Journal,* XXXXVI (1), 1992.

Rais, Rasul B., 'Pakistan in 1987: Transition to Democracy', *Asian Survey,* XXVIII (2), 1988.

Richter, William, 'Persistent Praetorianism: Pakistan's Third Military Regime', *Pacific Affairs,* 51 (3), 1978.

Robinson, Francis, 'Technology and Religious Change. Islam and the Impact of Print', *Modern Asian Studies,* XXVII, part 1, 1993.

Sayeed, Khalid Bin, 'The Jamaat-i-Islami Movement in Pakistan', *Pacific Affairs,* XXX (2), 1957.

——, 'The Political Role of Pakistan's Civil Service', *Pacific Affairs*, XXXI (2), 1958.

——, 'Collapse of Parliamentary Democracy in Pakistan', *The Middle East Journal*, XIII, 1959

——, 'Pakistan's Constitutional Autocracy', *Pacific Affairs*, XXVI (4), 1963–64.

—— 'The three worlds of democracy in Pakistan', *Contemporary South Asia*, I (1), 1992.

Syed, Anwar H., 'Political Parties and the Nationality Question in Pakistan', *Journal of South Asian and Middle Eastern Studies*, XII (1), 1988.

Talbot, Ian, 'The Growth of the Muslim League in the Punjab', *Journal of Commonwealth and Comparative Politics*, XX (1), 1982.

——, 'British Rule in the Punjab, 1849–1947', *Journal of Imperial and Commonwealth History*, XIX (2), 1991.

——, 'The Role of the Crowd in the Muslim League Struggle for Pakistan', *Journal of Imperial and Commonwealth History*, XXI (2), 1993.

Weinbaum, M. G., 'The March 1977 Elections in Pakistan: Where Everyone Lost', *Asian Survey*, XXII, 1977.

Weiner, Myron, 'Peoples and States in the World Order', *Third World Quarterly*, XIII (2), 1992.

Wilcox, Wayne A., 'Pakistan in 1969: Once Again at the Starting Point', *Asian Survey*, X, 1970.

Wright, Robin, 'Islam, Democracy and the West', *Foreign Affairs*, 7 (3), 1992.

Zaidi, S. Akbar, 'Regional Imbalances and the National Question in Pakistan. Some Directions', *Economic and Political Weekly*, 11 February 1989.

Ziring, Lawrence, 'Public Policy Dilemmas and Pakistan's Nationality Problems. The Legacy of Zia-ul-Haq', *Asian Survey*, XXVIII (8), 1988.

——, 'Pakistan in 1990: Fall of Benazir Bhutto', *Asian Survey*, XXXI (2), 1991.

Dissertations

Ahmad, Mumtaz, *'Class, Religion and Power: Some Aspects of Islamic Revivalism in Pakistan'*, Ph. D. thesis, University of Chicago, 1990.

Cheesman, David, *'Rural Power in Sind'*, Ph. D. thesis, University of London, 1980.

Husain, Imdad, *'The Failure of Parliamentary Politics in Pakistan, 1953–58'*, D. Phil. dissertation, University of Oxford, 1966.

Samad, A. Yunas, *'South Asian Muslims Politics, 1937–1958'*, D. Phil. dissertation, University of Oxford, 1991.

Newspapers and Magazines

Awaz International
The Daily Telegraph
Dawn
The Economist
Far Eastern Economic Review
The Financial Times

The Friday Times
The Guardian
The Herald
The Hindustan Times
The Independent
The Independent on Sunday
International Herald Tribune
Jang
The Nation
Nawa-i Waqt
New Statesman and Society
Newsweek
Newsline
The New York Times
Pakistan Profile
The Sunday Observer
The Sunday Times
Takbeer
The Times
The Times of India
The Washington Post
Time International
Viewpoint

Index

338

Objectives Resolution, 51
Ojhri arms-dump explosion, 104
Oman, 166
One-Unit scheme, 34, 62, 63, 64, 190,
    201, 206, 215
Operation Clean-up, 229, 245, 249
Orangi Pilot Project, 123
Oxford, 44

Pakistan(i), Afghan policy, 52; army
    17, 26, 53, 71–80, 103, 105–6;
    Christian women, 130; civic
    institutions, 12; civil service,
    58–72; civil society, 40, 115–38;
    Commission on the Status of
    Women, 150–8; Constitution of
    1973, 28–9, 51, 73, 74, 94, 147,
    161, 209; constitutional problems,
    34; coup of 1977, 95; creation,
    198; debts, 70; demand for, 33;
    economy, 22, 116–17; elites, 40;
    expatriates, 28; Federal Public
    Service Commission, 66; future of
    the country, 261; gender politics,
    139–67; generals in politics, 260;
    Girl Guides, 144; global policies,
    1; health and GNP, 130–1;
    historiography, 1; and India
    migration, 199–200; intelligence
    agencies ,260; in the 1990s, 24;
    land reforms, 90–3; languages,
    185; middle class, 115–16;
    Ministry of Kashmir Affairs, 22;
    Movement, 23, 26, 193, 200, 220,
    221; Muslim identity, 30; Muslim
    League, 30, 31; National
    Assembly, 36; nationalism, 15, 49,
    56, 186, 214; Navy, 69; political
    culture, 9, 11, 13, 19, 29; politics,
    24, 256; polity, 25; press, 107–8,
    133–8; Saudi-Iranian competition,
    33; society, 10; state, 4, 5, 10, 13,
    40, 55, 57, 80; Supreme Court, 2,
    29, 37, 53, 104, 110, 126;
    universities, 32, 123
Pakistan Steel Mills, 70
Pakistani(s), 9, 11, 17, 25, 27, 33
Paleejo, Rasul B., 209–10
Pan-Islamism, 35, 46

Patel, V., 26
PCO (Provisional Constitution Order),
    110–11
PDA (Pakistan Democratic Alliance),
    36, 102, 211
PDP (Pakistan Democratic Party), 34
PFUJ (Pakistan Federal Union of
    Journalists), 137
Persians, 14, 41
Peshawar, 21–2, 79
Palestinians, 172
PIA (Pakistan International Airlines),
    71
PID (Press Information Department),
    134–6
PIDC (Pakistan Industrial
    Development Corporation), 64
PIF (Pakistan Islamic Front), 38
Pir Ilahi Bakhsh, 87
Pir of Daiwal, 51, 87
Pir of Pagara, 31, 187, 212–13, 244
Pirzada, Abdul Hafeez, 209
Pirzada, Abdus Sattar, 206
PPI (Punjabi–Pukhtun Ittehad), 204,
    236, 237
PPP (Pakistan People's Party), 2, 31–2,
    38–9, 68, 85, 97, 98–101, 121,
    124, 146, 169, 187, 203–5, 207–8,
    211–13, 222, 223–59; PPP–MQM
    Accord (Karachi Accord), 238–9
PNA (Pakistan National Alliance), 74
Pothowar, 21, 79, 183
Press Commission of Pakistan, 136–7
Prophet, 141
Prussia, 173
PSO/PSF (People's Students
    Federation), 113, 123–5
Pukhtunwali, 21
Pukhtun Zalmai, 21
Punjab, 17–19, 21, 23, 30–1, 37–8, 82,
    141–2, 194; Legislative Council,
    18; National Unionist Party, 18,
    47–8, 48, 181; tradition/Indus
    Basin tradition, 9, 18, 55–6, 184;
    Southwestern, 19; University, 124
Punjabi(s), 14, 23, 48, 50, 65, 68, 217,
    219, 227, 254; Balochistan, 16;
    Baloch relations, 16, 183;
    domination, 19, 55, 78–80, 91,

Sindh – *continued*
presidency, 194, 197, 208, 225–56;
　University at Jamshoro, 124,
　216–17, 248
Sindhi, 14, 195; Hindus, 216, 218;
　middle class, 203; Muslim
　dynasties, 192–3; Muslims, 216;
　poetry, 216
Sindhi, Maulana, Ubaidullah, 45, 46
Sindhis, 23, 68, 254
Sindhi Shagird Tehreek, 209–10
Sindhi, Shaikh Abdul Majid, 194, 206
Sindhudesh, 210
Sipah-i Sahaba, 214
Siraj ud-Daula, 43
SITE (Sindh Industrial Estate), 235
Skeen Committee, 76
Smith, Adam, 6
SNA (Sindh National Alliance), 203,
　205, 209, 210, 217, 223, 237–8,
　240, 242
Soomro, Allah Bakhsh, 208
South Asia, 8, 9, 117; state of
　education, 128, 261
South Asian Muslims, 34, 41, 78, 140,
　174, 178–9
South Korea, 24
Soviet Union, 7, 15, 172, 177
Special Branch (police), 106
Sri Lanka(n), 48, 122, 200
Suhrawardy, H. S., 30, 62–3
Sukkur, 194, 197, 201, 204, 218, 231;
　airport, 239
Sultan Bahu, 187
Sultan, Tipu, 43
Suri, Sher Shah, 41
Swat, 258
Syed, Anwar, 3
Syed, G. M., 19, 20, 186–7, 194–5,
　204–6, 208–10, 212, 214–16, 219,
　221, 237
Sylhet, 200

Tablighi Jama'at, 43
Takbeer, 246, 251
Talpur, Bandeh Ali, 208
Talpur, Mir Ghulam Ali, 91
Talpurs, 192
Tamils, 48, 172

Tariq, Azeem Ahmed, 230, 234, 239
Tarkhans, 192–3, 196
Taxila, 235
Tehran, 96
Tehreek-i Nifaz-i Fiqh a-Jaafria, 214
Tiwana, Raheela, 113
Torkham, 21
Turks, 41

ulama, 50, 159; Brelvi and Deobandi,
　142; in politics, 34
Ummayyid Caliphate, 192
United Front, 62
UN, 120; talks on Afghanistan, 97
United Kingdom, 15, 224
UP, 18, 142, 173, 179, 181, 200
Urdu, 14, 55, 179, 185, 215, 217, 230,
　259; and politics, 20; press in
　London and Karachi, 245;
　Urdu–Sindhi controversy, 203
Urdu-speaking migrants/Muhajireen,
　20, 23, 198, 200; in Karachi, 16,
　170–1, 210
USA, 6, 15, 26, 28, 53, 219, 224, 231,
　245; and Pakistan, 75–6; and
　Pakistani armed forces, 77;
　diplomats in Karachi, 251
USAID, 123
USCIA, 96–7
Usmani, Shabbir Ahmed, 33

WAF (Women Action Forum), 146, 149
WAPDA (Water and Power
　Development Authority), 64
Wattoo, Manzoor, 19, 257
West Pakistan, 13, 57, 65, 108
Western Bengal, 15
Western civilisation, 81; democracies,
　1, 8
Women's Rights Committee, 146, 150
World Bank, 6, 120

Yusuf, Brigadier, Mohammad, 97

Zahir Shah, 53
Zardari, Asif Ali, 102, 110, 162
Ziaists, 35
Zia ul-Haq, General, 1, 3, 17, 18, 24,
　28–9, 31, 32, 33, 35, 51–2, 53, 61,